ALSO BY EVAN THOMAS

The War Lovers
Roosevelt, Lodge, Hearst, and the
Rush to Empire, 1898

Sea of Thunder
Four Commanders and the Last Great Naval
Campaign 1941–1945

John Paul Jones
Sailor, Hero, Father of the American Navy

Robert Kennedy: His Life

The Very Best Men
The Early Years of the CIA

The Man to See
Edward Bennett Williams: Ultimate Insider;
Legendary Trial Lawyer

The Wise Men
Six Friends and the World They Made
(with Walter Isaacson)

IKE'S BLUFF

PRESIDENT EISENHOWER'S SECRET
BATTLE TO SAVE THE WORLD

EVAN THOMAS

LITTLE, BROWN AND COMPANY

LARGE PRINT EDITION

Little, Brown and Company
Hachette Book Group
237 Park Avenue, New York, NY 10017
littlebrown.com

First Edition: September 2012

Little, Brown and Company is a division of Hachette Book Group, Inc., and is celebrating its 175th anniversary in 2012. The Little, Brown name and logo are trademarks of Hachette Book Group, Inc.

The publisher is not responsible for websites (or their content) that are not owned by the publisher.

The Hachette Speakers Bureau provides a wide range of authors for speaking events. To find out more, go to hachettespeakersbureau.com or call (866) 376-6591.

Library of Congress Cataloging-in-Publication Data
Thomas, Evan.
  Ike's bluff : president Eisenhower's secret battle to save the world / Evan Thomas.—1st edition.
      p. cm.
  Includes bibliographical references and index.
  ISBN 978-0-316-09104-6—ISBN 978-0-316-22416-1 (large print)
1. Eisenhower, Dwight D. (Dwight David), 1890–1969.   2. United States—Foreign relations—1953–1961.   3. Cold war—Diplomatic history.
4. National security—United States—History—20th century.   5. Nuclear weapons—Government policy—United States—History—20th century.
6. Nuclear warfare—Government policy—United States—History—20th century.   I. Title.
  E835.T44 2012
  973.921092—dc23   2012019640

10 9 8 7 6 5 4 3 2 1

RRD-C

Printed in the United States of America

To Oscie

The problem is not merely man against man or nation against nation. It is man against war.

       —Dwight Eisenhower, April 4, 1956

Contents

CONTENTS

IKE'S
BLUFF

Introduction
Tell No One

Ike (front), about age thirteen, with his gang (Dwight D. Eisenhower Presidential Library, Abilene, Kansas)

A T EIGHT THIRTY ON THE NIGHT of January 17, 1961, President Dwight Eisenhower gave his farewell address from the Oval Office. Even after years of coaching from actor Robert Montgomery, Eisenhower did not look comfortable giving his televised speech. He disliked using a teleprompter, and he began by glancing down and reading from the printed text on his desk. He paused, blinked, looked up at the lines on the screen, looked back down at the speech, lost his place, and tripped over a word.[1] At first, what he said was unremarkable, but then Eisenhower began to talk about what he called "the military-industrial complex." "This conjunction of an immense military establishment and a large arms industry is new in the American experience," he said. "...We must not fail to comprehend its grave implications.... The potential for the disastrous rise of misplaced power exists and will persist."

This was not the message most Americans expected to hear from a former army general, a hero of World War II. Eisenhower spoke in the flat twang of the Kansas prairie of his youth. The medium of television could not quite convey what came across so strongly in person. But there was a sense of urgency in his voice and an undertone of strength and power. After visiting with the president in January 1955, the diplomat David Bruce wrote in his diary that Eisenhower was "what the Romans meant by 'vir.'" The literal translation of *vir* is "a hero, masculine or manly person." Bald and gray-faced, peering through glasses as he struggled with the teleprompter, Eisenhower looked old. But he was still *vir*.[2] Eisenhower warned against "plundering, for our own ease and convenience, the precious resources of tomorrow. We cannot mortgage the material assets of our grandchildren without risking the loss also of their political and spiritual heritage. We want democracy to survive for all generations to come..." Then he turned to the subject that was closest to his heart. He spoke of the danger of war and the need for disarmament in the nuclear age:

"Because this need is so sharp and apparent I confess that I lay down my official responsibilities in this field with a definite sense of disappointment. As one who has witnessed the horror and the lingering sadness of war—as one who knows that another war could utterly destroy this civilization which has been so slowly and painfully built over thousands of years—I wish I could say tonight that a lasting peace is in sight [on his teleprompter script, he doubly underlined "wish" and "is in sight"].

"Happily, I can say that war has been avoided."

Two weeks later, at the inauguration, Eisenhower was a spent figure. His farewell address, despite good notices, had already been eclipsed. The attention was on John F. Kennedy, the incoming president, tanned and overcoatless, young and vigorous, as he summoned a new generation to national greatness. Eisenhower, bundled up against the cold, sat silently on the podium. When the ceremony was over, the ex-president and his wife, Mamie, climbed into the five-year-old Chrysler Imperial that she had bought for his sixty-fifth birthday, and their driver headed to their farm in Gettysburg, Pennsylvania. A single Secret Service car led the way. When they got there, Ike's grandson, David, recalled in a memoir, "the Secret Service honked the horn and made a U-turn, heading back to Washington."[3] Eisenhower hopped out of the car and opened the gate. That night, he tried to place his first phone call in twenty years. Frustrated, turning red as he clicked the receiver button to no effect, he yelled out, "Come show me how you work this Goddamn thing!"[4]

The greatest hero in the greatest war ever fought never saw combat. As a young officer in World War I, Ike, as he was universally and usually affectionately known, had been stuck stateside training troops, ending up in Gettysburg. It was an early lesson in forbearance. "I suppose," he commiserated with a fellow officer on November 11, 1918, when the news of the armistice broke as the two men eagerly waited orders to go overseas, "we'll spend the rest of our lives explaining why we didn't get into this war." Then he blurted out, in a rush of stilted syntax: "By God, from now on I am cutting myself such a swath and will make up for this."[5]

Eisenhower never shot at anyone, or was shot at, but he saw the effects of war, again and again, over the years. After World War I, he wrote a guide to the battlefields of France, where bodies were buried in mass graves by the thousands and shards of bone and skulls still poked through the soil.[6] During the Second World War, General Eisenhower was too valuable to the Allied cause to risk his life, and he had to avoid capture because he knew the highly guarded secret of ULTRA, the Allies' code-breaking operation.[7] But he often toured the battlefield, at times so soon after the fighting that he could smell the rotting flesh.[8] After Germany fell, he walked through the Nazi concentration camp called Ohrdruf-Nord, a subcamp of Buchenwald, near the town of Gotha, with his friend the tough-talking General George Patton. Patton threw up. Ike ordered the mayor of Gotha to turn out the townspeople to remove the dead bodies. The mayor and his wife went home that night and hung themselves. ("Maybe, there's some hope after all," Ike remarked, apparently relieved that the German conscience had not been obliterated by war and Nazism.)[9] In Germany, Eisenhower toured the squalid camps of the so-called displaced persons. They were homeless, but at least they were alive. As Supreme Allied Commander, Eisenhower knew that hundreds of thousands more had died in the giant firebombing raids on German cities. Later, on a low-altitude flight following the path of the warring German and Russian armies across the Ukraine to Moscow, Eisenhower did not see a single building left standing.[10] Eisenhower had witnessed how war brought out courage and comradeship, the best in men, and also the worst. During the Battle of the Bulge, Eisenhower knew that most men who were "separated from their units," in official jargon, were in fact trying to desert. He was vexed that American soldiers in jail for petty infractions almost always declined a pardon if it meant going to the front. As the American army liberated Europe in the winter of 1944–45, Eisenhower was so disturbed by reports that American GIs had raped local women that "at one point," wrote military historian Mark Perry, he "thought the only solution was to line up the perpetrators and mow them down."[11]

Always, inescapably, Eisenhower felt the weight of command. Before D-day, those close to him saw the strain. "He was as nervous as I had seen him and extremely depressed," recalled his driver Kay Summersby, who was emotionally fragile herself. She went on, explaining that Ike was smoking and drinking too much, his stomach was tortured with cramps, he was stricken with chronic throat infections and insomnia, and his blood pressure was spiking.[12] If he was not a mental wreck, he was certainly a physical one.

When Eisenhower came home after VE-day, however, Americans did not greet a haunted or burnt-out figure. They saw the famous smile, broad and beaming, wide-open and boyish in its delight, a man at ease. Eisenhower had a way of looking surprised, flattered, even a little amazed, when crowds cheered for him, as they did at an endless succession of parades and celebrations. It was becoming, and somehow perfectly suited for the moment, an expression that was part aw-shucks, but sincere. No need to fuss, Eisenhower seemed to be saying; this is what Americans do when the world needs saving.

Robert ("Bobby") Cutler, who went on to be President Eisenhower's special assistant for national security, was working at the Pentagon when Eisenhower returned one sunny day in late May 1945. All Pentagon employees, except those absolutely required for duty, were told to assemble in the courtyard.

The returning hero was not showy, but he could be vain. He used a sunlamp to keep his ruddy complexion. As Supreme Allied Commander, he did not wear a helmet or combat fatigues; he did not want to suggest he was in combat when he wasn't. He did, however, design the "Eisenhower jacket," a short, smart tunic that displayed his athletic build. In the manner of many senior commanders in World War II, he wore few decorations on his chest. On the other hand, he didn't need to.

Now, in the hot, bright courtyard at a minute

General Eisenhower (Eisenhower National Historic Site, Gettysburg, Pennsylvania)

before noon, the secretary of war, Henry Stimson, and the chief of staff of the Army, General George Marshall, appeared, along with various dignitaries and senior officers. There was applause, then silence. Then a single jeep emerged from the underground passageway. In the rear sat one officer. "From twenty-five thousand throats," Cutler wrote "a mighty shout arose, beating forward and back on the Pentagon walls. The deafening sound burst out like a thunderclap, and continued to roll on and on, unabated. It was he, Eisenhower—Ike—the conqueror of the conquerors of the world...come home."

The "tumult," wrote Cutler, "came to him as a complete surprise. He broke into his famous grin." Eisenhower was so sincere, so genuine—most of the time—that he may have been truly taken aback, notwithstanding the obvious stagecraft.[13]

Eisenhower frequently expressed a disdain for politics and politicians. He didn't vote, and for a long time, no one had known Eisenhower's political leanings. (Incredibly, in 1947 President Harry Truman had offered to be Ike's vice-presidential running mate if the hero general would agree to take the top of the Democratic ticket.)[14] He scorned patronage seekers and avoided Washington cocktail parties. He had no use for partisanship, and spoke only of duty to the country. All of this made him highly desirable to both political parties, who courted him as a presidential candidate in 1948 and 1952. All through 1951, delegations of kingmakers went to see Eisenhower in Paris, where he was reprising his role as Supreme Allied Commander, this time for the newly created North Atlantic Treaty Organization, the Western

Alliance shaped to stand up to the encroachments of Soviet Communism. Eisenhower politely declined, though he never quite shut the door.[15] In February 1952, a citizens' committee organized by financier John Hay Whitney (owner of the *New York Herald Tribune,* the leading moderate Republican newspaper) put together a midnight rally for Ike in Madison Square Garden. Some 18,000 people jammed into the arena, with thousands more standing outside, roaring over and over, "I want Ike!" An inventive PR man named Tex McCrary had staged a spectacular show: Humphrey Bogart, Lauren Bacall, and Clark Gable (making his first appearance on TV) waved to the crowd. Mary Martin, the star of *South Pacific,* sang "I'm in Love with a Wonderful Guy—Ike!" Irving Berlin ended the rally by leading the audience in singing "God Bless America."[16]

McCrary got Twentieth Century-Fox to produce a movie of the rally, and a handsome aviatrix named Jacqueline Cochran, who had test-flown P-38s during the war, was chosen to take the two-hour film to Eisenhower. Ike and Mamie watched it in a small movie theater in their château outside Paris near NATO headquarters. When the lights were turned back on, Cochran stood up and raised her glass. "To the President," she said.

Eisenhower "burst into tears," Cochran recalled. "Tears were just running out of his eyes, he was so overwhelmed and so overcome with the public demonstration." Eisenhower began to "talk about his mother and father, but mostly about his mother," she said. After a while, Ike told Cochran to go back to New York and tell his backers, "I'm going to run."[17] The next day he wrote his best friend, Swede Hazlett, "I can't tell you what an emotional upset it is for one to realize suddenly that he himself may be the symbol of that longing and hope."[18]

In 1952, many Americans regarded the Soviet Union, whose spies had stolen nuclear secrets, as an imminent and existential threat. American soldiers were embroiled in a bloody and seemingly interminable struggle in Korea. Americans did not want a man on horseback. They did not want a General Douglas MacArthur, as MacArthur himself understood. Once, after hearing Eisenhower launch into a lecture about the need for military separation from civilian politics and his own reluctance to run for office, MacArthur patted his fellow general on the knee and said, a bit sourly, "That's all right, Ike. You go on like that and you'll get it for sure."[19]

The American people were longing for security, for peace, and Eisenhower understood that he was the one person who could answer their call. That autumn, when Eisenhower ran for president on the Republican ticket, huge posters showed him smiling broadly and holding up two fingers in a V for victory. For many voters, that was all they needed to know.[20]

Most Americans thought the Korean War was a mistake. Soldiers fought and died for meaningless hills with names like Heartbreak Ridge and Bloody Ridge. One small promontory without any strategic significance, called Mount Baldy because it had been denuded by shellfire, changed hands eleven times. During the peak fighting, 1,500 Americans died near this barren hill every week.[21] A year into the war, on Memorial Day 1951, Eisenhower had quietly despaired over the waste. He wrote in his diary: "Another Decoration Day finds us still adding to the number of graves that will be decorated in future years. Men are stupid."[22]

As a candidate for president in the fall of 1952, Ike promised to find a way to end the slaughter. At a campaign appearance at the Masonic Temple in Detroit on October 24, less than two weeks before election day, Eisenhower declared, "I shall go to Korea!" He did not say what he would do when he got there, and in truth he did not know. But on the campaign train, when reporters were handed mimeographed copies of Ike's speech, one said, "That does it—Ike's in." And he was, beating Adlai Stevenson by a wide margin.[23]

In early December 1952, the newspapers dutifully recorded Eisenhower's tour of the bomb-cratered wastes near the 38th parallel, describing how the former Supreme Commander gazed out at the rocky hills honeycombed with North Korean defenses and took the measure of the battlefield. At one stop, he shared some frozen K rations with the men of his old army division. One of its officers was his son John. "The trip was mostly PR," John later recalled. "Dad could have seen there were hills by looking at a map."

Father and son had a loving but at times awkward relationship. Ike had lost his first child to an infant fever, and he had trouble showing his affection for his second. "I am certain I was born standing at attention," John Eisenhower wryly began a memoir, *Strictly Personal,* written in 1974, five years after his father died. Young Eisenhower had graduated from West Point on D-day, June 6, 1944, and could hardly avoid his father's shadow. Before John embarked for the front line in Korea, his father told him that if he was captured, he must kill himself. Stalin's son, he explained, had done so when captured by the Germans in World War II.

As General, now President-elect, Eisenhower made desultory small talk with the other troops that icy day late in 1952, John thought of the famous photograph of his father chatting with face-blackened airborne troopers on the eve of D-day. General

John Eisenhower, age six (Dwight D. Eisenhower Presidential Library, Abilene, Kansas)

Eisenhower had been told the paratroopers would suffer a very heavy casualty rate the next day, and he wanted to look them in the eye before sending them to their fates. Years later John Eisenhower, a retired brigadier general, ambassador, and author, pondered the two sides of his father, seemingly evenly balanced

President Eisenhower (Library of Congress, Washington, DC)

between open, sunny warmth and cold-bloodedness. He thought for a moment and said, with a slight smile, "Make that 75 percent cold-blooded."[24]

In his inaugural address, John F. Kennedy had boldly promised that the United States would "pay any price, bear any burden" to defend freedom around the world. But by the late summer of 1961, the young president was beginning to wonder what he had gotten himself into. Berlin, a flash point of the Cold War, was heating up with the erection of the Berlin Wall, and Kennedy realized that American soldiers might actually have to fight their Soviet counterparts. The Soviets held a huge advantage in tanks and troops. The only way to stop them would be to use nuclear weapons.

But how would the president know when to cross the line from fighting a World War II–type battle to using weapons that could—would—bring on the apocalypse? Kennedy summoned one of his informal advisers, Dean Acheson. The former secretary of state in the Truman administration was usually a vigorous hawk, impatient with dithering. But this time, when Kennedy asked Acheson when he thought the United States would have to resort to nuclear weapons, Acheson's response "was more measured and quiet than usual," recalled McGeorge Bundy, JFK's national security adviser. Acheson, Bundy later wrote, said that "He believed the president should himself give that question the most careful and private consideration, well before the time when the choice might present itself, that he should reach his own clear conclusion in advance as to what he would do, and that he should tell no one at all what his conclusion was."[25]

He should tell no one at all.... As Bundy recalled, Kennedy merely thanked Acheson, and the conversation ended. There is no record of what Kennedy was thinking, but the young president may have gotten his first inkling of the particular solitude of a nuclear-age commander in chief.

*   *   *

Dwight Eisenhower had long lived with this burden. He had been thinking about the question of when, if ever, to "go nuclear" throughout the eight years of his presidency and for several years before that. Eisenhower was an expert at bridge, an activity now associated in the American mind with middle-aged or elderly people sitting around a table, staring at cards. For Eisenhower, who played as much as possible, the game was a relaxing way of doing what he did all day: reading minds, weighing options (his own and others'), thinking ahead, and concealing his intentions. Eisenhower, who generally radiated warm sincerity and whose emotions were easy to read, was actually a great bluffer, and not just at cards.

Eisenhower's basic policy throughout his presidency was known as Massive Retaliation. It was, in essence, a threat to use nuclear weapons against Communist aggression wherever and whenever it might occur. Even in his most private councils, Eisenhower remained vague about what he might or might not do in a crisis. His closest adviser, General Andrew Goodpaster, guessed Ike would never use nuclear weapons, but others weren't so sure, and Eisenhower wasn't about to tell them.[26]

Indeed, Eisenhower sometimes sounded as if he regarded nuclear weapons as conventional weapons— "like bullets," he once said. Other times he seemed determined to rid the world of their scourge. To argue over which was the "real Eisenhower"—the nuclear brinksman or the peace lover—as many historians and scholars have done and still do, is to miss the point. Eisenhower's mission, which he achieved after he extricated America from the Korean War in 1953, was to avoid any war. As a general, Eisenhower had commanded a conquering army in a world war ended only by the use of two atomic bombs. Though he posed as a poor farm boy, he was a scholar who had closely read Clausewitz's treatise *On War*, and took to heart its basic, if overlooked, message: that small wars can become big wars, and that a nation fighting for survival will stop at nothing.[27] Eisenhower managed, by cleverness, indirection, subtlety, and downright deviousness—and by embracing the very weapon he could never use—to safeguard his country and possibly the rest of mankind from annihilation. As the United States and the Soviet Union created the power to end the world in the 1950s, the genial old soldier with a weakened heart contrived to keep the peace. He did so in his own distinctive way. He was honorable but occasionally opaque, outwardly amiable but inwardly seething.

This is not a general biography. The book covers Eisenhower's presidency but is almost entirely devoted to his foreign, not his domestic, policy. (I do briefly describe his civil rights record, because I think it reflects on his leadership style and worldview.) My concern is with Eisenhower's overwhelming, single, fixed preoccupation: the avoidance of war. Having done as much as any man to win World War II, Ike devoted the rest of his public service to keeping America and the world out of World War III.

As a World War II hero, General Eisenhower was remembered as a peacemaker among giant egos, his persona overshadowed by the likes of Churchill and Roosevelt, Generals Montgomery and Patton. As a president, he has been far less lionized than his predecessor, the salty, blunt Harry Truman, or his successor, the glamorous Jack Kennedy. It is easy to forget that Eisenhower was the first person in history to have the means to wreck civilization. Eisenhower did not shy from power. He used it. But he did so in a way that is still little understood.

Ike's method of leadership was subtle, to say the least. By early twenty-first-century standards, his approach to the presidency seems almost unimaginable. Eisenhower was the first president to use TV as a bully pulpit, but he was not particularly good at it, or effective in a way that would be easily understood today. The public trusted Eisenhower, not so much because of the words he spoke, which were often banal, but because of an aura he projected, an air of restrained, manly confidence. The people, most of them, judging from Eisenhower's high poll ratings, believed that he had sound judgment, that he would keep them safe, and they were right. But they had little idea what drove the man behind the warm, grandfatherly smile, or what he was really doing in between golf games and platitudinous speeches. Eisenhower's own colleagues were not entirely sure, either.

The 1950s were boringly peaceful (or are remembered that way) only because Eisenhower made them so. Eisenhower governed by indirection, not just because he preferred to, but also because he had to. His ability to save the world from nuclear Armageddon entirely depended on his ability to convince America's enemies — and his own followers — that he was willing to use nuclear weapons. This was a bluff of epic proportions.

In poker, when a player bluffs, he hopes his opponent will not "call" and force him to expose his weak cards. Eisenhower put tremendous — some would say risky — reliance on his own intuition about his former friends and contemporary foes in the Kremlin. He believed, as he once privately wrote a colleague, that the Russian leaders were not "early Christian martyrs."[28] But he did not widely express this view, or his belief that Nikita Khrushchev's menace ("We will bury you!") was mostly bluster, or that the giant rockets Khrushchev liked to conjure — stamped out in factories, like sausages! — were chimeras, frightening but not (yet) real. Nor did President Eisenhower try as hard as he should have to calm the fears of schoolchildren (like the author) about the threat of Soviet nuclear attack. To do so might have steadied nerves, but would also have shown cards. Public terror was a price—politically as well as psychologically—well below Armageddon. Yet by not publicly diminishing the fear, Eisenhower could give strength to those eager to strike first.

Ike's wide smile, open as the Kansas sky, concealed a deep secretiveness. Eisenhower preferred small-scale covert action over grand military maneuvers. In part, he was more realistic than civilian leaders about what could go wrong when armies took the field, but he was also temperamentally inclined to operate by sleight of hand. Unfortunately, Ike, who liked having a full grip on the reins, could not control his own Central Intelligence Agency. Under Allen Dulles and the brainy but reckless Richard Bissell, the CIA saw itself as the president's secret action arm, and its blundering would derail Ike's push, at the end of his presidency, for détente with the Soviet Union and lead to the most dangerous years of the Cold War.

Eisenhower was deeply human, a man in his sixties who had had too many cups of coffee, smoked too many cigarettes, slept badly, and worried far too much. His struggle to maintain his health and equilibrium is a major subplot of this story. He had a loving wife and friends and family, and he was genial and sociable most of the time. But he was coldly, ruthlessly pragmatic. He liked to be in the company of others, but he trusted no one but himself.

JFK's inauguration; Eisenhower bundled up (Library of Congress, Washington, DC)

PART ONE

Duty

1953–1956

1

Confidence

ISENHOWER'S INAUGURATION AS the thirty-fourth president of the United States on January 20, 1953, did not begin as warmly or triumphantly as his return home after VE-day in the spring of 1945. On a leaden, foggy winter's morning, sitting side by side in the presidential limousine on the drive from the White House up Pennsylvania Avenue, Eisenhower and President Truman rode in icy silence. Neither man liked the other and neither pretended otherwise.[1] In his final days in office, the president, who had been blamed for "Truman's War," was bitter about Ike's vow to go to Korea. After the election, he offered Ike a plane to fly there, adding, "that is, if he still wants to go."[2]

The sun broke through shortly before noon—"Eisenhower's luck," according to the pundits—in time for the swearing-in on two Bibles: one used by

Truman and Eisenhower (Dwight D. Eisenhower Presidential Library, Abilene, Kansas)

George Washington and the other used by Ike as a West Point cadet. Shortly after twelve thirty, as he stood on the speaking platform on the east facade of the Capitol, Eisenhower briefly flashed his grin and raised the V sign to the vast crowd, which cheered but otherwise remained mostly hushed throughout his inaugural speech. He looked "somber-faced," according to the *New York Times*. Eisenhower's twenty-minute address was lofty but abstract, framing the Cold War in Manichaean terms but offering no way out other than by persistence and vigilance. The address was not particularly memorable and is rarely quoted, but it did include a chilling line, intoned in Eisenhower's wintry, grating voice: "Science seems ready to confer on us, as its final gift, the power to erase human life on this planet."[3]

Eisenhower chose not to share with the American public how much progress the scientists were making. Three months earlier, on November 1, 1952, at a Pacific atoll in the Marshall Islands, sailors had watched agog as a giant, multihued pillar of fire rose five miles into the sky, completely obliterating everything beneath it. The bomb's fireball, four miles wide, would have incinerated San Francisco in a flash. The H-bomb, five hundred times more powerful than the atomic bomb, had been born. ("It's a boy!" exclaimed the bomb's champion, Edward Teller.)[4]

Eisenhower was on a postelection golfing vacation when he got his first formal briefing on the new weapon, code-named "Mike," from Roy Snapp, secretary of the Atomic Energy Commission. In the manager's office at the Augusta National Golf Club, Snapp handed Eisenhower a top-secret memorandum from the chairman of the AEC, Gordon Dean. Dean laconically wrote that the island base for the test was now "missing." The underwater crater was fifteen hundred yards in diameter.

As Supreme Allied Commander, Eisenhower had always been unusually open to new scientific research on weapons and intelligence gathering. To the briefer, the president-elect now said that, while he favored scientific research, he wondered at the reason "for us to build enough destructive power to destroy everything."[5] He brooded for a moment, accepted what he could not change, and began to think how he would handle this terrible new reality.

The scale of the blast and the technological leap from fission bomb to the far more powerful thermonuclear bomb were, at Eisenhower's request, kept secret at first. Once president, he ordered the word "thermonuclear" be kept out of government press releases. ("Keep them confused as to fission and fusion," he instructed.)*[6] Despite his open demeanor, at press conferences Eisenhower would from time to time pretend to know less than he did, leaving the illusion that he was distracted and ill informed about matters that deeply engaged him.

Indeed, Eisenhower was willing to appear less than sharp, even a little slow-witted, if it served some larger purpose. Unlike most politicians, he was not driven by an insecure need to be loved and recognized. He possessed an inner confidence born of experience. This is not to say, however, that he was serene. Accustomed to the "august calmness" of his old boss, General George Marshall, national security aide Bobby Cutler recognized that he was in for a

---

*An atom bomb uses fission only. A thermonuclear bomb uses both fission and fusion.

different experience when he went to work for Eisenhower. Ike would restlessly twirl his glasses, spin in his chair, doodle, jump up and pace, grab at the air with his huge hands, all while prodding and probing his aides in a sharp, flat, rapid-fire voice. When he was mad, which was often, a blood vessel in his temple would throb ominously. He hated wasting time and would terminate conversations, not because he was rude but because there was always something more to be done. "One could almost hear the whirring of a dynamo," recalled Cutler.[7]

After commanding in a world war alongside the likes of Winston Churchill, Franklin Roosevelt, Charles de Gaulle, and Joseph Stalin, Ike was not intimidated by anyone. The presidency was at some level more of the same. After his first full day in office, he wrote in his diary: "My first day at the president's desk. Plenty of worries and difficult problems. But such has been my portion for a long time — the result is that this just seems (today) like a continuation of all I've been doing since July 1941 — even before that."[8]

Pressure and anxiety were familiar companions to the sixty-two-year-old Eisenhower. He had learned to make light of hard choices, while subtly reminding others that he knew about stress in ways they could only imagine. In 1955, Eisenhower was invited to give the commencement address at Penn

State, where his brother Milton was president. As the big day arrived, rain threatened. Did Ike want to move the ceremony indoors or take his chances in the bigger outdoor stadium? Eisenhower shrugged and said, "You decide. I haven't worried about the weather since June 6, 1944."[9] This was not true; an avid golfer, he worried about the weather all the time. But it was useful to make others think that he was imperturbable.

And yet he knew that he was entering a new and uncertain world. Before he left the Oval Office on that first day, he received a brief phone call from General Omar Bradley, chairman of the Joint Chiefs of Staff. Turning to his secretary, Ann Whitman, Eisenhower said that he had just learned a lesson. His old friend Brad, who had entered West Point with him in 1911 and had been his comrade in arms throughout the Second World War, had addressed him not as "Ike" but as "Mr. President." From that moment, Eisenhower later wrote, he knew he would be "separated from all others, including my oldest and best friends. I would be far more alone now than when commanding the Allied forces in Europe in World War II."[10]

Vice President Richard Nixon had reason to resent President Eisenhower. Although Ike was friendly to his running mate on the 1952 Republican ticket,

Nixon couldn't help but feel like a junior officer in the presence of the commanding general. Ike's geniality masked a reserve, a coolness, which Nixon felt keenly. Nixon's insecurities had turned to anger when Ike kept his distance from Nixon during a campaign-fund flap just six weeks before election day. The California senator had been able to save his place on the GOP ticket only by appealing to the public with his maudlin but effective "Checkers speech."[11] Nixon understood and admired two important truths about Eisenhower. "He was a far more complex and devious man than most people realized," wrote Nixon in his 1962 memoir, *Six Crises*. (Nixon added, "in the best sense of those words.") And Nixon could see that Eisenhower identified himself with the nation. There was no point arguing "what's best for Eisenhower" versus "what is best for the nation," Nixon told friends and colleagues. In Eisenhower's mind, they were one and the same.[12]

Eisenhower had been taught at West Point to give credit to others and to avoid casting blame by name. Indoctrinated in the virtues of the team, he tried to convince himself that he was essentially replaceable. He went so far as to carry around a corny anonymous poem:

> *... Take a bucket, fill it with water,*
> *Put your hand in—clear up to the wrist.*

Now pull it out; the hole that remains
Is a measure of how you'll be missed . . .

The moral of this quaint example;
To do just the best that you can,
Be proud of yourself, but remember,
There is no Indispensable Man![13]

The evidence is overwhelming that he believed quite the opposite. Dwight Eisenhower recognized in himself the one man who could lead the United States in an era, when — for the first time in history — not one but two nations, mortal enemies, had the power to plunge the world into darkness. The image of Ike as a Cincinnatus, the citizen-soldier reluctantly but dutifully brought back from his retirement to lead his nation, glosses over Eisenhower's own fierce ambition. Eisenhower played hard to get in 1951 and into 1952, but he could easily have said no and retired with his honor intact. He wanted to be in charge because he believed he was the man for the age.

Eisenhower was not above politics; he had been a superb military politician and learned several valuable lessons from the experience. He was critical of the Democrats, who, he feared, were determined to spend the country into bankruptcy and risked that a totalitarian state might rise out of the ensuing chaos. Fascism was a very recent memory for the man who had, at a very high cost, defeated it. But he was even more disparaging of his own party, certainly its dominant wing, which was at once isolationist and obsessed with Communist plots.

Eisenhower disliked strutters and desk pounders, especially after working for General MacArthur in the 1930s. He preferred to operate by indirection and behind the scenes.

But he wanted to be in control. His first battle in life was to tame his temper. As a boy, denied permission by his parents to go on a Boy Scout event, he beat his hands against a tree until they bled. Fond of quoting scripture, his mother, Ida, had taken him aside and said, "He that conquereth his own soul is greater than he who taketh a city."[14] Shortly after Pearl Harbor, General Marshall informed Eisenhower that he was too valuable as a staff officer in Washington to be sent overseas to fight. Brimming with self-pity, Ike burst out bitterly that he would do his duty—"if that locks me to a desk for the rest of the war, so be it!" The next day Ike was full of regret. He wrote in his diary, "Anger cannot win. It cannot even think clearly."[15]

Ike credited the warm, pacifist Ida for teaching him self-control. "I thought to myself what a poor job she had done," recalled an aide, Bernard Shanley.[16] Ike's subordinates were awed by his capacity for rage. "It was like looking into a Bessemer furnace," recalled one of them, Bryce Harlow.[17] Ike's personal doctor, Howard Snyder, noted that during World War II a journalist had dubbed Ike "the terrible tempered Mr. Bang," and Snyder himself observed "the twisted cord-like temple arteries standing out of the side of his head" when Ike became angry.[18] If Ike felt an outburst coming on, he sometimes simply got up and—even more frightening to his staff—walked out of the room.[19] When he was president, Ike and Mamie would occasionally retreat to the small White House movie theater, though most feature films bored Eisenhower or were too mushy for his tastes. ("Can't you find a new western?" he would demand of the White House staff.)* An exception was a 1951 film entitled *Angels in the Outfield,* about an irascible baseball manager named Guffy McGovern, who is about to lose his job because his team is so awful. An angel appears from heaven to offer the manager a deal: God will let the team win if McGovern learns to control his temper. Through various twists and turns, redemption is achieved. Sergeant John Moaney, Ike's manservant, claimed to have run the movie thirty-eight times, according to Ike's grandson, David. As the lights

---

*A fan of the strong-and-silent type, Eisenhower watched Gary Cooper in *High Noon* numerous times in the White House theater.

came on, Ike would say "Wonderful show" almost inaudibly, and head for bed, resolved to keep his temper with difficult politicians in the morning.[20]

Eisenhower never entirely tamed his emotions. But he did not bully, and his outbursts would pass. On occasion, he used anger to advantage. As a five-star general, he took for granted the retinue of horse-holders in constant attendance, but at the same time he could be sweet with his staff, bestowing small kindnesses. In return, they were loyal; Eisenhower's White House staff turnover was very low. He was blessed with a natural likability. "He merely has to smile at you, and you trust him at once," conceded Field Marshal Bernard Law Montgomery, who was, by nature, suspicious and churlish.[21] "No one hated him. His enemies didn't even hate him," recalled Karl Harr, a national security staffer.[22]

Ike learned to keep up a genial manner, to seem interested, and, when necessary, to hide his true feelings and intentions. His motives were in no way malevolent. To the contrary, he was commanding himself to rise above pettiness, pride, and jealousy, human weakness he knew and understood. Eisenhower was confident in a way that transcended arrogance. He did not need to show off. He knew that he had a gift: the power to make people — indeed, whole peoples — trust him.

Certainly, his allies in World War II sorely tried

his patience. The British chief of the Imperial General Staff, Field Marshal Sir Alan Brooke, initially thought he had "only the vaguest conception of war." (Early in the war, British officers often referred to the Yanks as "our Italians.") In his dealings with the haughty Montgomery, Ike managed to be warm, open, and inclusive, even as "Monty" tested the limits of his short-fuse temper. "God damn it, I can deal with anybody except that son of a bitch!" Eisenhower once exploded.[23] But for the most part, Ike knew he could afford to be patient with the likes of Montgomery. Ike confided to speechwriter Arthur Larson that he had tremendous arguments with Prime Minister Churchill, who was demanding and impulsive. "But it didn't really matter," Ike added quietly, "because I was the boss."[24]

Eisenhower was sometimes even accused of being too agreeable. General George Patton railed that Ike was "damned near a Benedict Arnold" and groused that, as a result of Eisenhower's amiability, the British "are playing us for suckers."[25] But Ike's friendliness was often underwritten not by a sense of emotion but alliance. Indeed, Eisenhower put up with the bloodthirsty, anti-Semitic Patton, resurrecting Patton's career after he struck an enlisted man and relieving him of his command only after he announced at the end of the war that the Americans should join up with the Germans and invade Russia. Ike was fond of Patton and knew he needed him as a war fighter, especially as a tank commander pursuing a defeated enemy — but then, when the war was done, he needed him no longer.[26]

In one of his memoirs, *At Ease: Stories I Tell to Friends,* Ike portrayed himself as a somewhat lazy student who liked to relax by reading westerns and listening to his favorite dance band, Fred Waring and the Pennsylvanians. Elsewhere he described himself as a "simple country boy," and mournfully responded to a reporter's question, "That's just too complicated for a dumb bunny like me."[27] Eisenhower was, in fact, a well-read humanist. As a boy, he had become so entranced by volumes of Greek and Roman history that his mother, irked that he was neglecting his chores, locked the books in a closet. Eisenhower found the key and read while she was off doing errands (another of his heros, or in this case an anti-hero, was Hannibal, a magnificent loser). Ike's high school yearbook predicted that he'd end up as a history professor at Yale. His de facto graduate school was the three years he spent in the early 1920s under the command of General Fox Conner, a genius soldier-scholar, in a remote outpost in the Panama Canal Zone. (It was Conner who taught Ike, "Always take your job seriously, never yourself.") With Conner, Eisenhower read Plato, Tacitus, and Nietzsche, among other philosophers and thinkers.[28]

The younger Ike had also been shaped and hardened by personal suffering. His firstborn child, Doud Dwight, known as "Icky," died of scarlet fever in 1921, and he later wrote that he never really recovered from the loss.[29] During the war he declared to Mamie (but also to himself) that when "pressure mounts and strain increases everyone begins to show the weaknesses in his makeup. It is up to the Commander to conceal his; above all to conceal doubt, fear, and distrust."[30] The famous smile, Ike told his grandson, David, came not from some sunny feel-good philosophy but from getting knocked down by a boxing coach at West Point. The coach refused to spar anymore after Ike got up off the mat looking rueful. "If you can't smile when you get up from a knockdown," the coach said, "you're never going to lick an opponent."[31]

That smile had taken him far, as had the deep learning he shrouded under a mask of simplicity. Through self-control, he had been able to keep himself and the Allies together to liberate Europe. He would soon learn that winning the Cold War—or simply avoiding World War III—would be harder. Certainly, it would be lonelier.

2

The Card Player

The president practices his swing. (Dwight D. Eisenhower Presidential Library, Abilene, Kansas)

O N FEBRUARY 7, 1953, Eisenhower wanted to play golf "very, very badly," as his secretary, Ann Whitman, put it in her diary. The day was cold and rainy, and Ike kept wandering out of the Oval Office onto the porch by the Rose Garden to stare up at the clouds. "Sometimes," he told Whitman, "I feel so sorry for myself I could cry."[1]

Whitman knew her boss was not entirely exaggerating. It may have been the middle of winter, and Eisenhower had been in office less than three weeks, but golf was vital to him. Barred by his image-conscious handlers from venturing out on the links during the presidential campaign, he had been anxious to play as a way of dealing with the pressures of his work. Eisenhower had a healthy respect for the physical and mental toll exacted on the men who had occupied the Oval Office before him. "That damn job," he called the presidency when he was still a lowly staff officer in the 1930s, based in Washington. "Hell, the job killed [Woodrow] Wilson," Ike had exclaimed to Mamie.[2] As president, Eisenhower brought the same discipline to relaxation that he applied to everything else.

Golf was essential to his daily routine. When he awakened in the morning, he limbered up by taking a few swings in his bedroom with his favorite eight-iron. He sometimes swung the club when dictating to Mrs. Whitman. At 5:00 p.m. he would rise from Teddy Roosevelt's old Navy Department desk in the Oval Office, put on his golf shoes, and head out the door, leaving tiny spike holes in the floorboards. On the Ellipse, the greensward stretching south from the White House toward the Washington Monument, he would practice fairway approach shots. His faithful valet (or as he was known in military parlance, his striker), Sergeant John Moaney, would shag the balls while tourists peered through the iron fence.

Eisenhower teed off for a full round of golf about eight hundred times in his eight years as president. Almost every Wednesday and Saturday afternoon, he played three-hour, eighteen-hole rounds at Burning Tree, an all-male club in the Maryland suburbs. On twenty-three trips to Georgia, he played roughly two hundred times at Augusta National, where friends built him, on the 10th hole, a spacious three-story house known initially as Mamie's Cabin, then more commonly as the Eisenhower Cabin. (Mamie herself never played but approved of the game as a stress reliever for her husband.)[3] Ike was a respectable weekend golfer, usually shooting in the 80s, but he had a congenital fade and an unreliable putter, and he sometimes blew up with a torrent of *hell*s and *damnation*s.[4] (Ike almost never used stronger language, and he disapproved of off-color stories. He would turn and walk away if a friend unwittingly tried a dirty joke.)[5] The United States Professional Golf Association helped build a putting green and sand trap outside his office on the South Lawn in 1954. In the spring of 1955, when some unruly squirrels created divots in the green, Ike ordered them shot. Eisenhower was accustomed to having his wishes become commands, but in this case the offending animals were caught and removed.[6]

Eisenhower had grown up poor in Abilene, Kansas. As Army Chief of Staff, he had an office larger than the house in which he had lived with his parents and four brothers. Uncomfortable with ostentatious luxury, during the war he disapproved of his lavish suite at London's Claridge's hotel, with its gold-and-black sitting room, and moved out. ("Makes me feel like I'm living in sin," he said.)[7] But he wore custom-made suits (donated by New York clothiers) and cheerfully loud golf clothes. "He never seemed to wear the same thing twice," recalled Arthur Larson.[8] His clothes were carefully laid out every morning by Moaney. Dressing the president was a precise, half-hour ritual. (It was like seeing "somebody get ready for battle" in the movies, said his grandson, David, who as a boy watched with wonder. "He holds his hands out and puts his armor on, right plate armor, left plate armor...")[9] George Thompson, who filled in for Moaney on his days off, was astounded to find that he had to hold the president's undershorts for him to step into.[10]

Eisenhower was at once intimate and courtly with

his staff. He rose when his secretary entered the room and, for the first two years, addressed her as "Mrs. Whitman."[11] A tall, handsome woman in her early forties, Ann Whitman could instantly sense the president's mood; staffers would check with her in the morning for updates.[12] As she revealed to her biographer Bob Donovan, she knew the president's likes and dislikes—that he enjoyed classical as well as cowboy music, "though he was deathly afraid of being considered highbrow"; that he pretended not to like big crowds along his motorcade route; that he liked seeing old Abilene friends and classmates "for about ten minutes"; that he disliked visits by Republican ladies wearing corsages; also "abstract" paintings, "women who cry," "people who are afraid of him," "people who gush," and being physically touched by almost anyone.[13] Like her boss, Whitman was a shrewd judge of character and intention. Proud, sensitive, smartly dressed, a competent golfer and bridge player, she was devoted to Ike, drawn to him from the moment she first laid eyes on the general in 1945, during a victory parade down Broadway (she even left her husband, a United Fruit Company executive, behind in New York to work for the president). "When he passed he seemed to look right at me," she told Donovan, the *New York Herald Tribune* White House correspondent, who noted, "It was a

Mrs. Whitman (Dwight D. Eisenhower Presidential Library, Abilene, Kansas)

familiar comment. Eisenhower had a knack for conveying to individuals in a crowd the illusion that he was looking right at them."[14]

Mamie wanted Whitman fired almost as soon as she joined the Eisenhower campaign in 1952.[15] Eisenhower's wife recalled the rumors of an affair with Kay Summersby, Ike's pretty wartime driver, repeated by "sympathetic" friends in Washington, which was much speculated about but never proved. She did not want the experience to happen again.[16] Ike had rather coldly cut off Summersby after the war. (Hearing, in 1947, that his former aide was upset about a failed relationship, Eisenhower noted in his diary, "I trust she pulls herself together, but she is Irish and tragic.")[17] Eisenhower managed to allay his wife's fears about Whitman, and she remained his valuable and loyal secretary throughout his presidency. Yet the tension between Whitman and Mamie never really went away, and Mamie visited the Oval Office all of four times in eight years, never when Whitman was there.[18] Mamie had moved thirty-five times in thirty-five years as an army wife, and the White House was her reward (though less grand than the Supreme Allied Commander's château outside Paris). Some of the moves to wretched base housing had been almost unendurable. (In miasmic Panama, she made her husband kill a bat with his ceremonial sword.) The First Lady ruled a separate domain, the social White House. "They never talked business," said their son John. "They had a truce."[19]

In a 1972 oral history, Mamie recalled that "Ike was the sort of man that when he finished his day's work he left his work at the office. When he came home he was home and we didn't discuss what his big problems were."[20] Mamie could be a vivacious hostess—the Eisenhowers gave more state dinners than any of their predecessors—but her command post was her bed. She rarely arose before noon, holding forth to the staff while propped up against a massive custom-made pink headboard. She saw her husband over dinner, usually on trays in front of the

Ike and Mamie, wedding portrait (Dwight D. Eisenhower Presidential Library, Abilene, Kansas)

TV set, trying without success to stop him from eating too fast.[21]

Mamie was not physically strong. She had an inner ear condition that made her dizzy and walk with a slight stagger that gave rise to rumors that she was a tippler. She was a bit of a hypochondriac.[22]

But she maintained a strong physical attachment to Ike, who signed his letters "Your lover." Ike was proud of her. At whistle stops on the campaign train, he grinned broadly while introducing "my Mamie." Unlike most First Couples up to that point, they shared the same bed. (She told a reporter, in her cheery way, that she liked to be able to reach over in the middle of the night and "pat Ike on his bald head anytime I want to.")[23] Mamie was very feminine, frilly in her tastes. With her bangs, she could look a little dowdy to fashion writers, but she dressed to please her husband (she liked clothes that showed off her waist and bosom, according to granddaughter Susan), and loved pomp and ceremony. Her formal wardrobe was so large that extra closets had to be found at the White House (at the same time, she perused the morning papers looking for bargains on food and household items). She worked at sustaining the romance. "In a girlish way, she kept his handsome West Point picture on her dressing table," wrote Susan. She was delighted to have her husband home from the wars. "I've got my man here, right where I want him!" she exclaimed. Ike and Mamie were affectionate together, kissing hello and goodbye and holding hands, unbothered by the ubiquitous staff. But they did not talk much. Like the rest of America, they were captivated by a relatively new entertainment, television. (Mamie became a fan of *As the World Turns*.) President and First Lady wordlessly watched the news together before Ike went off to paint or read, usually a western or a whodunit.[24]

That she had to work on sustaining the romance was telling. Ike had returned from Europe "changed terrifically," according to Mamie—more impatient with frivolity, more entitled, but more metaphysical in his concerns.[25] She'd inserted herself back into his life, but there were strains. An open and vivacious hostess, she was "breezy" and "buoyant," recalled J. B. West, head White House usher, but she could also be "imperious," snapping off commands to staff "like a five-star general." Eisenhower counted on Mamie's devotion. ("I have one career," she said, "and his name is Ike.")[26] But there was a certain distance between them. Her grandson, David, once asked her if she had really known Ike. "I'm not sure anyone did," she replied.[27] Eisenhower never revealed himself entirely, not even to his own family. In 2010, John Eisenhower told the author that he never really knew his father. "I don't envy you trying to figure Dad out," he said. "I can't figure him out."

By his own testimony, Eisenhower felt the loneliness of command, especially after he became president. But while sometimes lonely at the White House, Ike was rarely alone. He spent almost every waking moment in the company of others. Though he had avoided Georgetown cocktail parties as too gossipy, he regularly hosted what he called "small, informal stag dinners" at the White House. The attendees, all male (it was the 1950s), were usually prominent businessmen or figures from academe or the sports world, rarely from government. The guest list might include a couple of big oilmen or a cattleman; some home appliance, publishing, or auto company executives; a top banker or insurance man; a golf champion; Cardinal Spellman or Bernard Baruch. At first, some small businessmen and even workingmen were invited, but they rarely spoke up so were dropped. If you were among the chosen, you received a personal letter from the president on stationery with a monogrammed DDE. "I shall probably wear a dinner jacket, but a business suit will be entirely appropriate," Ike would advise.

He was not a shy host. The evening began over drinks in the president's white, oval second-floor study, which he called "the trophy room" for its huge display cases filled with jewel-encrusted swords and various gaudy awards foreign governments had given him over the years. Ike would hold forth, sometimes with astonishing frankness. Trusting that it was possible to be off the record in that more innocent age, he once made the case for recognizing Red China just as his administration, under pressure from congressional conservatives, was refusing to do so. "The president does love to talk," Ann Whitman remarked in a letter to one of Ike's close friends, George Allen.[28]

Allen, a plump, jolly Mississippi lawyer who relished jokes at his own expense, was one of a group of wealthy businessmen Ike fondly called "the gang." In 1950, he had met some of them at Bohemian Grove, the boozy, convivial, quintessential white-male summer retreat in the California redwoods.[29] The gang members included William E. Robinson, publisher of the *New York Herald Tribune,* Ike's favorite paper, and Pete Jones, head of Cities Service Oil Company, a self-made man who always carried $10,000 in his wallet to remind himself of what he had accomplished. These men shared a deep appreciation of Ike. "Who would have ever imagined," Jones was fond of saying in Eisenhower's presence, "that I would ever walk in the White House as a guest, and know the greatest man in the world?" Ike shared Jones's reverence for the White House, and Jones's "praise for the Eisenhower presidency was, in Granddad's view, factual," wrote his grandson, David.[30]

Members of the gang were available to fly down to Washington or Augusta on short notice to play cards and golf with the president, amid much broad joshing and teasing. The product of an almost entirely male world of the early twentieth-century military,

Ike preferred male company, his love for Mamie and his appreciation of Ann Whitman notwithstanding. "Though Ike was sentimental," Mamie told David years later, "if they put a woman in his westerns he just closed the book—that's the way he liked history too, no goo—he believed in men's company."[31]

In mid-February 1953 Ellis Slater, head of a large whiskey distillery and a charter member of the gang, described the "First Weekend Visit to the White House" in his diary. There was a tour of the "deep bombproof shelter under fifteen feet of reinforced

"The gang": Robinson, the president, and Allen (Eisenhower National Historic Site, Gettysburg, Pennsylvania)

concrete" and some complaining by Mamie, who was having to make do with store-bought furniture from Truman's White House renovation in 1948. Mamie spoke of "the stingy, small bath towels which she felt she wanted to change" but lamented her budget was only $3,000 for the whole second-floor residence.

Bill Robinson flew in from New York, and on Sunday night the almost round-the-clock bridge game resumed. The president "lost sixty bucks," recorded Slater. "Ike is the one person who consistently holds bad cards. But it's probably just as well that he does; we need the edge in cards to make the game half interesting—he plays so much better than the rest of us."[32]

Eisenhower had been a card shark since his West Point days. Injured playing football, cast into a "brown study," as he called his depression, he had taken up smoking and poker. On graduation day, he went to New York City to the Astor Hotel, which loaned cash to West Point cadets, and used his winnings to pay back the $1,000 he owed (a big sum in 1915, roughly worth $22,500 today; Ike had borrowed the money from the Astor to stake his gambling). On dusty army posts during his long, slow climb through the ranks, he won so often and so much—sometimes his opponent's family savings—that he had to quit poker altogether to avoid a reputation for fleecing his fellow officers.[33]

At bridge, Ike was a fierce, take-no-prisoners player. He would mercilessly ridicule his partner for making poor choices and slam down his cards triumphantly when he won, rattling glasses and ashtrays. Mamie refused to play with him, and in time even members of his gang had to pretend to want to pair with him. His only true equal was General Alfred Gruenther, his successor as NATO commander, who possessed a cutting wit and could dish back.[34]

Eisenhower's skill at cards signifies much more than a proclivity for intense recreation. General Andrew Goodpaster, who served as Eisenhower's staff secretary and probably spent more time observing him than any other person with the possible exception of Ann Whitman, was close to his boss and perceptive about the way Ike's mind worked.* Ike, Goodpaster said, was an instinctive game player. He

---

* Wounded in action in World War II, Goodpaster had served as a staff officer to Army Chief of Staff General George Marshall. At the White House, Goodpaster stepped in after Ike's first staff secretary, Brigadier General Pete Carroll, died of a heart attack in September 1954. With roots in Midwest farm country, a strong sense of discretion and duty, and a keen understanding of human nature, Goodpaster was ideally suited to his boss and his job. After handing Eisenhower a letter for his signature that congratulated Harry Truman on his new presidential library, Goodpaster stood patiently while Ike, who disliked Truman, tore it up. "I'll get it retyped," said Goodpaster.

was always thinking several moves ahead, trying to read his opponent and figuring out how to lead him on or trump him. He was adept at operating on several levels, not showing all his cards and playing for bigger jackpots. His partners, let alone his opponents, could not always follow his moves. He was an expert at feints, both at the bridge table and as a commander in chief. Goodpaster made the connection between the card player and the master manipulator. Ike, he once said, "is a great poker player and an extremely good bridge player. He plays bridge very much in the poker style and he's a tremendous man for analyzing the other fellow's mind, what options are open to the other fellow, and what line he can best take to capitalize or exploit the possibilities, having figured the options open to other men."

Goodpaster could see that Eisenhower put enormous stock in his knack for anticipating his opponent's next move, or several moves. It was the key to Ike's success at bridge and poker—and at winning battles of every kind. Studying military history under his mentor Fox Conner, Eisenhower was less interested in the mechanics of the command process, said Goodpaster, than he was in "the analysis of what was in the commander's mind—what was in Lee's mind, for example, at Gettysburg."[35] It is noteworthy that Eisenhower did not like to use the telephone. He wanted to see people face-to-face, the better to read them.[36]

While the term "hidden hand" may overstate or oversimplify Eisenhower's leadership style, said Goodpaster at a 1983 conference on the Eisenhower presidency, Ike often did have a "tendency . . . to work to multiple objectives. He would be looking, as he would put it, at how you kill two birds or many birds with one stone. Some of his objectives he would be reluctant to show. I think on occasion he kept them deliberately concealed." Ike, he noted, was especially adept at getting others to do something he wanted done — sometimes without their ever being aware of his prodding.[37]

On their first Sunday in the White House, Ike and Mamie joined the National Presbyterian Church.[38] Although his parents had been deeply religious and taught him Bible verses as a boy, he had never settled on any one church. He went now mostly for appearances' sake. He believed the president should set an example; besides, a lot of voters, particularly Republicans, were regular churchgoers. To begin weekly cabinet meetings, Eisenhower instituted a prayer, usually delivered by his agriculture secretary, Ezra Taft Benson, an elder in the Mormon church. From time to time, in his haste to get on with the meeting, the president would forget to call on Benson, causing his churchly secretary of state, John Foster Dulles, to whisper a reminder. Ike once burst out, as the meeting was ending, "Jesus Christ, we forgot the prayer!"[39]

His staffers chuckled over this story, and Ike's close friends did not recall theological discussions or even any mention of church, other than Ike's irritation that his pastor was publicizing his presence after promising not to. But his family and his confidants believed that he was a deeply spiritual man, that he was awed by a power beyond man's own. His detachment at times suggested an otherworldly quality, as if he were communing with, or seeking out, some higher force.[40]

President Eisenhower's day usually proceeded with the precision of a military band. He pretended not to have read the newspapers, but he pored over them at breakfast. He was in the office by eight and worked until he took a light lunch at one. (He liked to stay at his football playing weight of 175 pounds.) He worked until five, then strapped on his golf spikes and polished his game for an hour. At six he often met for an hour with John Foster Dulles, and at seven he had a single cocktail before dinner. Then he might read a western (the staff was constantly looking for new ones without "goo") or paint. He liked to slip into a little room set up with his easel and paint pots (Mamie had given him some oils that Christmas of 1952) on the north side of the second floor, near the elevator. As Ike began the first full month of his presidency, he was working on a portrait of the legendary golfer Bobby Jones, who was his friend at Augusta.[41]

On February 17, Eisenhower had his first press conference, in the Indian Treaty Room of the Old Executive Office Building, a Victorian pile across the alleyway from the White House. He would meet with the press 193 times over the next eight years, more than any other president. He was often vague or rambling, and his syntax left something to be desired. (His private memos, by contrast, are sharp and to the point; he was a stickler for clear expression and demanded multiple drafts from his speechwriters.) He would tell reporters that he didn't know things when in fact he did, and refer them to cabinet secretaries for information...the same cabinet officers who had recently learned that precise information from the president. The reporters liked Ike, but they made fun of him, and some of them got together to write Ike's version of the Gettysburg Address: "I haven't checked these figures, but 87 years ago, I think it was, a number of individuals organized a governmental set-up here in this country, I believe it covered certain Eastern areas, with this idea they were following up based on a sort of national independence arrangement and the program that every individual is just as good as every other individual...."[42]

To Richard Rovere of *The New Yorker,* a high priest of the chattering classes in the 1950s, President Eisenhower was a bland "standard American" incapable of nuance or subtlety, who seemed a little bored by the government he ran. Another panjandrum of the Eastern Establishment press, Theodore H. White, at first thought the president was a bit of a simpleton. He would later change his mind.[43]

As a former army staff officer, Eisenhower believed in process, procedure, and organization. He revived the executive branch's cabinet system that Woodrow Wilson and FDR had let lapse or essentially ignored, and he created an elaborate process for national security planning. The heads of federal agencies came to the White House every week, and the president gave every appearance of actually listening to them. He was not pretending; still, as a wartime commander he knew that the best plan of attack rarely lasts longer than the first contact with the enemy. He liked to quote the elder Helmuth von Moltke, the champion of the German general staff: "The plans are nothing but the planning is everything." Ike routinely told associates, "Rely on planning, but never trust plans."[44] He would closely listen to the staffers and read their plans, and then, when it suited him, he would toss them out.

While President Eisenhower demanded a paper trail for official meetings and believed in the chain of command, he also ran what staffers called "the floating crap game," his informal consultations with friends and old comrades, usually with no notetaker present. He often used as an informal sounding board his brother Milton, who stayed many weekends at the White House (until he learned Ike was paying a guest charge for his room; from then on he stayed at the Mayflower Hotel).[45]

Planning and discussion bought Eisenhower time while he figured out what he wanted to do. The mere presence of a president can be intimidating; advisers tend to fawn or clam up. But because of his open and direct manner, his winning smile, and his determination to pass credit down while (most of the time) taking blame up, Ike was able to keep open a genuine dialogue with his staff. "He had an uncanny ability to enter directly and forcibly into a debate without squelching it," wrote Robert Bowie, the State Department's policy planning director.[46] At times, Eisenhower played devil's advocate against his own position. Advisers learned they could not always tell where the president stood on a close question — sometimes because he did not want to tip his hand, and sometimes simply because he had not decided. "Let's not make our mistakes in a hurry" was one of his standard sayings.[47]

*   *   *

Eisenhower was given to grand pronouncements about virtue and goodness that bordered on the banal. "There is no black and white except in morals and exact sciences," he liked to say. ("What's left?" wondered Rusty Brown, who helped him write *At Ease,* his informal memoir, in the 1960s.)[48] During the 1952 campaign, while dodging hard questions about how he would break the deadlock in Korea between the two armies dug in along the 38th parallel, he had told reporters, "The great problem in America today is to take that straight and narrow road down the middle." As historian William Manchester observed, "It wasn't that arresting a phrase to begin with, and when he used it the next day, and then the day after that, there was talk among correspondents of crossing the 38th platitude."[49]

To his son and grandson, he often said he most valued his "Germanic" traits: hard work, persistence, and thoroughness. But they noted that Ike himself had never been a bland corporate type and had always valued mavericks and individualists.[50] Eisenhower cared very much about being seen as a man of principle, the kind who never cut corners or resorted to expediency, and he often began sentences "I always..." and "I never..."[51] And he was, by and large, principled. But Goodpaster mordantly noted that Eisenhower "had a great inventory of principles, in order, some would say, to rationalize whatever he wanted to do."[52]

Though Eisenhower was famous for his displays of personal responsibility, he knew when to duck. He was not at all above letting his subordinates play the bad cop or take the fall. Eisenhower was close to his press secretary, a clever and resourceful Irishman and former *New York Times* reporter named Jim Hagerty. Recollected Hagerty: "President Eisenhower would say, 'Do it this way.' I would say, 'If I go to that press conference and say what you want me to say, I would get hell.' With that he would smile, get up and walk around the desk, pat me on the back and say, 'My boy, better you than me.' "[53]

On Harry Truman's desk stood a plaque declaring "The Buck Stops Here." Eisenhower replaced it with his own, reading *"Suaviter in modo, fortiter in re"*—gently in manner, strongly in deed. For Eisenhower it was critical to maintain a public image of the savior who was above the fray, the great warrior who kept the peace. For most of his presidency—though, as we shall see, not all of it—his efforts had the effect of keeping him enormously popular. His approval rating averaged 64 percent, far higher than that of most modern presidents.[54]

But someone had to do the unpleasant work. Eisenhower skillfully used a number of top aides and officials as buffers and as bearers of bad news. Chief among them was his chief of staff, Sherman Adams. A tightly wound, acerbic New Englander who was too busy to say hello or goodbye on the 250 phone calls he took or placed every day, Adams was known, not fondly, as "the Abominable No Man." He could be petty, telling staffers to keep their feet off their desks and issuing warnings about "general deportment."[55] But he uncomplainingly took on difficult jobs for the president, who was fond of Adams and grateful. Adams himself thought Ike was a little softhearted, though he noted, "Without saying much he could make you feel just terrible."[56]

Despite his temper, Ike always tried to maintain his generally sunny demeanor and claimed that he never held grudges or brooded over slights. He never attacked an opponent by name and was always careful to let even his vanquished enemies save face (except at the bridge table). As Jim Hagerty noted, he always tried to leave an escape route open "for himself and for the other guy."[57] And yet, recalled his grandson, David, "Well into retirement years, Eisenhower maintained a 'black book,' a registry of the living dead containing the names of people who, as far as Eisenhower was concerned, simply had ceased to exist." David's sister Susan doubted the existence of a black book but recalled being told by Ann Whitman that Eisenhower wrote the names of his enemies on pieces of paper, crumpled them up, and tossed them in a drawer. At an off-the-record dinner at the White House with *New York Times* columnist Arthur Krock, Eisenhower alluded to this method of anger management. Krock wrote in a memo to his files: "The President said he had an old professor who, admonishing his pupils that hate was an element always destructive of one's aims, told them how to expel it. The professor did this by writing on a card the name of one for whom he felt hatred and putting the card in a drawer, after which he forgot the location of the drawer and the name of the individual."[58]

3

Positive Loyalty

FOR SUCH AN EXPERT BLUFFER at cards and in life, Dwight Eisenhower possessed a face that was surprisingly easy to read. His features were animated, mobile, and "all too expressive," in the opinion of the president's most eloquent speechwriter, Emmet Hughes. On the trip back from Korea in December 1952 aboard the navy cruiser USS *Helena,* Hughes watched as Eisenhower's secretary of state–designate, John Foster Dulles, droned on about the nature of the Communist threat and then answered "at legalistic length" policy questions from Ike's advisers, gathered around a green baize table. Keeping an eye on Eisenhower, Hughes could clearly see that Dulles bored his new boss. "Time after time," wrote Hughes, "Eisenhower showed, in his face and mannerisms, gestures of impatience made almost more plain by his half-successful efforts to suppress them. His reactions were always the same—the brisk nodding of the head, in a manner designed to nudge a slow voice faster onward toward some obvious conclusion, the restless rhythm of the pencil tapping his knee, the slow glaze across the blue eyes, signaling the end of all mental contact, and finally, the patient fixing of the eyes on the most distant corner of the ceiling."

In the *Helena* instance, the president's eyes remained steadily focused on that corner. Hughes thought "the partnership of Eisenhower and Dulles would surely break, most probably within a year or two"—a "memorably erroneous conclusion," Hughes would later acknowledge.[1] Dulles, sixty-four, was a messianic moralist, or often posed like one. Raised in remote upstate New York, the son of a clergyman, he had been required to learn large segments of *The Pilgrim's Progress* by heart. He spoke slowly, almost painfully, pausing in midsentence, one eye twitching, his mouth opening and closing, his lawyer's mind sifting and searching for the precise word.[2] Dulles's Presbyterian rectitude and his many tics were a source of fun among his subordinates, who, as historian Michael Beschloss relates, enjoyed this story about his persistent blink: "Once, in a foreign hotel, with a twitch of the eye, he was said to have asked a room service waiter for some bottled water. The waiter returned with a tray of liquor. 'No,' said Dulles (another twitch), 'I said I would like some *bottled water*.' More minutes passed. A call girl arrived...."[3]

Ike was expansive, warm (in public), and instinctive; Dulles was crabbed, cold, and logical. One man was famously likable and the other infamously unlikable. Or so they appeared. Actually, Dulles's staff, though they poked fun, found him surprisingly affectionate and considerate in private, while Ike could be remote, even cold, to his subordinates.[4] Dulles was superficially stiff but privately eager to be liked. Eisenhower knew how to play on Dulles's insecurities, though in time he came to value his loyalty.

At the outset, Eisenhower found Dulles politically useful. During the presidential campaign, Dulles had taken a hard line, vowing to "roll back" Communism to liberate the "enslaved peoples" of Eastern Europe (many of whom had relatives in important voting blocs like the ethnic communities of Chicago). Eisenhower had to step in: Dulles, Ike told newsmen, had meant to say roll back by *peaceful* means. But it was handy for Ike to have Dulles play the role of tough guy; it allowed Eisenhower to sound like the voice of reason.[5]

Eisenhower also perceived that he could control his secretary of state. Dulles had long blended moral certitude and social insecurity. Though seemingly a pillar of the New York establishment—educated at Princeton and the Sorbonne, senior partner at Sullivan and Cromwell, member of the Council on Foreign Relations—he had been unclubbable at

Princeton and was known for bad manners and a kind of gracelessness. He would, among other awkward habits, stir his drink with a thick forefinger (then suck it); his socks drooped; and his breath was chronically bad.[6]

Dulles was jealous of power, and he made sure that he enjoyed private access to the president. He would irritate Sherman Adams by marching past the office of the chief of staff and into the Oval Office, stopping only to ask Mrs. Whitman if the president was free.[7] Dulles considered himself the president's personal lawyer, helping him shape arguments and argue his case, whether or not Dulles wholly agreed with it. The grandson of a former secretary of state, he had been with the American delegation at the Treaty of Versailles after World War I, and he was extremely knowledgeable about foreign policy. Ike joked that Dulles had been preparing to be secretary of state "since he was five years old." There was only one person who knew more people and had seen more of the world than Dulles, Eisenhower said to a friend, "and that's me."[8]

Their relationship was all substance: "I never, not once" saw Dulles socialize with Ike, recalled John. (In an oral history for the Dulles papers at Princeton, Eisenhower said he did play bridge with Dulles — once.) In their private conversations (no aides or notetakers; Dulles wanted no leaks), Eisenhower soon discovered that Dulles possessed a more subtle intelligence than his moralistic preachments suggested; that, indeed, Dulles possessed a private cunning not unlike Eisenhower's. Ike also saw, well hidden, an inner goodness and even a sense of humor in the shy, awkward Presbyterian. "Foster's a bit sticky, but he has a heart of gold when you know him," the president years later told British prime minister Harold Macmillan.[9] Within a few weeks of taking office in January 1953, Eisenhower began meeting with Dulles every evening at 6 p.m. in his study in the White House residence for a private conversation about the world. Eisenhower came to depend on those tutorials—a little too much, in the view of Eisenhower's son, who would work at the White House as an aide in his father's second term. Dulles's implacable distrust of the Russians seeped into the president's worldview. Dulles and Eisenhower often reviewed the history of East-West relations "and even took into consideration what they called 'Slavic temperament,' about which I doubt either man was a consummate expert," John Eisenhower wrote in an unpublished memoir.[10]

The East Coast foreign policy establishment had adopted Eisenhower after World War II.[11] He was seen as a bulwark against the rabid Republican far right, which preposterously—but with conviction—accused the Roosevelt administration

Eisenhower and Joe McCarthy (Dwight D. Eisenhower Presidential Library, Abilene, Kansas)

of enslaving Eastern Europe at Yalta and pilloried the Truman administration for "losing" China to the Communists. Eisenhower, on the other hand, was a member in good standing of the Council on Foreign Relations, Wall Street's bastion of internationalism, just as he was credible in small-town America. In that paranoid age, voters were looking for someone to blame. How *did* the Russians get the bomb? How were the Communists allowed to take over China? Ike could keep the Visigoths at bay, or so the citizens hoped.

Leading the yelping pack was Senator Joe McCarthy of Wisconsin, "Tailgunner Joe" in his largely made-up marine war-hero past. Using his sub-poena powers as a Senate committee chairman and his gift for manipulating lazy reporters, McCarthy led a nationwide witch hunt for Communists, or Communist sympathizers, or security risks, or homosexuals—all equivalently subversive to the demagogue from Wisconsin, who drank his lunch and imagined his facts.

The prize catch of the Red hunters had been Alger Hiss, a State Department adviser to Roosevelt at Yalta who had been recruited as a Soviet spy. Hiss was a Harvard Law grad and member of the Establishment—in 1946, he had gone to work at the Carnegie Endowment for International Peace, of which Dulles was then chairman. Lest this connection be used to show that Dulles, too, was soft on Communism, Dulles set out to demonstrate his anti-Communist bona fides. Declaring that he wanted not just loyalty but "positive loyalty," he turned loose a former FBI man named Scott McLeod to investigate his own State Department employees. Rifling through desks at night, McLeod and his men found "security risks" by the hundreds—foreign service officers who had once written critically about the Chinese Nationalists (and were thus, by inference, sympathetic to the Communists) or were cheating on their wives or behaving suspiciously in some way.[12] Before long, McLeod's labors started to threaten diplomats appointed by President Eisenhower. One of them was Ike's newly designated ambassador to the Soviet Union, Charles E. "Chip" Bohlen.

Eisenhower's posture toward McCarthy was hardly defiant. Campaigning in Indiana in early October 1952, Eisenhower had encountered Senator William Jenner, a McCarthyite who had called General George Marshall "a front man for traitors" because he had been Truman's secretary of state. (Marshall's successor, Groton-and-Yale man Dean Acheson, was "the Red Dean.") When Jenner threw his arm around Ike, the candidate visibly winced. "I felt dirty from the touch of that man," Eisenhower told his speechwriter, Emmet Hughes, but he did not shrug off the embrace.[13] His next stop was Wisconsin, McCarthy's own state, where Tailgunner Joe had called Marshall "disloyal" and "half loyal." Ike's friend Arthur Sulzberger, publisher of the *New York Times,* drafted a new paragraph for Eisenhower's speech in Milwaukee, praising Marshall. At the last minute, the candidate's advisers persuaded Ike to drop the insert; they were fearful of losing votes in the Badger State. But the speech had already been shown to some reporters, who immediately jumped on Eisenhower for the omission. "Do I need to tell you that I am sick at heart?" Sulzberger wired Sherman Adams. Eisenhower's aides thought their boss never got over his shame at failing to defend Marshall.[14] Still, though, Eisenhower held back. Although throughout his political and military career Ike dodged and delayed, covering his maneuvers with smoke screens of vagueness, when it came to using force he was all in or all out. He had a high tolerance for ambiguity and a willingness to compromise politically, but he only wanted to fight real battles, to engage in actual combat, when he was sure his side could win. In mid-March, rumors began to reach Capitol Hill that, over at the State Department, the Red hunters had found some "derogatory information" on Chip Bohlen. On March 21, McCarthy rose on the Senate floor to say that he had obtained sixteen "closely typed pages" of damning allegations in Bohlen's file, which, he did not have to say, had been conveniently leaked to him by McLeod, who kept McCarthy's signed photo on his desk ("To a great American..."). Bohlen's was "an ugly record of Great Betrayal," whined McCarthy.

At the Department of State, Dulles wavered. He summoned Bohlen to his office and asked if there was anything damning in his record. Bohlen assured him there was not. "I'm glad to hear this," Dulles responded. "I couldn't stand another Alger Hiss."[15]

At the White House, Eisenhower had been trying to deflate McCarthy by ignoring him. By then the Wisconsin senator was investigating the Voice

Dulles, Eisenhower, and Bohlen (Dwight D. Eisenhower Presidential Library, Abilene, Kansas)

of America and frightening embassy librarians into discarding and even burning books that might have a Communist taint. At a press conference on February 25, a newsman asked the president if McCarthy's efforts were helping the fight against Communism. Ike's answer was a classic of intentional vagueness and tangled syntax: "Well, I don't know exactly what he is aiming to do... because I haven't thought about his particular function—what he can do and what would happen if he didn't do it."[16]

Some of Ike's aides, like Emmet Hughes, implored the president to call out McCarthy. "I will not get into the gutter with that guy," Eisenhower muttered.[17] But on Bohlen, Ike stiffened. He liked and admired the State Department officer, an incisive but debonair Soviet specialist with a dry wit. He needed Bohlen in Moscow as quickly as possible; the Soviet dictator Joseph Stalin had just died, and no one was quite sure who would follow or with what consequences. The president called Dulles and privately instructed him that there would be no cutting and running on Bohlen.

The vice president, Richard Nixon, who had his own history as a Red baiter and could talk to McCarthy, was dispatched to the Senate. McCarthy told Nixon he had two speeches prepared about Bohlen, and had not used "the *real* dirty one."[18] Dulles called Bohlen back to his office. The White House would stand by him, he informed Bohlen. Indeed, he would go to Bohlen's confirmation hearing—but it would be better, Dulles said uncomfortably, if they traveled in separate cars. Bohlen realized the secretary did not want to be photographed with him.

On the Hill, Eisenhower's men worked out a deal: two senators would be allowed to inspect McLeod's file on Bohlen, the sixteen closely typed pages. They found almost nothing. Someone had claimed a "sixth sense" about Bohlen's attraction to "moral turpitude";

someone else said he associated with "some bad eggs." The rumor around Capitol Hill was that Bohlen had a "family problem"—code for homosexual behavior—but the file suggested nothing.

At a press conference, Ike blandly but nonetheless forthrightly said that he knew Bohlen and admired him, that he knew him to be a good family man, and that he had played golf with him. Eisenhower avoided any mention of McCarthy. ("Never get in a pissing match with the skunk," Ike told his brother Milton, who had pressed him to take on McCarthy by name.)[19] Bohlen was confirmed by the Senate the next day by a vote of 74 to 13. Dulles told the ambassador to make sure that his family accompanied him when he flew to Moscow. (Dulles's insecurities were exacerbated by a new quip going around the Georgetown set: "Dull, Duller, Dulles.") In his diary for April 1, Eisenhower wrote: "Senator McCarthy is, of course, so anxious for headlines that he is prepared to go to any extremes in order to secure some mention of his name in the public press. His actions create trouble on the Hill with members of the Party; they irritate, frustrate, and infuriate members of the Executive Department. I really believe that nothing will be so effective in combating this particular kind of trouble-making as to ignore him. This he cannot stand."[20]

Ike's careful maneuver had worked, but the victory was only temporary. The Senate majority leader, Robert Taft of Ohio, sent word to the White House: "No more Bohlens."[21] It was a blunt reminder that Eisenhower's new war would be fought on many fronts, one a short ride from the White House.

4

Cross of Iron

AT THE END of World War II, General Eisenhower had stood atop Lenin's tomb in Moscow with Joseph Stalin, viewing a seemingly endless parade of Russian gymnasts. "This develops the war spirit," Stalin told Ike as they watched the athletes marching by, gaily waving. "Your country ought to do more of this." According to Eisenhower's memoir of the event, Stalin spoke "stolidly," and he was "completely devoid of humor."[1]

When the Soviet Union exploded an atomic bomb on August 29, 1949, Stalin's chief of secret police, Lavrenty Beria, embraced the scientists who had built the bomb and kissed them on the forehead as the mushroom cloud rose in the distance. The scientists were well aware that for at least some of them, a fizzle would have been fatal. Instead they were rewarded with honors, cars, dachas, and the sort of consumer goods unavailable to less fortunate Russians (who soon dubbed the scientists *chocolatniki*). According to a possibly apocryphal story, wrote David Holloway in *Stalin and the Bomb,* "in deciding on who would receive which award, Beria was said to have adopted a simple principle: those who were to be shot in case of failure were now to become Heroes of Socialist Labor; those who would have received maximum prison terms were to be given the Order of Lenin, and so on down the list."[2]

Russians were so afraid of Stalin that when he collapsed with a massive stroke on March 1, 1953, he lay by his bed, soaked in his own urine, for almost twelve hours before anyone dared to enter his room. He died four days later.[3]

In Washington, March 4 was a cool and drizzly day. The CIA had learned of Stalin's stroke in the middle of the night, but White House aides, knowing Eisenhower's desire not to be disturbed about matters he could not control, did not awaken him with the news. Instead, he was told before breakfast. When the president reached the Oval Office at his customary hour of 8:00 a.m., Mrs. Whitman noticed he was wearing a brown suit, a bad indicator of the presidential mood and sign of a "hard day" ahead. Eisenhower's first words were, "What do you think we can do about *this*?"[4] His advisers had no useful answer.

At a cabinet meeting two days later, the president

spoke acidly: "For about seven years, ever since 1946, I know everybody who should have been concerned with such things has been sounding off on what we should do when Stalin dies.... Well, he did—and we went to see what bright ideas were in the files of this government, what plans were laid. What we found was the result of seven years of yapping was exactly *zero*. We have no plan. We don't even have any agreement on what difference his death makes. It's—well, it's *criminal,* that's all I can say." Emmet Hughes wrote in his diary, "No one contradicted him."[5] Eisenhower's mood had improved by the time Hughes found him pacing in circles in the Oval Office about a week later. Eisenhower had a speech scheduled in April for a group of newspaper editors, and he wanted to use it to make a peace overture to the post-Stalin Soviet Union. The president said to Hughes that he was "tired—and I think everyone is tired, of indictments of the Soviet regime."

As Hughes recalled the scene, Eisenhower wheeled and announced, "*Here* is what I would like to say."

The jet plane that roars over your head costs three quarters of a million dollars. That is more money than a man earning ten thousand dollars every year is going to make in his lifetime. What world can afford this sort of thing for long?... We are in an armaments race: everyone is wearing himself out to build up his defenses. Where is it going to lead us? At worst, to atomic warfare, and we can state pretty damn plainly what that means. But at the least, it means that every people, every nation on earth is being deprived of the fruits of their own toil. . . .

Now, here's the other choice before us, the other road to take—the road of disarmament. What does that *mean?* It means for everybody in the world: butter, bread, clothes, hospitals, schools—good and necessary things for a decent living. . . . [6]

The speech was one that he had been rehearsing in his mind, in one way or another, for a long time. As president, Eisenhower harbored two main fears. The first was nuclear war (or as it was still called, atomic war). The second was the fate that could befall a nation that devoted all its resources to preparing for war. In the 1920s and '30s, Eisenhower had been one of a new generation of officers who studied how nations mobilized for total war. (In 1925, Ike had finished first in his class at Command and General Staff School in Leavenworth, Kansas.) After World War I, the army's war colleges no longer instructed commanders about mere logistics—how to organize train timetables and so forth—but taught them to reorganize industries for war and even how to prepare the entire nation—politically and economically—for the terrible burden of all-out conflict. Eisenhower, a graduate of the officers' Army War College in Carlisle, Pennsylvania, later taught at the army's newly created Industrial War College in Washington, whose very name underscored this goal. In private conversation and in his public remarks, he often warned against what he called "the garrison state."[7] Military necessity would require citizens to give up their cherished freedoms—and, Eisenhower feared, to become automatons of the state. Ike had witnessed the turn toward fascism during the Great Depression. In one of his memoirs, he recalls once falling into a "brown study" as he rode around New York City, looking out his car window, wondering what would happen to all those people if they lived in a "master-planned society" ever girding for war.[8]

Eisenhower's passion to save America from becoming a garrison state was real, and Hughes was stirred by it. But the speechwriter, who had been an editor at Time-Life and was not always the subtlest reader of the moods and utterances of statesmen, was taken aback by the antimilitarism of the former Supreme Allied Commander. He was further confused as he juxtaposed Ike's dovish sentiments with the bellicose words he had heard, almost exactly twenty-four hours earlier, from the president's secretary of state. Visiting John Foster Dulles at his State Department office, Hughes had wondered aloud if the United States might not want to accept a peace settlement proposed by India to end the Korean War. "We'd be sorry," the secretary told him. "I don't think we can get much out of a Korean settlement until we have shown — before all Asia — our clear superiority by giving the Chinese a hell of a licking." (Dulles was, in fact, not quite so truculent; Hughes, who disliked Dulles, sometimes read too much into his declarations.)

Now, in the Oval Office, Hughes briefly pointed out to the president what his secretary of state had said about "licking" the Chinese. Still wound up, Eisenhower lashed out. "All right, then," he said. "If these very sophisticated gentlemen in the State Department, or Dulles and all his advisers, really don't mean they can talk peace seriously, then I'm in the wrong pew.... Because if it's war we should be talking about — I know the people to discuss this with, and it's not the State Department."[9]

In the Pentagon and the various military commands around the world were many officers who had fought for Eisenhower in World War II. In truth, Ike was just as wary of generals as he was of hawkish diplomats, if not more so. Eisenhower had a healthy skepticism about the grandiose schemes of the military. He knew how the top brass used worst-case scenarios to frighten their civilian masters into spending more on unnecessary new weapons systems and pet boondoggles. Hughes recalled Ike getting worked up during a review of the military budget and telling his advisers, "Look, let me tell you something. I know better than any of you fellows about waste in the Pentagon and about how much fat there is to be cut—because I've *seen* those boys [a favorite Eisenhower locution] operate for a *long* time."[10]

Eisenhower wanted to use his appearance before the newspaper editors in April to give his first truly important address on the most vital issue facing his presidency and the nation. Stalin's death presented an opportunity to send a serious peace feeler to the Soviets, and he wanted to let his own national security establishment know that he was looking for ways to get off the road to atomic war or the bleak alternative, turning the country into that garrison state. But as sometimes happened when Eisenhower was under real stress—when he faced a difficult decision or a critical speech—he fell ill.

Ike never wanted to be thought of as sickly. As a young officer, he had done chin-ups until he was a "real he-man," according to his friend Patton. But his stomach had bothered him at least as far back as his West Point days. According to a 1931 medical report, "For some time he has had sudden cramps, then followed by an intense desire to defecate." A year later: "Consider a neurotic element. Thinks he has something wrong with his bowels." His worst bout came in the winter of 1949, when he was working with Defense Secretary James Forrestal to unite the chronically feuding armed services. The stress was tremendous (later that spring, the mentally unbalanced Forrestal killed himself), and at one point Ike collapsed, so sick to his stomach he could barely raise his head from the pillow. He was forced to take a two-month sick leave. Chastened by the severity of the illness, Ike quit cold turkey his four-pack-a-day cigarette habit and vowed to play as much golf as possible to ward off further breakdowns.

Noting that various doctors had failed to diagnose the cause of Eisenhower's stomach upsets, his personal physician, Howard Snyder, observed that the attacks "usually develop after a period of nervously exhausting work, and have been precipitated by eating a highly spiced or 'rich and rough' meal."[11] On the night of April 15, on the eve of his speech to the American Society of Newspaper Editors, Eisenhower ate a large serving of heavily spiced fish in the dining room of the Augusta National Golf Club, where he had gone to play a round with Ben Hogan (who that summer would win the Masters and the British and US Opens). The next morning, back in

Washington, Eisenhower looked pallid and shaky. At eleven fifteen, Emmet Hughes and a few others were hanging around outside the Oval Office when Sherman Adams emerged and murmured to Hughes, "He's in bad shape, stomach backing up on him again." Oveta Hobby, the secretary of Health, Education, and Welfare, went in "and came out almost crying to me, 'Emmet, I don't think he can do it — he's dazed — he didn't hear a word I said,'" recorded Hughes in his diary.[12]

A half hour later, as the president made his way to the podium at the National Press Club, his national security aide, Bobby Cutler, "sensed something was terribly wrong." Sweat glistened on Ike's brow, Cutler recalled; "there was a slackness in his robust voice; its hearty earnestness seemed muted."

The president began reading the speech written by Hughes, which Eisenhower had heavily edited and which closely reflected his Oval Office expostulations of the month before: "The cost of one modern heavy bomber is this: a modern brick school in thirty cities. . . . We pay for a single fighter plane with a half a million bushels of wheat. We pay for a new destroyer with new homes that could have housed more than eight thousand people. . . . This is not a way of life at all, in any true sense. Under the cloud of threatening war, it is humanity hanging from a cross of iron. . . ." Cutler observed that Eisenhower was gripping the speaking lectern so tightly that his knuckles had turned white. Looking down at his mimeographed text, the national security adviser saw that the president was beginning to drop sentences from the prepared speech, then whole paragraphs.

Eisenhower was "experiencing one of the most miserable periods, physically, of my life," he later wrote. He described coming close to fainting while suffering chills and cramps "of a most disturbing kind."[13] After the speech, Cutler found the president half sitting, half lying on a sofa, clammy with sweat.[14] That afternoon, Ike insisted on throwing out the first pitch at Opening Day of the baseball season, "so as not to disappoint people." He smiled gamely, but reporters could see he was in pain, and muckraking columnist Drew Pearson began printing rumors that the president was suffering from "colitic poisoning" (while playing golf "at least three times a week").[15]

In the White House, Eisenhower searched for solitary pleasures that would divert him. He was so obsessive about getting onto his putting green in the morning that he had groundskeepers use fishing rods and lines to flick off the dew. His one sure retreat was the small room overlooking the North Lawn and Pennsylvania Avenue. There, for an hour in the late afternoon, he would stand at his easel, painting simple but energetic likenesses of friends and bright landscapes in primary colors. Ike may have been pondering his hard choices as he daubed on the oil paints, or he may have been thinking of nothing at all—or he may have been patiently and purposefully trying to make it look as if he was hardly working. In an age before instant communications and a twenty-four-hour news cycle, commanders in chief often tried to project an unhurried calm. Like all great poker players, Eisenhower could be almost ostentatiously imperturbable, only the momentary volcanism of his temper giving him away. But he also understood that a great poker player has to oscillate between intimidation and accommodation, depending on the circumstances. As a result, his real priorities were sometimes difficult to discern. Ike had the phone in the small room disconnected, and blew up once when the chief usher, J. B. West, stuck his head in to say, "Secretary of State Dulles is on the phone and says he *must* speak to the President." Ike, who was painting a coat sleeve on his portrait of Bobby Jones, threw his brush down on the little table and roared, "Damn, I can't do anything around this place!"[16] What he was "doing" was not always clear, often by intent.

Eisenhower's American Society of Newspaper Editors speech, entitled "The Chance for Peace," was the greatest of his career, wrote his chief of staff, Sherman Adams, in a 1961 memoir. At the time, Richard

Rovere of *The New Yorker* (showing more respect for Eisenhower than he had previously) called it "an immense triumph" that "firmly established" Eisenhower's "leadership in America and re-established American leadership in the world."[17] The Soviets, in an unprecedented gesture, published the entire address—which called for mutual disarmament—in *Pravda*. A sense of hope and possibility briefly flared in Washington and Moscow, and other capitals around the world.

But the moment passed. The Soviets, searching for Stalin's successor, were divided and confused. Eisenhower's own government was not really behind him. At Stalin's funeral, the new premier, Georgy Malenkov, had called for a period of "peaceful coexistence," but Secretary of State Dulles was skeptical. He was also wary of his own boss, lamenting to Hughes that Eisenhower was "falling in with the Soviet scheme of things."[18] Only two days after "The Chance for Peace," Dulles (with Eisenhower's approval) delivered a skeptical, scornful speech that began, "We are not dancing to any Russian tune."[19] Meanwhile, the military was doing its best to frighten Congress into spending more money on weapons.

During the Korean War, President Truman had invoked a document called NSC 68, prepared for the National Security Council, calling for a massive arms buildup to face the Communist threat. NSC

68 warned of a "year of maximum danger," when the Russians would have a hydrogen bomb and the means to deliver it. Ike regarded "target dates" as "pure rot," a "damn trick formula of 'so much by this date.'" Yet that didn't mean that those at the Pentagon agreed with him—or, if they did, that they would abandon the pretense.

Leading the demand for more money, particularly for the air force, was Democratic senator Stuart Symington of Missouri. Smooth, aggressive, and ambitious, Symington tested Eisenhower's patience, not least because he was a protégé of Harry Truman, whom Ike regarded, a little unreasonably, as his political nemesis. Eisenhower was determined to cut back defense spending, which had ballooned under Truman from $13.5 billion to a proposed $45 billion. Symington was loudly squawking, insisting that the air force must double its force to 141 air groups by 1954 to face the "year of maximum danger."

Meeting at the White House with congressional leaders in late April, Eisenhower did not try to hide his scorn. "I'm damn tired of the Air Force sales programs," he said. "In 1946, they argued that if we can have seventy groups, we'll guarantee security for ever and ever and ever." Now they had come up with this "trick figure of 141. They sell it. Then you have to abide by it or you're treasonous." One member argued that the air force knew better than the politicians how to measure its needs. "Bunk," Eisenhower scoffed. He knew the Pentagon "as well as any man living," he said, and he knew how the people who worked there routinely overstated their case.[20]

Eisenhower was simultaneously attacked by Senate Majority Leader Robert Taft for not cutting the military *enough*. The midwesterner's isolationist roots made him leery of international commitments. At a meeting with Republican leaders on April 30, Taft, a stiff, irascible figure, became exercised about Eisenhower's budget, which included a slight tax increase. Taft "exploded, losing control of himself, pounding his fist on the Cabinet table and shouting at the stunned president, who was sitting opposite him," recalled Sherman Adams. "With a program like this we'll never elect a Republican Congress in 1954," Taft shouted. "You're taking us down the same road Truman traveled. It's a repudiation of everything we promised in the campaign."

When Taft stopped talking, "a heavy and uncomfortable quiet fell upon the room," Adams recalled. "Eisenhower moved in his chair, flushed and upset, as if he were about to say something."[21] In his diary that night, President Eisenhower picked up the story: "Several of my close friends around the table saw that my temper was getting a little out of hand at the demagogic proceeding, and of course they did not want any breach that was unbridgeable. So

George Humphrey [secretary of the treasury] and Joe Dodge [budget director] in turn jumped into the conversation as quickly as there was the slightest chance to interrupt and held the floor until I cooled down somewhat."[22] Taft calmed down, too, and later made a joke of the incident. Ike invited Taft to play golf with him in Augusta, and the two became, if not close friends, good working allies.

5

Gentleman's Agreement

THE KOREAN WAR had begun because Joseph Stalin blundered. The Kremlin chief gave his North Korean client permission to invade its southern neighbor in June 1950, under the assumption that the Americans would not intervene. But the defense of South Korea quickly became a test of the Free World. Anti-Communism was peaking in the United States—the Cincinnati Reds baseball team changed their name for a time, and Miss America contestants were asked to state their opinion of Karl Marx. In Western Europe, where the threat seemed even more immediate, governments rallied to the American call to use the newly created United Nations to resist Communist aggression. Although the United States provided 90 percent of the troops in Korea, fifteen other nations joined the UN cause. By autumn, General Douglas MacArthur, at the head of a UN force, was driving deep into North Korea.

But then, in November, the Chinese Red Army stepped in and caught MacArthur by surprise, forcing a desperate retreat. The war bogged down around the 38th parallel separating North from South. The fighting in caves and trenches was grim and depressing, and Americans began to turn away. Suspecting that no one was reading about the war, the editors of an Oregon newspaper ran the same story about the fighting two days in a row, and no one seemed to notice.

The Korean War would become known as the Forgotten War, but at the time it seemed more like a festering sore. As political leaders talked and dithered, the toll of dead GIs continued to climb. By the time of Eisenhower's election in 1952, ending the war had become his highest priority.[1]

The President's National Security Council met once a week, usually on Thursdays at 10:00 a.m. The council—the president, the vice president, and the president's national security adviser; the secretaries of state, defense, and treasury; the chairman of the Joint Chiefs of Staff; and various undersecretaries and senior military officers as required—sat around an enormous mahogany table in the Cabinet Room, a large, airy chamber in the West Wing with southern light streaming through its tall windows. Eisenhower did not talk much at the larger and fairly pro forma weekly cabinet meetings, but he plunged in at the more intimate meetings of the NSC. Sitting relaxed in his chair, constantly doodling on a pad (pictures of coffee cups and saucers and the occasional sketch of a council member, one time with a bullet superimposed on the back of his head), he would often interrupt to dispute a point or float an idea. His mobile face was very expressive—his eyes would bulge when someone said something he regarded as stupid. Where his thoughts were taking him was often hard to tell.[2]

At an NSC meeting on February 11, only three weeks into Eisenhower's presidency, the question of using nuclear weapons in Korea had come up for the first time. General Mark Clark, the US ground commander, warned of a buildup of Chinese troops around Kaesong, the ancient Korean capital. The area was "chock full of troops and materiel" apparently massed for an attack, Clark reported. According to the NSC's official notetaker, Eisenhower "expressed the view that we should consider the use of tactical nuclear weapons on the Kaesong area, which provided a good target for this type of weapon."

The remark seemed to come out of the blue. General Omar Bradley, the chairman of the Joint Chiefs (and General Eisenhower's lead ground commander in Europe in World War II), offered a note of caution. Accustomed to Ike's provocations, knowing they were often intended to stimulate debate and not dictate policy, Bradley interjected that it was "unwise to broach the subject yet of possible use of atomic weapons." He reflected the view of many ground commanders that nuclear weapons were last-resort strategic weapons, unsuitable for the battlefield.*

Dulles spoke up next. He wanted to raise what he called "the moral problem." The secretary of state, who often sermonized, was not objecting to the use of nuclear weapons but rather to the opposite. According to the notetaker, Dulles brought up the "Soviet success to date in setting atomic weapons aside from all other weapons as being a special category. It was his opinion that we should try to break down this false distinction."[4]

That general taboo against using nuclear weapons had come not just from Soviet propagandists (who were calling for universal disarmament while racing to catch up to the American nuclear program) but also from Eisenhower's predecessor, Harry Truman.

---

*Bradley was accustomed to challenging his old boss. In their long but often tense partnership during 1943–45, he had viewed Ike as a great leader, but one who was sometimes too deferential to the interests of the British allies. Bradley in part blamed Ike's driver, the Irish beauty Kay Summersby, later recalling that "her influence over him was greater than is generally realized."[3]

In spite of, or because of, his willingness to use atomic bombs against Japan, Truman regarded such devices essentially as terror weapons or weapons of last resort. The American atomic bombs—about a thousand of them by the time Eisenhower took office—had not been given to the military but were stockpiled by the civilian Atomic Energy Commission. One of Eisenhower's first acts as president was to begin turning the bombs over to the military as part of their regular arsenal.[5] To be credible, Eisenhower knew, the threat had to be real: the bombs had to be positioned near warplanes ready to fly.

At the meeting on February 11, Eisenhower seemed to play with the notion of using the bomb as a lever to get more allied support for the UN forces. Bradley had warned that the allies would balk at Ike's gambit. Since at this stage of the Cold War, Europe was the most likely battlefield of World War III, London, Berlin, and Paris were understandably anxious to preserve the taboo on nuclear weapons. If the allies objected to their use, suggested the president, "we might well ask them to supply three or four more divisions needed to drive the Communists back, in lieu of use of nuclear weapons." But then Ike pulled back: he ruled out "any discussion with our allies of military plans or weapons of attack."[6] Eisenhower was never one to rush a decision, especially one as fraught as the use of atomic bombs.

Still, the issue kept surfacing. At another NSC meeting in late March, a civilian consultant, Deane Malott, president of Cornell University, argued that "we ought to use a couple of atomic weapons in Korea," despite the "public hysteria" over the bomb. "The President replied that perhaps we should," recorded the notetaker—but then Ike quickly added, "we could not blind ourselves to the effects of such a move on our allies." Even so, "the President and Secretary Dulles were in agreement that somehow or other the taboo which surrounds the use of nuclear weapons would have to be destroyed. While Secretary Dulles admitted that in the present state of world opinion we could not use an A-bomb, we should make every effort to dissipate this feeling...."[7]

Eisenhower did not quite share Dulles's zeal. In his memoirs of World War II, he suggested that he had opposed dropping the atomic bomb on Japan in 1945. After learning of the bomb from Secretary of War Henry Stimson, Eisenhower recalled, he "expressed the hope that we would never have to use such a thing against any enemy." Ike's son John recalled his father's "depression" that night over Stimson's news. But Eisenhower doesn't appear to have protested very hard (if at all) against dropping the bomb, and in any case by 1953 his views on nuclear weapons had evolved — as they would throughout his presidency.[8]

Eisenhower knew that Americans were losing patience and looking to him to end the war in Korea, any way he could. Ike was more realistic than Dulles, who seemed bent on unifying Korea, or at least enlarging South Korea, while giving the Chinese, as he had put it to Hughes, a "good licking." Sick of the stasis of trench warfare, more people were starting to accept the idea of drastic measures — in some polls, roughly half showed a willingness to drop the bomb on Red China, which was supporting the North Koreans with supplies and soldiers, and appeared to many as the real enemy.[9] Eisenhower's popular standing was high — his approval rating stood at around 70 percent, more than twice Truman's at the end of his presidency — and he seemed, in some White House conversations, to be willing to do whatever it took to terminate the war.

But with Ike, it was sometimes hard to know if he really meant what he said. There are no revealing diary entries from this period, no advisers' recollections of the president confiding or even guessing at his true intentions. There is the notetaker's record from the secret NSC sessions, but these paraphrased jottings can reveal only so much. Eisenhower was cagey, and he could be a provocateur, jumping into discussions to stimulate debate. He wanted to hear all sides, even if that meant arguing with himself. Ever the believer in planning (if not the plans), he required the military to come up with a massive order of attack, including nuclear weapons if necessary, to end the war.

In Moscow, Stalin had been perfectly content to let the war drag on, bleeding the West. The Chinese and North Koreans, however, were increasingly restive. The fighting was draining their resources. Both countries began to experience food hoarding, rampant inflation, and popular unrest.

With the death of Stalin on March 5, 1953, it did not take long for his successors, eager to ease tensions with the West, to signal their Chinese and North Korean comrades to sue for peace. On March 19, the Soviet Council of Ministers sent letters to China's Mao Zedong and North Korea's Kim Il Sung "indicating their willingness to resolve the outstanding issues in order to reach an armistice agreement."

For more than a year, peace negotiations at the desolate meeting ground of Panmunjom had been hung up over the seemingly arcane issue of prisoner repatriation. Americans had raw memories of forcibly returning Soviet soldiers held in German POW camps to the USSR, where there had been mass reimprisonments and suicides. Both sides in the Korean conflict claimed their prisoners did not wish to return home after the war. This was true for some, possibly many, who feared Communist rule or reprisal of some sort, but it was hard to know exactly how many, since there was coercion on both sides. Communist "brainwashing" was dramatized a decade later in a famous American movie, *The Manchurian Candidate*, but sadistic outrages also occurred in the South Korean prison camps, where some North Korean POWs were tortured to confess their hatred of Communist rule and forcibly tattooed with anti-Communist slogans.[10] Meanwhile, peace talks went nowhere.

The breakthrough came in late March 1953. Chinese foreign minister Chou En-lai returned from Stalin's funeral in Moscow to propose that prisoners who did not wish to go home be sent to a third country, at least for a period of time, to make up their minds. Talks resumed in earnest at Panmunjom, and sick and wounded prisoners began to be repatriated.

But then, in May, negotiations slowed again. Chinese and Americans were still killing each other in a pointless pitched battle at a place called Pork Chop Hill. The Chinese had become expert at building networks of impregnable tunnels, and they were able to avoid American artillery fire by tunneling right up to the American lines. The Chinese hid their artillery in caves on the back sides of mountains, rolling out the weapons for quick and maddeningly accurate barrages, then sliding them back into the rocks before the Americans could target their counterfire.[11]

Conventional forces were not enough, or so it seemed to the top commanders, who were frustrated by the long stalemate on the battlefield. The Americans could not win a World War I–style trench war without sacrificing more men than the public would tolerate; the only military solution, it seemed, was to strike with more devastating weapons.

Throughout May, the members of Eisenhower's National Security Council met, formally and informally, to decide what to do.[12] On May 6, the president again raised the possibility of using atomic bombs, but first he decided to bluff: to send some subtle warnings that American patience had run out and that the United States was making its final offer at the negotiating table.[13] If the Chinese and North Koreans failed to come to terms, American diplomats were to broadly hint, the United States would expand the war with nuclear weapons. China's leadership was willing to absorb enormous casualties, but a few atomic bombs would greatly raise the stakes even for the cold-blooded Chairman Mao.

Dulles headed to the Far East on a diplomatic grand tour later that month, and he stopped in New Delhi to see Prime Minister Jawaharlal Nehru. Discussing Korea, the American secretary of state said, according to his notes of the meeting, that "the United

States would probably make a stronger rather than a lesser military exertion, and that this might well extend the area of conflict. (Note: I assumed this would be relayed.)"[14] At the same time, Ambassador Bohlen in Moscow was instructed to give a similarly couched warning to Foreign Minister Vyacheslav Molotov.

Eisenhower and his lieutenants would later cite these secret signals as the carefully veiled threats that intimidated the Communists into giving up. Yet Dulles's warning seems fairly cryptic, and Nehru later denied that he had passed it on to the Soviets (and thence to the Chinese and North Koreans). Bohlen, likewise, was diplomatic to the point of opaqueness, saying only to his Russian counterpart that the failure of armistice talks would create "a situation which the U.S. Government is seeking most earnestly to avoid."[15]

What seems to have been more convincing to the North Koreans and their sponsors was not the threat of atomic bombs but the use of actual force — conventional, but aimed at civilians, and deeply destructive and demoralizing. In May, American warplanes started bombing hydroelectric plants, dams, and irrigation canals. Much of North Korea was blacked out and flooded, and with the rice crop ruined, the country faced famine.[16]

Eisenhower was an old hand at this sort of total

warfare. He was a believer in overwhelming force: if you have to fight, don't hold back, go all the way. Throughout 1942 and 1943, the British Royal Air Force bombed German cities by night, seeking to break German morale. But the American air force preferred "precision bombing," hitting military and industrial targets by day. Then, in August 1944, with the Germans in retreat, the RAF asked the Americans to join them in pasting Berlin in Operation Thunderclap, essentially leveling two and a half square miles of the German capital. The American air commander, General Carl "Toohey" Spaatz, was opposed to the mission; he did not want the United States to be "tarred" with moral opprobrium after the war. But the Allied Supreme Commander took a different view. On August 24, Ike wrote Spaatz, "While I have always insisted that U.S. Strategic Forces be directed against precision targets, I am always prepared to take part in anything that gives real promise to ending the war quickly." By February 1945, the Americans had joined the British in all-out bombing against Berlin.[17]

And there was no looking back, at least not consciously. During World War II, Ike never expressed any anguish over the orders he gave to burn cities and the people who lived there. He did broadly lament war itself. "It's so terrible, so awful," he wrote Mamie, "that I constantly wonder how 'civilization' can stand war at all." Once, he told a reporter that war brought on a sense of "exhilaration" from the "matching of wits with the enemy." He quickly caught himself and quoted Robert E. Lee, that it is "well that war is too terrible, lest we grow too fond of it."

In fact, some of his physical ailments may have been extreme manifestations of his internal feelings during World War II, a moral constipation and agony informed by waste measured in blood and rubble. "Ike complained that there was not one part of his body that did not pain him," reported Kay Summersby.[18] Unsettled, he would brood alone, lying awake at night, smoking cigarettes in the dark.

Exhilarated or not, Eisenhower was also apparently willing to consider using nuclear weapons in Korea. Certainly from the very beginning he spoke as if he were. He had been thinking about using the atomic bomb since the day the North had invaded South Korea, in June 1950. At the time, Ike was no longer a formal military adviser to the secretary of defense, but he had close Pentagon ties, and he found the top brass in a "dither," unsure how the United States would respond. In his diary on June 30, he recorded his advice to his "friends" in the Pentagon:

My whole contention was that an appeal to force cannot, by its nature, be a partial one. The appeal having been made, for God's sake, get ready! Do everything possible under the law to get us going.

Remember, in a fight we (our side) can never be too strong. I urged action in a dozen directions.... We must study every angle to be prepared for whatever may happen, even if it finally came to the use of an A-Bomb (which God forbid).[19]

A few days later, in a memo to the Army Chief of Staff, Ike suggested "the use of one or two atomic bombs in the Korea area, if suitable targets can be found."[20] The suggestion seems offhand, almost cavalier, but it could well have been made in typical Eisenhower fashion, as a prompt to debate. He did not pursue the suggestion. Ike was careful not to reveal his most intimate thoughts about a weapon he abhorred but might have to use. Eisenhower talked politics and, occasionally, about affairs of state with his millionaire friends, who joined him for marathon bridge games and golf at Augusta and Burning Tree Country Club. But there is no evidence that he plumbed his soul with them over the use or nonuse of nuclear weapons. And since Ike "never talked business" with Mamie, as their son John put it, unlike First Ladies from Abigail Adams to Lady Bird Johnson to Hillary Clinton, she did not play the role of informal adviser.

*   *   *

The war plan produced by the Joint Chiefs and ratified by the National Security Council on May 20, 1953, called for a massive bombing campaign, including hundreds of atomic bombs, against China as well as North Korea. As conceived by General J. Lawton Collins, the Army Chief of Staff, it also called for the use of mustard gas to drive the enemy from the caves into the open, where they would be targets for tactical nuclear weapons. The draconian proposal seemed to have given Eisenhower pause. He said he feared that the Soviets, looking for some way to retaliate against US interests and allies, might use A-bombs against defenseless cities in Japan, which lay within bomber range of Soviet airfields in East Asia. (Soviet long-range bombers on one-way missions could also conceivably hit the United States, but curiously, there was no discussion of this.)[21]

This was a contingency plan, to be used in case the Korean war dragged on. Earlier, on May 6, Eisenhower had suggested using nuclear weapons against four North Korean airfields. Such a move would "test the effectiveness of an atomic bomb," he said. The NSC notetaker recorded: "At any rate, said the President, he had reached the point of being convinced that we have got to consider the atomic bomb as being simply another weapon in our arsenal." Once again, General Bradley quickly stepped in: he "expressed some doubts as to the usefulness of any of these fields as a target for an atomic bomb." Bradley did not offer any damage assessment at the NSC meeting, but Eisenhower was probably aware that the Hiroshima-size atomic bombs in the US arsenal would take out not only airfields but the civilian population for miles around. Bradley said nothing more, and the president did not pursue his suggestion; he merely left it hanging.[22]

By 1957 or so, as nuclear weapons and their delivery systems became capable of raining down megatons of death, Eisenhower likely abandoned any thought of using nuclear weapons except in extremis. In 1953, it was still possible to imagine survivable nuclear exchanges and winning a prolonged war.[23] Yet even if Eisenhower had ruled out nuclear weapons, he never would have revealed it for one simple, if profound, reason: he knew that, to be credible about using the bomb as a deterrent to war or as a prod to diplomacy, he had to show a willingness to use nuclear weapons — not just in his public statements but *in his most private deliberations*. If he ever let on, even to his most intimate friends, that he had no intention of using nuclear weapons, he risked undercutting his entire strategy — in the slip of a tongue by a self-important staffer at a Georgetown cocktail party, or just because there is, over time, no such thing as a secret policy in Washington. The essence of effective deterrence is to never let on that you are not willing to use your ultimate weapon—*to tell no one,* as Dean Acheson, in McGeorge Bundy's presence, would later caution President Kennedy during the 1961 Berlin Wall crisis. For Ike, that literally meant no one. Such is the loneliness of nuclear command, but at least Eisenhower was accustomed to the burden—from those nights lying awake as D-day approached, wondering about the fickle weather and the fate of the liberation of Europe. "If any blame or fault attaches to the attempt it is mine alone," he had written in a note he tucked into the pocket of his uniform jacket the morning of June 5, 1944, shortly before going off to bid farewell to the paratroopers.[24]

Eisenhower's true intentions on nuclear weapons in Korea went untested. A few days after the NSC approved its war plan, the Communists accepted the US/UN peace terms. Eisenhower and his top lieutenants would always claim that the president ended the Korean War by artfully bluffing, by threatening to break the taboo against nuclear weapons. Sherman Adams recalled that when he asked Ike how an armistice had been achieved in Korea, the president instantly responded, "Danger of an atomic war."[25]

In his memoirs, Eisenhower wrote: "We would not be limited by any world-wide gentleman's agreement. In India and in the Formosa Straits area, and at the truce negotiations at Panmunjom, we dropped the word, discreetly, of our intentions [to use atomic bombs]. We felt quite sure it would reach Soviet and Chinese ears."[26]

At the time and in later years, Eisenhower wanted to believe that his nuclear threat was the key to ending a deadlock that had cost more than thirty thousand American lives. But John Eisenhower, who drafted his father's memoirs, told the author, "We were conjecturing."[27] Most historians now believe the nuclear threat was a factor, but not the most important one, in bringing the war to an end. More significant was the death of Stalin, the leader most responsible for the conflict.[28] It appears from recent scholarship that the Chinese most feared an amphibious landing by the Americans, not the atomic bomb. Mao had blustered that he was not afraid of nuclear weapons, which he called "paper tigers." China could lose millions in its coastal cities, he shrugged, and still have hundreds of millions more to rebuild the country (although, notably, he still got to work building China's own bomb).[29]

The war did not end right away. South Korea's president, Syngman Rhee, a Princeton-educated but fiercely independent strongman, threatened to sabotage the peace effort. He did not want a divided Korea. In a mad moment in the wee hours of June 18, Rhee opened the prison gates and allowed twenty-five

thousand prisoners of war to scatter before the nego-
tiators could resolve the sticky repatriation issue. It was
the only time during Ike's presidency when he was
awakened for a crisis in the middle of the night, and
he was, for a little while, flummoxed. "I can't recall
when there was ever a forty-eight hours when I felt
more in need of help from someone more intelligent
than I am," he remarked at the time.[30] But Eisenhower wheedled and flattered and bluffed some more
with Rhee and the Communists, and on July 27, an
armistice was finally signed. There were no church
bells or wild celebrations. Eisenhower was humble
and low-key with the press. A photographer asked
him how he felt. "The war is over," Eisenhower
answered, "and I hope my son is coming home soon."[31]
At the end of the year, writing in his diary, he would
rate ending the Korean War as his greatest accom-
plishment thus far as president.[32]

Like most of official Washington, Eisenhower was
eager to get away from the capital as August
approached. He liked to take long summer vacations —
a week or two in August and two or three more
weeks in September. He went to the Rockies to fish
and to Newport, Rhode Island, for the sea breezes,
and he played as much golf as possible in both
places. He was unapologetic about his vacations or
his frequent trips to the links (including his regular

Wednesday afternoon game at Burning Tree, in Washington). Jacob Potofsky, president of the Amalgamated Clothing Workers of America, told the president after visiting the Oval Office one day, "You know, Mr. President, we're keeping track of the number of times you play golf." As aides cringed, Ike smiled and said, "You go right ahead. I only wish I could play more."[33]

Eisenhower did not exactly bring a relaxed temperament to recreation. In Panama in the 1920s, he tried to learn the game of tennis on the private court of his mentor General Fox Conner. He could not master the strokes, and he alarmed Mamie by, as she recalled, "beat[ing] his head literally against the wall." He picked up golf more easily, and as an army officer he had plenty of time to master the game in the slow peacetime years between the wars. "Golf ran the army," recalled John Eisenhower. "At Leavenworth [the Command and General Staff College], officers scheduled their classes around the four hours a day they needed for golf."

Golf had never been mere recreation for Ike. It began as one more way to get ahead in the army, to ingratiate himself with other officers (especially after he stopped beating them at poker). But it became much more. The popular impression of Ike lazily whiling away his hours on the greens was a serious misperception. Golf for Ike, though he craved it, was grim. He was not highly skilled at the game (at least as measured by the standards of a perfectionist) and not much fun to play with. But he pursued it relentlessly.

For all his affability and capacity for humility, Ike craved control. In his daily life, he tried to control congressmen, his own advisers, and other politicians, allies, and Russians. Of course, he could not truly control them, any more than he could control his temper. So, as often as he could, he escaped to try to control a golf ball. That was equally maddening; golf is a notoriously fickle game, a mental nightmare for duffers and even more so for pros whose psyches are at all fragile. It is a contest at which even the greatest players suffer the "yips," an inexplicable inability to stroke a little white ball in a (more or less) straight line to a hole in the ground. A good but not great athlete, Eisenhower tortured himself at a game that possessed him.

Years later, John Eisenhower expressed a kind of bemused wonder at his father's obsession.[34] He recalled his father's "glee" as he arrived for his frequent weekends and holidays at Augusta National. "He would change his shoes in the Cadillac," on the way in from the airport, John recalled. Getting out of his limousine in his spikes, he would walk directly to the 10th tee by his house, "Mamie's Cabin," and play the back nine holes before coming up the front nine—and, if he was feeling energetic or frustrated by a mere eighteen holes, play nine more, hastening from shot to shot but nonetheless spending some five hours on the course.

Waiting for him, decked out in their loud golf shirts, would be several of his friends from the "gang." The foursome might include Robert Woodruff, chairman of the board of Coca-Cola; Cliff Roberts, an investment banker who skillfully managed Ike's money; and George Allen, who played the clown, though he was a brilliant corporate lawyer.

"He did not talk much," said John. "Only one thing mattered." There was usually some teasing in the president's foursome, but it was "one sided," John noted. "Dad teased George Allen for being fat. George was constantly making bets that he could lose weight." (Eisenhower's correspondence reflects that Allen rarely collected.) "Only Al Gruenther [an old army friend and Ike's successor as NATO Supreme Allied Commander Europe] teased him back, and if he did, it was pretty damn calculated." Other players knew not to try dirty jokes. "Dad was very Victorian. If he said 'damn' in the presence of a woman, he'd excuse himself. But there were no women on the golf course. He never played with one." Ike's cursing, while frequent, was not scatological.

John recalled, as a little boy on Sunday golf

Putting on his golf shoes (Dwight D. Eisenhower Presidential Library, Abilene, Kansas)

outings to the course at the Old Soldiers' Home in Washington, watching his father curse "Hell!" and "Damnation!" as he habitually sliced his first drive into a nearby alfalfa patch. Eisenhower had unusually large, strong hands, and he had little difficulty stroking approach shots onto the green, though his stiff left leg—his old West Point football and riding injury—meant his shots tended to fade to the right. Putting was more problematic. Ike's partners were generous about "gimmes," letting him pick up balls a few feet from the hole. (The caddies sometimes bet on the president's scores. On one hole, when an indulgent partner waved off Ike's four-footer with a casual "That's good for me," one of the caddies blurted, "Not for me!")[35]

On Augusta's gorgeous but challenging course, Ike was a "bogey golfer," usually a stroke or two above par. Of course, he "expected perfection. A good shot was normal. Hitting in the rough would bring an expletive," said John. Ike fretted over bad rounds and exulted over good ones. "You're the most cheerful winner I ever saw," a friend once told him. "If he sank a thirty-foot putt he would strut all over the place," John recalled. "He'd stick his chest out and pump his elbows up and down. He was quite boyish about the whole thing."

While he was president, Eisenhower did not have to wait for tee times or worry about groups playing ahead or behind. Secret Service men, carrying carbines in golf bags, roamed the woods to keep away the dangerous or merely curious. After Ike left the presidency he had to wait his turn, like all the rest. Playing at Eldorado Country Club near Palm Springs sometime in the early 1960s, the ex-president was signaled to play through by Jackie Cochran, the formidable woman who had helped persuade him to run for president in 1952 by bringing him the film of the "We Like Ike" rally. Cochran was playing in a women's foursome ahead of Ike and his pals. Before she allowed the men to jump ahead, Jackie said to Ike, "Watch this little girl." One of her partners, a young girl, lofted a perfect drive onto the par-3 green. This display of female prowess was apparently unnerving. "We sprayed our shots all over," recalled John. "God damn Jackie," grumbled Ike.[36]

Ike could be patient. But only when he wanted to be.

6

Deception

EISENHOWER WAS SINGLE-MINDED about getting his way. "When he decided to go anyplace, he just went," recalled a presidential aide, Bernard Shanley. On more than one occasion Eisenhower's doctor, Howard Snyder, had to drive at speeds up to a hundred miles an hour to catch up to his patient's motorcade on the way to the airport. His aides quickly learned that their boss could be manipulative and crafty. According to Shanley, Eisenhower spotted yesmen by tossing out "almost silly ideas" and watching their reactions. He pitted large egos against each other, figuring that competition would spur them to greater heights. His off-the-cuff remarks were carefully considered. The president even secretly tape-recorded conversations with people he didn't trust.

In public Eisenhower was calm but in private mercurial. In smaller groups, when he felt he could afford to speak more freely, his sunny mood could turn in an instant. If politics required, he could force himself to tolerate fools—but not for long. He regarded Alexander Wiley, the Republican chairman of the Senate Foreign Relations Committee, as a right-wing hack. Shanley recalled watching the president's neck turn beet-colored as Senator Wiley uttered casual profanities in the Oval Office during a meeting of Republican congressional leaders. The bright blue eyes hardened; the grin vanished. "Senator, don't you ever use that language again in this office," Ike growled, and the room grew silent.

But the genial smile returned. Once their sense of awe wore off, his aides found the president warmly human and sometimes disarmingly frank. Shanley, a Republican activist who became Ike's deputy chief of staff and then appointments secretary, had traveled with him on the 1952 campaign and noticed that Ike was amused, baffled, and flattered by the attention of women. Showing Shanley a rhinestone Ike button, Eisenhower remarked, "Do you know that women are always bringing me things?" "In Jersey City," recalled Shanley, "a nice looking girl came over and whispered to Ike and he said, 'I certainly will if you will.' She pulled out a bottle of Drambuie and the three of us had a snort." Ike was not ashamed to cry, and he let his staff see him do so. He openly wept when he was told that Senator Robert Taft, his new friend and sometime ally, had died of cancer. And he could laugh uproariously until the tears came, as he did once when press secretary Jim Hagerty got a fishhook caught on the fly of his pants while presenting a gift of fishing gear to Ike at a ceremony in the Cabinet Room. (Tears streaming down his face, the president finally suggested that Secretary of Health, Education, and Welfare Oveta Hobby, the one woman in the room, step outside so that Hagerty could take off his pants.) The president was intensely loyal. "Both with his friends and with his staff, he never wavered," recalled Shanley. Indeed, he was perhaps too loyal; he had trouble firing people, sometimes rationalizing that he would never let anyone go until he found an adequate replacement.[1]

Despite his experience with the gritty reality of war, Ike was also a romantic, an unabashed hero worshipper. As a boy growing up on the prairie with four brothers in a tiny house with no central plumbing, he was outdoors a good deal, and he naturally liked to play soldier. The Spanish-American War was fought when Ike was eight years old, so he and his brothers turned a small knoll in the flat Kansas farm country into Cuba's San Juan Hill and took turns playing Theodore Roosevelt leading his Rough Riders.[2] While it might be said that Eisenhower brilliantly employed Roosevelt's maxim—"Speak softly and carry a big stick"—as an adult he concluded that the blustery

East Coast cowboy was too guileless, and ranked him below Grover Cleveland when talking with his friends about "best presidents."[3] Ike revered George Washington, stoical and strong, but his more practical model was Abraham Lincoln. Honest Abe was much on Eisenhower's mind that first year in the White House. Daubing away in his second-floor studio, Eisenhower painted Lincoln's portrait, and, in a letter written in March, he recommended to a friend Alonzo Rothschild's *Lincoln, Master of Men: A Study of Character*. Before and during his White House stay, Ike closely studied Lincoln's elliptical style—in particular his ability to command headstrong political rivals and balky generals with a mixture of patience, firmness, and cunning.[4]

To be sure, Ike could be Boy Scoutish, brave and true; as a child, he did not shy away from a direct challenge. While a student at Abilene High School, he once stood as the champion of the south (wrong) side of the tracks against a stronger boy from the north side and survived a bloody two-hour brawl.[5] But there was a subtler, trickier, half-hidden dimension to his nature. Using a stolen key to find the history books hidden away by his mother in the parlor closet, the secret scholar spent hours reading about the clever and sometimes duplicitous methods and means of the ancient Greeks. Yet another Eisenhower hero, he later recalled, was Themistocles.[6] A man of the people who overcame the prejudice of the aristocrats, Themistocles (c. 524–459 BC) was a foxy general who used deception to lure the Persian fleet to its ruin at Salamis, the battle that launched ancient Greece to its greatest heights. In Eisenhower's adult universe, the Persians were the Nazis, then the Communists. To defeat them, almost anything was fair game. To lull your opponents into underestimating you was the art of a winning gamble.

Eisenhower had avidly used intelligence in World War II. He relied on ULTRA, the top-secret take from code breakers who gave the Allies an enormous advantage over the Germans. No stranger to dissembling, Ike was particularly delighted by the vast deception operation before D-day that fooled Hitler into believing the Allies would land at Calais instead of Normandy.[7] Eisenhower understood that intelligence gathering is difficult work, and that what is obtained is often wrong. His G-2 (intelligence) staff somehow missed the massive German buildup before Hitler's last-gasp counterattack at the Bulge in December 1944.[8] He had a high tolerance for error made in pursuit of noble goals, having learned from harsh experience to be patient about large organizations engaged in the arduous tasks of war.

Eisenhower knew he needed to be patient about the CIA's growing pains. Even the most devout defenders of the Agency (founded in 1947) cringe at its record from 1950 to 1952. Hundreds of agents dropped behind the Iron Curtain had either disappeared or were turned into double agents by the Soviets' ruthlessly efficient security services. From Poland to China, CIA case officers bought useless intelligence or "disinformation" from con men. A plot to overthrow the government of Albania was betrayed by a KGB mole, Kim Philby, the British intelligence services liaison to the CIA. Attempts to penetrate the Soviet Union utterly failed: the first CIA station chief in Moscow was caught in a "honey trap," thrown out after he was seduced by his chambermaid, who was actually a colonel in the KGB.[9]

Upon taking office, Eisenhower appointed Allen Dulles director of the CIA, replacing Walter Bedell Smith. In his baggy tweeds, waving his pipe and bellowing a hearty ho-ho-ho laugh, Dulles resembled a prep school headmaster, but he was an experienced conniver. Eisenhower had met him during World War II, when Dulles was the most effective spy in the Office of Strategic Services, the CIA's precursor. (Among his agents in Switzerland was Carl Jung—Agent 488—who analyzed the psyches of high-ranking Nazis.)[10] As the CIA's number two man during the Agency's troubled early years, Dulles bore some responsibility for its blunders. He was, however, the brother of John Foster—an immeasurable asset, given Eisenhower's desire for the CIA and the State Department to work together closely and discreetly.

The Dulles brothers conducted much of their most sensitive work "over cocktails, which they both liked," recalled Fisher Howe, who ran the State Department secretariat. They often relaxed while sitting by the swimming pool of their sister, Eleanor, at her home just across Chain Bridge in McLean, Virginia.[11] Outwardly, the brothers seemed quite different, but on closer inspection they complemented each other. Louis Auchincloss, the novelist and lawyer who worked with both at their Wall Street law firm, Sullivan and Cromwell, said of Allen, "He was a hale fellow, but his laugh was humorless. I thought of Foster as maladroit, but, beneath it all, warm. Allen was shrewd—but cold as ice."[12] Publicly and at meetings of the National Security Council, the two brothers were formal and correct; privately, they were partners in running what amounted to President Eisenhower's secret army.

It was all a little too cozy for some. Winston Churchill, Ike's wartime partner returned to power as prime minister, disliked John Foster Dulles and intentionally lisped his name. When he heard about Allen's appointment at CIA, he sniffed, "They tell me there is another Dullith. Is that possible?"[13]

Eisenhower had his own inside man to work with

and watch over the Dulles brothers. Walter Bedell Smith had been Ike's chief of staff in Europe. Missing half his stomach after an operation for chronic ulcers, Smith was said to be even tempered: always angry. In late 1950, "Beedle" (sometimes spelled "Beetle"), as he was known, had been appointed by President Truman as CIA director to ride herd on the cowboys at the Agency, whose amateurism had been exposed in the harsh light of the Korean War. Smith organized a "Murder Board" to weed out incompetents, and instructed, in his usual way, "I don't care whether they're blabbing secrets or not. Just get me the names of people at Georgetown cocktail parties."[14] Smith had inherited as his deputy Allen Dulles, whom he treated with irreverence bordering on disrespect. "Dulles, goddamn it, Dulles, get in here!" Smith would bellow, between sips of milk for his ulcers. (It didn't help that Allen Dulles was notoriously poor at running the Agency on a day-to-day basis. "He wasn't a good administrator or a bad administrator," said senior NSC staffer Karl Harr. "He was just totally innocent of administration.")[15] Dulles pretended to take it all in stride, winking at aides and breezily saying, "The general was in fine form this morning, wasn't he?"[16]

When Eisenhower was elected president, Smith had unrealistically hoped his old boss would make him chairman of the Joint Chiefs of Staff.[17] But Ike had different plans: he appointed Smith under secretary of state, the number two man at State, with oversight responsibility for CIA, and put a direct-dial phone on his desk to the White House. Smith, Eisenhower intended, would keep an eye on both Dulles brothers. Smith was not happy with Allen's appointment or his own role. "I was just Ike's prat boy," he would later tell Richard Nixon, who felt the same way. "Ike always had to have a prat boy, someone who'd do the dirty work for him."[18]

As under secretary of state, Smith did speak to Eisenhower several times a day—continuing to address the president as "Ike"—but the suspicious Dulles brothers were cleverer than Eisenhower might have anticipated, gradually managing to cut Smith out of most important decisions. Smith tried to stay in the game, in his gruff way. He scoffed at Allen Dulles's romantic love of cloak and dagger, and chastised him for neglecting the more productive side of intelligence—code breaking, analysis, and electronic eavesdropping. But Dulles loved his spies, known in CIA jargon as case officers, the men who would go into the field and hunt for agents, foreign nationals who could be recruited to betray their country, usually for cash though sometimes for ideology or personal motives of revenge. Beedle Smith sardonically gave him a nickname that would stick: the Great White Case Officer—but Smith no longer ran the

CIA; Dulles did, and the new director of Central Intelligence jealously guarded his power.*[19] Smith was never invited to Eleanor Dulles's swimming pool.

Beedle Smith and the Dulles brothers were like-minded in one crucial regard: they were staunch anti-Communists who wanted not merely to contain Communism but to roll it back, wherever it began to encroach. In 1953, they believed that place was Iran.

Ever since Winston Churchill, running the British admiralty in World War I, switched the Royal Navy from coal to oil, Britain had treated Iran as a protectorate and virtual colony, installing a shah and taking control of the country's vast oil reserves. Then, in 1951, the Iranian prime minister, a fervent nationalist and populist named Mohammad Mossadegh, seized control of the Anglo-Iranian Oil Company and effectively sidelined the shah. The British Secret

---

*By June 1954, Smith had despaired of trying to warn Eisenhower about Allen Dulles's shortcomings. C. D. Jackson, Ike's assistant for "psychological warfare," who was also cut out by the Dulleses and returned to his job at Time-Life, had a few drinks with Smith on June 1 and wrote in his diary, "Finally Beedle, almost sobbing, got on the subject of Ike, when he said, 'There are only two people who can give him professional but disinterested advice; you are one, and I am another. But you are gone and he won't listen to me.'"[20]

Intelligence Service (SIS) had a long history of getting its way with bribes and subterfuge, but in the aftermath of World War II, Britain was broke. The SIS turned to the CIA—"the cousins across the pond"—which had far deeper pockets. To get the attention of the "cousins," the Brits played up Mossadegh's ties to the Tudeh, Iran's Communist party. The Tudeh was not under Moscow's control; nonetheless, the SIS raised the specter that Mossadegh's weakness would invite in Soviet tanks and half the free world's oil supply would go to the Kremlin.

This was enough to persuade Beedle Smith that Mossadegh had to go and that the CIA should run the operation. In January 1952, a few days before Eisenhower's inauguration and while Smith was still at CIA, he summoned Kermit Roosevelt to his office. A canny operator in the Middle East, Roosevelt was every bit as brash as his grandfather Theodore, but he still had to put up with Beedle's harangues. "When are those fucking British coming to talk to us?" Smith demanded. "And when is our goddamned operation going to get under way? Pull up your socks and get going. You won't have any trouble in London. They'll jump at anything we propose. And I'm sure you can come up with something sensible enough for Foster to OK. Ike will agree."[21]

In fact, Ike did not agree, not right away. Eisenhower initially regarded Iran as the sort of mess to be avoided. At a National Security Council meeting on March 4, he wondered aloud why it wasn't possible "to get some of the people in these downtrodden countries to like us instead of hating us." Secretary of State Dulles weighed in that "Communists might easily take over" and "some sixty percent of the world's oil reserves would fall into Communist control." But Ike's initial instinct was to try to prop up Prime Minister Mossadegh and win him over from the Kremlin with a $100 million loan.[22]

During the spring of 1953, Eisenhower gradually changed his mind, though he never quite came out and said so. He signaled, more by what he did not say than what he did say, that he would not object to a CIA/SIS-run coup d'état in Iran. Eisenhower was very cautious about committing military forces, understanding from experience the risks of unintended consequences. But his fondness for deception tempted him to see covert action as a policy tool (and blinded him to the potential high cost of coups gone wrong). On June 14, Allen Dulles went to the White House to brief Eisenhower on the plot. Dulles sensed that the president did not want to know too much, so he gave him what Kermit Roosevelt described as "the most 'broad brush' outline of what was proposed." The president did not attend a meeting of top Agency and State Department officials on July 25 to hear the details of the covert operation. John Foster Dulles picked up the report and exclaimed, with some glee, "So this is how we get rid of that madman Mossadegh!" The plan was essentially to buy off enough Iranian military, religious, and political leaders to win their connivance. The coup, code-named AJAX, almost collapsed before it began. Security was poor, and Mossadegh, alerted to the plotters, began arresting them. The young shah, Mohammad Reza Pahlavi, who had been hiding in a CIA safe house waiting to resume his seat on the Peacock Throne, fled to Rome and the safer confines of the Excelsior Hotel. (By total coincidence, he checked into the hotel at the same moment as Allen Dulles, who was touring CIA stations in Europe. An awkward exchange took place.) Back in Washington, a vexed Beedle Smith sent a note to President Eisenhower that now "we'll probably have to snuggle up to Mossadegh."[23] CIA headquarters cabled Roosevelt to break off the plot and leave the country "at the earliest moment."

But Roosevelt was in too deep, or having too much fun, to give up. He had been smuggled around Tehran rolled up in a Persian carpet, and he seemed to relish intrigue. In his memoirs, he recalled waiting out the tense days sipping lime rickeys and listening to the Broadway show tune "Luck Be a Lady" on his Victrola.[24] He made some of his luck by spreading around cash to organize street protests. Tehran streets filled with thugs, and when Mossadegh ("the old bugger," Roosevelt called him) panicked and sent out his goons, the mob turned on him and stormed his house. Escaping over his garden wall, Mossadegh later surrendered, wearing a pair of pink pajamas and crying. Roosevelt was ready with his own strongman, General Fazlollah Zahedi, who was so nervous that a CIA man had to button his tunic. Informed at his hotel in Rome that he was back on the throne, the shah exclaimed, "Can it be true? I knew it! I knew it! They love me!"

An exultant Roosevelt was amused to receive another cable from Washington, always a beat behind, again admonishing him to flee instantly. Roosevelt puckishly wired back, "Yours of 18 August received. Happy to report R.N. Ziegler [Zahedi] safely installed and KGSAVOY [the shah] will be returning to Tehran in triumph shortly. Love and kisses from all the team." Then Roosevelt set off on his victory lap. In London, Churchill toasted him, and in Washington he provided a briefing to the Dulles brothers, Secretary of Defense Charles Wilson, Chairman of the Joint Chiefs Admiral Arthur Radford, and, from the White House, Eisenhower's aide Andrew Goodpaster. Roosevelt had set up an easel with charts and photographs, and as he spoke, he noticed that his audience "seemed almost alarmingly enthusiastic. John Foster Dulles was leaning back in his chair. . . . His eyes were gleaming; he seemed to be purring like a giant cat."[25]

Eisenhower was not there. In a memo-to-files, he wrote, "The things we did were 'covert.'" He praised Roosevelt and commented that his report "seemed more like a dime novel than an historical fact."[26] Yet Eisenhower may have been more involved than he let on. His memoirs speak of conferring "daily" with officials from State and CIA and note that he received from Beedle Smith a memo "prepared by an American in Iran, unidentified to me."[27] The American, as Ike knew, was Roosevelt. On September 23 he gave the dashing CIA man a medal at a secret ceremony. Roosevelt, at his earlier briefing of Dulles and other Eisenhower lieutenants, noticed that Foster Dulles was not only "purring" but, as he put it, "my instincts told me he was planning as well." Soon enough, Dulles was asking Roosevelt if he would like to stage an encore in Guatemala, which was also starting to drift toward the Communist orbit. Feeling that the conditions for a coup in Guatemala weren't right, Roosevelt begged off. Dulles began looking for someone else to do the job. From the shadows, Eisenhower watched and tacitly approved.

Allen and Foster Dulles (Library of Congress, Washington, DC)

7

Learning to Love the Bomb

ON AUGUST 12, 1953, the Soviet Union exploded its first thermonuclear bomb. It was a crude device, not nearly as powerful as the Americans' "Mike" shot that had eliminated a Pacific atoll the prior November, but the blast signaled that the Russians were catching up.[1] Eisenhower could not see very well behind the Iron Curtain, but he could guess that the Soviets were doing everything in their power to match or surpass the West. Indeed, Stalin had shown a mad scientist's lust for esoteric means of destruction. Among his favored ideas were the "antipodal bomber," a giant supersonic aircraft that would hurl itself beyond the earth's atmosphere before descending on America, and a huge "super torpedo," armed with an atomic warhead, to be shot by a submarine straight into US harbors.[2] More effectively, he put a group of captured Nazi rocket scientists to work on an intercontinental ballistic missile.

Eisenhower was well acquainted with atomic warfare. From the earliest days of the Cold War he had helped plan how nuclear weapons would fit into the nation's arsenal. Having read Clausewitz, and then drawing on his own experience in World War II, Eisenhower believed, almost as an article of faith, that war was ever-changing and surprising in its ways and weaponry, and that nations relied on old technology and tactics at their peril. On January 21, 1946, then Army Chief of Staff General Eisenhower, though warning against "excessive reliance" on nuclear weapons, urged, in a report to the Joint Chiefs, that "all possible methods of delivery of atomic weapons... be studied and developed." As technology improved, the bomb got smaller as well as bigger. In 1952, the air force commissioned Project Vista (named after a California hotel where the sensitive work was done), which recommended a range of small nuclear weapons that could be used on the battlefield — smaller atomic bombs and all manner of atomic artillery shells, mines, torpedoes, and antiaircraft missiles. The first of these, a large atomic cannon with a 15-kiloton shell (15,000 tons of TNT, roughly the size of the bomb used on Hiroshima), was tested in May 1953. In true Pentagon tradition, the Strategic Air Command, which coveted a nuclear monopoly, realized that most of these new tactical nuclear weapons would be controlled by the army and navy, and tried to recall every copy of the Project Vista report.[3]

When Eisenhower had taken office in January, he had found in his Oval Office desk a chilling report from a group of scientists on the future of the arms race. (The report was in a locked desk drawer; Eisenhower had to ask for a key.)[4] Commissioned by President Truman, the report predicted that both the United States and the Soviet Union would build thousands of nuclear weapons and missiles to deliver them. The United States might survive an onslaught of 2,500 atomic bombs, wrote the scientists, but survival would have "a rather specialized meaning," since much of the country would be radioactive ash.[5]

Eisenhower was intrigued by the report—appalled but fascinated—and took time to speak to its lead author, J. Robert Oppenheimer, the father of the atomic bomb. Ike encouraged Oppenheimer to write a public version, which appeared that summer in *Foreign Affairs,* the high-minded journal of the Council on Foreign Relations. The article included a chilling metaphor, that the Americans and Russians were becoming like "two scorpions in a bottle, each capable of killing the other, only at the risk of his own life."[6]

In July, before Eisenhower left Washington on vacation, Oppenheimer's warning was much on his mind. "The only thing worse than losing a global war is winning one," he told his advisers on July 16.[7] Though Eisenhower had been tempted to try to conceal the frightening power of the Bomb, to avoid scaring the public, he was changing his mind. With the Americans and now the Russians unlocking the secret to thermonuclear weapons—the so-called hydrogen, or H-bomb—Eisenhower told a group of aides, "We've just got to let the American people know how terrible this is."[8]

Most Americans had some idea. They had seen the photos of Hiroshima and Nagasaki. *Life* magazine ran occasional grisly stories on what atomic bombs might do to an American city. In an illustration for one feature, only the great stone lions on the steps of the New York City Public Library remain amid the rubble.[9] In January 1951, a Los Angeles construction company advertised the first fallout shelter. For $1,995, a family of five could have a concrete underground refuge equipped with its own Geiger counter. For $3,000, they could have a "Mark I Kidde Kokoon," complete with radiation charts, airblower, and pick and shovel "for digging out after the blast."[10]

But the public was getting confusing messages from the government. In the spring of 1953, in a series of tests in the Nevada desert, small atomic bombs blew away some buildings erected to test the force of the shock wave. Nevertheless, the radiation

Fallout shelter (© Bettman/Corbis)

menace was downplayed. In October, a *Newsweek* photo of an atomic shell bursting was dubbed "Atomic Annie: One of the Family" — just another weapon.[11] While film footage of the vastly more powerful

H-bomb blast was kept from the public, the air force made a movie of the Mike test and gave President Eisenhower and some staffers a private screening in June. "Much too long, much too Hollywood, stilted phony dialogue—but the last few minutes when bomb went off absolutely terrifying," wrote presidential adviser C. D. Jackson in his diary.[12]

Growing up in a God-fearing family at the end of the nineteenth century, Ike had memorized scripture. His parents had been evangelical Christians who divided the world between good and evil, and Ike never lost the language of right and wrong.[13] But as a central figure in the crises of the mid-twentieth century, he gained a profound appreciation for moral ambiguity. On his late-summer vacation, fishing and golfing high in Colorado's Rocky Mountains, President Eisenhower thought about the paradox of nuclear weapons: how they could end civilization or, perversely, save it.

As he drove, chipped, and putted around the Cherry Hills Country Club golf course outside Denver and fly-cast at the Byers Peak ranch of his friend Aksel Nielsen, Eisenhower could not distract himself. The H-bomb "was on his mind," national security adviser Robert Cutler reported to John Foster Dulles on September 3. "Even before that, he had doubts, he said, about how much we should poke the animal [that is, the Soviet Union] through the

140

bars of the cage."[14] Two weeks later, Cutler told Emmet Hughes, "I've never seen the president so concerned." Cutler quoted Ike as muttering, "My God, ten of these things and..." The president didn't finish the sentence.[15]

Despite the Soviets' quickening pace, Eisenhower knew that America had a lengthy head start in the arms race. But this perception led to an uncomfortable question: Should the commander in chief contemplate preventive war? Should the president order an all-out air assault to devastate the Soviet Union with nuclear weapons while the Soviets were still vulnerable, before they could muster an effective force of their own? Eisenhower was at least willing to entertain the possibility. In a letter from his summer vacation retreat to John Foster Dulles on September 8, with the Soviet thermonuclear test fresh in his mind, Ike anguished about the prospect of a relentless arms race that led either to war or "some form of dictatorial government" — that "garrison state" he had been worrying about. Very gingerly, in stilted language, he went on: "In such circumstances, we would be forced to consider whether or not our duty to future generations did not require us to initiate war at the most propitious moment we could designate."[16]

At a National Security Council meeting on September 24, the president used more plainspoken words as he and his senior advisers contemplated

"Joe IV," the code name given to the Soviets' ther-monuclear weapon. Would it be morally wrong, the president asked, to *not* attack the Soviets before it was too late? The notetaker wrote:

> It looked to him, said the President, as though the hour of decision was at hand, and that we presently really have to face the question of whether or not we would really have to throw everything at once against the enemy. The question could no longer be excluded, and it was the duty of the President and his advisers to find the best answer to it. The President concluded by explaining that he had raised the terrible question because there was no sense in merely shuddering at the enemy's capacity. We must indeed determine our own course of action in light of this capability.[17]

In September 1953 the reality of two enemies fac-ing off with weapons that could wipe out civiliza-tion was brand new. Eisenhower was the first man in history to make real the mythical power of a god. It should come as no surprise that, in the dawn of this terrible new age, he weighed the moral dimen-sion from all sides. A giant nuclear Pearl Harbor–style attack was too awful to contemplate — and yet it had to be contemplated. In later years, Eisenhower would formally outlaw preventive war, though he never de facto ruled out a preemptive strike if the Soviets seemed on the verge of attack.[18] There were others who worked for him who had fewer compunctions about the latter option.

Ike had asked the intelligence community to develop an estimate on how much damage the Russians and Americans could do to each other in a nuclear war. This doomsday document, issued annually beginning in 1953, was known drily as the Net Assessment. The first Net Assessment, in May, predicted that enough of Russia's propeller-driven TU-4 bombers (the rough equivalent of the B-29, America's workhorse long-range bomber in 1944–45) would get through on one-way missions to kill about nine million Americans.[19]

The fear of Soviet attack that gripped policy makers in the early 1950s seems exaggerated, even paranoid, from a post–Cold War perspective. It turns out that the Soviets were even more afraid of an attack than the West was. Stalin believed war between the Soviet Union and capitalist West was inevitable, and he knew that the West had superior armaments. "Stalin trembled with fear," his eventual successor Nikita Khrushchev told his son. "How he quivered! He was afraid of war."[20] Eisenhower had been more realistic than the jittery Pentagon planners who in the early days of the Cold War had predicted that the Red Army could—and would—roll virtually unimpeded to the English Channel, and even predicted the day: January 1, 1952. According to Army G-2 (intelligence) estimates, the Soviets could overrun Western Europe in two weeks. Writing in the margin of one such estimate in 1948, Ike jotted, "I don't believe it. My God, we needed two months just to overrun Sicily."[21]

As president, Eisenhower continued to doubt that the Russians would attack. Their people had suffered so much in world wars, but more to the point, the current Soviet leadership included some of the world's great survivalists. They had outlasted Hitler and the brutally lethal Stalin, who used the gulag and the firing squad almost indiscriminately. In a private communication to his World War II comrade Field Marshal Bernard Law Montgomery, Eisenhower had made his memorable remark that the Kremlin leaders were not "early Christian martyrs." Montgomery, who was now NATO's deputy commander, was worrying about a Soviet invasion. "Make no mistake, they like their jobs," wrote Ike.[22] Ike feared what he called a "powder keg war," started by miscalculation. Dulles, who thought the Russians more rash than Eisenhower did, especially feared setting off a tinderbox. "If we have another great war, that is probably the way it will come," he wrote in *Life* magazine.[23]

Eisenhower was also wary of his own military. "I know those boys," he liked to say. He did not so much worry that they would intentionally start a war; he thought they would respect civilian control, just as he always had. But he knew they would jockey and connive for more and better weapons and more men, and the mere building of great militaries carries the temptation to use them.

It was important to Eisenhower to get ahead of this dynamic—to build a structure that would allow him to control the burgeoning national security establishment, and not the other way around. Ike was in many ways an Organization Man. He had spent most of his career as a staff officer, and he had, or tried to have, mid-twentieth-century faith in progress and reason, the belief that if you put the right smart people in a room, they could figure out the answer to any problem. As president of Columbia University, his pet project was the American Assembly, which brought together prominent scientists, thinkers, and businessmen to solve the world's problems. At the same time, to a degree unusual for policy makers of his time, Ike had a healthy regard for *unreason*—for all the irrational forces that drive men. After South Korea's Syngman Rhee tried to thwart the armistice, Ike sent Winston Churchill a note mixing exasperation with philosophical resignation:

"It is remarkable how little concern men seem to have for logic, statistics, and even, indeed, survival: we live by emotion, prejudice, and pride."[24]

To create and run his national security staff, Ike brought in Bobby Cutler, a Boston banker recommended by his wartime boss, General Marshall, as "a rose among cabbages." A lifelong bachelor from a blue-blood family, Cutler was smart and devoted, and he was that rarity, a Washington insider who never leaked. He had a quietly ribald sense of humor, and he wrote funny doggerel, but he could be a little fussy—"a bit of an old maid," according to Sherman Adams.[25] At the beginning of every National Security Council meeting, Cutler, who spoke with a deep Brahmin accent, would herald, "Gentlemen, the President!" Eisenhower had to tell him to tone it down.[26]

Cutler was a little puzzled by Ike. In the 1952 campaign, Cutler had been hired to ride the train and act as an on-call sounding board and confidant. Ike was friendly with Cutler. But the candidate, Cutler found, was also enigmatic and kept his own counsel. At the White House, Cutler created an elaborate planning process for the NSC. The president paid close attention to the process and then, when it suited him, ignored it.

The exercise that emerged from Cutler's efforts, known as Project Solarium, is still studied as a model of policy planning. It is better understood as an exhibition of Eisenhower's sleight of hand. As Cutler recalled, Project Solarium got its start over Sunday lunch at the house of John Foster Dulles. Dulles lectured Cutler and Beedle Smith about the challenges facing America in a world in which the Soviets had achieved "atomic plenty" — one of those creepily bland phrases of the era, meaning enough nuclear weapons to devastate the United States. Cutler suggested they take the conversation to Eisenhower. In mid-May 1953, the president greeted the trio as he sat in the Solarium, a sunny, leafy penthouse on the third floor of the White House. "Here come the conspirators!" Ike exclaimed, as Mamie's canary chattered in a cage swinging beside him. Eisenhower suggested they get together "some bright young fellows" to present options. Cutler put his minions to work in the secret confines of the National War College.[27]

If Project Solarium was a conspiracy, as the president jokingly suggested, it was one he quickly hijacked. The findings for dealing with the Soviet Union were presented at an all-day conference in a projection room in the White House basement in mid-July. The president was given three proposals: A) he could essentially continue President Truman's policy of "containment"; B) he could draw a sharper line around the Soviet empire and threaten atomic war if the line was transgressed; or C) he could actively begin rolling back Communism by subversion, threats, and, if necessary, war. A "high stakes" game of chicken "must be played boldly," asserted the authors of Option C.

George Kennan had been drafted to write Option A. As Kennan sat there in the cool White House movie theater on a hot day in mid-July, he realized that his own role had been carefully and craftily cast by Eisenhower. A leading Soviet specialist and head of policy planning in Acheson's State Department, Kennan had been the author of the Truman administration's containment policy. By choosing Kennan, Eisenhower disarmed Democratic critics and showed his own Republican followers that he was serious about the idea. During the 1952 campaign, there had been a lot of loose talk by Republicans, especially by Foster Dulles, about "rolling back" Communism. Options B and C, drafted by an air force general and a navy admiral, exposed the riskiness of Dulles's bluster, because they led straight to war. As Eisenhower listened, he doodled and jotted a few notes:

```
GLOBAL WAR AS DEFENSE OF FREEDOM/
ALMOST CONTRADICTION IN TERMS
3 PLANS/BEAUTIFULLY PRESENTED (ALL SEEM TO
BELIEVE)/
C CONTAINS B.[28]
```

As the group convened in the White House library for a final meeting, the president stood and spoke without notes for forty-five minutes, artfully summing up the discussion and proceeding to chart his own course. Eisenhower wished to essentially continue the policy of containment, without calling it that. But there was a catch: containment, as practiced by the Truman administration, required a massive buildup of conventional forces, which was becoming ever more expensive — too costly, in Ike's view.

Dour and pessimistic, Eisenhower's father had nurtured, as Ike recalled, "an obsession against ever owing anyone a nickel." Though Eisenhower always tried to put a sunny face on his childhood poverty ("We were so poor we didn't know it"), he believed that his father, David, had gone broke as a small-store owner after being cheated by his partner.* Ike's normally cheerful mother, Ida, would grow bitter as she denounced "thieves, embezzlers, chiselers, and all kinds of crooks."[29] Eisenhower was determined to hold the line on government debt and to keep a sharp eye on the sort of people who profited from

---

*Or so went the family legend. A researcher at the Eisenhower Presidential Library concluded in 1990 that David Eisenhower, possibly mentally unstable, had inexplicably walked away from his investment, a fact later covered up by the family.

defense spending, some of whom would have aroused Ida's ire.

Thus the balance: Ike wanted to stop global Communism without spending America into bankruptcy or forcing it to become a garrison state, inevitably run by a military dictatorship. The answer, not immediately apparent and never entirely satisfactory, was to make a virtue of necessity, to transform the means of destruction into an engine of salvation. Kennan, who, like most Truman followers, had held a somewhat condescending attitude toward the smiling, platitudinous war hero, was astonished. "He showed his intellectual ascendancy over every man in the room," he recalled. It's doubtful that Eisenhower was truly educated by the Solarium Project, but it served to get his advisers, and even his potential critics, reading out of the same book. Project Solarium did not tell Eisenhower "anything that he hadn't thought through before," said Andrew Goodpaster, who worked on the project and would soon become Ike's staff secretary.[30]

In the spring of 1953, while he was launching the Solarium Project and thinking about his conversations with Oppenheimer, Ike had turned to C. D. Jackson, head of the Psychological Strategy Board ("psychological warfare" was an early Cold War buzzword) to look for ways to educate the public on the coming age of the H-bomb. Jackson was to prepare a speech, code-named "Operation Candor."

A protégé of Time-Life founder Henry Luce, Jackson was an ebullient, perpetually optimistic figure who saw himself as Eisenhower's general in the Cold War struggle for hearts and minds. Jackson had helped launch Radio Free Europe to keep alive the hope of freedom behind the Iron Curtain. He was seeking opportunities to, as he liked to say, "win World War III without having to fight it." Scaring people about the bomb didn't quite seem like the way to do that, but Jackson and his staff dutifully went about writing, as part of "Operation Candor," what they called "Bang! Bang! Papers."[31] As he read the drafts, Eisenhower realized the depictions of nuclear horror—"with everybody dead on both sides and no hope anywhere"—were just too frightening, and he decided to push Jackson in a different direction.

Eisenhower's ultimate, if distant, aim was disarmament—to rid the world of these "terrible" weapons. Dulles thought Eisenhower's dream was unrealistic and even dangerous. Ike's new head of the Atomic Energy Commission, Lewis Strauss, a charming but fierce Wall Street financier once described as looking like "a well-dressed owl," was very guarded about even publicly acknowledging the existence of America's nuclear stockpile. But Ike was determined to find some small confidence-building steps that would at least start the nation on a path to disarmament. Couldn't we, asked the president, create some kind of international authority that would use nuclear isotopes for peaceful purposes, like energy for the developing world? Both the Americans and Russians could donate from their stockpiles. Dulles and Strauss were extremely skeptical. But Jackson and his team went back to work drafting a speech, this time code-named "Wheaties," because its drafters met over breakfast at the Metropolitan Club, down the block from the White House.[32]

Eisenhower was eager to preserve his close wartime ties to the European allies; collective security, he firmly believed, was essential to checking Soviet aggression. In early December, he flew on his presidential plane, the *Columbine,* a souped-up four-engine Constellation, to meet with Prime Minister Churchill in Bermuda. (They stayed at the swank Mid Ocean Club, Churchill to paint watercolors and bathe in the sea, Ike to golf, though he fretted about public reaction to their staying at a golf club.)[33] Churchill, seventy-eight years old, recovering from a stroke and often cranky, had been privately sour about his wartime ally. After Eisenhower's election, Churchill told his secretary, John Colville, "For your private ear, I am greatly disturbed. I think this makes war much more probable. " In his diary on July 24, Colville wrote that his boss was "very disappointed in Eisenhower whom he thinks both weak and stupid"—a harsh judgment indeed, if it reflected Churchill's true opinion.[34] His frailty inconsistently masked, Churchill tested Eisenhower's affection and deep reservoir of goodwill. In May, C. D. Jackson recorded a ludicrous scene in his diary: "President spoke on telephone to Churchill, shouting at top of his lungs on account of Churchill's deafness and suggesting Churchill put somebody else on, which Sir Winston would not do. Considerable sorrowful speculation as to Churchill's motives."[35]

In Bermuda, Ike seemed to have shed his wartime smile. He disturbed Churchill by implying that he saw "no distinction between conventional weapons and atomic weapons: all weapons in due course become conventional weapons," Colville recorded. The secretary described Churchill, dressed in evening clothes, lying on his bed, listening to a reading of Ike's "Wheaties" speech—now proposed as an address to the United Nations, just three days hence. The speech was called "Atoms for Peace," and after describing the horrors of nuclear war (in less detailed fashion than the first "Bang! Bang!" drafts), it called on Russia and the United States to begin talking about ways to beat swords into ploughshares. Churchill, who certainly knew a good speech when he wrote one, insisted on removing a couple of "obnoxious" paragraphs (including a reference to the "obsolete colonial mode") but grumpily approved. It was at least a start.[36] Eisenhower, himself a heavy editor, fiddled with his speeches until the last possible moment, and in this case the *Columbine*'s pilot had to circle the airport in New York for fifteen minutes while Mrs. Whitman furiously typed the last draft on the flight from Bermuda on December 8.

The president's speech caused a sensation in the massive hall of the United Nations. Even the Russian delegates, perhaps forgetting themselves, rose to applaud as Eisenhower wound into his peroration: "...the United States pledges before you, and therefore before the world, its determination...to devote its entire heart and mind to find the way by which the miraculous inventiveness of man shall not be dedicated to his death, but consecrated to his life."[37]

As the waves of applause rolled over him, Eisenhower was reported to have shed a tear. The reaction around the world was universally positive at first. But then not much happened. Skeptics warned that Eisenhower's plan to provide the developing world with nuclear-generated electricity—the "Watts for Hottentots" program, as they mocked it—could lead to nuclear proliferation. No longer applauding, the Soviets became suspicious, seeing a plot to draw down their smaller stockpile of bomb-making materials to give the Americans a bigger relative advantage. Eisenhower tried to organize a conference to push along the international control of atomic energy, but there was so little interest that the president had to personally get on the phone and beseech scientists to come. Many years would pass before the Atoms for Peace program brought any real results. (It did ultimately lead to more open science in the search of nuclear fusion.)[38]

The hope initially spread by Eisenhower's address was quickly replaced by gloom over a speech delivered by John Foster Dulles on January 12. Speaking in the familiar wood-paneled rooms of the Council on Foreign Relations in New York, Dulles seemed to be warning the world that America would use nuclear weapons to stop Communist aggression wherever and whenever it occurred. To contain "the mighty landpower of the Communist world," Dulles said, it was necessary to impose "massive retaliatory power." He placed no restrictions on the use of this power.

Dulles's speech provoked widespread consternation. Did the Eisenhower administration intend to treat every border incident as a nuclear showdown? There was much backing and filling and clarifying in the days ahead, which confused things even more. Dulles explained what he called "the New Look" (a term taken, oddly, by administration officials from a Paris fashion show). The idea was to cut defense spending by relying on nuclear weapons as opposed to more expensive conventional forces ("More bang for the buck," quipped an alliterative administration official). "Official explanations of the New Look have become so voluminous that it is almost a career in itself to keep up with them," wrote columnist Walter Lippmann.[39]

The most chilling line in Dulles's speech was his perhaps overly succinct summation of the administration's impetus behind the New Look: "The basic decision was to depend primarily upon a great capacity to retaliate, instantly, by means and at places of our own choosing." Delivered in his Jehovah-like manner, the line seemed ghoulish, as if the Christian avenger Dulles relished having an apocalyptic hair trigger on his finger. The press immediately announced Dulles's policy of "massive retaliation," and the label stuck.

The language closely echoed a lurid piece Dulles had written for *Life* magazine in 1952, when he was trying to fan partisan flames against the Truman administration's "passivity" toward Communist aggression. But unknown to the press and all but a handful of White House insiders, the line had been inserted in the speech not by Dulles, but rather by President Eisenhower, once again exercising his hidden hand. Ike wanted to let the Russians know that, by spending less on defense, he was not in any way letting down his guard. Eisenhower desired to station a large, angry dog at the gate, and he was happy for Dulles to play the part, while the president floated above the scene, genial but vague as he parried and half responded to reporters' questions.[40]

Dulles was perfectly content to do the president's bidding. Though the secretary of state was outwardly formal and awkward, while Ike was at ease and seemingly comfortable, the two men had reached a kind of understanding that was mellowing into friendship. In October, while Dulles was at a foreign ministers' meeting in London, he wrote and underscored, among drawings of geometric shapes on a piece of scrap paper, "The President wants peace." The scrap paper with Dulles's doodlings and jottings found its way onto the front page of the *New York Times*. Dulles sent the newspaper clipping to Eisenhower and wrote, "Dear Mr. President, Someone slipped this away from the Foreign Ministers' Conference table. It represents my subconscious mind at work."[41]

The "Massive Retaliation" speech was the culmination of a secret debate that had gone on that autumn after the Solarium Project ended. Dulles had made his usual case for removing the "taboo" on nuclear weapons. The chairman of the Joint Chiefs, Admiral Arthur Radford, was even more aggressive. It was "high time," he said, for the administration to publicly declare its willingness to use nuclear weapons. Radford had commanded a carrier fleet that attacked Japan in 1945. His goal then, he had told reporters, was to "kill the bastards scientifically."[42]

Eisenhower went along with a statement in the official planning document, NSC 162/2, churned out by Bobby Cutler's bureaucracy, that nuclear weapons were to be treated like any other weapons. But Ike cautioned Radford that the military should not "plan to make use of these weapons in minor affairs." And Eisenhower insisted on a key qualification: the decision to use nuclear weapons would reside with the president alone. That finger on the nuclear trigger belonged to Eisenhower, not to Dulles or anyone else.[43]

8

The Chamber Pot

AT RAINY AUGUSTA National Golf Club over New Year's 1954, Eisenhower managed to get in four rounds. Ike loved the lush, rolling course, famous for its demanding greens and its azaleas in early spring. In the surrounding woods, the club dug a three-acre pond, where Ike could fish between golf and bridge, and religiously guarded his privacy on the course. Ike did not like to get golf tips during games. The coaching made him try too hard, ballooning his score, and those accompanying him from hole to hole learned to watch quietly. Once the great champion Sam Snead dared to say, "You've got to stick your butt out more, Mr. President." The bodyguards and other guests froze. "I thought it *was* out," said the president a little plaintively, according to Snead.[1] That was an exception in terms of both command and calm response.

That December, Mamie had been feeling ill, but

her mood brightened once she was ensconced in the roomy, comfortable cottage decorated in pink and green (her favorite colors), set in a stand of pine trees not far from the 10th tee, which had been built by Ike's supporters. "She spends the mornings in bed but sees everyone passing through the open venetian blinds," wrote Priscilla Slater in her diary. The wife of Ellis "Slats" Slater, the wealthy liquor distiller who had helped pay for the house and was a frequent golf and bridge partner of the president, Priscilla described the First Lady as "feminine, really luscious looking, dainty and loveable, appealing in the most childlike way." She noted, however, that "no individual would impose on her more than once. She has a strong personality."[2]

Eisenhower had been exhausted when he arrived in Augusta just before Christmas. He was fed up with congressional Republicans, whom he regarded as "cowards" for their endless favor-seeking and their fear of Senator McCarthy, whose Permanent Subcommittee on Investigations was still pretending to root out Communists and mostly casting a political pall. Following a legislative leadership conference in mid-December, Eisenhower angrily exclaimed to his staff that "his own greatest troubles always seem to come from the Republican party."[3] After House Speaker Joe Martin told reporters that he had "never heard of a President who didn't want a second term,"

Ike had written his brother Milton, "Brother! If he ever knew." On Christmas Eve, he had pledged not to seek reelection in a letter to Swede Hazlett. He had won Hazlett's friendship as a schoolboy by rescuing him from a gang of bullies and felt he could trust him with political secrets: "Of course I have no fear that you will ever reveal this information to anyone—but I want you personally to have it so that if a time ever comes when you see me even *appearing* to waver...you are to take drastic steps to see that I do not become more of a damn fool than I was in '52!"[4]

But he usually tried to hide his fatigue and anxieties from his friends. "No worrier is the president," proclaimed Slats Slater in his diary after staying up on New Year's Eve until 2 a.m., toasting with Ike.[5] That new year would test the president's ability to disguise his intentions and true feelings.

After a year in office, Ike's approval rating stood near 70 percent, roughly where it was when he was elected. In January, he gave an unremarkable State of the Union address, simply reaffirming that he wanted the country to take the middle way, neither abandoning the New Deal nor breaking the budget. The forty-five-minute speech was deemed a huge success, praised by newspapers on the left and right. The president is a "dominating presence," wrote columnist Ernest K. Lindley in *Newsweek,* because he projected "trust, good will, and visible and implied strength."

The president was not a polished speaker. During the 1952 campaign, he had sworn off teleprompters after an unfortunate experience with a technician who scrolled his speech too slowly. The television audience had heard him interrupt his stump speech to splutter, "Go ahead, go ahead, yeah, damn it, I want him to move up!" For his State of the Union address, his speech coach, actor Robert Montgomery, persuaded him to agree, grudgingly, to give the teleprompter another try, but the president still ended up looking down to read portions of his speech. (Montgomery raised the lectern so the audience would not see Ike's balding head bobbing down.) Montgomery did everything he could to make Ike less camera shy, even draping the camera and the bulky equipment in black sheeting in the hope that his client might be less aware of its intrusiveness. Montgomery also persuaded Ike to trade in his dark horn-rimmed glasses for clear plastic ones and to use stage makeup. Ike disliked makeup — "an old soldier doesn't feel very good under that sort of thing" — but relented because the bright newsreel and TV lights made his skin look pasty.[6] He kept himself spit-and-polish presentable. He had a vast closet of suits, and his shoes bore a mirror shine. To keep his nails from cracking, he applied three coats of clear polish, and, while sitting with his speechwriter in the Oval Office, unselfconsciously cut and cleaned his nails with foot-long scissors and a letter opener.

When editing his speeches, Eisenhower excised what he saw as rhetorical flourishes. He did not like words that "called attention to themselves" or seemed in some way overheated: "fatuous" became "futile" and "passionate" became "devout." Although Ike was a strict grammarian when it came to his speeches, he frequently mangled syntax in his spoken answers at press conferences. Trying to be precise, he sometimes became entangled in his words, recalled one of his speechwriters, Arthur Larson. "If the question was fraught with possible explosive consequences, he might in his answer start down one verbal path then, no doubt reminding himself of some possible impact on this or that interest of the country, he would backtrack and take a somewhat different turn," wrote Larson.[7]

These verbal meanderings amused reporters, who debated whether to quote Ike literally or straighten out his convolutions. But the public didn't care. They appreciated Eisenhower partly *because* he was not a flashy or smooth speaker. He was not an intellectual, an "egghead" like Adlai Stevenson, but a deeply reassuring presence. Television exposed and magnified

Meeting the press (Eisenhower National Historic Site, Gettysburg, Pennsylvania)

shifty looks and insincerity. Ike came across as calm and steady, but also quietly powerful. Ike disliked orators who overacted. He would make his advisers laugh by standing up and, arms flailing, imitating a windbag politician, denouncing some injustice, crying out, "How long, O America, how long?"

Ike rarely showed his whole hand, or if he did, it was only to offer a peek. In June, speaking without notes at Dartmouth College's commencement, he had reminisced about patriotism, golf, and college life, then suddenly implored the young men, "Don't join the book burners." He was obviously referring to Joe McCarthy, whose henchman Roy Cohn and

Cohn's sidekick David Schine had barged through US embassies in Europe removing "subversive" literature. But when Merriman Smith, the wire service reporter and dean of the White House press corps, asked him if he was referring to McCarthy, Eisenhower demurred: "Now, Merriman, you have been around long enough to know I never talk personalities."[8]

In Eisenhower's January 1954 State of the Union, most Americans heard, for the first time, an American president call for victory over Communism in the far-off country of Vietnam. Ike did not dwell on the subject, but promised only to offer US support to the French, who were embroiled in a wasting war in Indochina, as the region was then called.

Eager to restore their dignity after the shame of Nazi occupation in World War II, France clung to Vietnam, its longtime colony, despite a nationalist revolution led by Ho Chi Minh, who had studied Marxism as a student in Paris. The French wanted to draw the Vietminh, as the Communist rebels were called, into a conventional set-piece battle. The Vietminh were everywhere and nowhere. Talking to a Western reporter in 1952, the Vietminh top general, Vo Nguyen Giap, pointed to a dirt path and said, "Our boulevards." Smiling, Giap asked, "In our war, where is the front?"[9]

In the late fall of 1953, some 12,000 French para-troopers were dropped into a remote mountain out-post called Dien Bien Phu. They created a fort in a valley with a series of strongholds gallantly named after women — Beatrice, Dominique, Gabrielle (mistresses of the French commander, General Christian de Castries) — and invited the Vietminh to come out and fight. General Giap accommodated by marching in 50,000 men and hauling heavy artillery pieces over the mountains. The battle began on March 13, 1954, with barrages of shells into the French fort and onto the small airfield. French pilots were soon calling Dien Bien Phu *le Pot de Chambre,* "the Chamber Pot."[10]

Eisenhower was astonished at the foolishness of the French, whose army had allowed the enemy to occupy the high ground surrounding the fort.[11] He had no desire to get directly involved in Vietnam; having just extricated America from one Asian land war, he did not want to dive into another. The jungle, he had told the National Security Council in January, would "absorb our troops by divisions!" Normally, when Eisenhower became animated (as he often did) at meetings, the official notetaker would write, "the President spoke warmly." This time, the notation read, "the President spoke with vehemence."[12]

But Eisenhower had to tread very carefully. His

own political party had relentlessly chastised the Truman administration for "losing China" when the Communists took over in 1949. He did not want to be attacked by the Republican right for "losing Vietnam," setting off an intraparty fight that would provide a feast for Democrats. He also did not want to disappoint the French, who were essential, if difficult, members of the Western Alliance. In fact, the Americans were already paying for half of the French war effort.

On March 20, the French defense minister, Paul Ely, arrived to ask for more help from Uncle Sam. Ely was deeply depressed when his TWA flight arrived at Idlewild Airport in New York after the fourteen-hour Atlantic crossing. He was not looking forward to describing to the Americans the looming fiasco at Dien Bien Phu. Admiral Arthur Radford, chairman of the Joint Chiefs of Staff, was waiting on the tarmac with his personal plane for the flight to Washington. That Saturday night at his grand quarters at Fort Myer, in Virginia, Radford hosted a stag dinner for Ely. Guests included Vice President Richard Nixon and CIA chief Allen Dulles.[13]

A cocksure former aviator and carrier fleet commander, Radford was an "Asia Firster," who believed that a showdown with Communists there was unavoidable. He not only looked forward to it, he thought that when it came, America should use

Decorating Admiral Radford (Dwight D. Eisenhower Presidential Library, Abilene, Kansas)

nuclear bombs against the Communists. He was also a fearless bureaucratic infighter who had worn down defense secretary James Forrestal with his demands for more resources for the US Navy. In his admiral's quarters, over toasts to America and France, Radford lifted the spirits of the downcast French defense minister by telling him he proposed to fly B-29s, armed with nuclear weapons, from the Philippines against Vietminh targets and to send a carrier fleet to patrol off the Vietnamese coast.[14]

At 10:30 on Monday morning, Ely was escorted into the Oval Office. Ely had been a brave soldier in the Free French army, losing a hand in combat, and

Eisenhower treated him like a long-lost comrade. At the photo opportunity, the president exclaimed that they had won World War II together and would win this war, too. Eisenhower instructed Radford to fill Ely's immediate shopping list for twenty-five medium-range B-26 bombers. Technically, beyond providing the aircraft, Ike had made no real commitments, but Radford, hearing what he wished to hear, thought the president had made a fairly open-ended promise to give Ely "everything he asked for." Ely, too, thought he had heard Eisenhower offer to do whatever it took to save the besieged fort, "without limits." The French defense minister, no longer depressed and now almost giddy, had read too much into the presidential smile.[15]

At the National Security Council meeting that Thursday, March 25, the president was in a sardonic mood, joking about French military ineptitude and the deficiencies of French character. He also began laying down some important markers. If the United States were to intervene, it would be only after approval by Congress and as part of a UN-sponsored force.[16] As NATO commander in 1951, pondering the French predicament in Indochina, he had considered the ordeal of jungle warfare and ruefully decided that the situation was hopeless. He was "convinced," he wrote in his diary, "that no military victory is possible in that kind of theater."[17] But for now, the president did not want to acknowledge that victory was beyond reach. Instead, in his masterfully indirect way, he set down conditions that were impossible to meet. He knew that neither Congress nor the allies would want to plunge into an Asian land war to save France's colony. Indeed, he made Vietnamese independence another condition, which was sure to raise French hackles and thereby complicate a UN rescue plan.[18] At the NSC meeting, Eisenhower disguised his maneuvering by belittling the French some more. "If we could only sit down and talk to them man-to-man like we can with the British when things get tough. But not the French. It sure takes a lot of patience," said Eisenhower, who was, as noted, endlessly patient when he wanted to be.[19]

Secretary of State Dulles was scheduled to give a speech to the Overseas Press Club in New York that Monday night, March 29. Eisenhower saw an opportunity to cover his flank with a jeremiad from his most vocal anti-Communist. In his lugubrious, near-apocalyptic tones, Dulles warned against Russian and Chinese determination "to dominate all of Southeast Asia." The Free World was threatened by Communist aggression. What was called for was "united action" to stop the Red tide. The speech caused a stir, as Eisenhower knew it would (he had approved the draft). The pundits saw a call to action. But what, exactly, they asked, did Dulles mean by "united action"?

Eisenhower was ready with his usual practiced evasions for the reporters at his regular press conference two days later, on March 31. Dulles's "speech must stand by itself," he said, unhelpfully. He then launched into a general description of the New Look and his determination to defend America's "vital interests." But exactly *what* vital interests? the reporters wanted to know. Every local situation had "its own risk of degree and danger," Eisenhower blandly responded.[20]

While Ike equivocated, the situation at Dien Bien Phu grew more desperate. At the April 1 NSC meeting, Admiral Radford tried to force action, warning that without reinforcement the French garrison was finished. Gone now was the press conference vagueness, the blank expression Eisenhower had shown the reporters. Now his features twisted in scorn and his eyes widened. "Why had the French ever committed forces to a remote area where these forces could not be reinforced?" he raged to no one in particular. He knew that his cards were being called; he had to make some kind of decision, but he sidled toward it with notable lack of enthusiasm. "There was no reason for the Council to avoid considering the intervention issue," the president told his colleagues, according to the notetaker. This convoluted choice of words, as historian Melanie Billings-Yun put it, "must rank as one of history's most halfhearted preambles to a decision for or against war."[21]

Eisenhower may not have been entirely decided in his own mind. Earlier in March, he had listened while Radford proposed flying unmarked warplanes off American carriers and bombing the Vietminh positions for a day—then later pretending they were French ground-based aircraft. Ike had a soft spot for staging a *ruse de guerre,* and he was apparently still toying with Radford's idea that lunchtime, when he met with a couple of newspaper reporters from the Scripps-Howard chain. According to press secretary Jim Hagerty's diary, the president "said U.S. might have to make decision to send in squadrons from two aircraft carriers off coast to bomb Reds at Dienbienphu. 'Of course, if we did, we'd have to deny it forever.' French very difficult to handle. Almost impossible...."[22] Ike may have been plotting a dramatic covert action—or just bluffing with the two newsmen, trying to show that he was looking for ways to fight back against the Reds. In any case, the strategy he settled on qualifies as a classic case of artfully passing the buck. He would send Dulles up to Capitol Hill to ask congressional leaders if *they* wanted to intervene in Indochina.[23]

Dulles met secretly with eight top congressional leaders on Saturday, April 3. Only Senator William Knowland of California, a well-known Asia Firster, seemed inclined toward US intervention, and once briefed, he quickly backed off. The general refrain from the solons on the Hill was "No More Koreas." The *New York Times* quoted Senator Richard Russell of Georgia as saying, "I sat listening to him [Dulles] talk about sending American boys off to fight in a war like that and suddenly I found myself on my feet shouting, 'We're not going to do that!'" The blow-by-blow account of the secret meeting was leaked to the *Washington Post,* which ran a story headlined "The Day We Didn't Go to War."[24]

In later years, this would be called "spin." Congress had not exactly said no; rather, the congressmen had insisted that if America were going to intervene, other nations, particularly the European allies, had to jump in, too. Many Americans were confused and uncertain; they wanted to stop Communism and feared its spread, but they did not want to fight in far-off jungles. The subtext of the *Washington Post* story and others like it was clear enough: the administration's men wanted to intervene but couldn't, because Congress was tying their hands. The press play was exactly what Ike had hoped for. Ike routinely met with congressional leaders to make his case for one thing or another, but on this particular April Saturday, the president was not available. He had gone golfing.

On Sunday night, April 4, Eisenhower returned to the White House from Camp David. Eisenhower had renamed the presidential retreat, called Shangri-La by FDR, after his grandson. (Ike doted on little David, age six. When a friend said the boy "looked like presidential timber," wrote Slats Slater in his diary, "Ike said feelingly, 'Oh, no! Be kind to him.'")[25] The rustic camp in the mountains of western Maryland had grown shabby from neglect; Truman had preferred the presidential yacht, the *Williamsburg.* Ike sold the yacht,* and Mamie redecorated the camp's log cabins in a "1950s modern look," in greens, yellows, and beiges. A short par-3 golf course was laid out in a cow pasture.[26]

At 8:20 that evening, refreshed after a weekend in the mountains, the president met in his study in the Residence with Foster Dulles and several aides. Congress had insisted on international support before even considering intervention, Dulles gravely informed the president. Well, then, the president replied, go forth and get it.

Dulles was seen traveling across the Atlantic, earnestly but futilely trying to engage Great Britain with France in what he called "united action." The British foreign minister, Anthony Eden, shared Winston Churchill's low opinion of Dulles and was at best lukewarm to his overtures. Dulles in turn said

---

*He kept two smaller boats, named after his granddaughters Barbara Anne and Susan.

he had been "double crossed" by an Eden promise of help later reneged on. All this was carefully leaked and duly reported in anguished prose by American newspapers. To the picture of a reluctant Congress was added the image of recalcitrant allies. In the reporters' telling, Dulles was trying manfully to turn back the Reds, but the others were foot dragging. For Eisenhower, this provided more insulation from blame.[27]

By early April, Dien Bien Phu had nearly been overrun. The French paratroopers—"burrowed beneath mounds of dead corpses and excrement," in one account—were clinging to the base, but barely.[28] Now the French came begging for a loan of heavy B-29 bombers, waving Ike's "promise," as exaggerated by Admiral Radford, to "give them everything they asked for." Ike was furious. The Joint Chiefs chairman "should never have told a foreign country that he would do his best because they then start putting pressure on us," Eisenhower fumed. Just when Ike seemed to have succeeded in shifting responsibility to Congress and the allies, the buck was coming back.

At a secret emergency meeting of the National Security Council on April 6, Ike flatly declared that there would be no American intervention.[29] Publicly, though, he felt the need to show his bona fides as a crusader against global Communism. Meeting with reporters in the Victorian splendor of the Indian

Treaty Room on April 7, he spoke some words that would be taken a little too literally by later, less subtle presidents. Describing the US defense perimeter in the Pacific—Australia, New Zealand, the Philippines, Formosa, and Japan—he warned, slightly awkwardly but with an image that would last, "You have a row of dominoes set up, and you knock the first one over, and what will happen to the last one is the certainty that it will go over very quickly."*[30]

Ike's comments were tough talk to bolster the president's image as an anti-Communist *after* the inevitable fall of Vietnam. But some of Eisenhower's top advisers were not quite getting the message. At a National Security Council meeting on April 29, Eisenhower seemed besieged and surrounded by his own men. Not only was Admiral Radford pulling hard for intervention, but so were Under Secretary of State Walter Bedell Smith, Vice President Nixon, and Harold Stassen, the politically ambitious former governor of Minnesota who was head of the Mutual Security Administration, which dispensed foreign aid. Foster Dulles, who normally took his

---

*The memorable phrase that gave rise to the "Domino Theory" seems to have occurred to Eisenhower at a National Security meeting on April 6. In a handwritten note, he jotted "row of dominoes" and stated, "Indochina was the first in a row of dominoes. If it fell its neighbors would shortly fall with it, and where would the process end?"[31]

cues from the president, also began questioning his boss's reluctance to send in troops. For two hours, the advisers pushed and prodded, led by the outspoken Stassen, who had served as a staffer for Admiral William "Bull" Halsey during the Pacific war.

Eisenhower patiently rebutted the arguments. Then, ever the sly poker player, he upped the ante. He asked how his men felt about World War III. Why, he asked, "fritter away" your resources on "local engagements"? Why not go all the way? As the notetaker recorded it:

The President answered that before he could bring himself to make such a decision [for war in Indochina], he would want to ask himself and all his wisest advisers whether the right decision was not rather to launch a world war. If our allies were going to fall away in any case, it might be better for the United States to leap over the smaller obstacles and hit the biggest one with all the power we had. Otherwise we seemed to be playing the enemy's game—getting ourselves involved in the brushfire wars in Burma, Afghanistan, and God knows where.[32]

That was the end of the debate in the National Security Council. But there was still the last, nuclear card to play.

*   *   *

In his memoirs, Georges Bidault, the French foreign minister, claimed that on his trip to Paris in mid-April, Foster Dulles offered the French two atomic bombs to drop on Dien Bien Phu. Dulles later said he was "totally mystified" by the statement, but journalist and historian Ted Morgan found three credible French sources to buttress Bidault's claim. One said that he personally heard Dulles say to Bidault, in a low voice as they walked into a private salon in Paris on April 24, "Would you like two bombs?" The French deputy foreign minister, Maurice Schumann, claimed that Bidault, with a "chalky face," entered his office and "blurted out, 'Can you imagine what Dulles told me? He proposed atomic bombs to save Dien Bien Phu.'" The French said they declined; the fighting was so close that a nuclear weapon would annihilate both sides.[33]

Was Dulles operating on his own initiative? He rarely strayed too far from the president's views. The official record — a memo by Bobby Cutler — shows that, at a small White House meeting on May 1, Eisenhower and several of his top advisers discussed the use of what were politely referred to as "new weapons" on Dien Bien Phu. There was some doubt that the new weapons could "effectively be used in the jungles around DBP [Dien Bien Phu]." In his memoirs, Richard Nixon recalled that both he and the president thought conventional bombs and napalm would work better. But there is also the suggestion in Cutler's memo that if the French wanted some "new weapons...*now* for possible use, we might give them a few." Many years later, according to his biographer Stephen Ambrose, Eisenhower recalled that he said to his advisers, "You boys must be crazy. We can't use those awful things against Asians for the second time in less than ten years. My God."*

In recent years, Ambrose's accounts of his interviews with Eisenhower have been called into question. (At a minimum, Ambrose grossly exaggerated the number of times the two men met.) "We can't use those awful things" is a memorable quote, but as historian Richard Betts has written, what Ambrose purports to be Ike's "recollection does not seem quite consistent with Cutler's contemporary record." As he listened to Admiral Radford and others tout the efficacy of "new weapons," Eisenhower may well have *thought* that "you boys must be crazy," but it is unlikely that he *said* such a thing to his senior

---

*The talk of "new weapons" made Eisenhower's secretary, Ann Whitman, very anxious. Ike called Whitman to reassure her. As Whitman later wrote in her diary, "I thought the world was coming to an end....Later that night, the President...called me twice...to tell me things were not as bad as I believed them." One of the advantages of having seen so much history, Ike liked to say, was that things were rarely as bad as they seemed.[34]

advisers. Eisenhower was very careful not to rule out using nuclear weapons, even among his smallest, most intimate circles of friends or advisers. As always, the credibility of the New Look—his reliance on relatively low-cost nuclear weapons as a deterrent over vastly more expensive conventional forces that might be deployed in an ever-larger war—depended on the president telling no one his true intentions.[35]

Dien Bien Phu fell on May 7, the garrison, reduced to the size of a baseball field, succumbing to a final series of Vietminh human-wave attacks. In July, at a peace conference in Geneva, Vietnam was divided in half. The French colony was no more: the Communists took the north, and the south became a weak democratic state—and, increasingly, an American client.

Eisenhower was "an expert in finding reasons for not doing things," recalled Andrew Goodpaster, his staff secretary and the adviser who probably knew him best. "He never showed his hole card," Goodpaster told journalist John Newhouse. Of course, not doing was a kind of doing. It would be an oversimplification to suggest that Ike's handling of Vietnam was nothing more than an effort to foist responsibility for intervention onto Congress and the Allies, knowing they would never go for it. Eisenhower was willing to fight—but not a war he deemed unwinnable. The record shows that Eisenhower was truly worried about losing Vietnam to the Communists and actively looked for ways to hold the line. Had Britain and France been willing to join forces with the United States, had the military odds and timing seemed just right, Ike might have been willing to use force.[36] Still, Dean Acheson, viewing the game from the sidelines, was not being entirely cynical when he wrote his friend Harry Truman in June to describe the Eisenhower administration's gyrations and machinations: "... intervention, alone one day, and the next on conditions as long as a life insurance contract & involving no American boy anywhere on his feet—these shifts, twists and turns have people groggy."

The acerbic old statesman accused Eisenhower and Dulles of serving "prohibition hooch which makes some people go crazy and blinds others."[37] It's true that Ike could be sly. Some years later, at one of his stag dinners, the president was asked by a priest, "Tell me, why did you finally decide not to intervene militarily in the Indochina war?" Ike glibly responded, "No one asked us." It had not been so simple at the time. One adviser, Arthur Larson, recalled seeing beads of sweat on Eisenhower's forehead during the tense debate over whether and when to intervene. "Not this week, thank God," the president had muttered at one point.[38] In the pages of

Foreign Relations of the United States, the official record of government deliberations, Eisenhower hardly comes across as Machiavelli's coolly calculating prince. At times he does seem at sea, lurching about the tossing deck. But he had an almost instinctive sense of when to use indirection, when to shift blame and lie low. In the spring of 1954, at critical moments, he was able to find "reasons for not doing things" when less savvy and more impulsive leaders might have been sucked into a quagmire.

Eisenhower would later be lauded for keeping America out of a land war in Vietnam. At the time, he was seen as a somewhat passive figure who let his highly visible, pontifical secretary of state run foreign policy. For a strong man with a sizeable ego, Eisenhower was remarkably willing, on occasion, to let himself appear disengaged, even weak. He kept the presidency above the political fray, while pretending to be oblivious to the carping of pundits, a price he was willing to pay to further the larger end of keeping America out of war.[39]

Vietnam was not, of course, the only matter on Eisenhower's mind in the spring of 1954. On March 1, the United States took out another Pacific atoll with an H-bomb test code-named Bravo. This one was 750 times bigger than the blast at Hiroshima, and the radioactive fallout sickened some Japanese fishermen many miles away. The Japanese government protested, and Ike, with characteristic vagueness but uncharacteristic indiscretion, suggested at a press conference that the H-bomb testing had somehow gotten out of control.

When Lewis Strauss, head of the Atomic Energy Commission, tried to clarify matters, he made them worse. The H-bomb, Strauss said to reporters, with perhaps a hint of pride, "could be made as large as you wish...large enough to take out any city." The reporters looked up from their notebooks. "What?" they pressed. "How big a city?" "Any city," Strauss replied. "Any city, New York?" "The metropolitan area, yes."

Eisenhower anticipated the public alarm that Strauss would set off. "Lewis, I wouldn't have answered that one that way," he told his AEC director as they walked back from the Old Executive Office Building toward the Oval Office. Ike did not want to have a public debate about the morality of the H-bomb, and one big reason was J. Robert Oppenheimer. The father of the atomic bomb, Oppenheimer had opposed the creation of the H-bomb—the "super," as it was briefly known. Like many intellectuals in the 1920s and '30s, Oppenheimer had become acquainted with Communists as a younger man. In the feverish 1950s, he had been singled out as a security risk by Lewis Strauss and accused of intentionally delaying progress on the H-bomb.

Eisenhower had reluctantly agreed to yank Oppenheimer's security clearance, but he was afraid of a public scandal. He was especially worried that Senator McCarthy would come sniffing around the Oppenheimer case, which was highly secret. Even if Ike could honestly claim that he had taken steps to sideline Oppenheimer, he knew McCarthy would use the situation to make serious trouble.[40]

Instead, McCarthy, in his reckless way, made the mistake of attacking the US Army. For four years, McCarthy had blackened reputations and ruined careers, hounding government employees, even blameless ones like Chip Bohlen. Pouncing on a slightly pink army dentist named Dr. Irving Peress, McCarthy started wailing, "Who promoted Peress?" and began investigating his commanding officer, General Ralph Zwicker, denouncing him as "not fit to wear the uniform" and possessing "the brains of a five year old child." Zwicker had been a hero on D-day. At last, in the estimation of the commander in chief, Tailgunner Joe McCarthy had gone too far. "This guy McCarthy is going to get into trouble over this," said President Eisenhower to his aides. "I'm not going to take this one lying down."[41]

At the White House, there was a sense of relief. Some of Ike's more self-consciously principled aides, like Emmet Hughes, C. D. Jackson, and Ann Whitman, had been after the president to stop feigning indifference to McCarthy. ("This Three Little Monkeys act is not working!" Jackson had railed at a staff meeting in November.) Slowly, deliberately, secretly, Eisenhower began to explore his power to stop McCarthy. On March 2, he called Deputy Attorney General William Rogers. Mrs. Whitman, listening in on the call, took notes: "One thing people keep talking about is the authority of the President to protect people against McCarthy," Ike began. "No one has even suggested what kind of authority this is." He asked the Justice Department lawyers to work up a memo asking what steps he could take to keep McCarthy from "abusing" people.[42]

At the vortex of competing crises, from Indochina to McCarthy, all shadowed by the bomb, Eisenhower was feeling the pressure. "I realize I am more nervous than usual and a few days of trying to straighten out my drives and my putts would be good for me," he told Cliff Roberts of the Augusta "gang," as he stole away to his favorite course for a few days at the end of March.[43]

Behind the scenes, the White House orchestrated McCarthy's collapse, working with the demagogue's Senate foes to deny him information on the promotion of Dr. Peress and the deliberations of the secretary of the army. (Eisenhower cited "executive privilege," a term that would take on greater import during the Watergate scandal two decades later.) The maneuvering robbed McCarthy of essential fuel for his bonfire of the army, and, more important, signaled senators that the White House was finally engaging McCarthy, albeit from a safe distance. Still, Eisenhower was careful not to get the White House drawn into a direct, public confrontation with McCarthy. Over dinner, Senator Stuart Symington told Milton Eisenhower that "the real contest is between McCarthy and the President." On Milton's memo reporting this exchange to Ike, the president penned, "Or: artificial build up to urge me to act in a personal way."[44] As usual, Ike preferred to play a waiting game, to allow McCarthy to self-destruct. In late April, as Dien Bien Phu was heating up and the Army-McCarthy hearings began on television, Eisenhower got his wish. Whining and pathetic, McCarthy was exposed for his shallowness and petty cruelty. Millions of Americans watched on TV, including Eisenhower, though he denied it.

For someone who had become famous as a soldier who preferred to go on the offensive, Eisenhower as president seemed more informed by jujitsu and caution than by boldness. Perhaps Ike's wartime experiences informed his actions as president; he wished to avoid what would later be called "collateral damage."

Ike stayed mostly in the background throughout the Army-McCarthy hearings, but some months later, after McCarthy had been censured by the Senate, Ike asked at a weekly meeting of Republican congressional leaders if they had heard the joke around town about how "McCarthyism" was now "McCarthywasm."[45]

Ike was not joking much in the summer of 1954. Syngman Rhee of South Korea continued his belligerent feints at provoking a new war with the North, exasperating Ike, who tried to keep Rhee at arm's length. In February, Ike had noted in his diary, "Letter was delivered from President Rhee this morning to the State Department, and is of such a tone that the State Department is refusing to receive it and to pass it on to me. However, they will have a photocopy made of it. That copy I want to see—then it will become part of my unofficial records."[46] In July, when Rhee was once again agitating, Eisenhower at last took the direct approach, lecturing the South Korean leader, "Atomic war will destroy civilization. There will be millions of people dead.... If the Kremlin and Washington ever lock up in a war, the results are too horrible to contemplate."[47] To Jim Hagerty, he complained about Rhee's dangerous "stubbornness." He also went on about the "incredible selfishness" of congressmen and confessed he was feeling the "tension" of his office.[48] In his memoir, Chief of Staff Sherman Adams reported that Eisenhower had "spells of depression" that summer, "and the reason for them is not difficult to understand. Ann Whitman and I agreed that he was being faced with too many vexing problems that either had no solution or that required great personal concentration before making decisions for which he alone was responsible."[49]

At Camp David, summer 1954 (Eisenhower National Historic Site, Gettysburg, Pennsylvania)

9

Strange Genius

VERY FRIDAY, Milton Eisenhower would be driven from State College, Pennsylvania, where he was president of Penn State University, to the White House. The four-hour trip was boring, and Milton suffered from car sickness when he tried to read, but he knew that the president counted on seeing him. Ike thought so highly of his brother that he considered Milton as his possible successor in 1956. "I think my brother would do anything I wanted him to do," Ike told aides. "I think he would run for president."[1] Milton always insisted that he never tried to tell the president what to do; he did not want to be seen as a Svengali or even a Harry Hopkins, FDR's close adviser. Milton did share with Ike his expertise on Latin America, where he had studied and often traveled. In the spring and summer of 1953, Ike sent his brother on a fact-finding trip through Central and South America. Milton reported back that the small country of Guatemala had "succumbed to communist infiltration." Once again policy makers began hearing the click of dominoes.[2]

It has often been alleged that the Eisenhower administration staged a coup d'état in Guatemala in the summer of 1954 at the bidding of United Fruit, whose banana plantations were being nationalized by the leftist regime of President Jacobo Arbenz. Indeed, an astonishing array of Eisenhower advisers and appointees had financial interests in United Fruit, or close ties of one kind or another; these included John Foster and Allen Dulles (United Fruit had been their client at Sullivan and Cromwell) and Ann Whitman (whose husband, Ed, was United Fruit's spokesman).[3] The Eisenhower administration had worked from the beginning with United Fruit to oust Arbenz. Eisenhower even raised the issue of Guatemala with Ed Whitman at a lunch before his inauguration in 1953.[4] Educated by his brother, familiar with Central America from his service in the Canal Zone as a young officer, Eisenhower was genuinely worried about the spread of Communism to the Western Hemisphere. To Ike, the defeat of fascism in World War II was but prelude to a larger struggle. He understood how the world's poor and oppressed could be seduced by the false god of Marxism-Leninism. In his frequent correspondence with Winston Churchill, Eisenhower constantly appealed to his wartime comrade to lock arms in this new and greater test of good and evil. Ever (to Churchill) the aw-shucks boy from Kansas, Eisenhower was not above a little flattery and self-effacement, couched in the sort of grandiloquent appeals to history and destiny that he thought the prime minister might appreciate. In February 1954, Ike wrote "Dear Winston" that unless great leaders acted "soon...there will be no history of any kind, as we know it. There will be only a concocted story made up by the Communist conquerors of the world."

> *It is only when one allows his mind to contemplate momentarily such a disaster for the world and attempts to picture an atheistic materialism in complete domination of all human life, that he fully appreciates how necessary it is to seek renewed faith and strength from his God, and sharpen his sword for the struggle that cannot possibly be escaped.*
>
> *Destiny has given priceless opportunity to some of this epoch. You are one of them. Perhaps I am*

also one of the company on whom this great responsibility has fallen.

With warm personal regard, As ever[5]

With his own advisers, Ike was more down to earth: "My God!" he exclaimed to his cabinet at about the same time, "just think what it would mean to us if Mexico went to the communists!"[6]

Eisenhower's ambassador to Guatemala was Jack Peurifoy, a flamboyant figure who wore a jumpsuit with a shoulder holster rather than a diplomat's striped trousers. In October 1953, a month after meeting with President Arbenz, Ambassador Peurifoy gave his evaluation of the Guatemalan strongman: "It seemed to me that the man thought like a communist and talked like a communist, and if not actually one,

---

*In his response, Churchill seemed less anxious about the spread of global Communism than he was about the horrifying new weapons of war. If just one H-bomb were dropped in the sea windward of the British Isles, he wrote Eisenhower in March, "the explosion would generate an enormous radioactive cloud, many square miles in extent, which would drift over the land and extinguish human life over very large areas." Churchill understood that "human minds recoil from such facts" and retreat into a kind of "merciful numbness" that cannot "be enjoyed by the few groups of men upon whom such responsibility falls....I consider that you and, if my strength lasts, I, cannot flinch from the mental exertions involved."

would do until one came along." In May 1954, when Arbenz bought a shipload of weapons from Czechoslovakia, that was enough for Eisenhower.[7] On June 15, the president signed off on a CIA operation, code-named PBSUCCESS, to overthrow the Arbenz regime. "I want you all to be damn good and sure you succeed," Eisenhower told CIA director Dulles. "When you commit the flag, you commit it to win."[8]

To run the operation, Dulles chose Al Haney, an even more outrageous figure than Peurifoy. Haney's covert actions during the Korean War had usually ended in failure, but he covered up his shortcomings with macho swagger. Nicknamed "Zaney" by his unawed subordinates, Haney was assisted by a Groton and Yale man named Tracy Barnes, who had parachuted behind German lines in World War II and embodied the Ivy League brio of the early CIA. Barnes was a great favorite of Allen Dulles.

Operation PBSUCCESS at first looked like it was headed for failure. The army under the chief coup plotter, Carlos Castillo Armas, was tiny, ragtag, and pitiful, while Castillo Armas himself "might make sergeant in the American army," drily reported William "Rip" Robertson, a soldier of fortune hired by the CIA to whip the rebel troops into shape. On June 18, Castillo Armas "invaded" Guatemala from Honduras and promptly stalled just over the border without firing a shot. The people did not rise up.[9]

Not surprisingly, there was tremendous anxiety at CIA headquarters in Washington (the Agency did not move to Langley, Virginia, until 1961). "We were all at our wits' end," recalled Richard Bissell, a Dulles aide assigned to work on PBSUCCESS. In Guatemala City, the call came from Peurifoy to bomb the capital. Over at the State Department, Beedle Smith set about buying some unmarked surplus World War II planes to beef up the rebel air force, which consisted of a few pilots throwing grenades and empty or gas-filled Coke bottles out of a Cessna. (The empty bottles "made a satisfying whistling sound," wrote Bissell.) Incensed that the United States was trying to overthrow a democratically elected government, Henry Holland, the assistant secretary for Latin American affairs, demanded an audience with the president.[10]

At 2:15 p.m. on June 22, Allen Dulles and Holland appeared at the Oval Office. Eisenhower turned to Dulles and asked him directly, "What do you think Castillo's chances would be without the aircraft?" Dulles responded, "About zero." "Suppose we supply the aircraft. What would the chances be then?" Dulles answered, "About twenty percent." Eisenhower agreed to the planes, two old P-51s. When the meeting was breaking up, Eisenhower smiled to relieve the tension and said to Dulles, "Allen, that figure of 20 percent was persuasive. It showed me that you had thought this matter through realistically. If you had told me that the chance would be 90 percent, I would have had a much more difficult decision." Dulles was "equal to the situation," Eisenhower recorded in his memoirs. "Mr. President," he later said with a grin, "when I saw Henry walk into your office with three large law books under his arm, I knew he had lost the case already."[11]

In Guatemala City, the newly armed, CIA-backed rebel air force began dropping real bombs, which they called *sulfados* (laxatives). Drinking himself into a stupor at the presidential palace, Arbenz panicked and resigned. At CIA headquarters in Washington, a cheer went up. A special briefing was arranged for President Eisenhower in the White House theater.* Eisenhower had skipped Kermit Roosevelt's briefing after the Iran coup, less than a year earlier, but the president was an enthusiastic audience this time. "How many men did Castillo Armas lose?" Ike asked Rip Robertson. Only one, the CIA man replied. "Incredible," said Eisenhower. Robertson was lying (at least forty-three rebels had died in the invasion), but to a commander who had lost several thousand

---

*The night before, at a dress rehearsal at Dulles's house in Cleveland Park, Haney had inexplicably wandered off on a discussion of his exploits in Korea, largely made-up. "I've never heard such crap," said Dulles, and ordered a rewrite of the script.

men on the beaches of Normandy in 1944 and now faced a global war against Communism, the CIA's low-cost approach had great appeal.[12] In turn, the CIA basked in the president's approval. "We've been to see the Prexy and it was great!" exclaimed Tracy Barnes to his wife as he executed a little scuffling dance.[13] Dulles had a kind of blustery confidence that allowed him to appear frank; unlike other senior officials, he appeared relaxed in the presence of the president. Eisenhower had certainly appreciated his candor about the coup's low chances. Dulles's bluff charm did not fool some hard-eyed men, like the dyspeptic Beedle Smith. Eisenhower had a high tolerance for human foibles and eccentricity (he had put up with and forgiven George Patton for as long as possible), but he may also have been more in his element when judging soldiers than assessing smooth Ivy Leaguers. In 2010, his son John told the author, "Dad could be fooled. He was better when the guy was in uniform and knew him. But all those guys from Princeton and Yale..."[14]

Ike was not naïve; he was aware that he had few means to double check what the CIA men were telling him. In Iran and now Guatemala, the Agency had produced results, but at the same time, Eisenhower had recently been given reason to suspect that he was not hearing the whole truth from Dulles and Company.

On May 24—three weeks before he signed off on PBSUCCESS—Eisenhower received a six-page private letter, with a detailed twenty-page addendum, from a high-ranking former CIA man named Jim Kellis, who had run the Agency's paramilitary operations in the Korean War. "The Central Intelligence Agency is in a rotten state," Kellis warned the president. The ex-CIA man, who had quit the Agency in disgust, described a string of botched operations—agents rolled up or doubled, covert ops gone wrong or betrayed—that had been covered up by Allen Dulles.[15] Kellis offered a biting description of Dulles:

> He has been attempting for the past year through inspired magazine and newspaper articles to convey the impression of a scholarly affable Christian missionary bossing an Intelligence Agency and further that he is the country's outstanding intelligence expert. For some of us who have seen the other side of Allen Dulles, we don't see too many Christian traits. I personally consider him a ruthless, ambitious and utterly incompetent government administrator.

At Ike's instruction, his staff secretary, Colonel Pete Carroll, wrote back "to convey [the president's] appreciation," and to say the letter was being taken seriously. Reflecting his boss's views, Carroll did, however, defend Dulles. "Most certainly," he wrote, "a man of that caliber would never make any effort to cover up shortcomings for his own protection."[16]

Still, Kellis's letter was disturbing and reinforced doubts raised by Beedle Smith, who had long taken a dim view of the Agency's Ivy League cowboys. Eisenhower had been under some pressure from Capitol Hill to allow congressional oversight of the CIA, which operated behind a veil of almost total secrecy even to the committees appropriating its money (generally hidden as "black" funds in the defense budget). The president was loath to let Congress play watchdog, partly because he feared the Red baiters would go witch hunting. (He had told a congressman who proposed congressional oversight of the CIA that he would be "damned" if he would let Joe McCarthy "get a foothold.")[17] Moreover, he appreciated that the CIA served in effect as his own secret, quick-reaction strike force, a lean body that could operate without legions of bureaucrats, congressmen, or reporters second-guessing and slowing things down.

Ike preferred to use trusted friends for really sensitive assignments, so in July 1954, while PBSUCCESS hung in the balance, he asked General James Doolittle to conduct a discreet investigation of the CIA. Doolittle, a World War II hero, was close to Ike and the sort of no-nonsense soldier Eisenhower prized.

Doolittle delivered his conclusions to the president on October 19. The report itself was critical: the Agency was "bloated," filled with people who had "little or no training" and "dead wood" at all levels. In conversation with the president, Doolittle raised the awkward question of the "family relationship" of Foster and Allen Dulles. Naturally, warned Doolittle, the brothers were protective of each other and too easily influenced. Doolittle also raised the concerns of Beedle Smith: that Dulles was "too emotional to be in this critical spot" and that his "emotionalism was far worse than it appeared on the surface."

Here was a moment when Eisenhower should have listened closely to a friend. Instead, he was defensive about Allen Dulles. Perhaps Smith and Doolittle had chosen the wrong word. "Emotionalism" was not so much Dulles's problem; "deceitful bluster" and "overconfidence" were more accurate descriptions, as Eisenhower was painfully to learn. When Doolittle, quoting Smith, criticized Dulles for being too emotional, Ike interrupted: "I have never seen him show the slightest disturbance." (It was true; Dulles was all pipe smoke and ho-ho-ho around the president.) "Here is one of the most peculiar types of operations any government can have," Eisenhower said, "and it probably takes a strange kind of genius to run it."[18]

*　　*　　*

Ike was a believer in what he called the p-factor—psychology, propaganda, persuasion. He was determined to avoid war, and he was equally determined not to bankrupt the country preparing for war. Yet he believed that the United States was already at war—not a hot war, but a long-term struggle between East and West that had to be won. Ultimately, peace could not be negotiated, though negotiations were necessary; rather, the Western nations had to keep the pressure on the Communist bloc until Marxism-Leninism collapsed from its own internal contradictions.

In World War II, Eisenhower had learned to appreciate the value of what was melodramatically known as psychological warfare. Ike did not have much use for heavy-handed state propaganda machines. With his preference for the hidden hand, he believed that psychological war should be waged secretly—not by crude agitprop or Big Lies but by political action waged on many fronts, often by private CIA-backed and secretly funded groups like Radio Free Europe. For propaganda to be effective, said Eisenhower, "the hand of government should be carefully concealed, and, in some cases I should say, wholly eliminated." Morale was crucial: soldiers needed dry socks; allies had to be stroked and soothed and convinced of their common cause. Eisenhower did not buy the woollier ideas of his psychological-warfare adviser C. D. Jackson, who wanted to win World War III with black propaganda. Still, after Jackson, frustrated by bureaucracy, left in 1954, Ike stayed in touch with him and said, with at least partial sincerity, that he missed his former psy-war adviser's energy and ideas.[19]

The need for subtlety meant relying on the CIA, its front groups, and private organizations with no (discernible) link to the government. Much of the "psy-war" message put out by the CIA and the so-called radios — Radio Free Europe and Voice of America — in the 1950s was true or at least reasonably objective. But inevitably, the CIA felt the need to manipulate. Frank Wisner, head of covert operations at the CIA, bragged about his "Mighty Wurlitzer," which could play any tune he wanted, "from eerie horror music (Moscow is planning a purge of the Western parties!!!) to light fantasias," as Thomas Powers wrote in his history of the era, *The Man Who Kept the Secrets*. Perceiving their foe as devious and ruthless, the Cold Warriors of the age felt compelled to fight fire with fire, to counter Soviet subversion with dirty tricks. This ends-justify-the-means thinking was widely shared by the men around Eisenhower, including General Doolittle, whose critical report on the CIA nonetheless embraced no-holds-barred covert action.

Doolittle's report was memorably lurid when it

came to describing the Communist threat and condoning any means to stop it: "It is now clear we are facing an implacable enemy whose avowed objective is world domination by whatever means and at whatever cost. There are no rules in such a game. Hitherto acceptable norms of human conduct do not apply. If the United States is to survive, long-standing American concepts of 'fair play' must now be reconsidered."[20] This passage has long been regarded as a kind of official license for the CIA to blackmail, subvert, and assassinate. Less noticed, the report also emphasized that traditional spying and dropping agents behind enemy lines were unlikely to yield much useful intelligence in a "closed" society like the Soviet Union, with its effective secret police. What the United States needed was a more scientific, high-tech way to spy, by eavesdropping and photographing from afar. In the jargon of the trade, the CIA had to rely less on HUMINT — human intelligence, or old-fashioned spy versus spy — and more on SIGINT — signals intelligence and its cousins and offshoots, ELINT and COMINT, electronic and communications intelligence. In the future, already in the imagination of scientists, aerial photo reconnaissance by high-flying planes and satellites would become the most valuable spying techniques.

More than other top commanders in World War II, Eisenhower had been comfortable with scientific advancement in the art of war. He had been an avid consumer of intelligence produced by code breaking and pushed for high-tech advances in weaponry and radar. He knew firsthand how slow-moving bureaucracies and standpat military men could gum up the works. As Army Chief of Staff in 1946, Ike had stressed the importance of scientific breakthroughs in a memo to commanders: "Scientists and industrialists must be given the greatest possible freedom to carry out their research.... Scientists and industrialists are more likely to make new and unsuspected contributions to the development of the Army if detailed directions are held to a minimum."[21] If possible, Ike wanted to circumvent the army and its sister services altogether. Eisenhower did not trust the military to push the technological boundaries. Here was a job for an organization that disdained both bureaucracy and following the rules: the CIA.

Eisenhower's personal Pearl Harbor had been the Battle of the Bulge, in December 1944, when the Germans had secretly amassed a huge force to stage a counterattack just when they seemed to be on the run. The German attack "deeply impressed upon him the value as well as the limitations of intelligence, together with the dangers of being caught off guard," Andrew Goodpaster recalled.[22]

Eisenhower doubted that the Russians would be

foolish enough to attack the United States, but he could not be sure. Indeed, he was "haunted" by the threat of a surprise attack, he told his advisers in March 1954.[23] An April 1953 report by RAND (the initials stood for Research and Development), the air force's new think tank, predicted that if Russian bombers could deliver a knockout blow by dropping "only" fifty atomic bombs, they could take out two-thirds of the bombers of the Strategic Air Command and devastate several American cities. The CIA's 1954 Net Assessment offered a cooler appraisal: such an attack would be "desperate" and true surprise "unlikely."[24] Still, in July 1953, a military attaché at the American embassy in Moscow had spotted, on an airfield south of the city, a swept-wing, heavy, jet-engined bomber closely resembling America's new long-range B-52, which was just starting to come off the assembly line. These bombers could carry a conventional World War II payload with the explosive power of roughly 5,000 pounds of TNT. In the atomic age, that payload exceeded a million pounds of TNT, not to mention radioactive fallout.[25]

In the summer of 1954, Eisenhower turned to James Killian, president of MIT, to form a Techno-logical Capabilities Panel to look into the question of surprise attack.[26] The biggest problem was lack of intelligence on the Soviet Union. "There was an extraordinary absence of knowledge," as former CIA director Richard Helms later put it to journalist Phil Taubman.[27] The air force and CIA had tried to drop in agents (all lost), float experimental balloons (swept away by contrary winds), and fly secret reconnaissance missions with bombers (usually shot down or driven off, though some did collect valuable intelligence).[28] Killian was not a scientist, but he was superb at dealing with geniuses. One of them was his Cambridge, Massachusetts, neighbor, Edwin H. Land, a shy yet charismatic Harvard dropout who had founded Polaroid and, during World War II, produced miracles for the US Air Force with all manner of goggles and gun sights. Killian put Land in charge of conceptualizing a spy plane. Using high-powered optics, "Din" Land got to work on developing a camera that could photograph human figures from 70,000 feet. From the aircraft designer Kelly Johnson, who ran Lockheed's top-secret "Skunk Works," Land received drawings and design specifications for an airplane that could fly that high—a skinny, spidery, floppy-winged glider with a jet engine.[29]

The most powerful air force general wasn't interested. General Curtis LeMay, the cigar-chomping, tough-talking commander of the Strategic Air Command, walked out of a meeting set up to sell the new reconnaissance craft. Lacking guns or even full landing gear, the plane was a "pile of bullshit," in

LeMay's gruff opinion.[30] Discouraged, the plane's backers ran into the CIA's Richard Bissell (by accident, they later recalled; they were on their way down K Street in Washington to go duck-pin bowling). They told Bissell about their new invention.

Bissell was one of Allen Dulles's special assistants, his "boys" recruited from the upper crust, the sort of fellows who could slip seamlessly from their Yale secret societies to the real world of secrets. Like Tracy Barnes, his schoolmate at Groton and Yale, and fellow Dulles protégé, Bissell was highly confident, but in a different way. Handsome and fit, Barnes was a natural athlete, a scratch golfer and star hockey player, socially secure, always at the center of the popular crowd. Bissell had been awkward and ungainly, something of an outcast at Groton and redeemed at Yale only by his penetrating intelligence. Intellectually, however, Bissell was utterly sure of himself. He was, like Barnes, a lover of risk, as if the rules of gravity did not apply to these wellborn public servants. At college, the poorly coordinated, gangly Bissell loved to scale the steep roofs of his Collegiate Gothic dormitory at night. (When he fell, almost fatally, climbing a cliff outside New Haven, he recovered and climbed it again.) Bissell was an amateur yachtsman who enjoyed navigating without electronic instruments in the thick fog off the New England coast; Barnes was a weekend boater who didn't mind racing right into the mist.[31] Bissell, who had been a brainy economist recruited by Killian to teach at MIT in 1942, was very interested in the new spy plane.

His boss, Allen Dulles was not, at least not at first. The Great White Case Officer believed in human spying and covert operations like in Guatemala and Iran, and was a notorious technophobe; he could barely operate his phone.[32] Eisenhower, however, immediately saw the possibilities in an aircraft that could fly above Soviet air defenses and photograph planes and rockets on the ground. Ike, who was comfortable talking with scientists, took an instant shine to Din Land when the two men met in the autumn of 1954. (He would later exclaim to Land, "Oh I am so grateful to you fellows who are out of town! You can't think in Washington.")

Sometime in late October 1954, after he had read the Doolittle report calling for a higher-tech approach to spying, Eisenhower summoned Killian and Land to the Oval Office. No official record of the meeting was made; Ike did not want the national security policy machinery to kick in should word get out. The president told Killian and Land that he would approve the new spy plane, but as Killian later recalled, "he stipulated that it should be handled in an unconventional way so that it would not become entangled in the bureaucracy of the Defense

Department or troubled by rivalries among the services."[33]

"Unconventional" meant the CIA. The plane would be paid for by the Agency's special "reserve fund" for black operations. Written records were to be kept to an absolute minimum. Informed of the president's desires—and seeing a new realm of influence—Allen Dulles quickly dropped his earlier opposition and smartly saluted. At a meeting at the White House on November 22, Dulles was given formal authorization to build the spy plane that would be called the U-2 (literally, "utility aircraft number two," as U-1 had already been claimed). The code name of the project was Aquatone. The meeting took fifteen minutes. The president was in hurry to leave for a Thanksgiving weekend golf game in Augusta.[34]

Dulles put Bissell, his brightest boy, in charge. To develop the U-2, Bissell set up shop in an unmarked office across the street from the Metropolitan Club in downtown Washington. He moved with astonishing speed and efficiency, building the U-2 in less than eighteen months and $3 million under its $22 million budget. He accomplished this by "throwing the procurement rule book out the window," said Bob King, his assistant. "He ignored the lowest bid stuff. It took too long and you got a bad product."[35] Everything was kept secret from the Russians and even from the air force higher-ups. In his memoirs, Bissell proudly quoted his deputy, General Leo Geary, detached from the air force for secret CIA work: "The U-2 was built and flying before the commander of the Air Force research and development command ever even heard of it. If you wanted to see one ticked-off air force major general, you should have seen this guy."[36]

John Foster Dulles was kept in the loop; Allen Dulles did not keep secrets from his brother. Foster Dulles had been in the Oval Office that day before Thanksgiving 1954 when Eisenhower had formally signed off on building the spy plane. The secretary of state guessed that the U-2 might cause difficulties with Moscow, but, he predicted, "we could live through them."[37] According to an oral history Dulles later gave to his alma mater, Princeton University, Eisenhower sounded a more cautionary note at the meeting. "Well boys, I believe the country needs this information, and I'm going to approve it," he said. "But I'll tell you one thing. Some day one of these machines is going to be caught, and we're going to have a storm."[38]

10

"Don't Worry, I'll Confuse Them"

RIGHT AFTER SIGNING off on the U-2, Eisenhower boarded the *Columbine* to head to Augusta for Thanksgiving weekend. He had an unwelcome houseguest: Field Marshal, now Viscount, Bernard Law Montgomery, the vain and chilly British commander who had driven Ike to distraction on the way to defeating Germany. That evening in Georgia, the old generals discussed Robert E. Lee's decision to allow General George Pickett to make his disastrous charge on the third day at Gettysburg. "Do it if you can," Lee had said. Eisenhower was puzzled that the revered Lee had been so seemingly passive and tentative with a subordinate bent on attack.[1] In September 1944, however, Eisenhower had himself erred by signing off on Montgomery's plan to capture a bridgehead over the Rhine with an elaborate airborne thrust; the operation, called Market Garden, had been a fiasco. It was the sort of mistake Eisenhower would not make again.

Before leaving Washington, the president had spent a trying half hour with the Senate majority leader, William Knowland of California. Knowland was a very disappointing successor to Senator Robert Taft, who had died of cancer in the summer of 1953. For all his outward geniality and his willingness to overlook the personality quirks of outsize men like Patton, Ike could be (and often was) privately brutal in his judgment of men he disdained. He was repeatedly dumbfounded by Knowland. "In his case," Ike wrote in his diary, "there seems to be no final answer to the question, 'How stupid can you get?'"[2] Knowland was known as "the Senator from Formosa" because of his fealty to the so-called China Lobby, which provided favors to senators who backed the regime of Generalissimo Chiang Kai-shek, who had been driven from mainland China to the island of Formosa (now Taiwan). At a dinner at the Nationalist Chinese embassy in Washington, Knowland had stood and, with a shout, joined in the toast "Back to the Mainland!"[3] On November 23, after the Red Chinese sentenced some American fliers captured during the Korean War to prison terms for espionage, Knowland wanted to impose a naval blockade along the Chinese coast. "Knowland has no foreign policy," Eisenhower wrote in his diary, "except to develop high blood pressure whenever he mentions the words, 'Red China.' "[4]

The president was careful to tape-record his conversations with Knowland, whom he did not trust. Thinking, perhaps, of his recent engagement with the CIA, Eisenhower reassured Knowland that "there is a very great aggressiveness on our side that you have not known about, and I guess that is the theory of why put burdens on people that they don't need to know about." Eisenhower said that he himself "knew so many things that I am almost afraid to speak to my wife." But as for blockading Red China, "that is a step towards war; if you do that, then the next question is, are you ready to attack? Well, I am not ready to attack."[5]

Eisenhower was hardly above racial stereotyping, and he once said to the National Security Council, with some exasperation, that "we are always wrong when we think Orientals think logically as we do."[6] He was referring specifically to the Nationalist leader Chiang Kai-shek. Championed by the Republican right and the Time-Life publications of Henry Luce, Chiang had fled into exile in 1949 with crates of priceless Chinese art and his elegant, scheming, Wellesley-educated wife, Madame Chiang (who, like Mamie Eisenhower, stayed in bed until at least 11 a.m. and chastised her husband for eating too quickly).[7] Though routed by the Reds and not

The Generalissimo and Madame Chiang (© Bettman/ Corbis)

popular in his native land, Chiang entertained the illusion that he would one day return as the leader of all China. He had stationed 70,000 soldiers on two small islands called Quemoy and Matsu, one hundred miles west of Formosa and just a few miles from the Chinese coast. Quemoy meant "Golden Gate," and Chiang hoped to use the island as the jumping-off point for his invasion of the mainland, though it was more likely to be the target of a Red Chinese attack in preparation for their invasion of Formosa. Holding Quemoy and Matsu made no sense—unless Chiang hoped that by inviting a war, the United States would have to come to the rescue. That may not have been entirely logical, yet it showed the sort of cunning Dwight Eisenhower could understand.

Politics dictated that Ike support Formosa and at least give lip service to Chiang reconquering the mainland. President Truman had interposed the US Navy's Seventh Fleet in the Formosa Strait to keep peace between the "ChiComs" and the "ChiNats," as the followers of Chairman Mao and Generalissimo Chiang were known in the American press. Upon assuming the presidency, Eisenhower, by congressional resolution, officially "unleashed" Chiang to invade the mainland, though privately he made sure Chiang would not attempt something so foolish.

Eisenhower was committed to defending Formosa, but when it came to whether the United States would fight if China invaded Quemoy and Matsu, Eisenhower remained deliberately vague. He got a congressional resolution passed giving him the power to go to war to defend Formosa and "closely related localities," which might be interpreted to include Quemoy and Matsu—or not. Eisenhower evaded attempts to pin him down on what, exactly, he would do if the Red Chinese made a grab for the two small islands.[8]

In September 1954, the Red Chinese had begun shelling Quemoy and Matsu. Admiral Radford, still chairman of the Joint Chiefs and an ardent Asia Firster, saw the chance for the long-awaited showdown with China. In the National Security Council, he argued that the United States should defend the islands from invasion by attacking Chinese airfields and other targets with nuclear weapons.[9] Secretary of State Dulles talked about throwing a defensive perimeter around Quemoy and Matsu, until President Eisenhower quietly restrained him. Eisenhower ordered the Seventh Fleet to "get into position for reconnaissance"—but to "not be aggressive." Ann Whitman, taking notes as her boss passed instructions, wrote, "President: 'We are not at war now'—in a relieved tone."[10] The shelling had stopped and the crisis died down for a time.

At the end of the year, the Formosa Strait heated up again. ChiNats and ChiComs engaged in aerial dogfights, small naval engagements, and guerrilla raids. On New Year's Day 1955, Chiang predicted "war at any time," while the Red Chinese foreign minister, Chou En-lai, declared that war was "imminent."[11] President Eisenhower set out, in his usual hidden-hand, roundabout way, to stop it.

At a press conference on January 12, Eisenhower

delivered a lecture straight out of the pages of Clause-witz on the dangers of small wars turning into big wars: "Now, nothing can be precluded in a military thing. Remember this: when you resort to force as the arbiter of human difficulty, you don't know where you are going; but, generally speaking, if you get deeper and deeper, there is just no limit except what is imposed by limitations of force itself."[12] As ever, Eisenhower was careful to engage Congress — to demonstrate to the Republican right, in his elusive, evenhanded way, that he was not "an appeaser," while reassuring the other lawmakers that he was not about to start World War III over some remote rocks off the Chinese coast.

"This is the time for us to move patiently and slowly," he told congressional leaders at the White House on February 16. "We must not be too quick to say what we want to do." He told them he was sending Walter Robertson, assistant secretary of state for Asian affairs and a Chiang partisan, to Formosa to "sort of hold Chiang Kai-shek's hand." In his diary, press secretary Jim Hagerty wrote, "Then the President smiled wryly and said almost to himself, 'But those damn little offshore islands. Sometimes I wish they'd sink.' "[13]

Eisenhower needed time. He needed to know if Chiang's island outposts could hold out against a Red attack without American intervention. He could have gone through the regular channels and asked the Joint Chiefs, but he didn't trust Radford and his cohort to give him a straight answer. So he quietly sent his trusted staff secretary, Andy Goodpaster, to see the Pacific Fleet commander, Admiral Felix Stump, in Hawaii. Goodpaster reported back that the islands would survive anything short of an all-out amphibious invasion, and the Red Chinese were not on the verge of making one.[14]

Foster Dulles, as usual, was cast in the role of hawk. It suited his natural predilections, and his fierceness helped buttress Ike's right flank. In late January, he had told the Senate Foreign Relations Committee, "We have got to be prepared to take the risk of war with China, if we are going to stay in the Far East. If we are not going to take that risk, all right, let's make that decision and we get out and we make our defenses in California."[15] In mid-February, Dulles headed out to the Far East himself to take a look. Meeting with the powers-that-be on Formosa, he was given a gloomy spin.

The secretary of state returned full of foreboding. On March 10, he reported to Eisenhower and his assembled National Security Council, "The situation out there in the Formosa Strait is far more serious than I thought." The Red Chinese, he said, were determined to capture Formosa. The only way to make Beijing back down was by threatening to use nuclear weapons. In his gravest churchman's tones, he concluded that "before this problem is solved, I believe that there is at least an even chance that the United States will have to go to war."[16] Indeed, said Dulles, the United States might have to "shoot off a gun" to demonstrate American resolve by "deeds rather than words." This was Admiral Radford's cue to remind the NSC that the gun would have to be nuclear, that the only way to destroy Red Chinese gun emplacements and air-fields was by a nuclear strike. Conventional bombs dropped by carrier-based planes would crater the air-fields but not take them out of operation for long. If the islands fell before America acted, Radford warned, the administration—those officials in the room, who were already feeling anxious—would be the subject of a "Pearl Harbor–style" inquiry.[17]

Dulles had raised the specter of nuclear weapons in a speech to a radio and TV audience on March 8. He had wanted to report to the nation on his Far East tour and rebut Beijing's propaganda that the United States was a "paper tiger." He proclaimed that US naval and air forces were "equipped with new and powerful weapons of precision, which can utterly destroy military targets without endangering civilian centers." Eisenhower had signed off on this speech, though warning Dulles to be circumspect on the mention of nuclear weapons. At a press conference on March 16, Ike seemed almost blithe on the subject. "Would the United States," a reporter asked, "use tactical nuclear weapons in a general war in Asia?" Ike responded, "I see no reason why they shouldn't be used just exactly as you would use a bullet or anything else."[18]

This was a startling statement at the time and remains so. It is one of the main pieces of evidence that scholars still use to show that Eisenhower wanted to break the taboo against using so-called special weapons.[19] In his memoirs, Eisenhower merely stated that he wished to show the Chinese "the strength of our determination."[20] Certainly, Eisenhower wanted to be credible in his threats to use nuclear weapons. But as always with Ike, the context is important. At the March 16 press conference, the president added an important qualification: "I believe the great question about these things comes when you begin to get into those areas where you cannot make sure you are operating merely against military targets."[21]

Ike knew full well that the Chinese airfields were located in populated areas that would be devastated by the radioactive fallout of a nuclear weapon. So-called tactical nuclear weapons were not that small: at 15 kilotons (15,000 tons of TNT) they were only somewhat less devastating than the 20-kiloton atomic bomb used to destroy Nagasaki. Bothered by Dulles's claims about new "precision" weapons, a

State Department official, Gerard Smith, went to Dulles to tell him that even the smaller "tactical" nuclear weapons under development produced lethal fallout, and that air force strategy still contemplated taking out airfields with larger nuclear bombs of at least a megaton (one million tons of TNT). The director of policy planning at State, Robert Bowie, was also alarmed by Dulles's remarks, and got figures from the CIA and Atomic Energy Commission to show that if the United States struck the Communist airfields and gun batteries across the channel from Quemoy with atomic bombs, the civilian death toll in the populous area would exceed ten million. Dulles, a military neophyte, seemed surprised and chastened by this information, but it was not news to Eisenhower, who had been intimately involved in bomb development as Army Chief of Staff and NATO Supreme Allied Commander Europe.[22]

Nevertheless, war fever rose. Radford, who could barely constrain his eagerness, told reporters that "there is a distinct possibility that war could break out any time." Senator Knowland chimed in, "No appeasement!" And Dulles, his nuclear education notwithstanding, continued to make bellicose noises; in a speech on March 20, he declared that the Chinese were "an acute and imminent threat...dizzy with success," more dangerous than the Russians and as fanatical as Hitler.[23]

Reporters were beginning to write war-scare stories, and the public grew uneasy. The time had come for Eisenhower to cool things off, in his own way. On March 23, Eisenhower was scheduled for one of his regular weekly press conferences. Just as he was crossing the blocked-off street between the West Wing and the Old Executive Office Building, press secretary Jim Hagerty told him that he had just received a "frantic" plea from the State Department. The situation was exceedingly delicate in the Formosa Strait, and perhaps it would be best if the president said as little as possible. A grin spread across Eisenhower's face. "Don't worry, Jim, if that question comes up, I'll just confuse them."

Sure enough, Joseph C. Harsch of the *Christian Science Monitor* asked about using nuclear weapons in the Formosa Strait. Eisenhower's answer rambled on in memorable fashion. His first effort was incomprehensible, and Harsch had to interrupt. Asking for a clarification, the newsman apologized, "Sir, I am a little stupid about this thing." "Well, I'm glad you didn't say *I* was," Eisenhower began, his face splitting in a broad, indulgent smile.[24] For a moment he looked like a grandfather gently chiding a wayward teenager.

Eisenhower's personality was hard to capture in a painting or still photograph because he did not seem very impressive in repose. In person or on TV, his rubbery face became mobile and expansive. He had a sweet, genial, almost loopy grin. His power did not come from a strong jaw but from dark blue eyes that could flash with anger or twinkle with humor. With Harsch the president was perfectly open-faced and good-humored as he spoke in riddles:

> The only thing I know about war was two things: the most changeable factor in war is human nature in its day-by-day manifestation; but the only unchanging factor about war is human nature. And the next thing is that every war is going to astonish you in the way it occurred and the way it is carried out. So that for a man to predict, particularly if he had the responsibility for making the decision, to predict what he is going to use, how he is going to do it, would I think exhibit his ignorance of war; that is what I believe. So I think you just have to wait, and that is the kind of prayerful decision that may some day face a President.[25]

Eisenhower's answer has been called a classic of obfuscation, and it certainly baffled the press that day. According to one possibly apocryphal account, Eisenhower himself joked that he must have given fits to Russian and Chinese translators trying to explain to their bosses what he meant.[26] Yet his answer was precise in a more tactical sense, and was aimed at the American people. Eisenhower was mocked by reporters for his wobbly syntax ("the only thing I know about war was two things..."), but the American people saw a thoughtful man working through difficult problems. What he was really saying, in his own way, was: "I know war. Trust me." The public, by and large, did. Eisenhower's savvy press secretary Hagerty had reinforced Ike's direct, personal connection to the people by arranging to have press conferences recorded and televised.[27] The president's approval ratings stayed consistently over 60 percent in this period, a benchmark that more recent presidents would envy.

As Supreme Allied Commander, Ike had been deft at public relations. Reporters around his headquarters had made fun of Ike's linguistic garbling and temper, but they largely behaved as if they were on his staff. Other, stiffer military men lacked his PR touch. On Friday night, March 26, Admiral Robert "Mick" Carney, chief of naval operations and a disciple of Admiral Radford, gave a private dinner for some reporters at the Statler Hotel in Washington. Carney told them that the president was contemplating all-out war against Red China and said he expected hostilities to break out by April 15. The dinner was supposed to be off the record, but the news instantly leaked. Newspaper articles and radio and TV broadcasts predicted war in the Far East by April 15, or May 15 at the latest. "As a result of the Carney dinner," Jim Hagerty wrote in his diary, "the stories have gone somewhat hog wild over the weekend and threats of use of atomic bombs, invasion of the mainland, and everything else were written and spoken."

On Monday morning, March 28, Hagerty explained all this to the president in the Oval Office. Eisenhower took off his glasses "and characteristically chewed on the end of the earpiece," Hagerty wrote. "Are you sure this came from Carney?" he asked. Hagerty said he had picked up the story from some newsman friends. Eisenhower "exploded, got up from his desk, and walked around the room." Speaking rapidly, Eisenhower began, "By God, this has got to stop..." The president said he would be seeing Radford in an hour; in the meantime, Hagerty was to put the word out that "there is always danger in the Far East" but "we are trying to keep the peace. We are not looking for war." Ike calmed down, and recalled the information that he had received from Andy Goodpaster's backdoor mission to see Admiral Stump: there was no buildup of Chinese forces readying to attack the offshore islands. Eisenhower slyly told Hagerty, "I would also tell them you are not normally a betting man, but that if any of them wanted to bet a thousand dollars that we would be in war on any of the dates they wrote about, you would be happy to let them." Hagerty began laughing and said, "If you let me say a hundred dollars, I'll do it." Ike, smiling now, agreed.[28]

Gossip columnist Drew Pearson later reported in his widely read "Washington Merry-Go-Round" that Admiral Carney got "the bawling out of his life" from Eisenhower.[29] But that was not Eisenhower's style. He later told *New York Times* columnist Arthur Krock that Carney had "apologized," but "I told him to forget it, that I allowed all my subordinates to make one mistake a year. I make all the rest."[30] Carney arrived at the Oval Office "shaking like a leaf," recalled Ike's appointments secretary, Bernard Shanley, who told Carney to relax. "Mick, you'll come out of his office floating, so stop being nervous and go in and face the music." When Carney emerged, "he looked as though he had appeared before the Lord Almighty, he had such a glow on his face," recalled Shanley. That was "typical of the way [Eisenhower] handled people. He could chastise you very thoroughly yet you came away, as Admiral Carney did, feeling almost great that you had committed sin."[31] Nonetheless, when Carney's two-year term as chief of naval operations ended that month, Eisenhower did not renew it.

Privately, Eisenhower was not quite as confident

and offhand as he appeared with Hagerty and Carney. Writing in his diary on March 26, he noted, "Lately there has been a very definite feeling among the members of the Cabinet, often openly expressed, that within a month we will actually be fighting in the Formosa straits." This, Eisenhower allowed, was "entirely possible." The Red Chinese, he wrote in his diary, "appear to be completely reckless, arrogant, possibly over-confident, and completely indifferent as to human loss." But he had been thinking back to the days right after Pearl Harbor, when "every prophet was one of gloom." Eisenhower reflected, "I have so often been through these periods of stress that I have become accustomed to the fact that most of the calamities we expect really never occur."[32]

Eisenhower needed to find a way to calm down Chiang Kai-shek. He proposed that the Generalissimo treat Quemoy and Matsu not as "garrisons" but as "outposts"—and begin withdrawing his soldiers from them. To convey the message, Ike sent two pro-Chiang hard-liners, Admiral Radford and the State Department's Walter Robertson. These two were perhaps not the best messengers; in any case, Chiang remained defiant.[33]

In mid-April, Eisenhower got help from an unexpected quarter. In Bandung, Indonesia, twenty-nine former colonial nations of Asia and Africa held a diplomatic conference. Foreign Minister Chou En-lai of China was the surprise star, eclipsing, or at least competing with, the haughty Jawaharlal Nehru of India. Chou offered a forceful vision of "Asia for Asians," a slogan discredited by the Japanese in World War II but enjoying a second life in the postimperial age. Passions against nuclear war ran high, not just because of Nagasaki and Hiroshima but also because of the deadly fallout from the American H-bomb tests in the Pacific atolls. Although Chou wanted to publicly and ferociously blame the Americans, his nation came under pressure not to provoke a nuclear attack. Beijing's envoy pulled back, responding flatly by saying that China did not want war with the United States and calling for talks to relieve the tension. The showdown in the Formosa Strait was over.[34]

In hindsight, both sides probably miscalculated during the crisis. The Red Chinese had no intention of invading Quemoy and Matsu but wanted to frighten the Americans into abandoning Formosa. The gambit backfired: the outcome was a strengthened security alliance for Chiang Kai-shek as the Americans overreacted to the Chinese threat. Yet war was avoided, thanks in part to Eisenhower's deft maneuvering.[35]

"President Eisenhower, as a poker player, never made a public comment on what he would do if the Chinese communists attempted to take the little islands," noted his son John.[36] Eisenhower was able to bluff without showing his hand. Of course, he had been lucky; the obdurate Chiang might have dragged out the crisis had the Red Chinese not backed down. But they did. Such were the odds of the gambler. Eisenhower could not be sure about the motivations and intentions of his friends and enemies in the Far East, hidden as they were behind iron or bamboo curtains, beyond "Western logic," as he might have put it, and certainly beyond the prying of the CIA. Eisenhower did, however, know his subordinates in Washington. He had an instinctively clever feel for using his hawks to play at brinksmanship while he mumbled and dawdled and kept a tight rein. Eisenhower was playing several hands at once, and he needed to keep the game going while he figured out a strategy to trump his main enemy, the Soviet Union.

11

Meeting
Mr. Khrushchev

IN THE WINTER and spring of 1955, a maze of brick and concrete structures rose out of the Nevada desert. Reporters called the place Doomstown. On May 15, a nuclear bomb leveled the skeletal metropolis. Conducting a series of tests known as Project Teacup, the Atomic Energy Commission attempted to gauge the impact of a 40-kiloton bomb (about twice the TNT of the Nagasaki A-bomb) on a mock city. The blast was heard in Las Vegas, seventy-five miles away; when inspectors examined the site, they saw that only parts of some precast concrete structures were left standing. The "inhabitants" were pronounced dead, and traces of radioactivity were detected in the rainfall as far away as New York—this from a bomb that had less than 1 percent of the force of an H-bomb.[1]

Project Teacup's Doomstown test, widely reported

in the press, interrupted a happier reverie. Indeed, in so many ways (to white America at least), the American Dream seemed to be coming true in 1955; you could even watch it on TV. Television sets were flying off the shelves; the average American family was viewing four to five hours a night. Walt Disney had introduced Davy Crockett, "King of the Wild Frontier," on his Sunday-night television show in December 1954, and by the following spring, wrote historian William Manchester, "every playground and supermarket seemed to be populated by five-year-olds wearing coonskin caps."[2] America was growing prosperous in midcentury. Average income rose by an astonishing 50 percent between the late 1940s and mid-'50s. The middle class was burgeoning. As Manchester observed in his chronicle of the age, *The Glory and the Dream,* " 'big spender' became a term of approbation." People were buying phones, stereo FM sets, electric floor waxers and pencil sharpeners and electric blankets. They were driving to the new shopping malls in shiny "two-tone" new cars. Detroit sold two million more automobiles in 1955 than in 1954; the percentage of Americans owning cars jumped from 60 to 70 percent. At the White House, Mamie Eisenhower hosted five thousand wives of the National Association of Automobile Dealers. She told her husband she had never seen "so many furs and diamonds."[3]

America's love affair with the automobile inspired Eisenhower to launch what would become his principal domestic legacy: a massive program to build interstate highways. But his justification to Congress was a sign of the times: he wanted more multilane highways to evacuate American cities in case of nuclear war.[4]

This was the awakening from Lucy and Uncle Walt and tail fins: with the good times came a wavering sense of dread. Writing in the November 1954 issue of the *Bulletin of Atomic Scientists,* physicist Ralph Lapp warned that fifty of the new H-bombs could envelop the entire northeastern United States "in a serious to lethal radioactive fog." Fallout, wrote Lapp, "cannot be felt and possesses all the terror of the unknown. It is something which evokes revulsion and helplessness—like a bubonic plague." Lapp's warnings received widespread coverage in the press, and on February 15, 1955, the AEC issued a report on fallout, hoping to calm popular fears with soothingly dry bureaucratic prose. The report had the opposite effect: newspaper accounts drew attention to the finding that an H-bomb would produce a cigar-shaped cloud that would kill half the people living up to 160 miles downwind. In other words, a one-megaton H-bomb (roughly seventy-five Hiroshimas) dropped on Manhattan on a rainy day, with the breeze from the northeast, would also take out New Jersey—and that was just *local* fallout. *Global* fallout from radioactivity entering the jet stream could put a new poison called strontium 90 in mother's milk thousands of miles from the blast. In mid-March, with the chief of naval operations carelessly predicting nuclear war over the Formosa Strait, Southern California supermarkets began selling Survival Food Kits costing $5.40 to sustain a family of four for three days. Never mind that the AEC insisted that, in small doses, fallout was relatively harmless.

When the Teacup tests started up in February, Eisenhower wanted to view a nuclear blast. Lewis Strauss, the AEC chairman who was a booster of the project, encouraged him, but Jim Hagerty wisely persuaded the president to stay away.[5] Eisenhower tried to play down the scare stories that were spooking the public. "You have to look facts in the face, but you have to have the stamina to do it without being hysterical," he said at a press conference in late February.

In private, Eisenhower was not as sanguine as his public remarks suggest. At a national security meeting, he asked Dr. Willard Libby of the AEC if there was any theoretical limit on the size of an H-bomb. No, was the answer. How many megatons would it take to make the whole earth radioactive? About 10,000, Libby replied. Could a Soviet ship carry a thousand-megaton bomb to America's shores? Yes. Such a bomb might create a 200-foot-high tidal wave.

The notetaker did not record the look on the middle-aged male faces around the table, but one can imagine the expressions when the president asked how much atomic force it would take to knock the earth off its axis. The notetaker's dry recitation does capture the tension between Eisenhower's existential dread and his stoicism: "The President thought that we would soon get so far along in these scientific things that we get to the point where no one can win. There would be no use in talking much more. All life would lose its meaning, but, said the president, maybe we're not that badly off yet, so let's go on."[6]

During the standoff with Red China over the offshore islands, Eisenhower did not worry that Moscow's Politburo would join a war started by their Marxist comrades in Beijing. Indeed, Ike continued to doubt that the Russians wanted war. But it was hard to know for sure. Since Stalin's death, the Kremlin leadership had remained opaque. The Soviets were, however, testing ever-larger bombs.

On February 8, Hagerty went to see the president about the word, just breaking on news wires, of a leadership change in Moscow. Georgy Malenkov was out as premier, Nicolay Bulganin was in. He would rule as part of a troika with Marshal Georgy Zhukov, the Red Army general who had been Ike's ally in World War II, and the Communist Party secretary, Nikita Khrushchev, a relative unknown. Hagerty naturally wanted to know: did the leadership shuffle mean the Russians were moving toward war? According to his diary, the president "said he did not think so; that as a matter of fact, if the Army had more influence in Russia, it would probably be a conservative influence." Eisenhower went on:

> You know, if you're in the military and you know about these terrible destructive weapons, it tends to make you more pacifistic than you normally have been. In most countries the influence of the military is more conservative and so while I do not know for sure, I would not be surprised if the army influence would be just that within the Soviet Union. They're not ready for war and they know it. They also know that if they go to war, they're going to end up losing everything they have. That also tends to make people conservative.[7]

Eisenhower was reasonably confident about the intentions of General Zhukov, with whom in 1945 he had shared toasts for peace as well as horror at the destruction wrought by their armies in World War II. But he did not know Bulganin, and he was completely in the dark about Khrushchev.

For Eisenhower, it was important to know your

enemies as well as your friends, and to be alert to those occasions when the two overlap. Eisenhower wanted to personally take the measure of Moscow's new leaders, to see if they really did govern as a troika or whether one person was actually in charge. Though cautious, even passive at times, Eisenhower had an instinctive sense of when to take action. His earlier attempts at slowing the arms race, his "Chance for Peace" and "Atoms for Peace" speeches, had temporarily eased tensions, but Cold War exigencies kept the arsenals growing. He needed to find a way to reduce misunderstandings between East and West.

The heads of government of the great powers had not met for a decade, since the waning days of World War II. Secretary of State Dulles, supported by Eisenhower, strongly opposed bringing them together again. Dulles was skeptical of "summits" (the word was coined by Winston Churchill, who liked them) because he was afraid that Western statesmen, in a gush of generosity and good feeling, would squander their advantages over the threatening but still weaker East. Though he was not above horse-trading when he had to, Dulles tended to prefer moral pronouncements to negotiation. In June 1954, at a diplomatic conference in Geneva to divide up Vietnam after the fall of Dien Bien Phu, Dulles had refused to shake hands with Chinese foreign minister Chou En-lai or even, at first, to sit at the same table. A British diplomat later observed the American secretary of state "sitting at the conference table, not knowing where to look, his mouth drawn down at the corners, and his eyes on the ceiling, sucking on his teeth."[8]

Ever sensitive to the Republican right, Dulles remembered the charge that FDR had given away Eastern Europe to Stalin at Yalta in 1945. The secretary of state was wary of Eisenhower's supposed tendency to smile and placate his foes. Dulles played the role of stern nanny with Ike, shushing the president whenever he showed any sign—even rhetorical—of wishing to compromise with the devil. In his 1954 State of the Union address, Eisenhower wanted to say that it was "heartening" to see the Soviets express a willingness to negotiate. "No," Dulles protested in a phone call with the president, and the idea was dropped.[9] Most of all, Dulles was worried about losing control, about ceding his primacy among Ike's foreign policy advisers, and he feared that Eisenhower, in his quest for peace, might prefer more softhearted (and softheaded) counsel. "Dulles was not prepared to have anyone come between him and the president—anybody," recalled Robert Bowie, policy and planning chief at the State Department.[10]

Dulles was, for example, frosty with Harold

Stassen, the new assistant to the president for arms control. Tired of constant infighting between the Defense and State Departments and the AEC over arms-control proposals, Eisenhower had wanted someone to take charge, to goose the proposal-writing process along, and Stassen was single-minded and doggedly ambitious. When Stassen was dubbed "Secretary for Peace" by the press, Dulles instantly saw a usurper.[11] The secretary of state was even more suspicious of Nelson Rockefeller, brought in by Ike to come up with some initiatives for the Four Power Summit Conference—between the United States, the USSR, Britain, and France—scheduled over Dulles's objections for Geneva in July.* In June, Rockefeller holed up with a large team of technicians and idea men at the marine base at Quantico, Virginia. "He seems to be building up a big staff," Dulles grumbled to Sherman Adams. "He's got them down at Quantico, and nobody knows what they're doing."[13] The president had told his chief of staff that the only way to get lasting peace was through disarmament, and he needed a summit meeting breakthrough to overcome inertia

---

*Dulles would have preferred a meeting of foreign ministers, not the heads of government. At dinner at the home of Attorney General Herbert Brownell in June, he declared, tongue in cheek, "You know, fellows, God did not come to earth. He sent his Son."[12]

and resistance.[14] Adams, who regarded Dulles as a cold fish, ignored the complaint.

Meetings were insufficient without proposals and promises. Eisenhower wanted a bold stroke. He chose "Open Skies"—in essence, a license to conduct aerial espionage on an enemy. It's not clear who originated the idea; Stassen and Rockefeller claimed credit, though Eisenhower apparently thought of it before his advisers did. In any case, it was the sort of gambit that appealed to Ike because it had no real downside.[15] At the Geneva summit, the United States would propose that America and Russia allow each other's planes to fly freely over their countries, photographing each other's airfields and arsenals. The two nations (and any others that signed the treaty) would provide each other with blueprints locating and describing their military installations. As John Newhouse has observed, "Open Skies" had a "reassuring heads-I-win, tails-you-lose quality."[16] If the Russians said yes, the bugaboo of all arms control—verification—would be instantly solved. If the Russians said no, America still had the moral high ground—and soon, as Eisenhower winkingly told the very small circle privileged to know such things, it would have the U-2 spy plane, now close to production. Eisenhower told his aides that he would give "Open Skies" a shot—"then, if they don't accept, we'll fly the U-2."[17]

Still, Dulles, ever fearful that the West would be "lulled" into complacency, resisted any steps toward disarmament. In the preparations for the summit, Rockefeller and Dulles quarreled openly before Ike, who in turn lost his temper at both. This was far from his only outburst, the president was in a volatile mood in late spring and early summer. Indeed, he seemed to be blowing up every fifteen or twenty minutes, according to Bernard Shanley. (He even "bawled out" Ann Whitman when she failed to deliver some medicine by the exact time he expected it.) The pressure on his staff was "almost unbearable," recalled Shanley. "I saw Ann in tears more times than I care to say." He compared the president to a lawyer preparing for a big trial who is "disgustingly grumpy and takes out all his nervousness and upset on his family and partners."[18] As Eisenhower had shown by becoming physically ill before his "Chance for Peace" speech in March 1953, nothing was as nerve-racking to him as making the case for peace in a world perpetually driven toward war.

Eisenhower took his family with him to Geneva. Mamie was afraid of flying (she often went by train to Augusta) and suffered from her usual array of real or imagined illnesses, but her health and spirits had improved in the White House. "Mamie feels pretty well—in fact I think she is in better shape than she has been in some years," Ike had written a West Point friend in the summer of 1954. "She has picked up considerable weight and for some peculiar reason this seems to make her stronger and less subject to extreme fatigue. As you will recall, she used to suffer very greatly from indigestion and heart flutter, which would make her extremely nervous and fearful, and the results were sometimes alarming."[19]

Mamie was persuaded to make the trip to Geneva partly because son John would come along. Now an army major, John had just finished Command and Staff School at Fort Leavenworth and had a month's leave. As the *Columbine* headed out into the night sky on July 14 for the eighteen-hour flight to Geneva, mother and son played a distracting game of Scrabble.[20]

At the lakeside banking and resort city Ike rode to his villa, loaned by a perfume magnate, in the 1942 Cadillac he had once used during World War II. He and John hit some golf balls in the huge formal garden, and Ike assigned his son to do a little spying: Eisenhower wanted to learn if Marshal Zhukov was the real power or, as he suspected, window dressing. Ike asked John, who had no formal role at the conference, to tag along with Zhukov whenever possible.

Ike's hunch about Zhukov was right. During cocktails at the villa, as the two Eisenhowers and Zhukov spoke alone, Zhukov said softly, "Things are not as they seem." He had been a "cocky little rooster" when John first met him in Germany after the war as John traveled with his father. Now Zhukov seemed quiet and subdued, even shaky.[21]

The formal meetings were held at the cavernous Palais des Nations, home of the ill-fated League of Nations, rendered futile by World War II. When Eisenhower's limo arrived, bikini-clad girls rushed up from Lake Geneva to cheer him. The proceedings within were less festive. Speeches droned on; the participants circled each other at evening cocktails. Spotting the new British prime minister Anthony Eden and Foster Dulles in guarded and desultory conversation, John Eisenhower approached the two men and offered to get them a drink. Eden, a dapper Etonian, brightened and said, "Oh, no, thank you!" Dulles did not look up. "Had one," he said. Dulles had decreed no smiling or handshaking with the Russians. This was hard for President Eisenhower, recalled Stewart Alsop, a prominent journalist covering the diplomatic functions: "His whole instinct was to smile and be friendly. And then he'd kind of draw back, remembering what Foster had said."[22]

Finally, on the day before the six-day conference was to end, Rockefeller, sitting with John Eisenhower in the staff chairs off to the side, whispered, "Now listen. Here it comes." During the hum of speeches, President Eisenhower had sat staring out the great picture windows at the meadows and mountains beyond, and occasionally up at the vaulted ceiling. Giant murals showed man's struggle against famine and slavery, but his eye was led to the final panel, depicting "the one unconquered scourge, war," as he put it in his memoirs, "where subhuman beasts drop babies down the muzzles of monstrous cannons, tilted at crazy angles." The mural was outrageous and cartoonish but nonetheless disturbing.

It was late afternoon on Wednesday, July 21. At his seat at the massive conference table, Ike took off his glasses, laid them down, and spoke out, barely glancing at his notecards. In his flat but earnest and hopeful voice he said, "I have been searching my heart and mind for something that I could say here that could convince everyone of the great sincerity of the United States in approaching this problem of disarmament."

The greatest danger, in this age of "new and terrible weapons," said the president, was "surprise attack." To make that impossible, Eisenhower proposed "immediate practical steps," with each side providing the other with blueprints and charts of military installations as well as the airfields used by their planes. Under a treaty guaranteeing "Open

Skies," planes would be free to conduct permanent reconnaissance. In the spectator seats, Rockefeller gave John Eisenhower a triumphant grin and slapped his knee.

Just as Eisenhower finished his presentation, there was an enormous crash of thunder, the loudest, Eisenhower recalled, that he had ever heard. The lights went out, plunging the great hall into darkness. In the hushed silence, Eisenhower joked, "Well, I expected to make a hit but not that much of one." There was relieved laughter.[23]

The prime ministers of France and England spoke approvingly, even enthusiastically; then it was Russia's turn. As senior man in the ruling troika, Bulganin, a tall, smiling figure with a white goatee, wearing a white summer suit (he bore a striking resemblance to Colonel Sanders of the American fried chicken chain), declared that the American proposal had real merit and that the Soviet Union would give it complete and sympathetic study at once.

Eisenhower was elated. The statesmen rose and headed out, as was their custom, for tea (or, for most, martinis). Eisenhower, not by accident, fell in with Nikita Khrushchev. The two men were barely acquainted. They had nodded at each other when Eisenhower had gone to Moscow in 1945 to stand atop Lenin's Tomb with Stalin.

Khrushchev spoke first. "I don't agree with the

chairman," Khrushchev said, referring to Bulganin and rejecting the Soviet premier's apparent embrace of the American proposal. Khrushchev, recalled Eisenhower in his memoirs, was "smiling—but there was no smile in his voice. I saw clearly then, for the first time, the identity of the real boss of the Soviet delegation."[24]

In his diary kept at Geneva, British foreign secretary Harold Macmillan wrote, "Khrushchev is a mystery. How can this fat, vulgar man with his pig eyes and ceaseless flow of talk, really be the head, the head—the aspirant Tsar—of all those millions of people of this vast country?" The French foreign minister described Khrushchev as "this little man with his fat paws."[25] Khrushchev's father was a peasant, and his grandfather had been a serf. Before the 1917 revolution, Khrushchev had labored in the coal pits. He found his calling helping Stalin execute the Great Purge in the 1930s. ("I don't know where these people were sent," Khrushchev later said. "I never asked.") As party political officer with the Red Army at the Battle of Stalingrad, he was an eyewitness to the ravages of all-out war. After the war, he survived the dreadful all-night drinking sessions in Stalin's dacha. "Why don't you look me in the eye today, comrade?" Stalin once asked him in a dead cold voice. Khrushchev performed a Ukrainian peasant

Khrushchev (Library of Congress, Washington, DC)

dance, squatting and kicking out his heels, and tried, with his broad joking and jolliness, to be under-estimated. The moment passed, and Khrushchev survived.[26]

As a rising party apparatchik, Khrushchev had shown little interest in foreign affairs, barely reading briefing memos. On a trip to China in 1954, he felt that he had been patronized by Chairman Mao, and when he returned he told comrades, "Conflict with China is inevitable."[27] The US ambassador to Russia, Chip Bohlen, cabled home his opinion that Khrushchev "wasn't especially bright."[28] Among his obsessions — shared with his mentor Stalin — was a paranoid view that the Soviet Union was within target range of American bombers operating from airfields in Norway, Germany, Italy, South Korea, and Japan.[29]

Insecurity was the defining characteristic of Khrushchev's persona. He arrived at the Geneva summit ready to feel slighted. At the airport, he noted the large, four-engine planes of the Western statesmen. The Russians had flown to Geneva on a smaller, two-engine craft. The comparison, wrote Khrushchev, was "embarrassing"; the Soviet plane, he told his son Sergei, seemed like a mere "insect" next to the mighty airliners of the West.[30] The Communist Party secretary was intensely worried about what to wear at the summit dinners and whether he would use the right eating utensils. Finally he grumbled, "They'll have to take us as we are. We won't play up to them. If they want to talk with workers, they better get used to us."

Khrushchev could be cunning, and he covered his anxieties with a blustery and often earthy brashness. He liked to show that he would not be patronized. At his midnight drinking sessions, Stalin had taunted his comrades that after he was gone, the imperialists would strangle his successors "like kittens" or "baby calves."[31] Eisenhower did not seem so formidable to Khrushchev. Indeed, the American president seemed more like a target for bullying. In

his memoirs, Khrushchev recalled that he sat next
to the American delegation at Geneva:

> I watched Dulles making notes with a pencil,
> tearing them out of a pad, folding them up,
> and sliding them under Eisenhower's hand.
> Eisenhower would pick up these sheets of paper,
> unfold them, and read them before making a
> decision on any matter that came up. He fol-
> lowed this routine conscientiously, like a duti-
> ful schoolboy taking his lead from his teacher.
> It was difficult for us to imagine how a chief
> of state could allow himself to lose face like
> that in front of delegates from other countries.
> It certainly appeared that Eisenhower was let-
> ting Dulles do his thinking for him.*[32]

The newspapers, influenced by the diplomats, treated
the Geneva summit as a step toward what would
later be called détente. The Russians spoke of "peaceful coexistence," and there was much chatter about
the "spirit of Geneva." Eisenhower felt let down.
Andrew Goodpaster later recounted that at "tea" after

---

*"This was a tremendous exaggeration," recalled Chip Bohlen,
who was sitting behind Eisenhower. "He had Foster Dulles next to
him. He'd turn and talk to him, the way any president would
[with his] secretary of state."[33]

his "Open Skies" speech, Khrushchev had wagged his finger at the American president and said over and over, "*Nyet, nyet, nyet.*" The Russian translator had cleaned up his next remark, but the Soviet leader's crudeness came through—"You're simply trying to look into our bedrooms" was the polite version.[34] Ignoring the bluster, Eisenhower had tried to persuade Khrushchev that, with everything out in the open for all to see, it would be impossible for the NATO countries to sneak-attack Russia. Khrushchev responded, "Who are you trying to fool?" The Kremlin boss fulminated, "In our eyes this is a very transparent espionage device. You could hardly expect us to take this seriously."[35]

On the final afternoon of the summit, Ann Whitman found the president sitting at his temporary desk in one of the opulent offices at the Palais des Nations. He was disappointed with the results, he confessed. Maybe he could try an end run on Khrushchev by reaching out to Bulganin. Ike had no illusions about the real boss in Moscow—he had watched Khrushchev literally shove Bulganin aside as the Kremlin leaders climbed into their limousines.[36] Bulganin was at least still nominally the premier. With a translator in tow, Ike set off down the corridor to find Bulganin's office. "He just didn't want the summit to end in discouragement," Whitman later recalled to journalist Robert Donovan. "I think he

Welcome home from Geneva (Dwight D. Eisenhower Presidential Library, Abilene, Kansas)

simply intended to ask Bulganin to join us for a drink." But he was too late; the Russians had headed back to Moscow.[37]

On July 25, the *Columbine* landed at Andrews Air Force base outside Washington just ahead of a summer squall. Vice President Richard Nixon had organized a welcoming rally, but he had given an odd instruction: no umbrellas. Nixon, ever alert for symbols of appeasement that might inflame the Right, worried that umbrellas might remind people of British prime minister Neville Chamberlain, who, returning to London after meeting Hitler at the Munich conference in 1938, announced prematurely that "Peace is at hand." Chamberlain, as seen on all the newsreels, had been carrying a tightly wrapped umbrella. Now, as Nixon and his umbrellaless welcome-home committee stood on the tarmac, the heavens opened. "For whatever reason, the president did not carry an umbrella," recalled Whitman, "and he got soaked along with everyone else."[38]

12

The Devil's Grip

O N JULY 15, 1955, three days before the opening of the Geneva summit, the Red air force conducted its annual Aviation Day at Tushino airfield, outside Moscow. The military attaché to the US embassy, Colonel Charles Taylor, watched, eyes widening, as three waves of the Soviets' new M-4 Bison bombers flew over the field. He counted twenty-eight of the four-engine, long-range craft.[1]

Back at Wright-Patterson Air Force Base in Ohio, intelligence analysts went to work and made some hasty but dire projections — that within four to five years, the Soviet Union would have 600 to 800 long-range jet bombers. The first models of the American equivalent, the B-52, were just coming off the assembly line. The air force intelligence estimates of Soviet bomber strength were leaked to the press, and the so-called Bomber Gap was born.

Years later, more dispassionate intelligence analysts

guessed that Taylor had counted twice or thrice the same planes circling back around to impress the foreign attaché officers invited to Aviation Day.[2] The Soviets did not invest heavily in bombers; NATO forces encircled Russia, but Russia was far from America, and sending planes to bomb targets halfway around the world seemed like a high-risk, low-return proposition. When one airplane designer assured the Politburo that his plane could land safely in Mexico after bombing the United States, Khrushchev sneered, "What do you think Mexico is—our mother-in-law? You think we can simply go calling any time we want?"[3] By 1958, the Soviets had 85 long-range bombers. The United States, racing to close the mythical divide, had 1,769 bombers capable of striking the Soviet Union.[4]

The Soviets were concentrating their resources and engineering know-how on long-range missiles. The Nazi rocket scientists captured at the end of World War II had been put to work at Kapustin Yar, the Rocket Forces' top-secret missile testing site seventy-five miles from Stalingrad, on a dusty steppe along a bend in the Volga River. A Red Army general who defected to the British in 1948 disclosed the existence of Kapustin Yar, but Soviet fighters drove off a British bomber trying to photograph the site in 1953. The Americans and British did not know that the Soviets were already testing a medium-range ballistic missile with enough reach—eight hundred miles—to hit London from the USSR.[5] The Americans had been worrying about the wrong gap.

The CIA still lacked the ability to peer into Russia. There were, however, a few American savants who suspected that the Soviets were well along in building an even more powerful intercontinental ballistic missile that could reach the United States. They wanted the United States to be able to launch its own ICBM before the Soviets were able to hold the Americans hostage to nuclear terror. A brilliant Hungarian-born mathematician at the Institute for Advanced Study at Princeton, John von Neumann, had figured out that H-bombs could be made small enough to fit inside the nose cone of a missile. Using his expertise in game theory, the roly-poly, jolly von Neumann argued that the Soviets would be almost compelled to use their advantage in missiles, unless the Americans built their own weapons and struck first. It all became creepily impersonal in von Neumann's apocalyptic reckonings. War, once the imperfect pursuit of men, could now be made mechanical—predictable, total, and final—in effect, a doomsday machine activated by a short series of preordained and calculated decisions.[6]

Air force general Bernard "Bennie" Schriever, a handsome visionary running missile development out of a defunct Catholic girls' school in Los Angeles, pressed hard to build the ICBM (initially called the IBM, until the name was changed to avoid confusion with the computer company). Schriever's nemesis was the more powerful General Curtis LeMay, who had bombed and burned Japanese cities and industrial sites in World War II and was preparing to do the same to Russia on a far grander scale, if given the signal.[7] LeMay's Strategic Air Command was a superbly trained force of elite pilots and long-range jet bombers, the B-47 and later the B-52. LeMay had one war plan, the "Sunday punch," an all-out, preemptive strike against Soviet cities and airfields if it appeared the Russians were getting ready to attack first.[8] The United States had already dawdled too long, in LeMay's view. Before the Soviets got the bomb, "we could have completely destroyed Russia and not even skinned our elbows doing it," he grumbled.

LeMay was nicknamed "the Cigar" for his ever-present stogie and "the Diplomat" because he wasn't one. He was a showman, an orchestrator, and a verbal provocateur who sometimes made foolish remarks about how he wished to spark World War III. He accepted civilian control of the military, but just barely, and he ordered probes of Soviet airspace that were dangerous if not reckless. Giant portraits of the armies of Napoleon and Hitler retreating from Moscow hung in LeMay's office; the not-so-subtle message was that the only way to take Moscow was through airpower. To LeMay, bombers were the only means. He rejected missiles as too inaccurate and unpredictable, in large part because he didn't know much about them.[9]

President Eisenhower, too, was initially skeptical about missiles. He had regarded Hitler's V-1 and V-2 rockets as nuisances, terrifying to be sure, but a diversion of Hitler's resources from more useful tools, such as fighter planes.[10] Still, Eisenhower was open to new ideas in technology, and he was comfortable listening to scientists. At 10:00 a.m. on July 28, 1955, three days after he returned from the Geneva summit, Eisenhower's scheduler penciled in Schriever and von Neumann to make the pitch for developing the nuclear-tipped ICBM. They were allotted a half hour and told to present just the facts.

White House briefings were often delivered in a low-ceilinged space on the lower level of the West Wing known as the Broadcast Room. On this particular humid morning in July, recounts Neil Sheehan in his biography of General Shriever, it "was filled with rows of straight-back wooden chairs. The one exception to this austere seating was a capacious, plumply stuffed red leather armchair in the center of the first row for the comfort of the president."

The briefing started ten minutes late. Eisenhower entered, striding at a fast pace and looking angry about something. He sat down in his big leather chair, cupped his large hands together, and looked up. Trevor Gardner, a high-ranking air force official who was backing Schriever and von Neumann, went first. He described how an H-bomb on the end of a missile was a scientific breakthrough that "caused an irreversible change in the world power equation, in the waging of war." The mating of bomb to missile, he went on, "says loudly and clearly that not only is it technically feasible to develop a nuclear-armed ICBM, but, more importantly, it is now of overriding importance to the security and survival of the United States that we do it first—ahead of the U.S.S.R." He paused to let the message sink in. "Because, gentlemen, this technology is also known to the Soviets—and our intelligence tells us they are going full out to develop it." (Here Gardner was exaggerating an educated hunch into "intelligence," though the guess was correct.) "It means, gentlemen, that it is now possible to send a ballistic missile armed with a nuclear warhead from the continental United States to Soviet Russia—or vice versa—in roughly thirty minutes." Gardner paused again. As Sheehan reconstructed the scene, "The room was absolutely silent. There was no clearing of throats or shuffling of feet or shifting of chairs. Everyone in the room, including the president, had his eyes fixed on Gardner."

Von Neumann went next and walked the audience quickly through the science involved. He spoke of "nuclear blackmail" if the Russians got the ICBM first and added a fact that Gardner had neglected to mention: there would not be even a half hour of warning of a Russian missile attack. American radar would be unable to pick up the missiles until they were at the height of their parabolas. That meant only fifteen minutes before the first missile struck the first target, possibly the White House. One month earlier, air raid sirens had sounded throughout Washington as the administration practiced a nuclear alert. The president and Congress and top officials in the executive branch had been hustled out of town. This exercise had assumed a three-hour warning, which itself was not enough time, given the likely traffic chaos.

In the Broadcast Room, the time allotted to the briefing had long since run out, but Eisenhower signaled to keep going. General Schriever went into the costs involved, carefully lowballing them so as not to alarm the economy-minded Eisenhower. As Schriever finished, the president was not sitting back comfortably but sitting up straight. "This has been impressive, most impressive," he said, and began giving orders to Arthur Radford to run war games with long-range missiles. "Do it right away," the president instructed.

A new Frankenstein's monster had been born, and everyone in the room felt its presence. As the National Security Council gloomily discussed the implications a week later, Eisenhower remarked, "If the Russians can fire a thousand [missiles] a day, and we can fire a thousand a day at them, then, I, personally, would want to take off for the Argentine."[11] On September 13, 1955, Eisenhower signed NSC Action No. 1433, designating the ICBM project "a research and development program of the highest priority above all others," and ordered the secretary of defense to build it with "maximum urgency." Ten days later, on his annual summer vacation in Colorado, where he had gone to relax, he had a heart attack.[12]

President Eisenhower did not like to have his golf game interrupted. On September 23, he played a morning round at the Cherry Hills Country Club outside Denver. Ike was in good spirits; Ann Whitman recorded in her diary that she had never seen him "look or act better," possibly because he had just spent four days fishing in the mountains or because his popularity polls stood at an astronomical 80 percent in the afterglow of the "Spirit of Geneva."[13] By lunch, he was in a foul mood. Three times he had been summoned from the course to take a call from Secretary of State Dulles—only there was a mix-up, and Dulles (who spoke as often as eight times a day by phone with the president) had not been on the line. The president's game collapsed after the 14th hole. At lunch, Ike wolfed down a hamburger slathered with Bermuda onions and headed back out for nine more holes. Again he was interrupted to take a call from the secretary of state. "These onions are backing up on me," he told his golf partner, the club pro. At dinner, he felt some indigestion and skipped his usual cocktail. Ike was staying in Denver at the home of his in-laws, the comfortable eight-room house on a tree-shaded street where Mamie Doud had grown up. He retired early to read a western. At about 2 a.m., Mamie, sleeping in the next room, got up to go to the bathroom, and she heard her husband stirring in bed. Looking in, she thought he seemed troubled and asked if he was having a nightmare. "No dear, but thank you," he said. He complained of pain in his upper abdomen. Accustomed to Ike's stomach troubles, she gave him some milk of magnesia and called the president's doctor, Howard Snyder.

At age seventy-four, Snyder was old to be the president's personal physician, and Ike's millionaire friends fretted that he might not know the latest diagnoses and treatments. But the handsome, six feet three Snyder, whom Ann Whitman affectionately called "Old Duck," knew his patient, including his anxious stomach and mild hypochondria, and was attentively if sternly sympathetic. Arriving at the house shortly after 2:00 a.m., Snyder checked his patient's vital signs and decided, he later said, that the president was having a heart attack.

According to some notes that Snyder later made, the doctor engaged in a lonely bedside drama. He immediately injected Ike with morphine for the pain and drugs to stop his blood from clotting. He tried to put an oxygen mask on him, but the patient resisted. Ike began to sweat profusely. By about four o'clock, his blood pressure was dropping and he seemed to be going into shock. Snyder tried to warm him with rubbing alcohol and then told Mamie to climb into bed and wrap herself around her husband to keep him from shaking. Ike finally fell asleep at about five.

At eight, Snyder told the deputy press secretary to put out the word to reporters that the president was suffering from "digestive upset." He would later claim that he wanted to let the president rest, that he didn't want to unduly alarm Mamie (with whom he had not shared his apprehensions of a heart attack), or the staff, and that he wanted to wait to confirm his diagnosis.

All this was almost surely a lie. As historian Clarence Lasby has convincingly shown from the documentary evidence (which Snyder did his best to cover up), Snyder misdiagnosed Eisenhower in the early morning hours. "Indigestion" was not a cover story;

it's what Snyder mistakenly believed was causing Ike's suffering. He did not administer the anti-coagulants or try to fit the president with an oxygen mask. He probably did help him to the bathroom. Snyder did not realize that the president had suffered a coronary thrombosis until Ike was given an EKG after he woke up at 1:00 p.m. Then the president was finally driven to the hospital.

The Germans call heart attacks *der Teufel's Knotten*—the Devil's Grip. "It hurt like hell, Dick," Ike told his first official visitor, Vice President Richard Nixon, on October 8. "I never let Mamie know how much it hurt." Eisenhower may not have been aware of the seriousness of his condition until he was put into an oxygen tent on admission to the hospital. Then tears welled up in his eyes, probably not from the pain but from the recognition of the enormity of what was happening.[14]

Press secretary Jim Hagerty, back in Washington, felt as if he had been "slugged" when he heard the news. Whitman, as she worked the phones from Denver, could not stop weeping. Nixon exclaimed "My God!" On Wall Street, the stock market crashed, losing $14 billion, its worst dollar loss in history up to that time.[15]

A world-famous heart specialist, Dr. Paul Dudley White, was flown in from Boston on an air force plane. The bespectacled, soft-spoken White, no stranger to cameras or celebrity (his patients included Pablo Casals, Albert Schweitzer, Andrew Carnegie, Cornelius Vanderbilt, Jr., William Randolph Hearst, and the presidents of Nicaragua, Colombia, and the Philippines), soothed the press and deflected attention from the by-now dazed and shaky Dr. Snyder.

In his memoirs, Eisenhower recalled that when President Woodrow Wilson was disabled by a stroke, the public was kept in the dark. After awakening from a fitful sleep in his oxygen tent, he summoned Hagerty and ordered, "Tell the truth, the whole truth; don't try to conceal anything."[16] Hagerty proceeded to hold marathon press briefings, telling the reporters more than they wanted to know about the frequency of the president's bowel movements and the like. But as usual, the president and his men were crafty enough not to tell all the "whole truth." Eisenhower's recovery was not the smooth and sure progression that Hagerty made it out to be. Hagerty was reasonably forthcoming about Ike's physical condition, but he stayed away from the president's mental health.

Day by day, Hagerty recounted a stream of visitors to the president's bedside—sixty-six in all—making it clear that the chief executive was still attending to the nation's business. At the moment, the world was relatively calm; no immediate panic beckoned in Washington. For seven weeks, Eisenhower recuperated in a sunny private suite at Denver's Fitzsimons Army Hospital. What the press secretary did not disclose was that all visits were limited to fifteen minutes, and the president's doctors had forbidden the patient to read the newspaper or even listen to an Army football game on the radio. The medicos did not want to trigger his temper.* Eisenhower was a dutiful patient but not a happy one. As part of an experimental therapy four days after his attack, the heart specialists had tried to get him to sit up in an armchair. Ike took a turn for the worse, and a white-faced doctor ordered him put back in bed "at once!"[17] Bedridden in the hospital, Eisenhower, like many heart attack patients, sank into depression.

Eisenhower had always tried to stay fit. As a young officer, he could do five chin-ups with his right arm and three with his left. Mamie had admiringly called him a "bruiser."[18] Now he feared he would become an invalid, consigned to a wheelchair. On November 1, Bobby Cutler visited him and recorded some

---

*Still shaken by his role in the overnight drama, Snyder dwelled on a disturbing memory: the sight of Eisenhower's extreme vexation over his interrupted golf game on the morning before his heart attack. Ike's anger at the succession of bollixed phone calls had become "so real that the veins stood out on his forehead like whipcords," Snyder recalled.

unsettling impressions. Ike was sitting beneath a portrait of his mother, which he had just painted. He was wearing a jaunty green bow tie beneath his pajama collar. Cutler, who had resigned earlier that year, noticed that his old boss was smiling yet remained "very still — body, hands, and facial expression." He looked well enough, but "obviously he had trained himself to keep quiet." Cutler was bothered by Ike's "enforced placidity." The former White House aide remembered his vibrant chief, hands always moving, his restless body getting up and pacing as he made a point. Ike complained that his muscles had grown flabby. His doctors had told him that it would be four months before he knew whether he'd be "OK or a crippled man," wrote Cutler. Ike told Cutler that to be confined to a chair "would be just as good as being dead."[19]

Eisenhower was gloomy but not resigned. Indeed, as the days passed, he grew defiant. His mother had a saying he liked to quote: "The Lord deals the cards. You play them." Ike's bridge partners noted that Eisenhower did not whine about bad hands. In life, he told others, he was leery of the expression "with the help of God." He told friends, "I never say that. I won't say that. I don't believe that. I believe that the Lord dealt us a hand, that's right, but he expects *us* to play it."[20]

So Eisenhower pushed back. He began sitting

The patient recovers (Dwight D. Eisenhower Presidential Library, Abilene, Kansas)

under a sun lamp to get back his ruddiness. To his doctors he pretended, preposterously, that he had "conquered" his unhealthy impatience.[21] He even told them that he was determined to walk out of Fitzsimons and into the White House, no wheelchairs. With Ann Whitman, he went to a stairwell and practiced climbing fourteen steps; he wanted to make sure he could climb the ramp to his airplane because he knew there would be cameras everywhere.[22]

He chose Veteran's Day, November 11, to return to Washington. Some two thousand servicemen, standing ten feet apart, lined the route across the bridge from National Airport. A giant sign reading WELCOME HOME IKE stretched over Constitution Avenue. The NBC news van trailing the presidential limousine had so many cameras it looked like a tank bristling with gun turrets. Ike professed to hate motorcades, but his friends knew that he secretly liked waving to the crowds.[23] This time, he would have to do it from beneath a plastic bubble top fitted onto a Chrysler — doctor's orders, to protect him against the chill. As the cars glided along the avenues and the crowds cheered, Ike smiled and waved. When he got to the White House he blew up at Snyder. "Damn it, Howard, why did you not let me stand in the car? It would have been far less exhausting to me if I had been able to." Ike complained that he had to get down on his knees and "squeegee" around as he waved from side to side.[24] The patient was blowing up over small things. He was better.

Moving from post to post in the army, Ike had never owned his own home. But with the profits from writing his war memoirs in 1948, he bought a 189-acre farm in Gettysburg, spread out below Seminary Ridge, not far from the Civil War battlefield he liked to walk. Twenty miles from Camp David, the house was quarters for the cabinet when advisers came to consult.

Ike had considered a retirement home in the mountains or at the seashore, but Mamie liked neither (too many bugs), so they had settled on this farm in the rolling Pennsylvania countryside.[25] At a cookout at the farm in late July 1955, Ike had told his aide Bernard Shanley and his wife, Maureen, that he had "let the First Lady buy any farm she wanted," Shanley wrote in his diary. "'Otherwise,' he said, 'she probably would have had a nervous breakdown.'" Eisenhower "laughingly told us, 'I am very much in hock, and I wonder if I will ever get out of it.'"[26]

The fourteen-room white frame house had been restored by Mamie. "I just let Mamie go hog wild," Ike said. The most attractive feature was a glassed-in porch where the Eisenhowers could sit while he convalesced. Ike had wanted to head straight for Florida after a token appearance in Washington in November, but Mamie objected. So the First Couple drove north, eighty-one miles from Washington.[27]

The December weather turned raw and gray. Unable to walk outside, Eisenhower wobbled around inside, using a golf club as a cane. He was "brooding silently," according to Nixon, who came to visit.[28] The vice president had a particular interest in Eisenhower's ruminations. In the days and weeks after

Ike's heart attack, it was generally assumed that Eisenhower would not seek a second term. In a poll of Washington newsmen on November 12, some 88 percent predicted he would not run in 1956. Ellis Slater and George Allen, charter members of his "gang," hoped and believed he would retire after one term, and so did his brother Milton and his son John.[29] Ike had just turned sixty-five. In 1960 he would be seventy, an age no president had ever reached while serving in the White House. The heart specialist thought there was an even chance Ike wouldn't live that long (an opinion that was kept from the public).[30]

Mamie had moved into Fitzsimons Hospital with Ike and was happy to be with him in Gettysburg. She had been talking to Dr. Snyder, who disagreed with the experts and told Mamie that inactivity could be fatal to her driven husband. Snyder may have blundered in Denver, but he knew Ike; Mamie knew him even better. She surprised Milton and John by telling them she thought Ike should run for reelection. "I just can't believe Ike's work is finished," she said.[31]

For his part, Eisenhower seemed ambivalent. He had sworn not to run again after his first, draining year in office, but later told press secretary Jim Hagerty, whom he liked and whose instincts he trusted, that he might campaign after all.[32] Ike was bothered by irregular heart rhythms and residual discomfort, but he confessed to Ann Whitman that he was more inclined to run *after* his heart attack than before. Ike's brush with mortality seems to have heightened his sense of duty and ambition—one and the same with him. As the president tried to sit perfectly still in a hospital armchair or leaned on his favorite eight-iron for support, he had plenty of time to think about how the world would fare without his leadership. Eisenhower often wrote or spoke about a desire to "loaf," and he rightfully felt he deserved to lay down his burdens. Yet in his fitful dreams, he heard not taps but reveille.

"Of course you won't run—and I'm glad," wrote Swede Hazlett, Ike's most intimate correspondent, in mid-October. On December 23, Ike wrote Swede that the decision whether to seek reelection was "still unresolved, swirls daily around in my mind and keeps me awake at night." A month later, he wrote Hazlett that he was having trouble sleeping, waking up before dawn to stew over his problems. His doctors, he reported, had instructed him to take a half-hour nap before lunch and to rest, sitting up in an armchair, for an hour in the afternoon. Ike went on, with some exasperation, "I am supposed to take ten minutes each hour out of every long conference and to leave the room and either lie down or sit down by myself, allowing nothing to disturb me. Likewise, I am to avoid all situations that tend to bring about such reactions as irritation, frustration, anxiety, fear, and, above all, anger. When doctors give me such instructions, I say to them, 'Just what do you think the Presidency is?' "[33]

Eisenhower's mood was not improved by the news that the thick-headed, far-right Senate majority leader, William Knowland, was considering a run for the presidency. As Ike drove to Gettysburg at Christmastime, he grumbled to John, "I *told* the boys four years ago that they ought to get someone who'd want to run again for a second term." John thought he was still arguing with himself, testing himself.[34]

Eisenhower liked Dick Nixon well enough. Nixon had handled himself gracefully in a difficult spot while the president was recovering, neither seeking too much power nor shying from it as he chaired meetings of the NSC. Wisely, the vice president formed a close working relationship with Foster Dulles.[35] Ike was grateful for Nixon's yeoman service in both pandering to and spying on the Republican right. Ike's hand was not hidden to his closest lieutenants, men like Foster Dulles and Nixon. They did what the president told them to do. Nixon had been loyal; still, Eisenhower had trouble warming to his number two. "He *made* himself like Nixon," John recalled many years later.[36]

After looking at some poll numbers, Eisenhower questioned whether Nixon could beat Adlai Stevenson, the likeliest Democratic nominee, in 1956. The day after Christmas, the president summoned Nixon to a private meeting. Ike suggested that Nixon needed a little more seasoning to broaden his experience, and offered him any cabinet job in a second term except secretary of state, Dulles's domain, or attorney general (Nixon, in Eisenhower's view, lacked the necessary legal skills). How about secretary of defense? the president asked. According to his memoirs, Nixon felt he was being set up: Eisenhower was trying to dump him but wouldn't come out and say it. The Defense Department, with its vicious interservice, civilian-military crossfire, held no appeal. Nixon stalled and equivocated; so did Eisenhower. Nothing was resolved. Nixon was left to twist while Eisenhower, in a series of carefully hedged public statements over the winter, praised his veep but would not commit to keeping him on the ticket.[37]

On January 13, Eisenhower put together a secret meeting of his closest advisers to discuss whether or not he should run in November. There was a chorus of hosannas. Dulles declared that Ike was "God-destined" to protect the peace of the world, while Tom Stephens, the appointments secretary, chimed in, "We can't elect anyone but you, Mr. President." There was consensus that Ike had put together the finest group of subordinates ever to serve an administration and that the nation deserved their continued service.

Listening to the self-congratulatory cheerleading, John Eisenhower couldn't help but smile. His father was "hearing what he wanted to hear" from a group he had picked to deliver it. The only real dissenter was Milton. Ike allowed that as "an old soldier," he wanted to "die with his boots on." The decision had been made.[38]

Ike did not announce his intentions for nearly two more months. The president had a well-honed sense of drama, as well as a shrewd feel for timing. In mid-September, when questions about his reelection plans first surfaced in the press, he had written Milton that he had always thought it wise "to wait until the last possible moment before announcing any positive decision."[39] Eisenhower wanted to keep both his cautious heart doctors and potential political rivals guessing as long as he could, to give them less time to mount their opposition.[40] Insisting that he had not decided, he indicated that he would make up his mind by March 1. Incredibly, he seems to have kept Mamie guessing. This seems thoughtless, given her staunch support. Considerate if temperamental, Ike often showed small kindnesses to his helpmates, sending flowers and notes to staffers. He was especially generous with Mamie. That winter, the president personally designed a Tiffany necklace for the First Lady that was inscribed "For never failing help, since 1916, in calm and in crisis, in dark days and in bright. Love, Ike."[41] He was sincere, but that didn't mean he took her into his confidence. Bernard Shanley's diary records the First Lady fishing for information from the staff in late February as the deadline neared. On February 28, she finally braced herself to ask Ann Whitman, "What do you think the President is going to do tomorrow?"[42] The next day, Ike finally told reporters at a briefing that he would go on television to answer whether or not he would seek reelection, and that his answer would be "positive, that is affirmative." The reporters had to ask him a second time to be sure they understood what he was saying.

The public cheered. Before his heart attack, *New York Times* Washington editor James Reston had described a "kind of national love affair" with Eisenhower: "Everything he did was automatically wonderful." This was still true as Eisenhower gradually returned to the fray in the winter of 1956. A February 9 Gallup poll showed that 61 percent wanted him to run again, versus only 25 percent who believed he should retire; he led Adlai Stevenson by almost two to one.[43]

On January 10, after the president had returned from Key West, where he had rested and hit his first golf shots (only irons, no driver or fairway woods allowed), Foster Dulles and Ike had sat down to review the world's problems. Dulles had told the president that he was the most trusted leader in the world and the greatest force for peace. In his diary that night, Ike wrote, in a crabbed parenthetical, "I suspect that Foster's estimate concerning my own position is substantially correct."[44] He had been more forthright as he dictated a diary entry to Ann Whitman on January 11: "It looks to me more and more that if a fellow has a job he has to do it in his own way."[45] Eisenhower was the indispensable man, although he could never bring himself to admit it to anyone, at least not in so many words. But he knew it, and in his own indirect way acknowledged what his devoted followers told him. Another campaign had begun.

13

Bows and Arrows

ISENHOWER FELT A great burden to lead because he understood the peril of inaction. Without progress toward disarmament, Eisenhower wrote in his diary on January 10, 1956, "it would appear that the world is on the verge of an abyss."[1] The arms race, like war, had a dynamic of its own. The president had just read a study on the effects of a nuclear attack by the Soviet Union. The results, analyzing a hypothetical attack on July 1, 1956, were predictably horrific: tens of millions of Americans dead and dying, cities in ruins, social chaos or no society at all. "We might ultimately have to go back to bows and arrows," the president told a National Security Council meeting on January 12, his first since his heart attack.[2] Eisenhower continued to doubt that the Russians would launch such an attack, but he could not be sure. He worried that the fear and confusion in an East-West crisis would be exacerbated by the pressure of "use-it-or-lose it" in the new age of the ICBM. He knew that even a small confrontation could spin out of control and lead to "general war." Preventing such a doomsday chain reaction was his principal reason for wishing to remain president. His motivation was concocted from healthy intention and healthy ego: he had to find a way to leverage his unique standing, his power, the trust he commanded—and the respect and fear of his enemies—to keep the peace. The strategy he chose was not well understood at the time or later. It required enormous will and fortitude, a certain defiance of logic or at least conventional thinking, and a leap of imagination and faith. And it was by definition something he had to do alone.

Before his heart attack, on his fishing trip in the Rockies, Ike had stayed at the ranch of his longtime friend, Denver multimillionaire Aksel Nielsen. Visiting Nielsen's Byers Peak Ranch, near the crossroads of Fraser, Colorado, was a quasi-religious experience for Eisenhower. It was the place, he said, where he came closest to the mysteries of life. Ike spent happy hours at the easel, painting. The ranch was a modest cluster of outbuildings screened by some scraggly pines struggling to grow in the thin air. In such outdoor scenes, Ike liked to use bold, primary colors; he did not go for muted or subtle shadings. "The world he painted, like the world he saw, was one of sharp distinctions, of orderly and unmistakable transitions from one mood to the next, a world of right and wrong," his grandson, David, would write in a moving 2010 memoir.[3] Notably, on Ike's canvas the pine trees are flourishing, set off against towering mountains that protect the ranch from the outside world.

Eisenhower's strategy for protecting his own country was equally bold, but the way he pulled it off was extremely subtle. Ike's color palette may have been simple by necessity; he was an amateur painter. But no one was more sophisticated or nuanced at statecraft.

There was nothing subtle about the public persona of John Foster Dulles. In January, Dulles gave an interview that *Life* magazine turned into an article entitled "How Dulles Averted War." Dulles boasted that three times — in Korea, Indochina, and the Formosa Strait — the Eisenhower administration had bluffed the Communists into backing down by threatening to use nuclear weapons. His language was typically lurid. "You have to take chances for peace," said Dulles, "just as you must take chances in war.... The ability to get to the verge without getting into war is the necessary art. If you cannot master it, you inevitably get into war. If you run away from it, if you are scared to go to the brink, you are inevitably lost.... We walked to the brink and looked it in the face. We took strong action."[4]

Painting (Dwight D. Eisenhower Presidential Library, Abilene, Kansas)

Dulles's "brinksmanship," as his bravado was soon dubbed, caused an instant backlash. Many Europeans and Americans recoiled in fear and disdain; the secretary of state seemed to enjoy rolling the nuclear dice. And Dulles, in his public pronouncements, appeared to be almost eager to shock with his declarations. The secretary of state, wrote James Reston, "doesn't stumble into booby traps; he digs them to size, studies them carefully, and then jumps."[5] Dulles privately claimed that *Life* had hyped the article, but he couldn't deny his words, because the interview had been taped. Though he pretended otherwise, the secretary had seen and approved the article before publication.[6] At his first press conference after his heart attack, Eisenhower restated his "complete faith" in Dulles while trying to take some of the edge off the secretary's bluster. Taking a strong stand did not automatically mean "being at the brink of something," the president told reporters.[7]

Eisenhower did not protest too much, because Dulles's tough talk served his purpose. Ike wanted the world to believe that America would go to the brink of nuclear war if it had to—indeed, that the United States would be willing to use nuclear weapons in even a small conflict. This belligerent posture had been at the heart of Eisenhower's strategy for avoiding war, but now the stakes and risks were to intensify.[8]

By the winter of 1956, two years after Dulles proclaimed the concept at the Council on Foreign Relations, the doctrine of massive retaliation had no shortage of critics, many of them inside the Eisenhower administration. Civilian strategists in the universities and think tanks (notably Henry Kissinger at Harvard) were beginning to question the tenuous assumptions of Ike's all-or-nothing approach to Communist aggression. Before long, prominent statesmen like former secretary of state Dean Acheson and ambitious politicians like Senator John F. Kennedy of Massachusetts would take up the scoffing refrain. Was the United States really ready to wage nuclear holocaust to put out a brushfire war? Massive retaliation seemed to leave only two options: global war or surrender. Despite von Neumann's calculations, in the convoluted real world the extreme choice didn't seem realistic. The critics offered their own doctrine, which came to be known as flexible response. The United States, they held, needed to have the capacity and the will to fight limited wars, even limited nuclear wars. If the Russians rolled into western Germany, firing off some tactical nukes would buy time for heads to cool and statesmen to negotiate a ceasefire. Strong conventional forces could fight local wars without escalation into Armageddon.[9]

The chief apostle of flexible response was General Maxwell Taylor, a handsome, brainy World War II paratroop commander who enjoyed reading Shakespeare. Taylor was Army Chief of Staff, so he had a vested interest in flexible response. Massive retaliation had drained resources from the army; there was a diminished role for ground-pounding soldiers in the so-called New Look military. Indeed, reducing the military's claim to the nation's resources had been one rationale behind the New Look, as Ike sought to avoid a buildup that would lead to his dreaded garrison state.* But Taylor was not just angling for a bigger slice of the budget; he believed that massive retaliation was a clumsy, meat-ax approach, and that modern war demanded a range of weapons and the flexibility to use them.

Taylor was a suave and confident debater, unafraid to take on the president of the United States, even one who had been his commanding general in World War II. In the secret debates on the National Security Council, he had an important and surprising ally: John Foster Dulles. Privately, his *Life* magazine bluster notwithstanding, the secretary of state had abandoned the doctrine he had announced just two years before in his massive retaliation speech. The senior diplomat had heard too many European foreign ministers question whether Washington really would risk Chicago to save Paris. If the Russian tanks rolled, would America go all-out nuclear? The Europeans were doubtful. Britain, France, and West Germany wanted to see America put conventional forces on the line, divisions of American troops who would

---

*When Eisenhower heard how many army divisions Taylor wanted to fight a conventional war, he "nearly fainted," he told the National Security Council in March of 1956. After reading a synopsis of Henry Kissinger's *Nuclear Weapons and Foreign Policy*, urging a conventional-forces buildup, Ike wrote in a private memo, "This man would say, 'We are to be an armed camp—capable of doing all things, all the time, everywhere.' "[10]

stand in the way of the Red Army and fight the old-fashioned way, staving off global nuclear war as long as possible.

In the inner councils of the Eisenhower administration, Taylor and Dulles had considerable support for dumping massive retaliation. As the arguments went round and round that winter and into the spring, it appeared that the president was the only one left who really believed in his strategy. For political and bureaucratic reasons, Ike gave in here and there, hedging and fudging the language to allow flexible response into the policy-planning process; indeed, the official NSC documents in 1955 and 1956—confidential documents, for internal use, not public consumption—indicated that the policy of the United States *was* flexible response, or something close to it. Ike knew when to pick his fights and when to avoid them, and he knew that he held the trump card: the president had the final say over what to do in a crisis. On the eve of the election, Ike apparently calculated it was not worth getting into a policy battle with his chief advisers that could spill into the press and out into public view.

As an army major serving on a sleepy post in the Panama Canal Zone in the early 1920s, Eisenhower had read Clausewitz's *On War*—three times. His commander, the wise and literate General Fox Conner, had questioned him relentlessly about the book, forcing him to think through the slim but densely written volume that was regarded in the late nineteenth and early twentieth centuries as a kind of bible on the relationship between war and politics. *On War* is heavy going. Most readers (or skimmers) remember only Clausewitz's much-quoted dictum that war is an extension of politics by other means. But under Conner's tutelage, Eisenhower absorbed a deeper meaning. Politicians and policy makers may think they can control war by rational planning, but Clausewitz saw larger, irrational forces at work. The bias of war, Clausewitz wrote, is always toward violence; even the most well-meaning men will use whatever weapons they can find, including the sacrifice of citizens. Clausewitz, who witnessed Napoleon's invasion of and retreat from Russia in 1812, had firsthand experience with such "total war." Eisenhower, who was Supreme Allied Commander during the firebombing of German cities in 1945, understood total war as well.[11]

Eisenhower wasn't really a strategic thinker, not in the classical, formal sense of a Clausewitz or in the methodical, lawyerly way of Foster Dulles. Rather he was an intuitive operator who felt his way, tacking and turning, but always with an eye on his ultimate goal of avoiding war. The records of the heated internal debates in the White House in the winter and spring of 1956 reveal his independent if lonely genius—one based not on the rationality of smart men in a room but on his understanding of the *irrationality* of men in war.

Without quite saying so, Eisenhower made it clear he was going to do it his way, regardless of what the planning documents recommended.[12] Again and again, his lieutenants pressed him to prepare for limited war against the Soviets. Eisenhower responded by insisting that in the nuclear age there was no such thing as limited war. In one NSC debate with Dulles on February 27, Ike listened to the secretary drone on about "operations short of general war," and then "asked the Council," as the notetaker recorded the conversation, to "imagine the position of a military commander in the field. His radar informs him that a flock of enemy bombers is on the point of attacking him. What does the military commander do in such a situation? Does he not use every weapon at hand to defend himself and his forces?"[13]

Here was Eisenhower's central insight from reading Clausewitz so many years before, an insight made real by his own experiences in World War II. Military commanders will use "every weapon at hand" rather than accept defeat. As historian Campbell Craig observed in his insightful 1998 treatise, *Destroying the Village: Eisenhower and Thermonuclear War,*

"Any tempering of this tendency by moral, religious, or chivalric limitations on violence—well, the two World Wars had ushered that right out."[14] Small wars lead to big wars; in the nuclear age, to total war. The way to avoid small wars was to threaten big wars from the beginning and mean it. As for "brush-fire wars," Eisenhower was determined not to fight them; he didn't want to fight *any* wars that could escalate in unpredictable ways. He drew a distinction between small brushfire wars, which risked becoming larger confrontations, and covertly backing one side or another in a coup, even if that coup threatened to ignite a civil war. With the world divided between East and West, there was always the risk of conflagration. And even if the Kremlin hung back from actual combat, as in Korea, the fighting could drag on and sap the nation's spirits and resources.

On May 14, Eisenhower told Joint Chiefs of Staff chairman Radford that "we would not get involved in a 'small war' extending beyond sending a few Marine battalions or Army units. If it grew to anything like Korea proportions, the action would become one for the use of atomic weapons."[15] Ten days later, on May 24, General Taylor argued that since neither side was likely to go nuclear in a fight, it made sense to be able to fight limited wars with conventional weapons. Eisenhower flatly stated that

Taylor was wrong about human nature and failed to grasp the natural dynamic of war toward ever more violence. The president, wrote General Goodpaster, "said he thought General Taylor's position was dependent on an assumption that we are opposed by a people who think as we do with regard to the value of human life. But they do not, as shown in many incidents from the last war. We have no basis for thinking that they abhor destruction as we do. In the event they should decide to go to war, the pressure on them to use atomic weapons in a sudden blow would be extremely great."[16]

Would Eisenhower have ever *initiated* the use of nuclear weapons? If the Korean War had dragged on, he might have used them against Red China. And if Red China had invaded Formosa, he probably would have authorized the use of the atomic cannons he dispatched with American forces to defend the Nationalist Chinese island bastion. But in neither case did he expect the Soviet Union to retaliate with nuclear weapons. By 1956, as the Soviets built their nuclear arsenal and developed the means of delivery, it was highly unlikely that Eisenhower would order the use of nuclear weapons except in the most extreme of circumstances, like an all-out Soviet invasion of Western Europe. But he never said so — to anyone. The United States, he believed, needed to be credibly prepared to go all out. Eisenhower never, not even in the smallest forum, indicated that he would be unwilling to use nuclear weapons. Quite the opposite. The May 24 meeting at the White House was highly secret: only the president, Radford, Taylor, and Goodpaster were in the Oval Office. Eisenhower was clear with his military men, as Goodpaster quoted him: "Massive retaliation, though the term has been scoffed at, is likely to be the key to survival. He reiterated that planning should go ahead on the basis of the use of tactical atomic weapons against military targets in any small war in which the United States might be involved."[17]

Flexible response might seem like a reasonable approach, but in Eisenhower's view, it was likely to lead toward wars, not away from them. The president refused Taylor's request to build up conventional forces, the tanks, guns, and men to fight small wars. It was not just a question of saving money. By removing the means to fight limited war, the president meant to eliminate the temptation, the illusion—on both sides—that war could be contained.[18]

Ike's ultimate dream was disarmament, but the Soviet rejection of "Atoms for Peace" and "Open Skies" made him a realist: that dream was still a long way off. Convincing the Soviets not to even try their luck—by, for example, making a grab for Berlin—"required operational weapons," wrote Cold

War historian John Lewis Gaddis, "together with so credible an *appearance* of a determination to use them that even Eisenhower's closest advisers would not doubt his resolve."[19] In the meantime, Ike would go forward, foot on the gas, hand on the trigger.

As usual when Eisenhower grappled with doomsday questions, there was a physical price. Shortly after midnight on June 8, Mamie called Howard Snyder: her husband was experiencing severe stomach distress. Snyder gave Ike some milk of magnesia, then an enema to relieve his gas, but the cure didn't take. The president's abdomen became swollen and the pain grew worse. Despite his doctor's orders to avoid raw vegetables, Ike confessed that he'd asked the White House chef to prepare him a Waldorf salad for dinner.

Snyder became anxious. He had been keeping a secret from his patient: a gastrointestinal exam in May had detected an inflammation of the ileum, the section connecting the large and small intestines. Ike had, in fact, suffered from ileitis, also known as Crohn's disease, for years. The condition, usually mild and not life threatening, tended to flare up under stress. Now Snyder was afraid a piece of celery was stuck in the inflamed and narrow ileum, blocking his intestines.

At 11:00 a.m. an ambulance rushed the president to Walter Reed Hospital. Ike began vomiting dark green fluid. The patient, according to the admitting physician, appeared listless and apathetic, and was sweating freely. His blood pressure was dropping, and Snyder feared that he would go into shock.

Snyder remembered an old medical school adage: "Never let the sun set on an obstructed intestine." By early evening, a team of thirteen doctors had gathered. They were divided over what to do. X-rays showed a blockage, but left alone, the piece of celery might pass through naturally.[20] By midnight, the medicos had finally decided to operate. "If we don't move soon, we are going to lose the patient," Dr. Walter Tkach, the assistant White House physician, told Mamie and John Eisenhower, who had been waiting with growing anxiety.

Mamie clung to the idea that an operation was not necessary and refused to agree, but John signed the papers in her place. The surgeon, General Leonard Heaton, appeared at the president's bedside and told Eisenhower, "I think we had better go inside and look around." At first Ike seemed not to understand; then he gave the go-ahead.

The two-hour surgery, between 2:00 and 4:00 a.m., successfully inserted a bypass around the diseased piece of intestine. The press was naturally alarmed by the president's second medical emergency in nine months, but the unflappable Hagerty assured them his boss was doing well and in good cheer.

This was not true. For many days after the operation, John was shocked by how weak his father appeared. With his stomach muscles stitched together, he hunched over as he hobbled about. Unable to eat, he lost so much weight he looked gaunt.[21] He told Snyder he was "terribly depressed." He tried to control his temper but still blew up at Ann Whitman.[22] Devoted to her boss, she found the going hard. She confessed to a friend, "I am in one of my I-hate-people moods," and added, "I live on dexamyl.... We call them 'jolly pills.'" (Snyder freely handed out dexamyl, a potent mood enhancer containing a barbiturate and amphetamine, to staff and reporters, though not to the president.)[23]

Eisenhower was scheduled to attend a conference of heads of state in Latin America in late July. After that loomed the rigors of a presidential campaign. "If I don't feel better pretty soon, I'm going to pull out," Ike told Jerry Persons, his congressional liaison, before leaving for Panama. "The president questions whether he will be able to make the Panama trip," Snyder wrote in his diary on July 18, two days before he was due to depart. The next day Snyder reported the president "better"—and determined to go.[24]

Wearing a surgical drain beneath his clothes, Eisenhower rode in the motorcades he claimed to detest and hobnobbed with heads of state.[25] "He forgot his 'belly' troubles and seemed relieved of the anxiety which had depressed him for many months," wrote Snyder in his diary on July 23. "He goes down to Panama, almost gets crushed by the mobs, meets God-knows-how-many Latin American diplomats, suffers through all the damn receptions," said Persons to speechwriter Emmet Hughes, "... three days later he comes waltzing back looking like a new man."[26]

By August, Hughes, who had gone back to Time-Life at the end of 1953 but returned to write speeches for the campaign, found Ike looking bright-eyed and vigorous. The president's campaign appearances were sharply limited—seven major speeches—but he did a great deal of TV, and, with the help of a Madison Avenue advertising agency, projected an image of confidence and serenity. Oddly, it was his opponent, the fifty-six-year-old Adlai Stevenson, who appeared haggard and worn. Stevenson raced about the country, calling for a ban on nuclear arms testing.[27] John Eisenhower worried that Stevenson would make headway with the test-ban issue. Always eager for a horse race, the press was making the election seem close. "One day in early October," John recalled, "I marched into Dad's Oval Office considerably agitated. 'You've got to get moving,' I said. 'You're going to fall behind.'"

According to his son, the president "sat back and

roared with laughter. 'This fellow's licked and what's more he knows it! Let's go to the ball game.'" It was the first game of the 1956 World Series, Yankees versus Dodgers. The two Eisenhowers flew to New York with John Foster Dulles. A photograph shows the trio at the ballpark watching the game. Dulles looks grim and distracted, and John looks self-conscious in his army major's uniform. The president is leaning forward, hands on the box-seat rail. He looks to be having a wonderful time.[28]

14

Rising Storm

THE 1950S SEEM staid only in hindsight. To the people living through the era of beatniks, rock 'n' roll, and the first stirrings of the sexual revolution, change was coming fast, too fast for many. On their new TV sets, Americans were watching a thrilling, gyrating, disturbing new entertainer named Elvis Presley. "Elvis the Pelvis" was creating a national frenzy just by pouting and bucking his hips. Hysterical teenage girls were carving Elvis's name on their forearms with penknives. Television producers refused to show him below the waist. "They called him lewd, and they were right," wrote William Manchester. "That was the secret of his appeal." Parents were anxious, though not a few fathers and certainly their teenage sons were starting to buy a new magazine called *Playboy* (circulation 600,000 by the end of 1956).[1]

More than anything, most Americans wanted to

be protected, to see their families safe. If Ike seemed conventional, even a little boring, he also came across as calm, steady, and strong. To the American people, who knew nothing of his inner turmoil, he was steady when it mattered.

That spring of 1956, Eisenhower had been wrestling with a decision he described to aides as "one of the most soul searching questions to come before a President."[2] The U-2 spy plane was ready to fly. Did Eisenhower dare send it over the Soviet Union? The rewards were potentially immense; so were the risks.

Project Aquatone, the development of the U-2, was a triumph of engineering and vision. Eisenhower was proud of his scientific advisers—he called them "my scientists"—and he was receptive to their ideas and grateful for their contributions. He gave them freedom to work and protected them (though he did not always trust their discretion or political instincts). The inventions spurred by the Technological Capabilities Panel to meet the threat of surprise attack—the U-2 and the ICBM—were mighty swords in his arsenal, but, as Eisenhower was well aware, they were double edged.

In the Nevada desert, a top-secret government-controlled facility called Area 51 would become known to generations of science fiction fans and conspiracy theorists for UFO sightings. It was here, beginning in August 1955, that project director Kelly Johnson, a slick-haired, bulbous-nosed engineer with a profane tongue, pushed his paper-thin, jet-propelled aircraft ever higher into the sky. Johnson's motto was KISS, for "Keep It Simple, Stupid," and he told his engineers he would trade his grandmother for a few pounds less weight in the airframe. Johnson's engineers struggled with fuel that froze or, perversely, boiled at high altitudes and engines that flamed out. In less than eighteen months, they managed to build a photo-reconnaissance plane that could fly all day long at 70,000 feet—out of range of Soviet air defenses.[3]

Johnson disdained federal bureaucrats, which is why he appreciated Richard Bissell, the CIA man who was his government boss. Bissell was just as contemptuous of petty rules and foot-dragging, and just as confident of his own genius. "Bissell distrusted all bureaucracies," recalled his assistant, Bob King, "including his own." At Yale, the gangly, awkward Bissell had published a wickedly funny, subversive magazine. The Big Men on Campus recognized his gifts and invited him to be one of them, but Bissell turned down their tap at Skull and Bones, a rare act of independence in his day. Bissell liked to play the rebel iconoclast—he would do it his way. At the CIA he terrified his secretary, Doris Mirage, by driving her the wrong way down a one-way street en route to an office party. Why not? No one was coming the other way.[4]

Bissell knew that President Eisenhower would have misgivings about flying a spy plane over Soviet airspace, so in May 1956, the spymaster came up with a stunt: a U-2 flew over the Eisenhower farm at Gettysburg, shooting photographs from 70,000 feet with its specially designed camera. Looking at images so precise that he could see his cows feeding at a trough, the president exclaimed, "This is close to incredible."[5]

Eisenhower still was wary. He insisted that civilians pilot the U-2. If uniformed military men were captured flying over the USSR, it would be an act of war, "and I don't want any part of that," said the president. Eisenhower was always careful to keep covert operations "deniable." A group of air force pilots was "sheep-dipped"—clandestinely transferred to the CIA—and given cover as civilian employees working for the National Advisory Committee for Aeronautics, a precursor to NASA. A dozen of the new spy planes were matched with sheep-dipped pilots and designated "the First Weather Reconnaissance Squadron."[6]

On May 28, Bissell and his boss, Allen Dulles, went to the White House to seek permission to fly the U-2 over Russia. Ike was inclined to say yes. He sorely needed the intelligence only the spy plane could provide. On Capitol Hill, two powerful Democratic senators, Stuart Symington and Washington's Henry "Scoop" Jackson, were rumbling about the Bomber Gap. Eisenhower suspected that the Bomber Gap was exaggerated, if not a myth, but he needed proof. Otherwise he would be forced to spend hundreds of millions more on building B-52s. It gnawed at the president that he knew so little about the Soviets' capabilities and intentions. Accurate aerial reconnaissance could go a long way toward allaying his fears of a surprise attack. Still Ike remained nervous about the U-2. He quizzed Dulles and Bissell: what if the plane went down and the pilot was captured? The CIA men assured the president that the plane would disintegrate and the pilot would be dead. At worst, they said, the pilot would pop a suicide pill if he somehow survived the crash. The CIA had repeatedly advised the president that the Soviets' World War II–era radar would not be able to pick up the high-flying plane. Bissell neglected to tell the president then or later about a report issued the day of their meeting by the CIA's Office of Scientific Intelligence that revealed that detection of the U-2 by the Soviets was actually probable.[7]

The president dismissed Bissell and Dulles without making a decision. He needed more time to ponder the problem. Ten days later Eisenhower was in the hospital undergoing intestinal surgery. A wound-up Bissell, who had been nicknamed "the Mad Stork" by his assistants, shambled around Project Aquatone's messy and decrepit offices; his secretary had to trot to keep up.

On June 21, Bissell met with Andy Goodpaster, the presidential staff secretary who handled highly sensitive matters. Bissell was impatient to get going with U-2 operations; a spell of clear weather was predicted for much of the USSR in early July. On July 2, Bissell was granted a secret audience with the recuperating president, who said that the missions would be "close to an act of war, and very hard for the Soviets to swallow." Still, he seemed to be close to giving the go-ahead. Bissell and Dulles had already shown the president pictures of downtown San Diego taken by the U-2 from 70,000 feet. "We could easily count the automobiles on the streets and even the lines marking the parking areas for the individual cars. There was no doubt about the quality of the information to be obtained," Eisenhower later wrote in his memoirs.[8] The president was persuaded. On July 3, Goodpaster called with the go-ahead. He told Bissell the president had approved a ten-day period of operations. Always aggressive, Bissell asked if that meant ten days of good weather. "Absolutely not," said Goodpaster. The president meant ten days, not more.

On July 4 and 5, 1956, the first two missions

took off from an air base in Germany and successfully flew deep inside Russia. On July 5, Bissell told Dulles, as the CIA director was returning from the holiday, that the missions had flown directly over Moscow and Leningrad—the Kremlin and the Winter Palace. Dulles usually gave Bissell a long leash, but he was taken aback by his subordinate's audacity. "Oh my Lord," said Dulles. "Do you think that was wise the first time?" Bissell replied, "Allen, the first is the safest."

The first flight photographed MiG fighters climbing to meet the U-2, then falling away in the high altitude, unable to reach the American craft. The Soviet radar had clearly picked up the U-2. In an omission that bordered on insubordination, the president was not told; Bissell was intent on packing in as many flights as possible before anyone objected. The U-2 flew three more times, five in all, before Bissell's luck ran out. On July 10, the Soviets filed a formal protest. They did it secretly, through diplomatic channels. The Kremlin, ever loath to reveal weakness, did not want the world to know that American planes could crisscross Soviet territory with impunity.

One Kremlin leader was especially indignant: Nikita Khrushchev. The Communist Party secretary and, as Ike had discovered at Geneva, the true Kremlin boss, had been attending a Fourth of July reception at Spaso House, the American embassy in Moscow. Egocentric and sensitive to slights, Khrushchev told his son Sergei that the Americans had intentionally humiliated him. (In truth, Bissell, in his cone of supersecrecy, had not known about Khrushchev's visit to the embassy.)

Eisenhower was upset to learn only after the fact that Soviet radar had tracked the U-2. "I don't like a thing about it," he exclaimed to Andy Goodpaster on July 10, when the Soviet protest was received at the White House. On July 19, Ike bluntly told Dulles that he felt he had been misled by the CIA and said that he had "lost enthusiasm" for the U-2 program. He suspended missions for an indefinite period, and said he would need to personally approve any future flight. The president was mindful, Goodpaster told both Dulles and Bissell, of how the United States would have reacted "if this had been done to us."[9]

Sometime in July (it's not clear when; U-2 briefings were not recorded on the presidential calendar), Bissell brought Eisenhower the blown-up intelligence photographs on large poster boards. The U-2 had flown over Soviet air bases without finding more than a handful of Bisons, the Russians' new long-range jet bombers and the source of great anxiety in the American intelligence community. The air force had estimated that the Soviets already owned at least a hundred Bisons. The president's skepticism had been confirmed by just five days of aerial reconnaissance. The Bomber Gap was a myth.

The president's eyes were unusually expressive, noted speechwriter Emmet Hughes, "icy with anger, warm with satisfaction, sharp with concern." Years later, when Dino Brugioni, the CIA's photo interpreter, was writing his memoir, he borrowed Hughes's phrasing. When Ike heard about the Soviets' ability to track the U-2, his eyes were "sharp with concern," wrote Brugioni, who was present at the briefings. When the president learned that there was no gap— and that he would not be railroaded into busting the budget to buy hundreds more B-52s—"his eyes were warm with satisfaction."[10]

Barred from flying over Russia, the U-2 proved useful for spying on friends. In early October, the CIA reported something odd. A U-2 flight over Israel had spotted a surprisingly large number of French Mystère fighter jets at Israeli airfields—sixty in all, far more than the dozen or so that CIA analysts expected to find there.[11] The finding should have raised more suspicions than it did, and by the time the reason became clear, events had already spun out of control.

The Middle East was roiling in the fall of 1956. Egyptian strongman Gamal Abdel Nasser had seized the Suez Canal, which had been controlled since its opening in 1869 by Egypt's former colonial rulers,

Britain and France, which had financed and over-seen the canal's construction. The reaction in both countries to the seizure was outrage. More than two-thirds of Europe's oil flowed through the canal. Nasser thus had the power, if he wished, to turn off the heat and lights of the Continent. With the govern-ments of Britain and France threatening Egypt with military intervention, the international crisis had wound up in the United Nations, where the United States was anxious to find a peaceful settlement.

On October 12, President Eisenhower appeared on a television show called *The People Ask the President,* one of the vehicles Ike was using to avoid the rigors of the campaign trail while still reaching large audiences. "I have got the best announcement that I think I could possibly make to America tonight," a benignly smiling Ike told viewers. He reported that at the UN, Britain, France, and Egypt had agreed on a set of negotiating principles to resolve their dif-ferences. "It looks to me like here is a very great cri-sis behind us," he said, adding that he had spoken to Secretary of State Dulles, who had joined him in a "very great prayer of thanksgiving."[12]

In fact, the Americans had been deceived by their allies. At almost the same moment Ike was praising the peacemakers at the UN, the governments of Brit-ain and France were secretly plotting with Israel to attack Egypt and take back the canal. The United

States may have emerged from the world war as the world's great superpower, but the old empires wished to show they could protect their interests, by force if necessary. The Suez Crisis of 1956 would rank as one of the great blunders of history, and it sparked the first direct threat of nuclear war between the Soviet Union and the West.

The mess was partly of America's making. After General Nasser and his fellow Arab nationalists overthrew the corrupt regime of King Farouk in 1952, the Americans tried to buy his favor. The CIA—in the person of Kermit Roosevelt, mastermind of the 1953 Iranian coup—funneled millions in payments to Nasser, who used some of the money to build a minaret on the Nile jokingly known to CIA officials as *el wa'ef rusfel,* Roosevelt's erection.[13] Nasser, alas, did not stay bought. He began to drift toward the Soviet orbit, purchasing Communist bloc weapons with shipments of cotton. The United States had offered to help Nasser build an enormous hydroelectric project, the Aswan Dam, but to punish Nasser for his perfidy, John Foster Dulles cut off its funding in June 1956. In a rage, Nasser responded in July by nationalizing the Suez Canal Company, which sparked the crisis.

Ike was ill with his intestinal attack when all this happened. In two memoranda that John Eisenhower found when he was drafting his father's memoirs a decade later, Ike questioned Foster Dulles's handling of Aswan and the secretary responded with a torrent of defense and denial.[14] Years later, in an oral history, Foster's brother Allen was more honest about his own performance as chief intelligence officer. "I don't think I was very good on the Suez thing," the younger Dulles recalled. "I didn't think they were going to move in on the Suez Canal at that time."[15]

As the British and French schemed with Israel to stage a provocation to take back the canal, the CIA was clueless. The National Intelligence Estimate, the intelligence community's formal oracle, blithely predicted that hostilities were "highly unlikely." At the State Department, Foster Dulles, at least, was jumpy. On October 18, he called his brother at the CIA to complain that the British and French "are deliberately keeping us in the dark."[16]

The CIA was distracted by another crisis. In Eastern Europe, the Soviet satellites were astir with riots and talk of freedom. In Poland and especially Hungary, people were agog over the leak of a sensational secret speech by Nikita Khrushchev, denouncing the crimes of Stalin and promising—or appearing to promise—a looser grip on the Eastern Bloc states. In Budapest, cheering, chanting students filled the streets. Fearing a revolution, on October 24 the Kremlin sent troops to the Hungarian capital to restore order. This further inflamed the situation. Just as popular resentment against colonialism was fueling the Arab nationalism of Nasser, hatred of Soviet rule was boiling up among Hungarian citizens, who were suddenly "freedom fighters."

From central Europe to the Middle East, events were spinning and colliding in a "perfect storm," as historian David Nichols put it in his history of the crisis.[17] Eisenhower, who had just turned sixty-six, rose to the challenge, even as his body failed him in familiar ways: he needed a sleeping pill, Seconal, some nights. Already suffering from a persistent respiratory infection and an irregular heartbeat, he was racked with abdominal cramps. On October 25, he developed a case of diarrhea that would last the better part of a month, during some of the most intense days of his presidency.[18]

At the National Security Council meeting on the morning of Friday, October 26, CIA director Dulles reported that street fighting had broken out in Budapest. Hungarian students were throwing Molotov cocktails at Russian tanks. Dulles, who had a flair for the dramatic, said he was reading a cable from a CIA officer who had been lying on the floor of the US embassy in Budapest to dodge the bullets. Dulles predicted that the crisis would drive Khrushchev from power. (Khrushchev lasted in office seven more years, three more than Dulles.) Remembering Hitler, Eisenhower reminded the NSC that dictators could be even more dangerous when cornered. Would the Kremlin "be tempted to resort to extreme measures, even to start a world war?" the president wondered aloud.[19]

As the president was worrying his advisers, a few yards away his press secretary was chiding the media. Through one of his many friends in the press corps, Jim Hagerty had obtained an advance copy of Drew Pearson's syndicated "Washington Merry Go-Round" column, scheduled to be published in hundreds of newspapers the next day. Pearson reported that a couple of days earlier, riding in a motorcade through Minneapolis on a western campaign swing, Ike had said to his advisers, "I can't take any more of this. Let's get out of here." The president, according to the muckraking columnist, had spent the next twenty-four hours holed up in a hotel room. "I am trying not to get mad," Hagerty told the assembled scribes in the press room, "but I think this is about as worse a job of reporting as I ever saw." With election day less than two weeks away, Hagerty wanted to keep the health issue under wraps. The press secretary artfully contrived to confuse the reporters with a jumble of dates and times, but in fact Pearson had gotten the story mostly right: Ike had gone to ground for twenty-four hours. He was "quite exhausted," according to Howard Snyder's notes. "The president was emotionally upset because of exhaustion of these three days and the prospect of requirements for days to come," Snyder recorded in his log. The president's pulse, he found, was "100 and irregular."[20]

By Sunday, October 28, it was clear that Israel was mobilizing its forces for some kind of military action, but the Dulles brothers, fed disinformation by Israeli intelligence, were convinced that Israel's target was Jordan. That afternoon, Emmet Hughes found Ike in the Oval Office, stewing. "The whole Middle Eastern scene obviously leaves him dismayed, baffled, and fearful of great stupidity about to assert itself," Hughes wrote in his diary. He quoted Eisenhower as saying, "I just can't figure out what the Israeli[s] think they're up to." After complaining about the British and French as well, the president broke off and—"with a not very cheerful smile"—headed out the terrace door back to the Residence. He sighed "a bit heavily," wrote Hughes, and said, "I better get out of here or—despite all those doctors—these things will have my blood pressure up to 490."[21]

The next morning, hoping to make inroads in the Democrats' "Solid South," the president headed off on a quick campaign tour of Florida, Georgia, and Virginia. He was boarding a plane in Jacksonville shortly after 3:00 p.m. when he got the news: Israel had invaded Egypt. Soldiers and tanks were rolling across the Sinai. By 7:10 p.m., Ike was back in the White House, angrily ordering John Foster Dulles to send a message to the Israelis: "Foster, you tell 'em, God-damn-it, that we're going to apply sanctions, that we're going to the United Nations, we're going to do everything there is so we can stop this thing!" Israeli forces had already driven seventy-five miles into Egypt and were within twenty-five miles of the Suez Canal. Misled, shocked, and (though he did not know it yet) gravely ill, Dulles looked like a "broken man," recalled a State Department official.[22] According to John Eisenhower, Ike seriously considered using force to stop Israel. "Won't you lose the election?" asked John, who was thinking about Jewish voters. Ike couldn't resist the comeback: "I might pick up a couple of southern states."[23] And if America did not intervene on the side of Egypt, he feared, then Russia would.

The next morning, Eisenhower looked "drawn, eyes heavy with fatigue, worry, or both," recalled Emmet Hughes. Throughout the day, as cables flew back and forth across the Atlantic, it slowly dawned on the president's men: America had been double-crossed. The British delivered an "ultimatum" to both Egypt and Israel to cease fighting and cede control of the canal to an Anglo-French force, so that maritime traffic would not be disrupted. It was all an elaborate ruse, a staged provocation giving Britain and France a pretext to step in and claim what they regarded as their own. Eisenhower still did not know the precise details of the plot or how it had been secretly hatched, but as his anger rose, so did his resolve. If Britain and France were counting on their long bonds of friendship with the United States, they would be disappointed. "I've just never seen great powers make such a mess and botch of things," Eisenhower fumed. "Of course, there's just nobody, in a war, I'd rather have fighting alongside me than the British.... But—this thing! My God."[24] Meanwhile, he was beginning to do a little scheming of his own. He knew that Britain and France would soon run short of oil if, as seemed entirely likely, Egypt sabotaged the canal rather than give it back.

At 4:25 p.m., Eisenhower met with Arthur Flemming, director of defense mobilization and the official who handled strategic issues like oil supplies. Eisenhower told Flemming he was "extremely angry" at the British and French, who were presenting the United States "with a fait accompli, then expecting us to foot the bill." As Eisenhower explained the situation, the British and French "would be needing oil from Venezuela, and around the Cape, and before long they would be short of dollars to finance these operations and would be calling for help." At that point, London and Paris would be in for a rude surprise: Eisenhower instructed Flemming to resist any entreaties from the allies for help. "You'll be under pressure by some of your colleagues in the capital to move," the president told Flemming. "Don't pay any attention to them until you hear from me." Flemming realized that he was getting a direct order from his commander in chief. "Those who began this operation," the president told him, "should be left to work out their own oil problems—to boil in their own oil."[25]

The next morning, Tuesday, October 30, the *New York Times* reported "the largest naval concentration seen in the Mediterranean since World War II." The navies of Britain and France were slowly steaming toward the Egyptian shore. After sleeping fitfully the night before, Eisenhower was feeling low about the rift in the Anglo-American "special relationship" that he had done so much to strengthen as Supreme Allied Commander in World War II. "I am about to lose my British citizenship," he said at a meeting with the Senate Republican leadership that morning. Playing to Asia Firster William Knowland, Ike sighed, "I have done my best. I think it is the biggest error of our time outside losing China. I am afraid of what will happen."[26]

The mood in the White House lightened with some unexpectedly good news from Hungary later that morning. The American legation in Budapest was reporting that Soviet troops were withdrawing from the city. In Moscow, the Communist Party's house organ, *Pravda,* oozed conciliation: the Kremlin vowed not to interfere with the "internal affairs" of its Eastern Bloc satellites and apologetically observed that troops should be stationed in other socialist countries "only with the consent" of the host state.

Allen Dulles was thrilled. "This utterance is one of the most significant to come out of the Soviet Union since the end of World War II," said the CIA director at a White House meeting. Could this be the turning point in the march of Communism, the crack in the Iron Curtain? Eisenhower was more guarded: "Yes," he replied to Dulles, "if it is honest."[27]

The CIA director had no real way of knowing. The Agency had no effective spies inside the Kremlin, or much, if any, useful intelligence out of Hungary. A secret in-house CIA history later found that the Agency's clandestine service was in a state of "willful blindness" during the Hungarian Revolution. "At no time," the report concluded, "did we have anything that could or should have been mistaken for an intelligence operation."[28]

The Agency was better served by its new U-2 spy plane. CIA photo interpreters had been picking up signs of an Anglo-French buildup in the Mediterranean, yet Allen Dulles had not heeded the warning signs. Now, on October 31, a U-2 pilot passed over

the Cairo airfield just as British bombers were beginning to attack; swinging around and flying over the
field twenty minutes later, the spy plane photographed
rows of burning aircraft. Shown the briefing boards
at the White House, the president recalled his wartime reliance on aerial reconnaissance. ("Twenty-
minute reconnaissance!" he exclaimed. "Now that is
something to shoot for.")[29] Meanwhile, Nasser was
sinking old Egyptian ships in the canal—thirty-two
in all—and blaming the British for the impassable
wreckage.

The White House was tense and chaotic as afternoon bled into evening. The president was scheduled to address the nation at 7:00 p.m., but at about
3:15, Secretary of State Dulles's first draft of the
speech was deemed useless by the president. The
secretary, exhausted, was stricken with stomach pain
and could barely stand. As Emmet Hughes and other
aides struggled to craft something that made sense
of the surprising and confusing crisis, Ike went outside to hit golf balls. At four minutes before 7:00
p.m., Hughes handed Eisenhower the last page as
the president sat at his desk in front of the TV cameras. Eisenhower joked, "Boy, this is taking it right
off the stove, isn't it?" Under the glaring lights, the
president seemed surprisingly calm to Hughes. Eisenhower's manner was "grave," the *New York Times*
observed, but he seemed measured and reassuring.

"There will be no United States involvement in these present hostilities," he promised the public.[30]

In the Mediterranean, the Anglo-French invasion force was gathering off the Egyptian coast. The American Sixth Fleet shadowed the defiant allies. At the White House ("another day of great crises," wrote Ann Whitman in her diary), Secretary of State Dulles asked Chief of Naval Operations Arleigh Burke if the Sixth Fleet could somehow obstruct the troop landings. "Mr. Secretary, there is only one way to stop them. But we will blast the hell out of them," said the hard-charging World War II hero and destroyer commander known as "31-Knot Burke."[31]

Eisenhower was looking for subtler tools. He knew that America, if it was to be true to its anticolonialist principles, could not stand by and allow the British and French to attack Egypt. Eisenhower continued to worry about Soviet intervention; here was the Kremlin's chance to play savior in the Arab world and gain a foothold in the oil-rich region. At another in a series of emergency meetings at the White House, the president asked Arthur Radford whether the Russians could have "slipped" the Egyptians some atomic bombs. The Joint Chiefs chairman was doubtful, but there was no way of being sure. The Americans needed to find a way to make the British back off.

Britain did have an Achilles heel. It had never fully recovered from World War II, and London's fragile finances provided the United States with a way, as Eisenhower said to Foster Dulles, "to do a few things quietly" — to let Britain and France, as Ike had put it to Arthur Flemming, "boil in their own oil." The first step was to let Britain know that the United States would not come to the rescue when British oil supplies ran low. This was done without fanfare. The Eisenhower administration simply canceled the weekly meeting of an obscure group, the Middle East Emergency Oil Committee, and several other meetings necessary to get the oil flowing. Oil importers, expecting news on the availability of tankers, were told to take a "wait and see" approach. The press barely noticed this low-key but critical squeeze play (the *New York Times* put the story on page 22).[32]

Publicly, the president took the high road, declaring in a speech to eighteen thousand GOP partisans cramming the Philadelphia Convention Hall that the United States "cannot and we will not condone armed aggression no matter who the attacker, and no matter who the victim. We cannot — in the world, any more than in our own nation subscribe to one law for the weak, another law for the strong; one law for those opposing us, another for those allied with us. There can be only one law — or there will be no peace." The speech over, Eisenhower was done in. He rarely had more than one drink in the evening, but as he headed back to Washington that night he had two Scotches before dinner and three afterward.[33]

Back in the White House, he found time to dictate letters to his closest friends, Swede Hazlett and Al Gruenther. He told both men that he was having trouble sleeping. "I seem to go to bed later and wake up earlier," he wrote Gruenther. "Life gets more difficult. I could really use a good bridge game." He fantasized, as he often did, about retirement—going shooting and fishing, raising his cattle, playing bridge and golf and "doing it with abandon and no sense of responsibility whatsoever." If he lost the election, now just four days away, he wrote Gruenther, "you can be sorry for anyone you want in this world *except me*."[34]

15

Subtle and Brutal

A T TIMES OF crisis, Eisenhower willed himself to relax. He had long since determined that overwork was counterproductive and that his shaky physical health demanded physical and mental diversion. So, on the weekend of November 3–4, in the middle of two violent crises and an election, he played cards.

Thanks to private and corporate airplanes, his gang could assemble quickly for a game of bridge at the White House. Ann Whitman's call went out on Friday, November 2, and by Saturday afternoon, Bill Robinson, Pete Jones, George Allen, and Slats Slater were watching the Navy–Notre Dame football game on TV with the president as White House stewards set up the bridge table. The card game began. The chaos of Hungary and Suez echoed only faintly through the high-ceilinged West Hall on the second floor of the Residence, where the table of prosperous-looking, middle-aged men intently stared at their cards and occasionally baited each other. No news bulletins disturbed them; the only references to the far-off fighting came in the occasional joke as the gang, joined by John Eisenhower, rotated in and out of the bridge game. Slater recorded in his diary that he "ended up the big winner—with much complaint from everyone—when I was particularly annoying I was referred to as Ben-Gurion, who wasn't very popular right now." (Israeli prime minister David Ben-Gurion had concocted the Suez plot with the British and French.)

While Ike was counting cards, Foster Dulles was undergoing an operation for stomach pain that had become unbearable. That afternoon, Eisenhower reported the troubling news that surgeons had removed a large tumor from Dulles's intestines. "What a hell of a time for Dulles to be taken sick," Slater wrote in his diary. Ike's friend reported, overoptimistically, that the doctors "felt they were able to clean it all up and expected a good recovery." Suffering from colon cancer, the secretary of state had eighteen months to live.

Ike played rubber after rubber of bridge as the gang was served meals on trays late into Saturday night and again on Sunday. The men were waited on hand and foot, in the manner to which Ike had become accustomed. "There seems to be an almost endless group of servants always doing something, pressing clothes, bringing water, or announcing telephone calls, or just waiting," observed Slater. Despite the mounting pressures, he wrote, the president seemed "completely composed."[1]

Budapest meanwhile was in a state of upheaval. Soviet concessions had only whetted a demand for more. In the Hungarian capital, more than 300,000 people marched on the government buildings demanding complete withdrawal of Soviet troops and free elections. Workers with acetylene torches sawed off the giant bronze statue of Stalin at the knees. The Hungarian secret police opened fire with machine guns, but still the crowds came.[2] Student revolutionaries grabbed plainclothes security policemen, whose regulation light-colored shoes gave them away, and hanged them from the city's fin-de-siècle lampposts. Newsreels of the gruesome scenes from Budapest were shown in the Kremlin, embarrassing and infuriating the leadership. At his Lenin Hills residence, Khrushchev couldn't sleep. "Budapest," he recalled, "was like a nail in my head."[3]

On Sunday, November 4, the Soviet empire struck back. More than 200,000 Soviet troops and 4,000 Red Army tanks and armored cars rolled across the border to end the dream of revolution. The Soviet reaction caught the CIA by surprise. Just three days before, at a National Security Council meeting on

Thursday, November 1, Allen Dulles had been exclaiming over the "miracle" of Budapest. The apparent withdrawal of Soviet troops had disproved the theory that "a popular revolt can't occur in the face of modern weapons," Dulles had claimed. Briefing the NSC on the situation, Dulles said that 80 percent of the Hungarian army had gone over to the revolutionaries and most Soviet troops were showing "no stomach for shooting down Hungarians."[4] By Monday morning, November 5, Soviet tanks were mowing down citizens by the hundreds. (About 30,000 Hungarians would die, and thousands more were shipped off to the gulag.) The Hungarian "freedom fighters," encouraged by CIA-backed clandestine radio stations to fight tanks with Molotov cocktails, were begging for help.[5] But it was too late. By this point, armed intervention by the West was out of the question. As Eisenhower later noted in his memoirs, landlocked Hungary was "as inaccessible to us as Tibet."[6]

At dawn that same Monday, British and French paratroopers began landing in Egypt. Eager to make a permanent ally of Egypt and pose as the friend of Arab nationalism—and to divert attention from Hungary—the Soviet Union weighed in as Nasser's protector. Moscow sent a message to Britain and France warning that the Middle East conflict could escalate "into a third World War." Boasting of their new "rocket weapons," the Kremlin leaders strongly hinted that the attack of the old colonial powers on Egypt could be matched "by more powerful states possessing all types of weapons of destruction." The message vowed to "crush the aggressor and reestablish peace in [the Middle East] by using force."[7] In Egypt, rumors flew that Soviet troops were on the way to the rescue. With clumsy coyness, the Soviets appeared to be attempting nuclear blackmail.

Here was the risk of small wars leading to a much bigger one. The time for studied neutrality or equivocation was over. Eisenhower was determined to send a series of clear messages to the Kremlin, while quietly but sternly leaning on his World War II allies to abandon their attack on Egypt.

Ann Whitman had noticed that Ike was spending "all the moments he had free" rereading his own World War II memoir, *Crusade in Europe*. Eisenhower had always tried to plumb the psychological state of his enemies, and the president clearly had Hitler's last days in mind when he met with top advisers at 5 p.m. The book seemed to put him in a good mood, and his manner was bluff and confident.[8] "Listen, those boys," he said of the Kremlin, "they're furious and they're scared. And just as with Hitler, that's the most dangerous state of mind they could be in. We better be damn sure that every intelligence point and every spot in our armed forces is absolutely right on their toes."

Eisenhower was not going to be intimidated. "You know," he said ("tautly," according to Emmet Hughes), "we may be dealing here with the opening gambit of an ultimatum, and we have to be positive about what we say. If those fellows start something, I'll have to hit 'em—with *everything* in the bucket if necessary." Eisenhower emphasized that *"everything."*[9] The White House released a strong statement that warned the Soviet Union to stay out of the Middle East. The Sixth Fleet was put on war alert; its ships began to mingle with the British and French fleets so "an attack on one would be an attack on all."[10] Eisenhower was so wound up, so intent on showing his resolve, that he told Howard Snyder that "if he were a dictator, he would tell Russia if they moved a finger, he would drop our entire stock of atomic weapons upon them," according to Snyder's medical diary.

Snyder was a witness to all this because beneath his iron mask, Ike was worried about his health. That afternoon, he had his pulse and blood pressure taken seven times, more than on any other day of his presidency. His heart was skipping as many as eight times per minute and his pulse was revved up to ninety beats a minute. That night he could not sleep, and he called on his indefatigable physician to feel the abdominal scar from his intestinal operation. It was red and distended; Ike feared that it would need lancing to ease an infection. Snyder gave Eisenhower a pill, a mood stabilizer, along with a "tall glass of Scotch and water."[11]

On election day, Tuesday, November 6, the president was determined to appear ready for anything. At 8:37 a.m., he and his men gathered to hear the latest intelligence report. According to CIA director Dulles, the Soviets had told the Egyptians that they would "do something" in the Middle East. But what, exactly? The president's men speculated that the Soviets might try sending fighter planes into Egypt. Eisenhower ordered Dulles to send "high altitude reconnaissance flights" (meaning the U-2) over Syria to look for Soviet planes and pilots. "Our people should be alert in trying to determine Soviet intentions," Eisenhower instructed. "If the Soviets should attack Britain and France directly, we would of course be in a major war."[12] Congressional approval would not be necessary, he added (the United States was bound by the NATO treaty to fight). Eisenhower recognized that if the Soviets were sending planes into the region, the British and French would have reason to destroy them. "General war" seemed closer than at any time since the Cold War had begun. There were reports of Soviet submarines near the Anglo-French invasion fleet. To show his advisers that he meant business, the president inquired whether American warships in the Mediterranean were equipped with "atomic anti-submarine weapons."[13]

While it seemed highly unlikely that the Kremlin would unleash its rockets on Paris and London, the Soviets had 500 bombers and 2,000 fighter planes in the Black Sea region. At 10:44 a.m., Ambassador Bohlen sent a cable reporting that the Soviet attitude was becoming "more ominous." The Soviet leaders were looking for "psychological cover" for their brutal repression in Hungary, but "perhaps more importantly" they were positioning themselves for a more active role in the Middle East if the fighting spread.[14]

Ike was on his way to his farm in Gettysburg to vote. White House aides were so worried about the news from the Middle East that they decided to bring him back, though without telling him why.[15] By the time he returned, the jittery mood had calmed a bit. Goodpaster met Ike's helicopter with the reassuring information that the U-2 had spotted no Soviet planes in Syria.

The president was closeted with his advisers, pondering ways of ratcheting up American war preparations to get the Soviets' attention, when at last some good news arrived. The British had declared a ceasefire against Egypt, effective at midnight. With unexpected suddenness, the slide to a greater war had stopped.

At 12:55 p.m., on a newly installed direct phone line between the White House and Number 10 Downing Street, the president and British prime minister Anthony Eden conferred over the dramatic new turn. Eisenhower was firm but gentle. "I can't tell you how pleased we are," Eisenhower began, nudging the British PM toward not just ceasing fire but withdrawing his troops. Over the scratchy transoceanic connection, Eden seemed terse and beaten.[16] He had experienced trench warfare in World War I, and he was now a physical and emotional wreck. Sleeping less than five hours a night, he had become addicted to amphetamines.[17] The opposition Labour Party was staging monster rallies in Trafalgar Square calling for him to resign, and his government faced a vote of no confidence that evening in the House of Commons. "If I survive here tonight," he told Eisenhower, "I will call you tomorrow."

Eden's ministers had been shaken by another behind-the-scenes squeeze play by the Americans. The English pound was weak, and speculators were driving it lower. Eden's chancellor of the exchequer, Harold Macmillan, feared a run on the currency and suspected that the US government was behind it. "How far this was due merely to the desire to avoid loss and how far this followed the lead of the United States Treasury is hard to know," Macmillan later wrote in his memoirs. "But certainly the selling by the Federal Reserve Bank seemed far above what was necessary as a precaution to protect the value of their own holdings." Macmillan said he might not have been "unduly concerned," but Britain had been unexpectedly blocked from getting a repayment of a large loan to the International Monetary Fund. He urgently called Washington and was informed that there would be no return of the IMF loan until Britain agreed to a cease-fire.[18] No documentation of Eisenhower's role in this has ever emerged. As one Eisenhower scholar later observed, the president was presented with the perfect opportunity for coercion: in order for the desired effect to take place, Eisenhower needed only do nothing, and the economic calamities would naturally occur.[19] In his own invisible way, Eisenhower had been playing hardball with his wartime ally. It was thanks to moments like this that Eisenhower earned his reputation among Cold War scholars, in the words of John Lewis Gaddis, as "at once the most subtle and brutal strategist of the nuclear age."[20]

After his call with Eden, Ike took a two-hour nap, followed by a one-hour nap in the early evening, accompanied by some grousing that the Suez Crisis would deprive him of his scheduled postelection vacation at Augusta. "He's as disappointed as a kid who has counted out all the days to Christmas," Ann Whitman told Emmet Hughes.

Eisenhower's chief speechwriter was sitting outside the presidential suite at the Sheraton Park Hotel in Washington shortly before midnight, waiting for Stevenson to concede, when the president slumped down beside him on the hard bench and began "murmuring aloud, as if half to himself, 'Boy, I've got to sit down. Oh, I had my rest this afternoon, but, you know, the thing for me is to take it easy so I *don't* have any trouble. It's funny, you know. *Emotions* are the thing you gotta watch out for. So all the doctors say. The worst is anger. . . . Of course, I haven't had a twinge since the first, but you just gotta be careful.'" Hughes could hear the noise from inside the hotel suite—voices babbling, glasses clinking, the TV droning. Suddenly the president's deputy chief of staff, Jerry Persons, cried out, "I want you to know that the cradle of the Confederacy—Montgomery, Alabama—has just voted for a Republican for the first time in its history!" Cheers and laughter. Ike "thr[ew] back his head to roar appreciatively," wrote Hughes.

The returns piled up: Eisenhower was on track to win at least forty states. Some twelve hours earlier, Ike had told Anthony Eden, "I don't give a damn how the election goes." Now he said to his speechwriter that he wanted to win them all. "There's Michigan and Minnesota still to see," he said. "You know—when [Admiral Horatio] Nelson lay dying, he looked around and asked, 'Are there any of them still left?' And when I get in a battle, I just want to win the whole thing…six or seven [states] we can't help, but I don't want to lose any more. Don't want any of them 'left,' like Nelson. That's the way I feel."

The minutes passed. The landslide mounted. Still, Stevenson did not concede. "What in the name of God is the monkey waiting for?" Ike fussed. "Polishing his prose?" Finally, word arrived that Stevenson was coming on the television. Eisenhower rose and drily told his aides to "receive the surrender." Then he disappeared into a bedroom and came out a few minutes later in a new blue suit to head down to the ballroom to claim victory. He had beaten Stevenson by ten million votes, more than two times his margin in 1952, and carried forty-one of the forty-eight states.[21]

At 8:43 the next morning, Eden called Eisenhower in the family quarters. The British prime minister wanted to fly to Washington to discuss the Soviet threat in the Middle East. Eisenhower at first seemed to welcome the overture—"after all, it is like a family spat," he soothed Eden—but he called Eden back two hours later and told him he'd have to wait. The president laid the rebuff on his advisers: Secretary of State Dulles, weighing in from his hospital bed, had opposed Eden's visit, and Eisenhower was willing to accede.[22]

For the next few days, Ike deftly coaxed the British and French to withdraw their troops. He was chummy with Eden, greeting him on one phone call "with the warmth of one old friend getting together with another after being out of touch with one another for quite a while," wrote Sherman Adams, who recalled, with some amusement, overhearing the conversation. " 'Well, Anthony, how *are* you?' " the president cheerily inquired, "a question which, it seemed to me at the time, would have required a long and involved answer," Adams noted.[23] Meanwhile, Ike signaled the British and French that if they wanted America's help meeting their needs for oil, they must pull their troops out of Egypt. Winter was coming; it would take months to clear the blocked-up canal. London and Paris had no choice but to accept the reality of American hegemony. Physically broken, Eden resigned and was replaced by Macmillan. In Cairo, as the last of the British and French troops departed on Christmas Eve, triumphant crowds cheered as the statue of Ferdinand de Lesseps, the French builder of the canal, was dynamited.

In the fall of 1956, CIA director Allen Dulles had taken a fifty-seven-day, around-the-world trip to review the Agency's far-flung empire of "stations" and to meet with foreign officials, a number of whom were on the CIA payroll. "It was one of the most highly publicized clandestine missions ever made," recalled Ray Cline, a CIA officer who accompanied Dulles. Flying in a VIP-configured cargo DC-6, Dulles passed, like a global pasha, through London and Rome, Athens and Islamabad, Bangkok and Sydney. In the Mediterranean, aboard the 190-foot yacht of Greek shipping magnate Stavros Niarchos, Dulles sighed, "You know, all my life I've wanted a yacht like this. And I know I'll just never have one." In Bangkok, he declined a full-sized sampan, a gift to his wife from the Thai chief of police. "I will not go back to Washington with a gift as big as my plane," he declared. (For years to come, the spurned boat adorned the lawn of the ambassador's residence.)[24]

Dulles was still gently mocked as "the Great White Case Officer," but he didn't seem to mind. Indeed, Dulles seemed to relish his dark celebrity. Soviet propagandists deemed the CIA director the most dangerous man in the world, more dangerous than his brother, the secretary of state. According to *Izvestia*, if Allen Dulles ever succeeded in getting into heaven, he would "be found mining the clouds, shooting up the stars and slaughtering the angels." Dulles gleefully borrowed this quotation to introduce his public lectures and speeches.[25]

Dulles felt comfortable in the Oval Office. "Personally, Eisenhower and I were very close to each other," he later recalled in an oral history.[26] With good reason, Dulles had great faith in his power to coax and charm. He was a master at placating, if not conning, senators and congressmen. He managed to paper over the CIA's intelligence failures during the Hungary and Suez crises, insisting to credulous congressmen that the Agency had been right on top of the Franco-British-Israeli scheme. Before a private session with the Senate Armed Services Committee chairman, Senator Richard Russell of Georgia, Dulles said to an aide, "I'll tell the truth to Dick. I always do." He chuckled; his eyes twinkled. "That is, if Dick wants to know."[27] When he visited the Russell committee or Representative Clarence Cannon's House Appropriations Committee, he brought along an aide, Colonel Lawrence "Red" White, who carried an enormous black briefing book. White recalled:

> Sometimes a congressman or senator would actually ask a question, usually something they had just read in the newspaper. Just as often as not, Senator Russell or Cannon would interrupt, "Now don't tell us about that if we don't need to know." If he actually had to refer to the black book, Dulles would usually make a

big deal about the confidential nature of what
he was about to reveal. He would ask for a
delay while I was sent out of the room. Me!
I'd brought the damned thing into the room
in the first place. I knew everything in that
book. But out I'd go and they ate it up.[28]

Eisenhower liked Dulles and valued his experience and broad range of contacts. He appreciated, as
he had memorably put it to General Doolittle in
October 1954, the "strange kind of genius" required
to run an intelligence agency. "Allen could have
walked into the President's bedroom any time he
wanted," Sherman Adams said.[29] Still, with Beedle
Smith gone (fed up with his role as Ike's "prat boy,"
he had retired in September 1954), Eisenhower
wanted to keep an eye on Dulles and his sometimes
too-merry band of men. At the recommendation of
Doolittle, Eisenhower had created an informal advisory board of "wise men" to quietly oversee the work
of the CIA and report back from time to time. On
December 20, 1956, as Dulles was busily spinning to
reporters that the CIA had performed capably during
the crises just past, the president received a report
from his civilian intelligence advisers that was eye-
opening and should have been alarming. The document was written by David Bruce and Robert Lovett,
charter members of the foreign policy establishment.

Bruce, the courtly Virginian who served as ambassador to a series of important European capitals, and Lovett, a Wall Street investment banker and former high-ranking State and Defense Department official, were biting in their criticism. They wrote that the Agency, which they described as "busy, monied and privileged," had become infatuated with "King making," to the neglect of tedious, uncelebrated intelligence gathering. Bruce and Lovett described the seductive appeal of covert action. "The intrigue is fascinating—considerable self-satisfaction, sometimes with applause, derives from successes—no charge is made for 'failures' ..." The authors asked, with a mix of pleading and exasperation, "Should not someone, somewhere in an authoritative position in our government, on a continuing basis" be calculating "the long-range wisdom of activities" which have led the United States to abandon the international "golden rule"? The report noted that if the covert actions had been "successful to the degree claimed for them," then they were "responsible in great measure for stirring up the turmoil and raising the doubts about us that exist in many countries of the world today." The authors plaintively asked: "Where will we be tomorrow?"[30]

There is no record of Eisenhower's response to this significant warning and complaint. Having long tasted the sour grapes of bureaucratic rivalry, he may have thought that Bruce and Lovett, both former State Department men, were reflecting the view of disgruntled diplomats who had been marginalized or outmaneuvered by the CIA swashbucklers. Except for his occasional explosions, Eisenhower disliked direct personal confrontation, and he sometimes rationalized the shortcomings of problematic subordinates. John Eisenhower regarded his father as overly indulgent of Allen Dulles, too unwilling to meddle with the "Dulles act," as CIA officials described the tight axis between Foster and Allen.[31] President Eisenhower knew from long experience to keep his expectations low when it came to covert action. Most of the operations staged by the CIA's World War II precursor, the Office of Strategic Services, had failed to produce useful results or had backfired.[32] But, like presidents who came before and after him, Eisenhower wanted to have a secret action arm, a capacity to strike quickly and in ways that were, in the jargon of intelligence, "deniable."

Ike's mentor General Fox Conner had advised him to acquire a hatchetman to kill what he called "fool schemes."[33] Eisenhower did set up a secret oversight board, called the 5412 Committee and later the Special Group, to act as a check on CIA covert operations.[34] But Dulles was skillful at playing or evading his overseers, and effectively turned the committee into a rubber stamp. Covert operations, admitted

Andrew Goodpaster to historian Michael Beschloss, "were very weakly controlled." The lax oversight would prove costly.[35]

On February 19, 1957, as Eisenhower began his second term in office, Henry Wallace, FDR's third-term vice president, wrote the president and generously compared him to George Washington, in part because the two shared "a combined military-agricultural background" as well as a "profound faith in God." Eisenhower by no means shrugged off the comparison; rather, in his reply to Wallace, he expanded on it. He disparaged "those who so glibly deprecate [Washington's] intellectual qualities. I think that too many jump at such conclusions merely because they tend to confuse facility of expression with wisdom; a love of the limelight with depth of perception." He was writing about himself. "I've often felt the deep wish that The Good Lord had endowed me with his clarity of vision in big things, his strength of purpose and his genuine greatness of mind and spirit."[36] Like Washington, Eisenhower would need his deep reserves of wisdom and spirit in the final, testing years of service that lay ahead.

PART TWO

Honor

1957–1961

16
Dark Star

The first couple, 1957 (Eisenhower National Historic Site, Gettysburg, Pennsylvania)

AFTER WORLD WAR II, a black newspaper, the *Pittsburgh Courier,* published an article entitled "Ike's Way" that recounted how Dwight Eisenhower as a high school football player had taken a strong stand on civil rights. According to the story, the other players on the Abilene High team refused to play against a team that had a black player. The reporter portrayed Ike standing tall in the locker room, nobly lecturing his teammates on justice and human rights until they were shamed into playing. The story was partly true. Some of the Abilene players refused to line up opposite the black athlete, who played noseguard and center. In response, Ike moved from end, his normal position, to play center for the only time in his life. Ike shook hands with the black player before and after the game. But as he wrote in a private letter correcting the account in the newspaper, "I did *not* make a speech."[1]

Eisenhower has been widely criticized by historians for failing to take the lead on civil rights. He was "no leader at all," according to Stephen Ambrose.[2] But as David Nichols has shown in his revisionist work *A Matter of Justice: Eisenhower and the Beginning of the Civil Rights Revolution,* the conventional interpretation misreads the facts. Eisenhower did advance the cause of civil rights, in ways that seem cautious only in retrospect. But he avoided moralizing, and as usual he operated by indirection. He cared about deeds more than words, though he sometimes overlooked a fundamental truth about his job: in matters of national conscience as well as in moments of national crisis, the president's words do matter.

The most damning story of Eisenhower's attitude toward civil rights comes from Earl Warren, the former governor of California whom Eisenhower nominated as chief justice of the United States in 1953. Warren wrote the court's unanimous opinion in *Brown v. Board of Education,* its 1954 decision ruling that segregation in public schools was unconstitutional. On February 8, 1954, while the court was deciding the Brown case, Warren was invited to one of Eisenhower's stag dinners at the White House. The president sat the chief justice near John W. Davis, the famous New York lawyer who was arguing for the Topeka, Kansas, school board that separate-but-equal schools were permissible under the Constitution. Warren implied that Eisenhower was fostering a little ex parte lobbying, a form of impermissible special pleading with the judge outside the courtroom. "The president went to considerable lengths to tell me what a great man Mr. Davis was," Warren recalled. After dinner, the president took the chief justice's arm and, sounding like a small-town Deep South mayor talking about his constituents, said, "These are not bad people. All they are concerned about is to see that their sweet little girls are not required to sit in school alongside some big overgrown negroes."[3]

Or so Warren told the story. He may have exaggerated; the language seems crude for Eisenhower, and in any case the timing of the dinner seems too late for any serious attempt to sway the court's decision.[4] To be sure, Ike was not free of the sort of racist stereotypes and humor common among his Augusta golf partners. (At a surprise birthday party for Slats Slater attended by Ike, his gang arranged to have a five-year-old black girl step out of a large gift box, put her arms around Slater, and exclaim, "Happy birthday, Papa.")[5] But he did not believe in segregation, and he actively opposed it. One of his first moves as president was to desegregate the nation's capital, which still had whites-only laws in 1953. Mamie desegregated the White House Easter egg roll, and the First Couple publicly refused to attend any segregated movie house in Washington. Harry Truman officially desegregated the armed forces in 1948, but it was President Eisenhower who actually forced the services to integrate their units.

It is perhaps not surprising that Eisenhower was more decisive about integrating the military than society at large. The army was his entire world for almost half a century—a world apart, very unlike a civilian existence. When Ike became president of Columbia University, he needed to buy a car. He had never owned one before. He had to sell off Mamie's nest egg of stocks and bonds to purchase a Chrysler; it was their one real possession after all those years of service.[6] On the other hand, as Ike rose high in the ranks, his material needs, down to the smallest want, were attended to by a retinue of aides and enlisted personnel. Newspaperman Merriman Smith and some of his cronies on the White House beat calculated that Ike had not been inside a regular barbershop or bowling alley, a drugstore or a grocery store, for decades.[7] He rarely experienced or even saw how regular people lived. His old friends were all former servicemen. When he made some new civilian ones in the late 1940s, they were millionaires and captains of industry.[8]

Ike was thus far removed from the social forces bubbling up in midcentury America. His experience with blacks was certainly of an earlier time. The one African American he saw routinely was his valet, John Moaney. He considered himself close friends with Freeman Gosden, who in blackface and on the radio was the voice of Amos on *Amos 'n' Andy,* and his most frequent off-hours companion was George Allen, a proud Mississippian and self-styled son of the Confederacy. His most trusted adviser on domestic affairs, treasury secretary George Humphrey, owned a hunting plantation in Georgia that faithfully replicated the Old South. (Fred Morrow, Ike's only black White House aide, whose vaguely defined title, Administrative Officer for Special Projects, included civil rights, lamented that Humphrey heavily influenced Ike's views on race.)[9]

No wonder Eisenhower did not feel what Justice Oliver Wendell Holmes called "the felt necessities of the time" when it came to interpreting the Constitution, much less "the fierce urgency of now," in the words of Martin Luther King. At a gathering of black leaders, Jackie Robinson, the first black major-league baseball player, heard Ike call for "patience" on civil rights. He wrote Eisenhower that he had "felt like standing up and saying, 'Oh no! Not again.'"[10]

Eisenhower was not aloof from the struggle when it percolated up to his level. He appointed supporters of desegregation to the federal bench, including some courts of appeals judges who played critical roles in striking down separate-but-equal. And he was actively engaged in the landmark civil rights case of his time. Whatever Earl Warren believed about Ike's motives at that White House dinner with John W. Davis in February 1954, Eisenhower had already decided in the fall of 1953 that the federal government would take the side of the black schoolchildren, whose representatives were suing to end separate-but-equal in *Brown v. Board of Education*.[11] He scrutinized the Justice Department briefs on desegregation cases and wrote marginal notations. One of these — that desegregation should be implemented "with all deliberate speed" — even found its way into the court's decision.[12]

As the phrase suggests, Ike was a gradualist who wanted to take measured steps. He did not think it was possible, as he put it, to "change people's hearts merely by laws." He was not wrong about that. But Eisenhower missed a chance to inspire their hearts by using the president's bully pulpit. Witness to malevolent orators from Hitler to Joe McCarthy, he easily equated political rhetoric with demagoguery. When his advisers urged him to repeat a message in a speech, he would bristle or grumble, "I've already said it." It was as if he expected "people listening to his speeches to take notes on a yellow pad," said his son.[13] Typically, out of modesty or because he was looking for cover, he wanted others to play the inspirational role. In a letter in 1956, he urged evangelist Billy Graham to encourage the election of qualified blacks to public office and their admission to university. When Graham widely shared the president's "personal" letter, Ike chided him for breaking a confidence.[14]

In 1957, Eisenhower introduced the first meaningful civil rights act since Reconstruction, a measure to give the Justice Department more power to protect the voting rights of blacks. Some historians, most notably Robert Caro, have given Senate Majority Leader Lyndon Johnson the credit for passing the measure, even though LBJ watered down the bill. At press conferences, Eisenhower did not improve his place in history by sounding vague and dependent on the advice of others. It was an old Eisenhower trick designed to share credit or deflect blame, but it could also make him look weak. He was probably shrewd to operate behind the scenes on civil rights legislation, although his invisible hand was often mistaken for detachment.[15]

Governor Orval Faubus of Arkansas was not the first person to underestimate Eisenhower, but he was one of the more obdurate. In early September 1957, the governor cavalierly defied a federal court order issued by an Eisenhower-appointed judge to desegregate Central High School in Little Rock. Through his attorney general, Herbert Brownell, Eisenhower warned Faubus that he could be held in contempt and that federal troops could be used to enforce the court order. Faubus had the gall to complain to Eisenhower that the FBI was harassing him. He asked the president for his "understanding and cooperation." At the time, Ike was enjoying the salt air on a rolling golf course near the US naval base in Newport, where he had turned a Victorian mansion into a "summer White House" after his heart condition ruled out the Rockies as a vacation place. The president shot back: "The only assurance I can give you is that the Federal Constitution will be upheld by me by every legal means under my command."

Eisenhower brought to civil rights his firm belief

in the doctrine of overwhelming force: avoid fights if you can, but if you can't, go all-out to win.[16] When angry mobs began attacking reporters outside Central High and frightening the first black schoolchildren to enter the school, Eisenhower chose to go beyond deputizing the police or national guard: he sent in the 101st Airborne, the tough but disciplined paratroopers he had seen off on the eve of D-day. With bayonets drawn, the federal troops broke up the mob (which, possibly ignorant of the 101st Airborne's recent history, screamed "Heil Hitler!" at the soldiers) and escorted the brave students to school. Eisenhower may have been a gradualist, but he would not brook defiance of the federal courts. Almost reverently, he regarded the federal judiciary as the guardian against abuse of power. "If the day comes when we can obey the orders of our Courts only when we personally approve of them," he wrote a friend that fall, "the end of the American system, as we know it, will not be far off."[17]

Eisenhower groused to his brother Arthur, "My vacation this year was hardly worth the name."[18] His golf games were constantly interrupted or curtailed, and his self-control was frequently challenged. James Schlesinger, who later served as secretary of defense and CIA director under President Gerald Ford, was teaching at the Naval War College in Newport during the Little Rock crisis. Passing by Eisenhower's summer residence, he recalled seeing Ike near a boat landing, speaking to an aide. Turning bright red with anger, Eisenhower grabbed the man by the lapels and seemed to be about to shake him. Then, suddenly aware that he was being watched by a small crowd that had gathered, the president stopped and, just as if nothing had happened, grinned broadly and gave a little wave.[19]

In early October, back from Newport, Eisenhower escaped to the golf course as much as possible. On Saturday, October 5, playing his fifth eighteen-hole round in seven days, he teed off at the Gettysburg Country Club at 10:22 a.m. and, riding an electric golf cart, raced around the course in two hours and three minutes. "It was a bleak afternoon," the ever-present Snyder wrote in his diary. The next day, Snyder recorded, was too "rainy, bleak" to play golf.[20] The clouds concealed a tiny new star in the heavens.

Like Eisenhower, Nikita Khrushchev felt comfortable around scientists. Awarded an engineering degree from the Stalin Industrial Academy, he was "very creative and curious" about technology, according to his son Sergei.[21] Khrushchev was inordinately proud to be the first to suggest that missiles could be safely launched from silos (the designers worried they would burn up; Khrushchev correctly suggested lining the silos with steel to dissipate the heat). An all-purpose engineer, he also took an interest in building shelter for the masses. In the 1950s, Russia still suffered from a severe postwar housing shortage. At Khrushchev's instigation, a hundred million people were housed in standardized five-story apartment houses stamped out by assembly lines. People were grateful—until the floors sagged, the roofs leaked, and the plumbing gave out. The apartment houses were called *khrushchobi,* which combined Khrushchev's name and the Russian word *trushchobi*, for "slums."

Khrushchev was the ruler of a poor, weak country, and he was fearful the Americans would find out. Russia's muddy collectivized farms were barely producing enough food to feed the people. The Russians would periodically jam radio broadcasts from the West, but Russian musicians began making crude records of American rock 'n' roll songs, dressing in jeans, and calling themselves *bitniki.* (Teenagers bid each other "See ya later, alligator," after the Bill Haley and the Comets lyrics they heard over Voice of America.)[22] Other intrusions from the West were more disturbing to Khrushchev. In March of 1956, the Strategic Air Command's Curtis LeMay launched Operation Home Run, sending squadrons of bombers, their undersides painted white to deflect the heat from a nuclear blast, several hundred miles into Siberia just for practice.[23] Then, beginning in June 1956 and continuing off and on, there were those mysterious high-altitude flights of some kind of American spy plane, still out of range of Soviet air defenses.

Khrushchev's power had been threatened with an attempted coup in June 1957. The party secretary was rescued by Marshal Zhukov, Eisenhower's old World War II comrade, who rallied to Khrushchev, flying loyal members of the party's Central Committee to Moscow on a long-range bomber.[24] As things worked in the Soviet hierarchy, by October Khrushchev had sidelined Zhukov, who was becoming a little too popular, and finally secured his place as solitary ruler of the Soviet Union. But he needed a way to show his people and the world that he was not afraid of the West.

The answer lay on a launching pad in the desert wastes of Kazakhstan. The place had no name and showed up on no map, though it would become known to Western intelligence as Tyuratam. Trees did not grow there. Temperatures in winter plunged to 35 degrees below zero and in summer soared to 135. On buried railroad trestles sat an odd, tulip-shaped set of metal claws. Into them, on October 4, 1957, was hoisted a massive, slightly hourglass-shaped rocket with four giant boosters. It was called the R-7, and it would become the hope and pride of the

Soviet Union as well as the big stick of Nikita Khrushchev.[25]

Kremlin leaders had been given a sneak preview of the rocket twenty months earlier. On February 27, 1956, the Politburo had been driven in their ZIL limousines (modeled after the 1954 Cadillac), to the secret missile laboratory of N11-88, home to the Soviet rocket engineers, in the birch forests of the Baltic. There, the chief designer, Sergei Korolev, a brilliant, angry, profane man with a pomaded pompadour, greeted them. Korolev showed the Politburo members the Soviets' medium-range ballistic missile, the R-5, which was capable of reaching London and Paris. Khrushchev asked how many nuclear-tipped R-5s it would take to destroy England. The confident answer was five. "Terrible," said Khrushchev, delighted. "We have seen the past and present of Soviet rocketry," declared Korolev, leading the delegation to a set of giant doors. "This is the future." The doors of the hangar swung open, and the chief designer dramatically announced, "The R-7."

The rocket inside was five times the size of the R-5. It stood as tall as a Kremlin tower. "I was amazed. I had never seen anything remotely like it, no one had," said Sergei Khrushchev, recounting the scene to journalist Matthew Brzezinski some fifty years later. Khrushchev asked how quickly the R-7 could reach targets in the United States. A half hour, came the reply.

The missile was only a prototype. In the spring and summer of 1957, three real ones were launched from the Kazakhstan desert, only to quickly crash and burn. But on the fourth shot, on August 21, 1957, the rocket sailed three thousand miles, all the way to Russia's Pacific coast. The heat shield failed and the dummy warhead was incinerated, but the age of the ICBM was close at hand.[26]

Khrushchev couldn't resist bragging about the R-7. On August 26, the Soviet news agency TASS reported, papering over the failures:

A few days ago a super-long-range, inter-continental multistage ballistic missile was launched. The tests of the missile were successful; they fully confirmed the correctness of the calculations and the selected design. The flight of the missile took place at a very great, hereto unattained altitude. Covering an enormous distance in a short time, the missile hit the assigned region. The results obtained show that there is a possibility of launching missiles into any region of the terrestrial globe.

The Western press picked up the report, but with curiously little fanfare. With the exception of the

New York Times, which seemed to grasp the millennial significance of the TASS report ("if true," the paper added), the newspapers failed to recognize that Russia had taken a first step into a new era. The American ICBM, the Atlas, was still a year away from a full flight test.[27]

Korolev had planned a more dramatic way of getting the world's attention. In the tip of another R-7, hoisted into its launcher on October 4, sat a 184-pound object known as PS-1, better known to the world as Sputnik (the Russian word for "fellow traveler"). Korolev wanted his satellite to be seen in the night sky over America, so he had its aluminum skin polished to a mirrorlike sheen to better reflect the sun's rays.

The R-7 shuddered off the pad before midnight on Friday, October 4, 1957. Inside a van near the launching pad, operators cupped their headphones while officials clamored for information. "We have the signal," shouted one operator. "We have it." In the crowded van there was hugging, dancing, singing, crying. "This is the music no one has ever heard before," exulted the chief designer. It went *beep-beep-beep.*[28]

"Listen now for the sound that will forever separate the old from the new," intoned NBC, broadcasting Sputnik's beep on Saturday, October 5. "Here in the capital responsible men think and talk of little but the metal spheroid that looms larger in the eye of the mind than the planet it circles around," CBS's Eric Sevareid announced in his somber tones on October 6. America's politicians and pundits were full of gloom: "A great national emergency"..."A grave defeat"... "A technological Pearl Harbor." In the United States Senate, Henry "Scoop" Jackson of Washington declared a "National Week of Shame and Danger." In Texas, Senator Lyndon Johnson swore, "I'll be damned if I sleep by the light of a Red Moon."[29]

The White House tried to play down Sputnik. The satellite was no surprise, announced Jim Hagerty, which was mostly accurate, though he could not spell out how the Americans knew this: the U-2 had photographed the Tyuratam test site in August. Additionally, along the Russian border giant radars, built on an Iranian mountainside for the National Security Agency (so secret that NSA was said to stand for "No Such Agency"), had tracked the failures and lone success of the R-7. Since none of that could be revealed, the only option was to appear nonplussed. There was some truth to the unruffled American stance. Launching a satellite didn't mean much for national defense; Sputnik was but "a neat technical trick," scoffed defense secretary Charles Wilson. And the idea of a "space race" had not caught on, at least not at the White House. America had no interest in getting caught up "in an outer space basketball game," said the sardonic White House chief of staff Sherman Adams. (In his memoirs Adams would later recall, "I was only trying to reflect the President's desire for calm poise but I had to admit on reflection that my observation seemed to be an over-emphasis on de-emphasis.")[30]

Eisenhower was perplexed by the almost instant public hysteria. "I can't understand why the American people have got to be so worked up over this thing. It's certainly not going to drop on their heads," he told Andrew Goodpaster.[31] To the president's way of thinking, Sputnik actually brought some good news. Eisenhower was pleased to note that there had been no international protest against what he saw as a Soviet overflight. This was a relief because, in deepest secrecy, the Americans were developing their own spy satellite. Eisenhower knew that it was only a matter of time before Soviet air defenses could reach the U-2, and he wanted to be ready with a reconnaissance backup. The United States actually had two satellite programs in the works. There was a public one, the Vanguard booster and satellite, being built by the navy to do scientific research. There was also a top-secret option, known only as WS-117L, under development by Lockheed, creators of the U-2.

Its supervisor was the CIA's ambitious and ubiquitous Richard Bissell.[32]

Eisenhower had enjoyed a jocular, amiable relationship with reporters, so he was startled by their hostility at a press conference on Wednesday, October 9. The senior man in the pressroom, UPI's Merriman Smith, had always been friendly, or at least fair-minded, to Ike. But on the subject of Sputnik, Smith curtly demanded, "I ask you, sir, what are you going to do about it?" Scowling, Eisenhower went into his wandering, mildly evasive mode. The Soviet satellite was just "one small ball," he said. It didn't prove that the Russians had an operational ICBM that could hit targets in the United States. After a lot of back-and-forth, an NBC reporter asked, "Mr. President, in light of the great faith which the American people have in your military knowledge and leadership, are you saying at this time that with the Russian satellite whirling about the world, you are not more concerned nor overly concerned about our nation's security?" Eisenhower seemed to stumble, then recovered and gave the direct answer that grabbed the headlines: "Not one iota," he said.[33]

The press pounced. "A crisis in leadership," announced *Time*. "The president must be in some kind of partial retirement," wrote Walter Lippmann, the most influential columnist in the country.[34] Cartoonists suggested that Ike was golfing while the world burned. The governor of Michigan, G. Mennen Williams, mocked the president in light verse:

Oh little Sputnik, flying high
With made-in-Moscow beep,
You tell the world it's a Commie sky,
And Uncle Sam's asleep.

You say on fairway and on rough,
The Kremlin knows it all,
We hope our golfer knows enough
To get us on the ball.[35]

Around the country, odd events began to occur. People reported that their automatic garage doors (a new gimmick of the automated age) were mysteriously opening—set off, somehow, by that *beep beep* signal from Sputnik. At two and three in the morning, small and then ever larger groups would gather on rooftops and in the street, straining to catch a glimpse of the Red Moon. A remarkable 4 percent of Americans claimed to have seen Sputnik in the night sky, although what they probably saw was the hundred-foot-long R-7 rocket casing trailing some six hundred miles behind it—Korolev, ever the clever propagandist, had fitted the casing with reflective prisms.[36]

At first, Khrushchev did not realize what Sputnik had wrought. But as he read newspaper accounts from the West, he was ecstatic. "People all over the world are pointing to the satellite," he exclaimed, according to *Time* magazine. "They are saying the U.S. has been beaten."[37] The Kremlin leader summoned James Reston, the *New York Times* man in Moscow, and gave him an exclusive. "When we announced the successful testing of an intercontinental rocket, some American statesmen didn't believe us," Khrushchev said. Now, he said, only "technologically ignorant people can doubt us." The ICBM used to launch Sputnik was "fully perfected," he boasted, and could strike anywhere in the world. Soon, Soviet factories would be cranking them out "like sausages." These claims were not true, or even close to true, but the Kremlin did have a powerful rocket that could fly across oceans and launch objects into space.[38] Khrushchev asked Korolev for an encore.

Sputnik II, launched on November 4, had a top-this quality. The rocket carried a small dog named Laika. The dog died shortly after launch (the heat shield failed, a fact the Soviets covered up), but the headlines were enormous and panicky. "A real circus performance," John Foster Dulles grumbled to Eisenhower. But the secretary was worried about "the weight of this thing." With reason: the satellite, dog and all, totaled over 1,000 pounds, six times as much as Sputnik weighed, offering convincing evidence that the Soviets could boost warheads — big ones.[39]

Sputnik awakened America from its complacent mid-1950s dream. After a long boom, the economy was starting to turn down, and many Americans were feeling queasy, hungover from their postwar materialistic binge. The Sputniks were "an intercontinental outer-space raspberry to a decade of American pretension that the American way of life was a gilt-edge guarantee of national superiority," said Clare Boothe Luce, whose husband owned *Time* and *Life*. Older voters who had lived through the Depression and two world wars fretted that America had somehow lost its grit and will to sacrifice. Coincidentally, Ford's shiny new car, the Edsel, was introduced that fall and promptly flopped, a symbol in its own way of the demagnetized American compass. "It's time to stop worrying about tail-fins," preached Edward Teller, a father of the H-bomb.[40] At the time, fewer than one high school student in eight studied physics. America, declared *Life,* had the world's best baseball players and TV comics, and in a few years the Russians would have the world's best teachers and scientists.[41] At a conference in Barcelona, Leonid Sedov, Russia's chief space scientist, taunted,

"You Americans have a better standard of living than we have. But the American loves his car, his refrigerator, his house. He does not, as we Russians do, love his country."[42]

Sputnik stirred emotions deeper than mere guilt over materialism. Stephen King, the phenomenally successful author of horror novels, was ten years old in 1957. He was sitting in a movie theater in Stratford, Connecticut, watching a sci-fi thriller called *Earth v. Flying Saucers,* when the theater manager turned on the house lights and came onstage to announce that the Russians had launched a satellite that was orbiting over the United States. Something clicked in King, he later recalled. The line between fantasy terror and real terror had been crossed.[43]

So it seemed to millions of Americans. The rumors that flew after Sputnik—the Russians will soon be firing death rays from the moon!—seem wildly far-fetched now, but they seemed credible enough in the autumn of 1957. The federal government's ongoing attempts to make the atomic bomb a fact of life had by now frightened a generation of schoolchildren, not to mention their parents. One civil defense film showed a little boy riding his bike, and intoned: "Here's Tony on the way to his Cub Scout meeting." Suddenly, a flash. Tony leaps off his bike and hurls himself against a wall, careful to cover his neck so it won't be burned ("like a really bad sunburn"). The moderator exclaims, "Attaboy, Tony! Tony knows it can come at any time."[44] What was intended to reassure merely reinforced the idea that everyone was at risk.

The mood inside the White House was not nearly so hysterical. But it was at times grim. When Neville Shute's best-selling 1957 novel, *On the Beach* (later a movie), spooked people with its vision of slow global annihilation from radioactive fallout after a nuclear war, White House officials debated whether the scenario was realistic. No, they decided; life would probably be eliminated in the Northern Hemisphere, but not entirely in the Southern one.[45]

James Killian, the MIT president who had run Ike's brilliant Technological Capabilities Panel ("my scientists") and now served as the president's chief science adviser, observed that Ike was "startled that the American people were so psychologically vulnerable."[46] Throughout his presidency, Eisenhower had understood that a large majority of the American people trusted him as their protector. Now he was not so certain. His approval ratings were dropping, from nearly 80 percent to under 60 percent. Eisenhower himself seemed a little discomfited. He was never a great wit, and now his jokes fell flat. To a National Security Council meeting he wisecracked, "Any of you fellows want to go to the moon? I don't.

I'm happier right here." The laughter around the table was forced.[47]

Eisenhower wanted to find some way to rally the people, to restore their confidence, and he settled on pushing schoolchildren to study science.[48] His worried aides cast about for a suitable pep talk. On October 22, the president ad-libbed while giving a speech, harking back to his comrades in World War II. "I don't believe that there's a single one of them that ever saw victory won by growing pessimistic and putting your chin on your chest. You have to get it up," said Ike. That, said his advisers, was just what the country needed—"chin up" speeches. The White House scheduled three of them.[49]

For the first, on November 7, Eisenhower showed off the nosecone of a Jupiter-C test rocket that had been successfully shot into space. He soberly warned against "going off in all directions" and spoke of the need to balance "what we must have and what we would like to have." It was a sound, measured speech, and it didn't work. "Public reaction to the president's efforts at national reassurance ranged from biting criticism to lukewarm praise," wrote historian Robert Divine. *Life* credited him only with a "faltering step forward."

Eisenhower stubbornly refused to play his trump card: the U-2 spy plane had found nothing to suggest that Russia was building a great nuclear strike force. In fourteen flights over Russia, the U-2 had discovered very few long-range bombers and had pinpointed the Soviets' lone ICBM launchpad, which was now on Strategic Air Command charts as a target. Secretary Dulles urged Ike to reveal that the U-2 had provided solid evidence that America was not behind in the arms race. Eisenhower "reluctantly" refused.[50] Even though he knew that the Russians were aware of the overflights, he did not want to force a public confrontation. Ike was always sensitive to the mind-set and feelings of his opponents; he did not want to "poke the Bear in his cage," as he once put it to Bobby Cutler.

More than cool calculation was at work. "You can understand that there are many things that I don't dare to allude to publicly," he wrote his friend Swede Hazlett on November 18, "yet some of them would do much to allay the fears of our own people.... While I am often urged to be more assertive, to do a little more desk-pounding, to challenge Russia more specifically and harshly, I do not do these things for the simple reason that I think they are unwise. Possibly I do not always control my temper well, but I do succeed in controlling it in public. And I still believe that a frequent exhibition of a loss of temper is a sure sign of weakness."[51] Eisenhower knew that he could, in the short term, calm the public's fears by taking the easy way out. Patience and privacy were virtues of leadership, vices of politics. There was no choice for Ike: he was the lonely keeper of the nation's secrets.

He was human, though. Eisenhower intensely felt the weight of so much pressure, external and self-imposed. "Since July 25th of 1956, when Nasser announced the nationalization of the Suez, I cannot remember a day that has not brought its major or minor crisis," he wrote Hazlett. Ticking off all the speeches and "endless conferences" ahead, he continued, "The only hope I see for any real letup is some time around next July." Such tiny bouts of self-pity were rare for Eisenhower. He, too, had to be chin up.

Eisenhower was not weak, of course, not in an emotional or spiritual sense. Psychologically, he could handle the pressure. But physically, he could not.

17

The Great Equation

WHEN EISENHOWER WAS feeling down or under stress, he sometimes lashed out at his doctors, the only people he could safely blame. On New Year's Eve 1956, with the Suez and Hungary crises still smoldering, Howard Snyder had found his patient "in an evil state of mind." The president, his doctor recorded at the time, also had high blood pressure and a "quite irregular" pulse. "These experts," Ike grumbled, referring to his various heart specialists, "don't know anything about my heart. It isn't as good as they say."[1] Eleven months later, exhausted and frustrated by his inability to calm public anxiety about Sputnik, Eisenhower blew up at Snyder for letting him play too much golf. "The president again, as he has on a number of occasions in the past, accused the doctors of letting him in for something he was not physically competent to handle," Snyder wrote in his diary on November 19.[2] (It is hard to imagine that Eisenhower would have heeded a command to stop golfing—and easier to understand why Snyder would have been reluctant to offer one.) His outburst to Snyder came only a day after Ike had written Swede Hazlett to vent about the unrelenting pressures he faced, so physical overexertion was not likely his only, or even real, complaint. The unrelenting mental strain took a physical toll. "No man on earth knows what this job is all about," Ike had uncharacteristically whined to Field Marshal Montgomery during Monty's December 1954 trip to America. "It's pound, pound, pound. Not only is your intellectual capacity taxed to the utmost, but your physical stamina."[3]

"Doc" Snyder was not a submissive caregiver. "My rejoinder was that I felt he 'pushed' himself a little too hard at these quasi-vacation times; that especially here at Augusta indulged in too much and too vigorous golf practice...," Snyder wrote. Of course, Ike's real problem was not excessive golf or faulty medical advice. It was the essential conundrum Eisenhower faced as the great peacemaker, trying to appear calm when the world, or his psyche, was not. Eisenhower has been so often described as a political moderate that it is easy to overlook his intense effort at personal and emotional moderation. And yet without a healthy way to vent his feelings, he was faced with a choice between stretching ever tauter as a result of the building pressure and intermittently blowing up. That night in his diary, Snyder recorded the president's frustrations: "He stated that the doctors said he would be perfectly all right if he didn't allow tensions to affect his health, and then he commented, 'How in the hell can anyone carry the load of the Presidency without permitting the tensions to affect his physical self?' "[4]

Six days later, when Ann Whitman looked out her window and saw the president walk by on his way from the Residence to the Oval Office, she noticed something odd. He appeared to be listing a little to one side. She went into his office and found him holding a letter from a friend, Pete Jones, the head of the Cities Service Oil Company. The president tried to speak to her but only jumbled words came out. She went out to the outer office and instructed the secretaries to find Andy Goodpaster and seal off the office. When Goodpaster appeared, she slipped him a note that read, "Something terrible has happened." Alerted by the secretaries, Snyder appeared and found the president angry and upset. Ike dropped his reading glasses and couldn't find them. Snyder could see that Eisenhower was "aphasic," meaning that he was having trouble using or understanding language. This time, unlike the long night in Denver in September 1955, Snyder instantly and correctly diagnosed his patient: the president was having a stroke.[5]

Gently, slowly, Snyder and Goodpaster coaxed the president upstairs and into bed in his dressing room, where he fell asleep. An hour or so later, chief of staff Sherman Adams, joined by Snyder and John Eisenhower, were meeting with the First Lady in her high-ceilinged bedroom when the president walked in. "What are you doing up, Ike?" gasped Mamie, who was "deeply disturbed," according to Adams. The president was wearing his brown checked bathrobe and smiling as if nothing had happened. Mamie, Adams, and Snyder looked up in astonishment. "I suppose you are dis—" the president began. He stopped, unable to find the word. "...talking about the dinner tonight," he finally said, visibly laboring. The president was supposed to be hosting a state dinner for King Mohammed V of Morocco. Eisenhower became agitated. "There is nothing the matter with me! I am perfectly all right," he bellowed. The president struggled to speak some more and spluttered instead. Mamie looked horrified. "We can't let him go down there in this condition," she said.

Snyder and Adams tried to reassure Eisenhower that Vice President Nixon and the First Lady could fill in for him at the dinner. "Flushed and upset," recalled Adams, "he shook his head abruptly and said, 'If I cannot attend to my duties, I am simply going to give up this job. Now that is all there is to it.'" (In his medical diary, Snyder recorded the president as saying, "If I can't go to that dinner, this spells the end of it for me. We'll be farmers from this time on.") Vexed, spent, the president turned around and shuffled off in his slippers. In his memoirs, he described his retreat more jauntily: "It soon appeared to me that a retirement in good order was called for; I went back to bed."[6]

The First Lady was shaken but duty bound, and so she put on her gown and soldiered on. "It was a ghostly white Mamie Eisenhower who descended the elevator with the Vice President and Mrs. Nixon that night," recorded the White House chief usher, J. B. West. "She sat in her throne-like chair at the head of the E-shaped banquet table, visibly nervous, obviously wishing to be by her husband's side."[7]

John Eisenhower spent the night of November 25, 1957, by the bed of his father, whom he called "the Boss." When Ike awoke, he looked around the dimly lit bedroom and pointed to a favorite painting, a watercolor by Turner. Trying to name the painting, Ike could only burble. "The more he tried, the more frustrated he became," recalled John. "He thrashed on the double bed, beating the bedclothes with his fists. By this time Mother and Doc Snyder had joined us and each was shouting any word that came to mind. Finally, Mother hit upon the official title of the picture, 'The Smugglers.' When she blurted it out, Dad shook his finger at her in a gesture demanding a repeat. But even having heard the word, he still couldn't say it."[8]

In the lobby of the West Wing, reporters had been baying for information. For the third time in two years, the president was incapacitated. The fear of another heart attack permeated the White House, and, though the country had rallied to Ike after his two prior illnesses, a third might be too much. The night before, a deputy press aide (Hagerty was in Europe) became flustered and garbled the diagnosis, so that one wire service reported that the president had suffered "a heart attack of the brain." Fortunately, Eisenhower's heart was unaffected; he had suffered a spasm in one of the capillaries running through the cerebral lobe that handles speech. The stroke was mild.

Eisenhower was determined that he would not be bedridden. Later that day he sat in his tiny studio near the second-floor elevator, working on a portrait of Princess Margaret (the British royal family had just visited; Ike enjoyed a warm, avuncular relationship with the young Queen Elizabeth). He insisted that he would be well enough to go to a NATO conference in Germany less than three weeks away.[9] On Saturday, November 30, Ike read an article in the *New York Times* suggesting that Nixon was taking over. He turned to Snyder and said, "Howard, there can't be two Presidents of the United States. I think I'll go down to the Cabinet meeting Monday morning."

Ann Whitman had been desperately worried about her beloved "Boss." On November 22, as the post-Sputnik pressure to spend wildly on the military continued to build, she had written in her diary, "Just about the worst day ever—two very tough meetings, full of doom and gloom." She was enormously reassured when Ike put on one of his shows of indomitable good cheer on his first day back to work. In her diary on December 2, she wrote, "He seemed chipper and entirely sure of himself when he left to go over to the house. He set his hat at a jaunty angle, said he thought the business of an atomic cruiser was 'nuts,' and walked firmly home, not nearly, seemingly, as tired as he had every right to be."[10]

Eisenhower suffered from bad headaches for weeks, but the stroke caused no serious damage or impairment. He would sometimes stumble over a word, a vestige of his aphasia ("I might say 'desk,' when I mean 'chair,'" he wrote Swede Hazlett), but for the most part, he regarded the disability as a minor irritant.[11] By December 3, Snyder was back to squabbling with Ike over his dietary restrictions, writing in his diary, "I cancelled the President's dinner menu of spare ribs and sauerkraut and substituted broiled steak, string beans, and boiled potatoes. This aggravated the President." Normalcy had returned.[12]

The next day, December 4, the White House opened a telephone line to the Long Range Proving Ground at Patrick Air Force Base, a sandy, swampy patch of Florida seashore that would become better known as Cape Canaveral. A countdown was scheduled to begin early that morning.

Well before Sputnik, America had become fascinated by outer space. General Motors cars were beginning to resemble fantastic rocket ships, with high fins and sleek, swept-wing designs. Drive-in movie theaters illuminated their screens with interplanetary adventures, and pulp magazines and comic books devoted page after page to worlds beyond our own. In California, at the new Disneyland theme park, tourists were flocking to Tomorrowland, which imagined space travel through the universe. On March 9, 1955, Walt Disney himself had appeared on television to intone, as his image faded into the Milky Way, "One of man's oldest dreams has been the desire to travel in space. Until recently, this seemed to be an impossibility. But new discoveries have brought us to the threshold of a new frontier."

More than forty million people watched the Disney show, called "Man in Space." The narrator, Wernher von Braun, was an instant star — wavy-haired, broad-shouldered, upbeat, with an odd Teutonic

Texas twang to his voice. What the audience didn't know was that von Braun had polished his showmanship in Nazi Germany. In 1943, the physicist had used charts, models, and film to pitch Adolf Hitler on the virtues of rocketry. The result was the V-2, built with slave labor, a missile that terrorized London in World War II. When the war ended von Braun was working on a rocket to hit New York and Washington.[13]

Welcomed to the United States along with a number of other German rocket scientists, von Braun built an improved version of the V-2 known as the Redstone rocket for the army. With some added boosters, von Braun ventured, the new rocket could put a satellite in orbit. He even began work on Project Orbiter, but politics and secrecy intervened. Scientists from twenty-two countries were observing the International Geophysical Year in 1957–58 — good cover, it seemed, for launching a rocket that could put a satellite in space, while not disclosing that the orbiter the United States really cared about was Lockheed's WS-117L spy satellite. The job of building an IGY rocket was given to a team of civilian and navy scientists. The other two services had further divided the missile pie: the air force — strategic bombing — was developing a long-range ICBM, and the army — artillery — was restricted to shorter-range missile duty. The Eisenhower administration may also have

Von Braun (Library of Congress, Washington, DC)

been reluctant to feature von Braun because of his Nazi past.

But the navy Vanguard rocket program was beset by technical glitches and delays.[14] With the launches of Sputniks I and II, the pressure was on the navy to put its satellite into orbit. Mockingly nicknamed "the grapefruit" by Khrushchev, it was only 2.9 pounds, far smaller than the Soviet's 1,000-pound flying dog kennel. The Eisenhower administration, eager for a success, hyped the launch, scheduled for December 4. Tourists filled motels called the Sea Missile, the

Satellite, and the Vanguard, hastily thrown up around the mosquito-infested dunes of Cape Canaveral. The launch was postponed to December 6, then delayed. Finally, just before noon, the engines roared to life and the rocket rose about four feet, then exploded in a gush of flame. Later, the small satellite could be seen lying in the twisted, smoking metal.[15]

The foreign press had a field day. Headlines around the world hooted over Flopnik, Kaputnik, Goofnik, Oopsnik, and Dudnik. On the floor of the Senate, Lyndon Johnson wailed, "How long, how long, oh God, how long will it take us to catch up?" In the Cabinet Room at the White House, John Foster Dulles muttered that America had become a "laughingstock to the free world."[16] Eisenhower was not particularly disturbed, however. He had lost a hand but not the pot, and he knew enough about his own cards and Russia's to feel confident about the long run. "Was a bit downcast yesterday afternoon because of our failure in the attempt to launch a satellite," wrote Dr. Snyder in his log the next day, December 7. "Doesn't seem to be taking the matter too seriously this morning."[17] Eisenhower knew that before long America would launch a satellite; he had been briefed about von Braun's Redstone, which was being recruited into satellite duty as the Jupiter-C and would be ready to go in January. Eisenhower had a bigger worry: that the politics of fear would force the country to spend too much money on civil defense—weakening rather than strengthening the nation.

The threat of atomic attack, with its attendant radioactive fallout, had heralded in a great age of shelter building. The ultimate Cold War ziggurat, begun earlier in 1957, was a massive underground structure dug into a West Virginia mountain near the Greenbrier resort, to house members of Congress and their staffs. The walls of the 120,000-square-foot bunker, equipped with chambers for the House and Senate, a hospital and a crematorium, were hung with four gigantic photomurals of the Capitol—one for each season of the year, with appropriate foliage.[18]

Recognizing that the members of Congress and other federal employees might get stuck in the massive traffic jams sure to follow the sounding of an alert, the federal government in its wisdom had decided to give its forty thousand essential employees a thirty-minute head start.[19] (On an evacuation drill in the summer of 1955, as Eisenhower's motorcade raced down country roads, it was stymied by a slow-moving pig truck.)[20]

But what to do about everyone else? Like the previous film that had showed young Tony dodging radiation damage behind a sturdy wall, the *Duck and Cover* film, which demonstrated the proper posture in a nuclear attack (squatting with nose between knees and arms), didn't seem to offer much hope for schoolchildren. Produced by the federal government, the film featured a cartoon turtle named Burt, who hid behind his shell when a wicked monkey threw firecrackers at him.[21]

It all seemed darkly absurd to the president of the United States, who used the underground bomb shelter at the White House to practice golf on rainy or cold days. Early in his presidency, Eisenhower was led to a secret bunker in the North Carolina mountains, a command post in case of nuclear attack. As he descended through the blast doors, he turned to an aide, Dillon Anderson, and remarked, "Good God, I didn't realize we were this scared."[22] In August 1956, as the National Security Council debated the need for a national shelter program, "the president wondered how far we could go until we reached a state of complete futility," wrote the official notetaker.[23]

Privately, Eisenhower could not imagine life after a nuclear attack. In 1961, after leaving office, he was asked if he wanted to contribute to a bomb shelter at the Palm Desert country club he had chosen for his retirement. He declined, writing a friend, "I am not sure whether I would really want to be living if this country of ours was ever subjected to a nuclear bath." (He added that if the club did build a shelter, it should remember to make room for the caddies and maids.)[24]

A national program to build shelters would be fantastically expensive, and Ike did not want to spend the money. As always, he was thinking of what he called the Great Equation, balancing the cost of security against the cost to freedom. "We could lick the world if we were willing to adopt the system of Adolf Hitler," Ike said, ever wary of that garrison state.[25] But by 1957, the pressure was growing on the president to gird the country in every possible way for world war. In the mid-'50s, national security experts debated the virtues of "active" versus "passive" defense—roughly, bombs and warheads versus shelters. "Piss on shelters," said the Strategic Air Command's General Curtis LeMay, who wanted no rivals for resources.[26] Ike's approach was characteristically more roundabout: he proposed that a citizens' commission examine the matter, figuring that he could thank the members for their efforts and politely deepsix any proposals that were too costly.[27]

At the recommendation of his science adviser, James Killian, in the spring of 1957 Eisenhower appointed Rowan Gaither, head of the Ford Foundation, to run the commission. A wealthy San Francisco lawyer, Gaither seemed a safe choice. But Gaither was also chairman of the board of RAND, the West Coast think tank established by the air force after World War II. Gaither stocked his commission with RAND employees, who viewed the problem and the solution more expansively than Eisenhower had bargained for.

The Soviet news source *Pravda* referred to RAND as "the academy of science and death."[28] For once, Soviet propaganda was not entirely exaggerating. RAND was an early textbook example of why brains do not guarantee wisdom. At RAND, the article of faith was the power of reason. The RANDites believed that man was an essentially rational being, and that it was possible, by virtue of logic and reason—through game theory and "systems analysis"—to predict what men would do. As historians Fred Kaplan and Alex Abella have shown, this faith led to brilliant insights, but also to some dangerously irrational conclusions. The founding father of nuclear strategy at RAND was Bernard Brodie, who brought a clever if mildly outrageous sexual analysis to war-gaming. Brodie believed nuclear wars could be fought and won. He advocated pausing after a first-round nuclear exchange to allow time for the enemy to surrender, and in a private memo widely circulated at RAND he used the metaphor of withdrawal before ejaculation. Brodie likened General LeMay's heavy-handed Strategic Air

Command strategy—the hit-'em-with-everything-you've-got "Sunday punch"—to a "wham-bam-thank-you-ma'am" climax. Brodie's RAND colleague Herman Kahn, a corpulent and jolly showman on the nuclear war lecture circuit, stretched this analogy, telling an assembly of SAC officers, "Gentlemen, you don't have a war plan, you have a *war-gasm!*"*[29]

The reigning genius at RAND was Albert Wohlstetter, a superb mathematician and aesthete who revered classical music. Presiding in his all-white modernist office in Santa Monica—white furniture, white shag rug—he created a small empire of acolytes.[31] They traveled first class, ate in the best restaurants (government contracts were lucrative), yet, fatalistically, saw no point in investing in their retire-

---

*With what Fred Kaplan called "mock sincerity," Kahn imagined a "Doomsday machine," a vast computer wired to H-bombs that would kill billions around the world with fallout at the first sign of a Soviet attack. Kahn and Albert Wohlstetter were the inspirations for Dr. Strangelove in the 1964 Stanley Kubrick film. RAND produced more serious ideas with practical applications, like the concept of counterforce—a second-strike capability to deter surprise attack—and "positive control," better known as "fail-safe." Sent aloft on news of a Russian attack or already in the air, B-52s were to abort their retaliatory missions unless they received a go-order at the "fail-safe" point near the Arctic Circle. The fictionalized failure of fail-safe made for a best-selling novel in 1962 and a movie in 1964. The real fail-safe system helped keep America safe with a twenty-four-hour nuclear umbrella.[30]

ment.[32] There was a sense among the RAND wizards that they were living for the moment, because Armageddon beckoned. Wohlstetter and his minions warned that the United States was highly vulnerable to a sneak attack by the Soviet Union. This central fear became the animating notion behind *Deterrence and Survival in the Nuclear Age,* the Gaither Commission's twenty-nine-page report that would add mightily to President Eisenhower's headaches.

As the commission was readying its report, its deputy director, Robert Sprague, who ran an electronics firm that fashioned atomic bomb parts, took a field trip to SAC's Omaha headquarters in September 1957. Sprague asked General LeMay to stage a spontaneous alert of the command's bomber forces. After six hours—about the time it would take Soviet bombers to reach SAC airfields after detection by the polar Early Warning System—not a single SAC bomber had lifted off. As Sprague later told the story, LeMay seemed completely unconcerned. He wasn't going to wait to be surprised; he was going to launch a preemptive attack. "If I see the Russians are massing their planes for an attack," he told Sprague, "I'm going to knock the shit out of them before they take off the ground." "But General LeMay," protested Sprague, "that's not national policy." LeMay replied, "I don't care. It's my policy. That's what I'm going

LeMay (Library of Congress, Washington, DC)

to do."[33] The hawkish Sprague didn't know whether to feel relieved or alarmed.

The author of the Gaither Commission report was Paul Nitze, a former Truman administration official. In later years, Nitze would become a significant Cold War figure, a resourceful and patient arms control negotiator in the Reagan administration, but at this stage of his career he was better known for his hair-raising prose. In 1950, Nitze had written NSC-68, possibly the most famous, or infamous, of all Cold War documents, calling for a massive increase in defense spending and warning darkly of a "year of maximum danger," 1954, when Soviet superiority would tempt the Kremlin to attack. That year had passed peacefully, but Nitze and the commission found a new year— 1959—when the United States would be highly vulnerable to a Russian ICBM attack.[34] With melodramatic urgency—"if we fail to act at once, the risk, in our opinion, will be unacceptable"—Nitze laid out the threat in *Deterrence and Survival in the Nuclear Age.* "It was like looking into the abyss and seeing hell at the bottom," recalled Robert Lovett, a former secretary of defense and Gaither Commission member.[35]

The findings of the Gaither Commission were presented to President Eisenhower informally on November 4 and formally to the National Security Council on November 7. The commission called for an extra $44 billion in spending over five years— more than the entire defense budget for 1958. Half the money would go for more missiles and bombers, including measures to protect them, and half for a massive fallout shelter building program and other civil defense.[36]

With a yellow pad on his lap, Eisenhower listened impassively. In an oblique, folksy way, he signaled his resistance by noting that a billion dollars was a stack of ten-dollar bills as high as the Washington

Monument. He made a disparaging reference to the public mood. "I can't understand the United States being quite as panicky as they are," he said. As before, Eisenhower knew something that the public, and for that matter the Gaither Commission, did not. The U-2 spy planes had not found the Soviet Union massing missiles and planes for war. Indeed, aerial reconnaissance showed that the Kremlin lacked the capacity for an effective surprise attack. Eisenhower very much doubted that the Russians were readying to deliver a "bolt from the blue." Yet, as before, he couldn't reveal any of this. At the same time, he did not want to alarm and provoke the already paranoid Kremlin leaders by building shelters, an indication that America believed war was inevitable and hence was preparing to start one. He seemed trapped.[37]

Ever secretive about the U-2, instead he used John Foster Dulles as his surrogate naysayer. At the NSC meeting, the secretary of state huffed dismissively at the conclusions of the report and peremptorily dismissed the commissioners (so antagonizing them that Nitze wrote Dulles a letter demanding his resignation).[38] For his part, Eisenhower swept aside the doomsday war-gaming that made for coffee-hour chatter at RAND and that had informed the commission's recommendations. Jerome Wiesner, one of the scientists on the commission, recounted a telling scene to historian Gregg Herken. As Eisenhower thanked the members for their six months of work, the president recalled that he had asked them, back in April, to advise him on what course to take if there was going to be a nuclear war. Eisenhower now realized that he had asked the wrong question. "You can't have this kind of war," the president declared as the commission members were being ushered out of the Oval Office. "There just aren't enough bull-dozers to scrape the bodies off the streets."[39]

Eisenhower did not want to make public the Gaither Commission report, but he was not naïve about leaks. "It will be interesting to find out how long it can be kept secret," he told his advisers.[40] The wait was short. On November 23, two days before Ike's stroke, a slightly garbled reference to the report appeared in the *New York Herald Tribune.* On December 9, at a dinner party in Georgetown, Gaither Commission members discussed the need for bigger, better leaks. The first came on December 11 in the *New York Times,* followed by a really sensational one on December 20 in the *Washington Post* with a headline that read: "Enormous Arms Outlay Is Held Vital for Survival." The first three paragraphs of the story by Chalmers Roberts (almost certainly fed to him by Paul Nitze) were pure hype: "The still-top-secret Gaither Report portrays a United States in the gravest danger in its history. It pictures the Nation moving in frightening course to the status of a second-class power. It shows an America exposed to an almost immediate threat by the missile-bristling Soviet Union."[41]

The story made a mockery of Eisenhower's tepid public engagement. The leaks about the Gaither report caused an uproar in the press, which largely received the reported findings as statements of fact. Ike's "chin-up" speeches were part of a White House PR plan called Operation Confidence. In response, the editors of *Life,* the nation's most prominent mass-circulation magazine, wrote an editorial: "Arguing the Case for Being Panicky."[42]

Among those who had been watching the skies was a group staying at the LBJ Ranch, on the Pedernales River in the Texas Hill Country. On hearing the news of the Soviet satellite, Senator Lyndon Baines Johnson and his dinner guests had gone for a walk on a dirt road, staring up into the night sky, "straining to catch a glimpse of that alien object," Johnson recalled.[43]

LBJ didn't spot Sputnik that night, but soon enough he saw political opportunity. Johnson was Senate majority leader (the Democrats had main-tained a slim majority in the Senate despite Ike's near landslide in 1956), and he hoped to be elected president in 1960. Sputnik, he saw right away, was the sort of epochal event that favored a man with big ambitions. So LBJ seized the chance to sail into the great sweep of history by making fun of the Eisenhower administration. Two days into the Age of Sputnik, he flamboyantly proclaimed: "The Roman Empire controlled the world because it could build roads. Later—when men moved to the sea— the British Empire was dominant because it had ships. In the air age, we were powerful because we had airplanes. Now the Communists have established a foothold in outer space. It is not very reassuring to be told that next year we will put a 'better' satellite in the air. Perhaps it will even have chrome trim and automatic windshield wipers."[44]

As chairman of the Senate Preparedness Subcommittee, Johnson began calling witnesses who could explain how America got caught flat-footed in a space-age Pearl Harbor. The leadoff witness on November 25, the day of Ike's stroke, was Edward Teller, promoter of the H-bomb and a reliable purveyor of gloom and doom. (If America ever did get to the moon, Teller was asked, what would we find there? "Russians," he answered.) General LeMay, also testifying, charged that the president's budgetary inclinations were hurting national security, claiming that SAC had nearly been grounded at the end of the fiscal year by a shortage of funds to buy fuel.[45]

Learning of the secret Gaither Commission report, LBJ demanded that the president release it to the public. Citing executive privilege, a constitutional power of the president, Eisenhower refused. A quiet compromise was worked out: Johnson's staff was given an off-the-record briefing.[46] The leaks about the report in the *Times* and the *Post* inflamed LBJ to preempt the president's State of the Union address in January with his own over-the-top jeremiad about the stakes involved — nothing less than the control of the "high ground" of space. "Control of space means control of the world," Johnson said. "From space, the masters of infinity would have the power to control earth's weather, to cause drought and flood, to change the tides and raise the levels of the sea, to divert the Gulf Stream and change temperate climates to frigid." *Life* put LBJ on the cover. "In a week of shot and shell in Washington...Lyndon Johnson went a far piece toward seizing, on behalf of the legislative branch, the leadership in reshaping U.S. defense policy," *Life* asserted.[47]

Shrewdly, Johnson insisted that he was not playing partisan politics, that he had only the interests of the nation at heart — and said this so often that cynical reporters half believed him. (The Senate Preparedness hearings were a "minor masterpiece," wrote widely read columnists Robert Novak and Rowland Evans.) With high-minded magnanimity, LBJ even admitted that Democrats shared some of the blame for America's second-place status in space. Racing from camera to camera and microphone to microphone, his lights on in the Capitol late at night, glad-handing favored reporters over bourbon and barbecue at the ranch, Johnson was energetic, vigorous, vibrant, determined, defiant, and bold—everything, it seemed, President Eisenhower was not.

Ike, who regarded LBJ as a "phony" in most circumstances, grudgingly told aides after meeting with Johnson, "He said all the right things. I think today he is being honest."[48] Eisenhower's seemingly tepid response to Sputnik intensified the criticism of him as a do-nothing president. Newspaper columnists had picked up the refrain after Eisenhower's reelection in November 1956. The president was seen as too passive, inert, distracted, vague—in short, too old and worn-out for the job. In Augusta, while the president rested between sessions of golf and bridge, his gang fretted over the carping in the press. "It is a subject of general discussion in small groups when the President isn't around," wrote Slats Slater in his diary on April 24, 1957. "I am sure everyone agrees what is needed is a more positive and forceful position by the boss himself." Slater, a barometer of business-class conventional wisdom, continued, "I contend that the only men who go down in history with any kind of reputation are the dominant leaders, men of decision. The public thought of Ike as that kind of man, and he cannot afford to lose even a minute part of that reputation."[49]

18

The Strong Say Nothing

B Y JANUARY 1958, Eisenhower's approval ratings notably accelerated their descent. They would fall almost 30 points before bottoming out at 52 percent in March.[1] *Harper's* magazine called for his resignation. America, declared the magazine's editors, was "a leaky ship, with a committee on the bridge and a crippled captain sending occasional whispers up the speaking tube from sick bay."[2] In December, flying to Europe to attend a NATO meeting less than three weeks after his stroke, Eisenhower had risen to the challenge of high-intensity diplomacy, as he so often did. But afterward, he undercut the positive perception in a disastrous television appearance with Secretary of State Dulles. As Dulles droned on, Eisenhower tapped his pencil, stared up at the ceiling, and looked bored. Worse, he came across as an underling to Dulles—sitting sullenly, like a reluctant student who had been summoned to the headmaster for a stern talking-to.[3]

Eisenhower's advisers noticed a slackening in their sixty-seven-year-old boss. Visiting the White House in October, Emmet Hughes wrote, "I thought I detected—and it was the first such occasion I could recall—a new deepening of lines in the strong face, a slightly lower bent to the shoulders. Whatever the visible evidence, there was somehow in the office a troubling sense of—age." In January, White House chief of staff Sherman Adams confided to James Killian, the president's science adviser, "This man is not what he was."

Still, Ike snapped out strong opinions, "curt and tart as ever," wrote Hughes, "sputtering indignation at the Democrats: 'The idea of *them* charging *me* with not being interested in *defense!* Damn it, I've spent my whole life being concerned with the defense of our country.'"[4] Ann Whitman's diary records blue moods and outbursts of anger, but also resilient good cheer.[5]

Eisenhower suffered from a bad cold he could not shake. *Time* magazine was running snippy items about his golfing and napping. Once, discussing a complex matter with Killian and Goodpaster, Ike laid his head on his arms, which were folded on the desk. According to Killian, he "looked up and remarked that he didn't know whether his poor brain was going to be able to take it or not."[6] Trying to get over his cold, in mid-February he flew down to Thomasville, Georgia, to shoot quail on George Humphrey's plantation and soak up some sunshine. It had snowed there for the first time in forty-six years, and Ike spent most of his time in bed or playing bridge, 180 rubbers. The trip, Ann Whitman recalled, was a "miserable fiasco."[7] Mamie was worried. During a discussion about whether to enlarge the library in Gettysburg for Ike's retirement office, she confided to Slats Slater, "I'm not so sure we're ever going to be able to live in Gettysburg." She was especially anxious about the engorged arteries in Ike's temples. Slater tried to reassure her that they had always been prominent.[8]

At about this time, Ike welcomed an unusual visitor to the White House. Robert Frost came to give the president a book of his poems. On the flyleaf, the poet wrote: "The strong are saying nothing until they see." Eisenhower was moved and grateful. "I like his maxim perhaps best of all," he wrote.[9] Ike's illness, the sniping in the press, and the president's wishy-washy "chin-up" speeches concealed his great strength, but he consciously concealed that strength, too. Eisenhower had retained an unusual capacity, for a man of such large ego (and being president had not deflated that ego), to wait and see—to resist the pressure to act merely for the sake of action or for political reasons. It was a quiet, confident kind of muscularity, and he showed it in subtle ways in the winter of 1958.

Eisenhower had yet to utter the expression "military-industrial complex," but he had been fighting the incestuous relation between the military, congress, and industry for years. He was especially alert to the military's desire to build as many new weapons systems as possible, regardless of need, and he struggled against the unwillingness of the services to work together to assign priorities. In August 1956, Eisenhower wrote Swede Hazlett at length about his constant effort to make the Joint Chiefs of Staff strike "the balance between minimum requirements in the costly implements of war and the health of our economy."

The top brass—most of them old warrior comrades of Ike—"habitually, when with me, give the impression that they are going to work out arrangements that will keep the military appropriations within manageable proportions and do it in a spirit of good will and of give and take. Yet," Ike continued, "when each Service puts down its minimum requirements for its own military budget for the following year, and I add up the total, I find that they mount at a fantastic rate. There is seemingly no end to all this."

"Getting tough," Eisenhower went on, was not the answer. Rather, Ike wanted strong military leaders who would swallow their parochial loyalties. Admiral Radford, for all his Asia First fanaticism, was one, said Eisenhower. It was a slow, frustrating, demanding business, finding others and trying to herd the rest. "Some day there is going to be a man sitting in my present chair who has not been raised in the military services and who will have little understanding of where the slashes in their estimates can be made with little or no damage," Eisenhower wrote to Hazlett. "If that should happen while we still have a state of tension that now exists in the world, I shudder to think what could happen in this country."[10]

The "state of tension" had increased dramatically since Ike had confided in Hazlett, and it was all he could do to restrain military spending on the scale called for by the Gaither Commission. But he did resist. He refused to support a nuclear-powered airplane and a new high-altitude bomber, the B-70. He ordered up some more intermediate-range missiles, but not more ICBMs. Well advised by "my scientists" (the advisory board overseen by James Killian), he was savvy enough to see that the first-generation, liquid-fueled ICBMs would be vulnerable and quickly obsolete; they would need to be replaced by solid-fuel missiles that could be protected in subs and silos and more readily fired. Ike was willing to be patient, despite the cries of "missile gap," which he knew from fragmentary U-2 evidence and more so from his own intuition to be exaggerated, if not bogus. Modern weapons, Ike groused to his advisers at the end of January, "were just so damn costly." It was foolish to believe that "money is the cure," he burst out. "It's just not right!"[11]

On the night of January 31, the administration got a break when von Braun's Jupiter-C rocket finally put a US satellite into orbit. The news found Ike playing cards with his gang in Augusta shortly before midnight. "That's wonderful," he exclaimed. "I sure feel better now." But he instructed an aide: "Let's not make too great a hullabaloo about this."[12]

In early February, he resisted congressional demands to order up lunar probes to match the Russians, who were preparing to launch a "Lunik." Explained Eisenhower, "We don't have an enemy on the moon."[13] In early March, he told his aides to be on guard against "useless things" proposed in the name of national security.[14] Later in March, he told congressional leaders, who were clamoring for more defense spending, "I'm trying to be Horatius at the bridge to keep from going out of bounds."[15]

The pressure on the White House in the winter of 1958 can be measured by the toll it took on

Robert Cutler, the president's national security aide. The charming, witty Cutler, who delighted in limericks and clever after-dinner toasts, was a fanatically hard worker. But, a sensitive man, he blamed himself for letting the Gaither Commission get out of control, and he was swamped with conflicting and adamant advice.[16] "By the spring of 1958, I was beginning to harvest my whirlwind of overwork," Cutler recorded in his memoirs. Increasingly unable to sleep, the lonely bachelor lay awake through one long night in April, "my mind busy with problems confronting me in my work, those dark watches filled with futility and melancholy." Cutler went to see the president, who was "discerning and kind," he recalled. Eisenhower remembered too well his friend James Forrestal, the defense secretary who, overwhelmed by his private demons and his inability to tame the four-star lions at the Pentagon, had killed himself in the spring of 1949. At about the same time Eisenhower, then an adviser to Forrestal, was suffering such a severe physical collapse that he had to take a month off from work. Ike counseled Cutler to go away for a "rest" as soon as he could. Cutler would resign and return to Boston at the end of the summer.[17]

Eisenhower kept on. He repeatedly told lawmakers that the Cold War would be a long haul, that the nation needed to pace itself, and he periodically asked what America would do with all these new weapons. "How many times do we have to destroy Russia?" he demanded more than once.[18] Eisenhower could have done more to publicly quiet fears of the missile gap. But, operating behind the scenes in his customary fashion, he stood up to extraordinary political and bureaucratic pressure to spend profligately on armaments. The raving to buy more missiles, planes, and shelters eventually died down, although the fever would return. "Eisenhower's calm, common-sense deliberate response to Sputnik may have been his finest gift to the nation," wrote Stephen Ambrose, "if only because he was the only man who could have given it."[19]

As for Lyndon Johnson, after all his bombast about the High Ground of space, he quickly got bored with Sputnik. "In the early spring [of 1958]," recalled his press secretary, George Reedy, "he just plain lost interest."[20]

In April 1956, Richard Simon, a founder of the New York publishing house Simon and Schuster, wrote President Eisenhower urging him to build up US airpower. Simon likened America to Britain on the eve of World War II. Britain's decision to go on a crash program to build fighters in 1938, Simon argued, won the Battle of Britain in 1940. Eisenhower sent back a thoughtful response, his essential insight into the matter most crucial to his presidency. The problem, Eisenhower wrote, "is not merely man against man or nation against nation. It is man against war."

I have spent my life in the study of military strength as a deterrent to war, and in the character of military armaments necessary to win a war. The study of the first of these questions is still profitable, but we are rapidly getting to the point that no war can be *won*. War implies a contest; when you get to the point that contest is no longer involved and the outlook comes close to the destruction of the enemy and suicide for ourselves — an outlook that neither side can ignore — then arguments as to the exact amount of available strength as compared to somebody else's are no longer vital issues.

When we get to the point, as we one day will, that both sides know that in any outbreak of general hostilities, regardless of the element of surprise, destruction will be both reciprocal and complete, possibly we will have enough sense to meet at the conference table with the understanding that the era of armaments has ended and the human race must conform its actions to the truth or die.[21]

Eisenhower did not merely wish to hold the line of armaments to preserve "the Great Equation." He wanted to *dis*arm. He had eloquently expressed this desire in his "Chance for Peace" and "Atoms for Peace" speeches in the first year of his presidency, and he had suggested a critical first step in establishing trust with his "Open Skies" proposal at the Geneva summit in 1955.

He was saying what the world, including the Russians, wanted to hear. The Soviet Union was not against disarmament. Indeed, Kremlin leaders routinely, if not always sincerely, advocated total disarmament. The post-Stalin generation dropped the Marxist-Leninist belief in the inevitability of war against capitalism, choosing "peaceful coexistence" as the goal instead. The Kremlin did so chiefly because Soviet scientists began telling their leaders as early as 1953 that an all-out thermonuclear war could terminate life on earth.[22] Khrushchev was posturing when he waved his rockets; he believed that nuclear weapons were so deadly that mankind would never employ them. (When he first learned "all the facts about nuclear power," he once said, "I couldn't sleep for several days. Then I became convinced we could never possibly use these weapons, and... I was able to sleep again.")[23]

So why then did the two great antagonists of the Cold War make so little progress toward the "conference table" envisioned by Eisenhower, where both sides could agree to lay down their suicidal weapons? Much of the fault lay with the Soviets, whose paranoia was profound and who feared that any inspection regime would expose the humiliating weakness of the Soviet state. That is why, in Geneva in July 1955, Khrushchev instantly dismissed Eisenhower's "Open Skies" proposal as "espionage."

But Eisenhower also bears blame. His follow-through after his great disarmament pleas was weak. He was a brilliant crisis manager, but he was not always forceful about pushing the bureaucracy along when it came to stubbornly intractable issues. He was willing to take great personal responsibility, almost more than any man could bear, and he could be a master manipulator. Yet he was also deferential: willing to defer decisions and to allow others to execute, but without forceful direction. Eisenhower's management style was to delegate: to trust his subordinates. He liked to say he also held them accountable, though he had a hard time firing anyone. Ike would bear down on subordinates who arrogated power to themselves or used poor judgment, but he did it sparingly. After Interior Secretary Fred Seaton unilaterally announced a tariff on copper in April 1958, Eisenhower called Secretary Dulles and blew up: "God damn it, he is not running the foreign affairs of the United States. I am." A week later, the Strategic Air Command announced a world tour of its bases for forty newsmen. Ike called the air force chief of staff, General Thomas White, and protested, "I disagree with the plan 100 percent. We once had the reputation of being weak. We are now getting the reputation of being a war-mongering nation." But rather than cancel the press tour, Ike ordered a review by "higher authorities." (SAC may have gotten the message this time, but throughout the 1950s it was a publicity machine, cooperating with Hollywood on at least three movies.) Needless to say, Ike did not fire either Seaton or White.[24]

As Supreme Allied Commander during World War II, Eisenhower had learned the necessity of delegation, and he usually chose his subordinates wisely.[25] The problem, in the case of arms control, was that he picked the wrong men.

During the Cold War, the development of America's nuclear weaponry was overseen by the chairman of the Atomic Energy Commission. When Eisenhower named Lewis Strauss to run the AEC in 1953, he instructed him, "My chief concern and your first assignment is to find some new approach to the *dis*arming of atomic energy." Ike "could not have found a worse person to advance that goal," wrote historian Benjamin Greene. Strauss became an unwavering foe of doing anything that might diminish or retard the development of nuclear weapons.[26]

Strauss was fascinated by science, but he was not a scientist. The son of a prosperous shoe wholesaler, he skipped college and headed straight for Wall Street, where he made millions as a young man. Given a temporary senior rank in the naval reserve as an aide to then secretary of the navy James Forrestal during World War II, he insisted thereafter on being addressed as "Admiral."

Strauss was capable of deep resentments, and he could be vindictive. In 1949, he clashed with Robert Oppenheimer on the technical question of whether sending Norway some radioisotopes would reveal atomic secrets. At a closed AEC hearing, Oppenheimer mocked Strauss's concerns as uneducated and paranoid. A beer bottle, Oppenheimer testified, would provide as much nuclear information. The room erupted in laughs and titters. Strauss never forgave Oppenheimer and later led the witch hunt to strip the father of the atomic bomb of his security clearance.[27]

Strauss could also be charming. "I am completely in love with Admiral Strauss, who is a sweet man if ever I saw one," wrote Ann Whitman, who was no pushover, to a friend in December 1953.[28] Strauss possessed a cagey, secretive side that appealed to Eisenhower. Eisenhower liked scientists, but more for their scientific than policy advice. He did not fully trust them to keep secrets. Eisenhower was obsessive about leakers. In London during World War II, a West Point classmate named Henry Miller had spoken about D-day preparations at a cocktail party. Eisenhower demoted him and sent him home the next day.[29] Ike counted on tough-minded bosses like Strauss to keep a lid on the scientists.

Strauss obliged too well. He zealously kept the AEC's nuclear scientists from speaking out, thereby ensuring that the president heard only what Strauss wanted him to hear. Any information that might incline the president toward arms control was kept under wraps. Strauss held a fiercely Manichaean view of Soviet perfidy and wickedness. He was convinced that the Kremlin would use arms control as a subterfuge to get ahead in the arms race.

As early as 1954, Eisenhower began to look for ways to cease or somehow limit nuclear testing. From even before that moment in June 1953 when he had visibly blanched as he watched the film of the first H-bomb detonation, Eisenhower had wanted to explore a test-ban treaty. Strauss vigorously, and effectively, objected: it would only allow the Russians to catch up, he insisted. During the 1956 election, when Adlai Stevenson darkly warned of strontium 90 poisoning mother's milk, Ike and his spokesmen castigated the Democratic candidate for fearmongering and politicizing national security. In truth, Ike was comparably concerned.[30]

Eisenhower prized balance in all things, and he sought to even out Strauss's influence. In 1955, before the Geneva summit, the president had tapped Harold Stassen to be his arms control adviser. The "Boy Governor" of Minnesota, the nation's youngest at the age of twenty-nine, Stassen was willful and determined, and Ike thought he might have the force of personality to break through the bureaucratic snares created by Strauss and the AEC, as well as opposition at Defense and State, where Secretary Dulles scorned deal making with Russia. But Stassen's strength would prove to be his weakness.

By 1957, Eisenhower was determined to achieve an arms control breakthrough. At the May 23 National Security Council meeting, Eisenhower "very forcefully" spoke about "the absolute necessity of some kind of a halt in the arms race," according to the official notetaker. The president emphasized "we have got to do something."[31] Stassen was heading to London for a United Nations conference on disarmament in June, and Eisenhower gave him clear room to maneuver. Overruling Strauss's objections and the protests of the Defense Department, the president for the first time agreed to seek a temporary nuclear test ban *before* all sides agreed to an inspection regime, always the sticking point with the Soviets. The strong-willed Stassen promptly threw away the opening, committing what Eisenhower later peevishly described as "one of the most stupid things that anyone on a diplomatic mission could possibly commit." Disregarding White House orders, Stassen prematurely showed the Soviet representative at the London conference an "informal memorandum" detailing the Americans' change of policy. America's allies, France and Britain, who were then preparing to test their own nuclear weapons, were blindsided. Their diplomats were outraged.[32]

In Washington, Stassen already had many enemies. John Foster Dulles had been trying to leash and muzzle him ever since the press had created a potential rival for the secretary of state by dubbing the new disarmament adviser "Secretary of Peace" in 1955. He had antagonized both Nixon and Sherman Adams by announcing a "Dump Nixon" movement in 1956. With Stassen's blunder in London, his foes saw their chance. Eisenhower did not need much persuading. Indeed, presidential aide Bernard Shanley had already been summoned to the Oval Office, where Eisenhower angrily told him to get Foster Dulles on the telephone. Turning an unhealthy shade of red, Ike picked up the phone and started yelling at his secretary of state, "What are you doing letting this fellow Stassen run wild behind the backs of the French and British, dealing with the Russians without letting you know he's doing this?"[33] Effectively demoting Stassen, Eisenhower required the arms control adviser from now on to report directly to Dulles, cutting his access to the president.[34]

The bureaucratic infighting frustrated Ike. Still, he kept casting about for an idea. He conducted a thoughtful, wide-ranging correspondence with two test-ban proponents, Norman Cousins, the editor of the *Saturday Review,* and the famous scientist Dr. Albert Schweitzer.[35] When Strauss asked him for more tests and more weapons that June, the president responded, "You've been giving us a pretty darn fine arsenal of atomic weapons," and wondered why Strauss wanted still more. Strauss told the president that the United States needed many small nuclear warheads for air defense. (The Pentagon was proposing to knock down incoming Soviet missiles with nuclear airbursts.) The president told Strauss he wanted to reduce, not expand, the nuclear program. At the time, the United States possessed over 6,000 atomic warheads, while the Soviet Union had 600. Reducing the nuclear program "would be a fine thing," Ike insisted. He saw no point in adding to the program or racking up more costs. But Eisenhower did not *order* Strauss to stop production. It was a moment of weakness uncharacteristic for a man who showed courage in so many ways, but not atypical of his dealings with the vast and growing nuclear weapons bureaucracy. Brushing aside Ike's reservations, Strauss and the AEC kept building warheads.[36]

Curiously, it was Sputnik that finally diminished Strauss's sway over Ike. There were two deeply technical questions about testing: Was it possible to monitor Soviet underground tests? And what were the long-term dangers of radiation from tests aboveground? Scientists, naturally, disagreed. Fierce as ever, Strauss branded test-ban skeptics as lefty peaceniks and did his best to keep them away from Eisenhower. But Sputnik opened the Oval Office door to scientists who favored a test ban. In reaction to the clamor to "do something" about the Soviet leap into space after Sputnik, Eisenhower reached out. He formalized and expanded the power and reach of the president's Scientific Advisory Board, earning Killian the nickname "Missile Czar." Meeting with eighteen scientists in the wake of the Gaither Commission report, Eisenhower said, "Why don't you help me with this nuclear test ban? Everybody in the Pentagon is against it."[37] Some of the scientists were able to convince Ike that aboveground nuclear testing really was a threat to the health of the planet, and that it would be possible to catch the Soviets if they cheated on a treaty ban with tests belowground.[38]

A significant convert tipped the balance against nuclear tests. John Foster Dulles had adamantly opposed a test ban, but after a dispirited Stassen quit in the winter of 1958 to run for governor of Pennsylvania, where he had been a university president, Dulles began seriously to look for a way to at least bring about a pause in atomic testing. The man who had undercut the "Chance for Peace" speech and tried to stop "Open Skies" in Geneva was suddenly the leading advocate for bargaining with the Russians over arms control.[39]

Dulles's about-face came as a surprise to almost everyone involved in arms control in or out of government, but maybe it should not have. He was always a more complex and sympathetic character than he seemed in his dogmatic and preachy public statements. Dulles was an easy target. Reporters sneered at him as a "hymn-singing creep," according to columnist Marquis Childs.[40] Eisenhower was mindful of Dulles's lawyerly tricks and sometimes exasperated by his tendency to play "the international prosecuting attorney" toward the Russians.[41] But Ike also valued Dulles's analytical mind and knew that his secretary of state was not the uncompromising hardliner he appeared to be. Dulles's mind was more supple than he let on. Although he saw Communism as a force of evil, he was sophisticated enough to know that it was not monolithic. He looked, for instance, for ways to alienate the Soviet Union from Red China.

While often brusque and awkward, Dulles had an endearing side, even a well of disguised tenderness. He delighted in goofy practical jokes, and on his rare weekends off, he was a sportsman who loved rough-weather sailing and good whiskey.[42] In time, Ike grew to like Dulles as well as to value him. Though the president did not hesitate to use him as a bad cop and lightning rod, he felt sorry for him when the press ganged up. John Eisenhower recalled a later afternoon when "My father made an amazing statement to me as we were walking down the portico between the White House and the West Wing. 'Well,' he said, 'I've got to go give Foster some encouragement. He doesn't look it, but he takes the public criticisms hurled at him to heart. I've got to reassure him.'"[43]

Dulles needed constant support from Ike; indeed, the secretary had a "hold my hand attitude," observed Slats Slater.[44] Dulles's close attention to the president's desires may explain why he switched sides and decided to seek a test ban; he knew Eisenhower wanted one. His uncharacteristic dovishness may have stemmed from a deeper, possibly unexamined source. Dulles had undergone surgery for a malignant tumor in his stomach in November. He knew that the tumor could return, and that his chance to be a peacemaker might be short. On August 22, 1958, the Eisenhower administration declared a one-year moratorium on nuclear testing while it pressed for a test-ban treaty with the Soviet Union.[45]

In 1952, as Harry Truman was getting ready to leave the White House, the soon-to-be ex-president had a mordant chuckle at the expense of the soon-to-be president. "He'll sit here and say, 'Do this! Do that! *And nothing will happen.* Poor Ike—it won't be a bit like the Army. He'll find it very frustrating."[46]

By August 1958, Admiral Strauss, his six-year term over, was out as chairman of the AEC. His successor, John McCone, a conservative California industrialist, was just as opposed to a test ban. On August 27, five days after Eisenhower announced the temporary halt to nuclear testing, McCone came to the president and asked for "one more test." Eisenhower was irritated. He told McCone he had just announced the testing suspension, and already here was the AEC demanding just one more. The president grudgingly gave in, aware of the uproar he'd caused in the British government, which was beginning a series of H-bomb tests in the southern Indian Ocean, and of the views of influential pro-nuclear-testing advocates, including Henry Kissinger of Harvard and Hanson Baldwin, the widely read defense correspondent of the *New York Times*. "One more" turned out to be nineteen. All told, there were eighty-one nuclear detonations around the world in 1958, before a pause in the testing on October 31.[47] One of the tests was of a bazooka-like launcher device called "the Davy Crockett." The small, .01-kiloton (10 tons of TNT) warhead could be launched off the back of a jeep. The launch crew might survive the blast but probably not the fallout. The Davy Crockett, which was to be operated by a sergeant, was, Pentagon jokesters observed, "the only weapon in world history whose lethal radius was greater than its range."[48]

Eisenhower had ordered strict presidential control over nuclear weapons, and elaborate protocols governed "pre-delegation" of his authority to far-flung commanders in time of war. But with so many weapons out there, what was to stop a madman or an accidental launch?* The army was being equipped with thousands of tactical nuclear weapons (the navy too — including nuclear mines and torpedoes). The risk for a president in the nuclear era was not just that he would give an order and nothing would

---

*Mechanical locks called "permissive action links" would later help make nuclear weapons more secure, but in the 1950s a single pilot could have started a nuclear war. At Incirlik Air Force Base in Turkey, beginning in 1958, an American pilot flying for NATO would sit in the cockpit of a nuclear-armed F-105 fighter-bomber on runway alert, guarded by a single Turkish enlisted man with an unloaded sidearm.[49]

happen. It was that he would order something *not* to happen and it would anyway.[50]

A small incident involving balloons vividly illustrated this risk. That August, Eisenhower received a formal protest from the Soviet Union against balloon flights over Soviet territory. Twice he had ordered the air force: no more balloon flights.[51] Since he was trying to launch an exceedingly delicate negotiation with the Soviets on arms control, this was no time to be feeding their paranoia about overflights and espionage. Yet the balloons kept going up. Ann Whitman noted Eisenhower's angry phone call to the Pentagon, full of "salty language" (for Ike) and suggestions that the secretary of defense "fire a few people." Servicemen "ought to obey orders or get the hell out of the service," the president stormed. Next he sent a formal memorandum to Defense Secretary Neil McElroy, stating that "there is disturbing evidence of a deterioration in the processes of discipline and responsibility within the armed forces." He cited the balloon flights and, perhaps more disturbing, U-2 flights over routes "that contravened my standing orders." He demanded action "at once" to tighten discipline. "If he had done some of the things that had been done in the last few days," Mrs. Whitman recorded the president spluttering, he would have "shot himself."[52]

19

Guns of August

O<small>N A SUNDAY</small> morning in early August of 1958, Ike decided to skip church and instead cooked breakfast for his White House guests, Ellis and Priscilla Slater. Over stacks of hotcakes and sausage links, they chatted for three hours. "The president talked about how tough 1958 had been to him— the worst of his life," wrote Slater in his diary that night. Eisenhower had an odd theory that the eighth year of every decade was somehow especially arduous and climactic for him. He ticked off the decades ("1918—First World War…1938—Back from the Philippines and Mamie's illness…") until he got to 1958. "All hell broke loose," he said.[1]

Eisenhower's chief of staff, Sherman Adams, was in serious trouble that summer. Although he was a stern Calvinist, as governor of New Hampshire, Adams had begun accepting small favors—clothes, a rug, free hotel rooms—from a New England industrialist named Bernard Goldfine. At the White House, Adams would from time to time intercede on Goldfine's behalf with federal regulators, mostly just requests for information. The peccadilloes were minor, measured by the standards of the place and time, but reporters were irresistibly drawn to the favors-for-gifts story line. Much was made of Goldfine's gift to Adams of a vicuna coat, tailored from the soft furry hide of a rare South American animal. Summoned to explain his questionable ties to the White House, Goldfine came across as sleazy and boorish as he testified before Congress. Sherman Adams himself had few friends on Capitol Hill or anywhere else in Washington, with the exception of the president, who needed and liked him.[2] Adams's brusque manner, his habit of dispensing with traditional greetings or goodbyes, did not bother Eisenhower. He "hung up on me once," joked Ike, and even Adams's wife, Rachel, called him "the Great Stone Face."[3]

The matter of getting and keeping gifts was a potentially awkward subject for Eisenhower. The president himself had been given lavish presents, including the house on the Augusta golf course. There is no record that Ike ever performed favors for friends in return, and he would have been offended by the mere suggestion. Nonetheless, it might have raised the eyebrows of voters, who by the summer of 1958 had heard all about Adams's coat, to read a letter Ike had written to his friend Slats Slater on April 16, 1956: "Dear Slats, come next winter when my new vicuna sports coat is made up, I shall dazzle my friends—and feel pampered myself. Thanks for bringing me the wonderful material."[4]

By September, with the November midterm elections approaching, Adams had become too much of a political liability. Eisenhower couldn't bear to fire his chief of staff in person, so he had Republican National Committee chairman Meade Alcorn and Vice President Nixon drop heavy hints, which Adams finally took.[5]

In his memoirs, Eisenhower bitterly regretted sacrificing Adams, but he faced more pressing issues. By the late summer and early autumn of 1958, the president was engulfed in a series of foreign crises.[6] In mid-July, for the first and only time in his presidency, Eisenhower had ordered US combat troops to land in a foreign country.[7] On July 16, about 3,500 US troops arrived on the shores of Lebanon. It was a show of force carefully calculated to impress foes at home and abroad; Eisenhower was not looking for a fight, and indeed made sure to avoid one. Emboldened by the Suez Crisis, Nasser was trying to form a pan-Arab state and calling for regicide against the feudal regimes (and staunch US allies) in Jordan and Saudi Arabia. In Iraq, the Hashemite king was assassinated and his regime overthrown on July 14. Camille Chamoun, the weak but pro-Western prime minister of Lebanon, claimed that Egypt and Syria were conspiring against him and asked for American intervention.

Surprisingly, Eisenhower sent in the marines. Lebanon was tiny and had no oil, and it is not even clear Chamoun was in danger. But the president wanted to send a message to Nasser, who had been flirting heavily with the Soviets and buying their arms. He also wanted to show the Democrats and other critics of massive retaliation that America was, when need be, capable of flexible response, of using limited force to make peace. Eisenhower banged the drums by sending troops into Lebanon; the marines and navy were equipped with tactical nuclear weapons, so-called Honest John rockets (under strict presidential control). But his innate caution emerged when General Maxwell Taylor, Army Chief of Staff, recommended sending US troops into the mountains behind Beirut to drive out infiltrators. Absolutely not, responded Eisenhower. "They stay on the beaches so they can get away just as fast as they can if anything goes wrong," he ordered. Eisenhower was not going to get the army bogged down in guerrilla fighting.[8] The incursion was mostly theater; Eisenhower still had no interest in brushfires. Nasser may have been chastened for a time, though he went on trying to build a pan-Arab empire, with himself in charge.

The short-lived Lebanon crisis—order restored, the US troops had left by October 25—seems to have lifted Ike's spirits. When the crisis first arose, he joked about putting on his uniform to see if it still fit. At a council of war on July 14, Eisenhower had already made up his mind to invade, he recalled in his memoirs. He "sat sprawled back in the chair behind his desk in a comfortable position, the most relaxed man in the room," observed Robert Cutler.[9] The day after the invasion, Slats Slater stayed with the president at the White House. "I commented on how well he looked, which he did," Slater wrote in his diary. "He went on to say things had been a little tough." Later, Ann Whitman told Slater that "things had been hellish," but that the president had been completely calm under the pressure.[10] The lingering headlines were less complimentary, accusing the United States of gunboat diplomacy. After the ignominious retreat of Britain and France from Suez, America had understandably but perhaps unwisely chosen to fill the power vacuum. With the so-called Eisenhower Doctrine, the president vowed to protect Middle Eastern nations from aggression by Communist-controlled countries, pulling America deeper into a region where oil was the reward but the costs of engagement were very high. Eisenhower was perfectly capable of using rhetorical fudges and deliberate inaction to avoid armed conflict and overcommitment, but his successors, who had to live with his words, were often not quite so nimble.[11]

On August 25, President Eisenhower was deep in a bombproof shelter in the North Carolina mountains when he got the news that Red China was bombarding the island of Quemoy. The Formosa Strait crisis of 1954–55 had come back like a bad dream. Ike was at the time participating in the federal government's Operation Alert, an annual drill to evacuate policy makers from Washington in a simulated nuclear attack. The news from the Far East added a touch of reality to the exercise. Once again, Eisenhower had to decide how close to take the United States, along with the rest of the world, to the nuclear brink.

No national leader talked, or possibly thought, more belligerently about nuclear war than Red China's Chairman Mao. Under the misimpression that Sputnik signaled the superiority of the Communist bloc over the West, on November 18, 1957, he told Chinese students in Moscow that "the international situation has now reached a new turning point.... The East Wind is prevailing over the West Wind."[12] The Soviets were too ashamed of their inferiority to set him straight. That same November, Mao blustered to Khrushchev that a nuclear war would be a victory for Marxism: "If worse came to worst and half of mankind died, the other half would remain, while imperialism would be razed to the ground and the world would become socialist." The Kremlin leader was dumbfounded. "I looked at him closely," Khrushchev later recalled. "I couldn't tell from his face whether he was joking or not."[13]

When the United States Marines landed in Lebanon in July 1958, Mao was disappointed with the Soviet response. He scoffed at Khrushchev's qualms about setting off a nuclear war. To show his Kremlin comrades how to deal with the imperialists, Mao ordered Red Chinese forces to resume shelling the islands of Quemoy and Matsu in August and vowed that Red China would take the offshore islands and then invade Formosa.[14]

Sworn to defend the islands and protect the Nationalist Chinese on Formosa, the Eisenhower administration uneasily pondered its options. The Joint Chiefs of Staff informed President Eisenhower, as they had in 1955, that it would be necessary to destroy Chinese airfields on the mainland with nuclear weapons. Eisenhower was publicly more circumspect than he had been in the winter of 1955. There was no more loose talk equating atomic bombs with bullets. Now that the Soviets were developing

ICBMs, he had to be more careful in his public utterances. Eisenhower knew that neither the American people nor America's allies could stand the risk of starting a global war over some small islands off the Chinese coast.[15]

As he so often did, Eisenhower chose studied ambiguity. The president told the military to prepare to fight with conventional weapons, but also to be ready to use atomic bombs in a worst-case scenario. At a press conference on August 27, Ike made clear that he alone would decide if and when to use those weapons. On Formosa, Generalissimo Chiang Kai-shek fumed that Ike seemed to be hedging. In early September, Foster Dulles went to Ike's summer White House in Newport to press the president on whether he would be willing to use tactical nuclear weapons on Chinese airfields. Ike stalled and wandered off into a marginally relevant reminiscence about D-day. When it came to nuclear bluffing, Eisenhower followed his own lonely counsel. *Tell no one.*[16]

Fortunately, Ike's bluff worked. Mao was perhaps not as cavalier about nuclear war as he pretended to be. On September 5, the Communist Party chairman told the Supreme State Conference in Beijing, "I simply did not calculate the world would become so disturbed and turbulent."[17] With both sides looking for a way to pull back from the brink, the crisis quickly wound down. By the end of September, secret diplomacy was working toward a deal. The Americans were quietly persuading Chiang to reduce his large army (100,000 men) on the offshore islands. In a near parody of saving face, the Red Chinese announced they would fire on the Nationalist convoys only on odd days of the month, allowing them to sail on even-numbered days. In his memoirs, Eisenhower, who had seen almost everything, wrote, "I wondered if we were in a Gilbert and Sullivan war."[18]

Yet amid this absurdity was a victory of sorts: Eisenhower and Dulles had been hoping to drive a wedge between Russia and China, and the second Quemoy-Matsu crisis aided this cause. Khrushchev had promised to provide Mao with a prototype atomic bomb. After listening to Mao's tirades and watching him goad Uncle Sam, he began to think better of the idea. In 1959, Moscow told Beijing that no bomb would be forthcoming.[19]

In the spring of 1958, the Wham-O Manufacturing Company of San Gabriel, California, makers of the Frisbee, began marketing three-foot hoops of colored plastic tubing. The hula hoop was born. By summer dozens of firms were selling tens of millions of hula hoops all over the world. European medical journals warned of hip injuries, and Japanese emergency wards filled with slipped disks, but waiting lines to buy more hula hoops stretched down city blocks from Piccadilly to Ginza. Returning from Europe, Queen Mother Zaine of Jordan brought one in her luggage. In Finland, there were hula hoop marathons, and in Communist Warsaw, a weekly newspaper reported, "If the Ministry of Light Industry and the Chamber of Artisans do not embark upon the production of hoops, we will be seriously delayed in hula hoop progress, especially on the international level." As William Manchester noted, it was just a fad: by the summer of 1959, "discarded hoops had begun to pile up in city dumps." Never mind that the Russians were ahead in space and too few American high school students studied physics. American culture was dominant the world over.[20]

Even with the dread of nuclear war, the American Century was deeply felt in 1958. America was the world's policeman, too materialistic and perhaps even a little lazy, but all in all very much the world's last, best hope. At least that was the way it felt to men who manned the top jobs at Defense and State, the White House and the Justice Department. There was a sense of duty but also fulfillment, even exultation. The stakes seemed enormous. Karl Harr, a Princeton Rhodes Scholar, left a promising career at a Wall Street law firm to serve in the Defense Department and later as a senior national security staffer at the White House. He recalled: "I felt, what's the sense of spending your life in the traditional way trying to make money for your kids if they are to end up living in a slave camp?"[21] He was far from alone in his American messianism.

The sense of American triumphalism was nowhere giddier than in the upper reaches of the Central Intelligence Agency. True, the CIA was locked in grim struggle against global Communists, and the KGB was a ruthless foe. Still, there was an esprit among the Ivy League–bred senior officers of the Agency, a feeling of doing righteous work (albeit in underhanded ways) and having a lark while doing it. "We went all over the world and we did what we wanted," the CIA's Al Ulmer told journalist Tim Weiner. "God, we had fun."[22]

Ulmer, a charming Princetonian, had been CIA station chief in Athens, "with a status somewhere between a Hollywood star and a head of state," wrote Weiner in *Legacy of Ashes,* his critical history of the CIA. Ulmer had helped Allen Dulles nurture a romantic infatuation with Queen Frederika of Greece and had sailed the Aegean on the yachts of magnates. In 1956, Ulmer became head of the CIA's Far East division. His assignment was to overthrow Indonesia's President Sukarno.

Ike had a cultural contempt for tin-pot dictators in the developing world. With a certain West Point stiffness, he considered most of them decadent as well as corrupt. If they also leaned toward Moscow, or even if they were guilty of neutralism in the great moral struggle of the Cold War, Eisenhower regarded them as dispensable.

An organizer of "nonaligned nations" in 1955, Sukarno had toured Moscow and Beijing in 1956. The Indonesian strongman made no attempt to disguise his sexual appetites ("As an artist," he said, "I gravitate naturally towards what pleases the senses"). Foster Dulles, the good Presbyterian, found Sukarno "disgusting," and signaled his brother Allen to start looking for ways to unseat him. The CIA considered assassination and tried to embarrass Sukarno by making a pornographic film showing a look-alike in the carnal embrace of a Russian spy (the blue movie seemed only to enhance Sukarno's reputation). On September 25, 1957, President Eisenhower, hoping the Agency would repeat its successes in Iran and Guatemala, signed off on a coup.

Indonesia proved more intractable. The army remained mostly loyal to Sukarno even though many of its officers had been trained in the United States and styled themselves "Sons of Eisenhower." By April 1958, the coup had clearly fizzled. Eisenhower wanted deniability, but the American role was exposed when a CIA pilot named Al Pope was shot down after mistakenly bombing a church. Pope was captured with all his ID, including his PX card from Clark Air Base in the Philippines.[23]

Eisenhower was furious. It was not the first CIA-backed coup that had gone awry. In 1957, a veteran spy named Rocky Stone, a hero of the Iranian coup, was caught in a sting operation trying to bribe officers in the Syrian army to overthrow the Nasserite government. ("A particularly clumsy CIA plot," huffed the US ambassador to Syria, Charles Yost.)[24] Ike understood that covert ops were inherently risky, but he was beginning to wonder whether Allen Dulles was losing his grip at the Agency. The president was miffed about an April 1958 article in *Harper's* magazine on the CIA's shaky role during the Hungary and Suez crises. The magazine repeated Dulles's rather disingenuous defense — that the president would have known what was going to happen if he had only read the CIA reports. According to unnamed sources, the article recounted, Eisenhower had demanded simpler briefings, with red arrows and headline summaries. That part of the article was true, but not because, as the story implied, the president was simple-minded or superficial. Rather, Eisenhower had grown impatient with Allen Dulles's discursive ramblings, especially in his reports to the National Security Council.[25]

In fact, it was sometimes difficult to tell if Dulles

was paying attention to his own briefings. Art Lundahl, the CIA's chief photo interpreter, would come to Dulles's cluttered office to show him the latest U-2 photos and find the director of Central Intelligence listening to a Washington Senators baseball game on the radio. Dulles did not turn off the radio, and it wasn't always clear to Lundahl whether the director was listening to him or to the game. In the middle of one briefing about aerial reconnaissance, Lundahl could hear in the background the baseball announcer exclaiming over a strikeout. Dulles muttered, "He couldn't hit a bull in the ass with a banjo."[26] In the summer of 1958, Ike took the unusual step of cutting the director of Central Intelligence out of meetings with his inner circle and insisting that an aide be present when the two men met one-on-one.[27]

Ever the roué, Dulles pursued his Greek infatuation, Queen Frederika, right into the small dressing room off his office, where he kept a daybed for naps. In December 1958, the queen came to Washington, escorted by the CIA's Athens station chief, and went to visit Dulles. When the time came to leave for the next appointment, the CIA man looked into the director's office — empty. He heard a muffled sound from the dressing room and, with some trepidation, knocked on the door. Inside Dulles and the queen were laughing in embarrassment. They had locked themselves in.[28]

The same month, the President's Board of Consultants on Foreign Intelligence tried, one more time, to address Dulles's shortcomings. Speaking for the board, Robert Lovett—the Wise Man who had joined with David Bruce to write a damning report on the CIA in December 1956, two years earlier—urged Eisenhower to force Dulles to hire a chief of staff to run the Agency better. But Dulles refused, and Eisenhower did not force the issue. (As an alternative, the board suggested stripping the director of Central Intelligence of his power over the whole intelligence community; "pistol at Allen's head," wrote Robert Cutler in the margin of a briefing paper.)[29] John Eisenhower, then an army major, had gone to work as a deputy to Andy Goodpaster, who was still serving as the president's staff secretary. He recalled: "I was there for the Lovett briefing. They said [to Dulles], 'You have to get an administrator.' Dulles said, 'I won't do it.' That put Dad in the position of firing him or giving in."

Many years later, the whole episode seemed to gnaw at John Eisenhower, who recalled that he and his father had "a couple of real fights" about Dulles. John Eisenhower's closest friend at the time ("my twin") was a CIA officer named George "Bo" Horkan. A lawyer, Horkan worked for Lyman Kirkpatrick, the CIA's inspector general, investigating the Agency's increasingly numerous covert-action failures and "flaps." John recalled, "He'd harangue me when he was over at the White House about 'this idiot Allen Dulles.' He'd be sarcastic and personal." Standing in his friend's tiny West Wing office, Horkan would imitate the director of Central Intelligence pompously holding forth in the Cabinet Room, telling the National Security Council "We're moving effectively" when in reality, according to Horkan, "they weren't doing anything." John wasn't sure what to do with Horkan's information. "I wasn't about to run in and tell Dad," he said. He spoke to Goodpaster in general terms about Dulles but doubts that Goodpaster passed on the CIA man's misgivings to the president. "Goodpaster might have been too good a soldier to tell [the president]. He was very military. He'd consider it unethical to warn Dad that this guy you like so much is not very competent. Goodpaster was very correct. He'd figure that Dad had official advisers."[30]

Although Dulles resisted or deflected attempts to undermine his authority, he could see that he was in some disfavor at the White House. The solution, to Dulles, was to look within the CIA, to find a strong right arm and possible successor, a master spy who was to his liking and in his image. In September of 1958, Frank Wisner, the CIA's mercurial and, as it turned out, manic-depressive chief of covert operations, was collapsing under mental strain so great that he entered Sheppard Pratt psychiatric hospital. Among intelligence professionals the betting was that Dulles would choose Richard Helms, Wisner's more prudent deputy, as the new chief of covert operations. Instead Dulles picked Richard Bissell, the brilliant if willful chief of the U-2 program.

Bissell knew very little about spies or covert action, aside from his brief involvement in the Guatemala coup. Helms had essentially run the CIA's clandestine service during Wisner's decline. But Helms was cautious and bureaucratic. The risk-loving Bissell was far more Dulles's type. (It is telling that Bissell, alone among men, regarded Allen Dulles as a *good* administrator, largely because he did not administer much.)[31] Bissell's trump card was his high standing with the White House. For the past four years, Bissell had run the most successful operation in CIA history. The U-2 had given President Eisenhower what he needed most: hard, real-time intelligence on the existence and pace of Soviet bomber and missile capabilities. The U-2, of course, was vulnerable, and Eisenhower mightily feared a shoot-down as the Soviets perfected their air defense missiles. Bissell was the answer to that problem, too: Eisenhower had put him in charge of developing the top-secret reconnaissance satellite, which Bissell had code-named

Corona (after the favorite cigar of one of his staffers). The cover story was that it was a weather satellite named Discoverer; the CIA hoped to be using Corona by the spring of 1959.[32]

The CIA may have embarrassed the president with the occasional ill-conceived plot, but it was performing its primary mission of effectively spying on the main enemy's capacity to strike the United States. True, Eisenhower was not entirely happy with the intelligence product that crossed his desk. Reading a CIA "Estimate of the World Situation" in March 1958, he remarked to Ann Whitman that "page five could have been written by a high school student."[33] But overall he was appreciative of the intelligence community's efforts to penetrate the Soviet Union (the code breakers never achieved the success of ULTRA in World War II, but not for lack of trying), and he continued to tolerate Dulles.[34] In August 1958, when Gordon Gray was taking over from Robert Cutler as the president's special assistant for national security, Eisenhower explained his attitude toward Dulles. In a private memorandum, Gray wrote that the president complained about "the briefings by the director of Central Intelligence, which he felt were too philosophical, laborious, and tedious. He said, however, that one must recognize the personality of the individual involved and that he really had not sought to do anything about it."[35]

The President's Board of Consultants on Foreign Intelligence continued to warn the president about the CIA's shortcomings. Ike by and large shrugged them off, telling aides he was "allergic" to consultants and at one time confusing the foreign intelligence advisory board with another: when Gray rattled off the names on the board, most of them Ike's friends, Ike continued to be puzzled, though he might have been pretending.

By now, Dulles was starting to think more seriously and more urgently about his legacy. Bissell was part of it; so was the gleaming new CIA campus going up in the woods across the Potomac in Langley, Virginia. Dulles wanted to make sure his name was on the cornerstone (and not just on a bronze plaque, which could be removed), so he pressured the White House for a cornerstone-laying ceremony. Gray recorded that Eisenhower agreed, "but expressed his hope that he would not be called upon to make an address at that time." Dulles could keep his job, but Ike did not feel like publicly singing his praises.[36]

20

Missile Gap

I N THE SUMMER and fall of 1958, Eisenhower
needed good intelligence on the Soviet Union to
ward off his political foes. He was resisting the
avatars of what he would later describe as the
military-industrial complex; the story of the "missile gap" almost perfectly illustrated what Ike was
up against. It started with a *New York Herald
Tribune* column on Friday, August 1, 1958, by
Joseph Alsop, a source of particular vexation to
Eisenhower.

"At the Pentagon they shudder when they speak
of the 'gap,' which means the years 1960, 1961,
1962, and 1963," the column began. "They shudder
because in those years, the American government
will flaccidly permit the Kremlin to gain an almost
unchallenged superiority in the nuclear striking
power that was once our specialty." In 1959, pre-

dicted Alsop, citing anonymous but "highly placed" sources, the United States would have zero ICBMs while the Soviets would have 100; in 1960, just 30 ICBMs to the Soviets' 500; in 1961, 70 ICBMs to the Soviets' 1,000; and so on. Alsop placed direct blame on Eisenhower, saying that he was either "consciously misleading the nation" about this dire state of vulnerability, or, more likely, "misinformed about the facts." In other words, he was either lying or gullible, deceitful or weak, not to mention "flaccid."[1]

The president was known to throw offending newspapers and magazines against the Oval Office walls, and on this morning he may have hurled Alsop's contribution. It certainly put him in a foul mood. Two days later, over Sunday breakfast with the Slaters, he launched into his soliloquy about bad years that ended in 8 and pronounced 1958 the worst year ever.

The consequences of the Alsop column were immediate on Capitol Hill, where senators voted to spend a billion dollars more (out of a total defense budget of some $40 billion) than Eisenhower wanted, on bombers and missiles. At a press conference on August 27, the president blandly denied that the United States was in danger of falling behind the Soviet Union in striking power but offered no specifics. Privately, he seethed to his aides: "Alsop is the lowest form of animal life on earth."*[2]

Although Eisenhower enjoyed an easy, bantering relationship with the White House press corps, who tended to be middle class, regular-Joe types, he wanted his staff to have nothing to do with the sophisticated columnists found at Georgetown cocktail parties. Karl Harr of Ike's national security team was approached by his Ivy League–educated social friends in the press, Charles Bartlett, Rowland Evans, and Joe Kraft, who proposed "a quiet little dinner" once a month or so, for "background." Absolutely not, decreed press secretary Jim Hagerty; he would handle all press himself.[4] At the beginning of the Eisenhower presidency, Joe Alsop had proposed the same sort of arrangement with Bobby Cutler; the two had been members of the Porcellian Club at Harvard; maybe they could have a confidential relationship. Cutler said no, and, he recalled, "Joe appeared annoyed." Alsop put the request in writing, and Cutler showed the letter to the president. "Do you know

---

*Alsop was set up in a homosexual "honey trap" by the KGB while reporting in Moscow in 1957. He bravely refused to be blackmailed into spying for the Soviets, but he needed the US embassy to rescue him from arrest. In 1959, White House press secretary Jim Hagerty, "fed up" with Alsop's articles, threatened to lift his White House press pass. "He's a fag and we know he is," Hagerty told *New York Herald Tribune* bureau chief Bob Donovan.[3]

Alsop?" asked Eisenhower. Cutler explained that they had been clubmates, but that he had turned him down. "In fact," said Cutler, "I told him I could not talk with him again about a matter of this kind." According to Cutler, "The President said sharply: 'That goes for me too.'" For the next seven years, noted Cutler, "the Alsop column had no good word for me." (In an oral history given in the 1960s, Alsop described Cutler as "rather like the eunuch of the sacred bedchamber" who had enmeshed national security policy making in "the most byzantine procedures.")[5]

Alsop did what newsmen do: he found other sources. One was Lyndon Johnson, who cultivated Alsop with leaks and trips to his ranch. Top officials in the air force and their champion on Capitol Hill, Ike's old antagonist Senator Stuart Symington, were only too glad to give Alsop secret scoops. In a speech in early August, the Missouri Democrat asserted that the Pentagon was studying possible terms of surrender following a Soviet attack. A clearly exasperated Eisenhower felt compelled to tell Republican lawmakers he knew nothing about such studies and that "he might be the last person alive, but there wouldn't be any surrender."[6] Symington was swinging wildly, but not altogether blindly. He had an industry mole.

The handsome, confident, politically ambitious Symington was friends with a World War II hero

Symington (Library of Congress, Washington, DC)

Alsop (George Thames / New York Times / Redux)

named Thomas Lanphier, an ex–fighter pilot who in 1944 had led the aerial ambush of Japan's naval commander in chief, Admiral Isoroku Yamamoto. When Symington had been secretary of the air force under Truman, Lanphier was his aide. Now Lanphier was assistant to the president of Convair Corporation, manufacturer of the Atlas ICBM missile. Convair had a strong financial interest in frightening Congress into paying for more missiles.[7] Lanphier was routinely fed intelligence, some of it grossly exaggerated, by his friends in the air force, which also wanted more money for planes and missiles. Symington, Lanphier, and the air force formed the perfect Iron Triangle, the congressional-industrial-military triad that drove defense budgets ever higher, whether the increases strengthened national security or not.

The Iron Triangle needed the press to win public support, and Alsop, with his nationally syndicated column, was the perfect megaphone. Sometime in the summer of 1958, a leaker slipped the newspaperman a top-secret National Intelligence Estimate with the frightening numbers that formed the basis of his "missile gap" story on August 1. What Alsop did not know, or at least did not report, was that the CIA was having serious second thoughts about the alleged missile gap and was beginning to revise the figures downward. The Soviets had conducted only six ICBM tests in 1958, hardly enough if the Kremlin were to field a hundred missiles the next year and five hundred the year after that. The Agency knew this because it could detect test firings with its massive radars directed across the Black Sea from Turkey. The U-2 had tracked rail lines looking for ICBM launch sites and found none besides the Sputnik launchpad at Tyuratam. The NIE was a consensus document that combined estimates of intelligence analysts from the armed services and the CIA. Air force analysts, eager to juice up the Soviet numbers to justify more spending, argued that the Soviets had already moved past testing and were now deploying, hiding the missiles in barns and churches. CIA analysts were highly doubtful. To the air force, scoffed one CIA man, "every flyspeck on film was a missile." Allen Dulles, who as director of Central Intelligence had ultimate authority over the NIE, disliked confrontation and tried to get along with everyone. In the summer of 1958, he split the difference and ordered up somewhat less sensational estimates.[8]

That was not good enough for Symington, a powerful member of the Senate Armed Services Committee. In August he demanded an audience with President Eisenhower. The CIA, he charged, was seriously lowballing the Soviet threat.

Eisenhower was reluctant to meet with Symington, whom he regarded as a headline seeker too close to the arms makers. On August 25, he recorded in a memo-to-the-files that Andy Goodpaster "gave me a long and detailed story of the activities of a certain Col. Tom Lanphier. . . . Every bit of evidence we have indicates that Lanphier is dealing in falsehood." Lanphier, Eisenhower wrote, could be "honestly mistaken"—but there was a "very strong implication of self-interest somewhere along the line."[9]

Eisenhower could not refuse to see the powerful senator, but when he finally did meet with Symington on August 29, the president was politely dubious. He reminded Symington that the last "gap"—the "bomber gap," which Symington had widely proclaimed—had turned out to be a false alarm. Eisenhower said he would look into Symington's charges that the CIA was somehow covering up. But in later conversation with Allen Dulles, Eisenhower was skeptical that Symington's source, Thomas Lanphier, could possibly have access to the full extent of US intelligence on the Soviet ICBM threat. Lanphier was trading in air force gossip, Dulles replied.[10]

Eisenhower was an avid and expert consumer of aerial reconnaissance data. The CIA's Art Lundahl recalled his intense concentration at Oval Office briefings on the photos from the U-2. In many sessions over nearly five years, Lundahl learned to read Eisenhower's body language. When Ike didn't understand something, Lundahl recalled, "he would lift one of his eyebrows in an inverted V and keep the other horizontal." During the Suez Crisis, Lundahl had produced four-by-eight-foot masonite boards covered with U-2 photos of the blocked canal and laid them out on the floor of the Oval Office. Ike got down on his knees with a magnifying glass and crawled over the boards, muttering, "Stupid. Stupid. Damn stupid."[11]

In the autumn of 1958, Eisenhower badly needed more photographic evidence from U-2 overflights into Soviet airspace. The missile gap was taking hold as a political issue. Democrats drubbed the Republicans in the November midterm elections, thanks in part to the post-Sputnik hysteria revved up by Lyndon Johnson and the fears spread by Senator Symington. Ike had long since learned to be wary of estimates from military intelligence analysts with an agenda. The Joint Chiefs wanted a 1960 defense budget of $50 billion; Eisenhower wanted to hold the line at $40 billion. Surveying America's retaliatory power at a high-level meeting in November, Eisenhower, as he had before, asked, "How many times do we have to calculate that we need to destroy the Soviet Union?"[12] The president personally began nicking out big-ticket items, like a second nuclear aircraft carrier. "Eisenhower knew the defense budget," recalled his aide, William Ewald. "He knew where the fat was. He knew where the people were trying to load extras on...things you didn't need."[13]

Eisenhower was, in effect, his own secretary of defense. When Defense Secretary Neil McElroy warned him that further budget cuts would harm national security, Eisenhower acerbically replied, "If you go to any military installation in the world where the American flag is flying and tell the commander that Ike says he'll give him an extra star for his shoulder if he cuts his budget, there'll be such a rush to cut costs that you'll have to get out of the way." He would periodically sigh to Andy Goodpaster, "God help the nation when it has a President who doesn't know as much about the military as I do."[14]

Whatever his instinct and judgment told him about the paltry scale of Soviet rocket forces, Eisenhower could not be sure that the Russians weren't hiding something in the vastness of the Russian landmass. A score of U-2 flights had followed rail lines and covered great swathes of territory in 1956 and 1957, but there was more to see. Eisenhower did not want to press his luck, however. The Russians were not publicly complaining about the overflights by the American spy plane—that would be too embarrassing—but they were privately warning the Americans that their radars were picking up the U-2s. The Russians were slow to build ICBMs, but they had the intermediate-range missiles needed to hit European capitals, and they were testing antiaircraft missiles that would one day, maybe soon, be able to reach the U-2. In all of 1958, Eisenhower dared authorize only one U-2 flight over Russia, and, against the vehement protests of Richard Bissell, he had begun to talk about canceling the program or transferring it to the air force.[15] That would be as good as ending U-2 flights over Russia, because Eisenhower would not take the risk that a military pilot flying a military plane into the enemy interior might get shot down.[16]

At the CIA, they called the U-2 "the angel."[17] Its godfather was Bissell. His staff joked about the RBAF—Richard Bissell Air Force. Bissell moved the U-2 operation away from CIA headquarters and into an office building in a nondescript industrial space downtown. Of his staff of 225, 30 handled security. His communications were so secret that even Allen Dulles, Bissell later said, was unaware of most of them. (Dulles preferred human spies to technology; "you're taking all the fun out of intelligence," he told Bissell.)

Ever bold, Bissell chafed at President Eisenhower's caution. In an extraordinary act of lese majesty he set up a separate line of authority through British intelligence and the Royal Air Force so he could fly

U-2 missions with just the permission of the British government, not Washington. (He never got to use this runaround to fly over Russia; the Brits were careful not to cross Eisenhower.)[18]

Bissell was part of a social set in Georgetown that sniffed at the president's circle. At the "Sunday Night Supper," a weekly, well-lubricated maids-night-out party, old Harvard and Yale classmates and clubmates would argue and make fun of John Foster Dulles and talk of the Democrats' return to power. (C. D. Jackson had warned Ike about "the Bohlen clique," which included Bohlen's Porcellian clubmate Paul Nitze and other Truman-era refugees.)[19] Eisenhower and his self-made-millionaire friends were regarded by the Georgetown crowd as a little dull and provincial. They were not as refined or clever as the kind of people you would find at a dinner party hosted by, say, Joe Alsop. "Eisenhower's Washington will, I think, be unbearably boring, although rich," Alsop had written a friend in January 1953.[20]

Alsop and Dick Bissell were good friends, and had been since childhood. They had gone to Groton together, where they had overcome their lack of skill at games by showing how smart they were. Bissell regarded Alsop as his peer, not like other journalists. When he was writing his memoirs in the early 1990s, Bissell told Jonathan Lewis, who was helping him, that he disapproved of leaking to the press. Lewis asked about Alsop. "Oh well," Bissell replied, "I did talk to Joe."[21]

If Bissell was talking to Alsop, that raises an interesting question: why did he let Alsop write those scare stories about the Pentagon "shuddering" over the missile gap? Why didn't he steer him away from such hyperbolic, if not wrongheaded, journalism? Bissell, more than anyone in the United States government, knew that the missile gap was almost surely a fiction. It is hard not to conclude that Bissell *wanted* Alsop to raise alarms about a gap. Why? Because he knew that would keep the pressure on Eisenhower to allow the U-2 to fly, the risks be damned. Bissell wanted to keep flying the U-2 over Russia, and he was willing to do almost anything to get his way.

21

Looking for a Partner

NIKITA KHRUSHCHEV HAD spent a lifetime covering up fear and weakness. Through the purges and show trials of the 1930s, through the Great Patriotic War against Hitler, through the long drunken nights playing the dancing clown with Stalin, Khrushchev had taken courage from bluster and cunning. At times, he was even able to convince himself that he was bolder than other men. After the Suez Crisis he claimed, and may have even believed, that his intervention, and not America's, caused Britain and France to cease and desist. He scoffed at John Foster Dulles's "brinksmanship." To an Egyptian journalist, Khrushchev boasted that "when we dispatched an ultimatum to London and Paris, Dulles was the one whose nerves broke." Those, he continued, "with the strongest nerves will be the winner.... That is the most important consideration in the power struggle of our time. The people with the weak nerves will go to the wall" — to be executed.[1]

Since the end of World War II, the divided city of Berlin had been the place where those Cold War nerves were tested. In 1948, when the Soviets tried to close off West Berlin (one hundred miles inside Russian-controlled East Germany) by shutting the autobahn across East Germany to Western traffic, the allies kept West Berlin supplied by a massive round-the-clock airlift. A decade later, Berlin was a reproach to the Soviet system. In the Western-controlled sectors, shiny new buildings arose from the rubble of World War II and commerce thrived. In the bleak Soviet-controlled eastern half of the city, scientists and doctors and lawyers were packing their bags and moving to the West (the Berlin Wall would come later, in 1961). West Germany was not just an embarrassment to the Kremlin but, as Khrushchev saw it, a potential threat. He and his comrades lived in fear of the day when the West Germans might obtain or build nuclear weapons to aim at their historic enemy to the east.[2]

On December 1, 1958, Senator Hubert Humphrey of Minnesota spent eight hours with Khrushchev at the Kremlin, one manically ebullient politician trying to one-up the other. Four days before he met with Humphrey, Khrushchev had delivered an ultimatum to the West. In six months, declared the Soviet ruler, he would allow the Kremlin's puppet state of East Germany to control its own borders. In practice, that meant that the Western powers would have to leave Berlin; West Berlin would cease to be an enclave of freedom. With Humphrey the Soviet leader brought up Berlin twenty times, referring to the city as "a thorn," "a cancer," and a "bone in my throat"—a further warning of his growing impatience with the Western presence. The Soviets had a new missile, he claimed, which could fly nine thousand miles, all the way to the American Midwest. Khrushchev asked Humphrey to name his native city, and then, with a sly smile, went to a map of the United States on the wall and circled Minneapolis with a fat blue pencil. "That's so I don't forget to order them to spare the city when the rockets fly," he said. Humphrey said he was sorry, he could not reciprocate when it came to Moscow. Humphrey read Khrushchev correctly as a man who is "defensive in an offensive way, insecure in a superconfident way." The Kremlin leader, reported the Minnesota senator to Ambassador Llewellyn Thompson, "thinks that [we] are rich and big and keep picking on [him]."[3] Like a schoolyard bully, Khrushchev talked big to compensate for his own weakness. "Berlin," Khrushchev would later say, "is the testicles of the West. Every time I give them a yank, they holler."[4]

Khrushchev's Berlin declaration was completely unacceptable to the United States, Britain, France, and West Germany; they had long since agreed that an attack against one was an attack against all. Already, East German troops were harassing Western convoys on the autobahn. US policy was clear: any Soviet move to deny access to western Berlin would risk what the policy makers still called "general war."[5]

Major John Eisenhower was sent by his White House boss, the president's staff secretary Andy Goodpaster, to Augusta, Georgia, over Thanksgiving weekend to brief the president. John found his father restlessly fretting in his office above the golf shop overlooking the 1st tee. "What the hell do you want?" Ike angrily demanded when he saw his son carrying an armful of black briefing books. John was accustomed to his father's moods, but Ike seemed particularly cranky. "What the hell are the British up to?" the president roared as he leafed through the official documents. (The British, fearful of war, were casting about for any diplomatic solution, including diplomatic recognition of East Germany, which had previously been shunned by the West as illegitimate.)[6] Eisenhower admitted to John Foster Dulles that he had been lying awake late into the night, worrying over the fate of Berlin.[7] For a man who had suffered a heart attack and a stroke in recent years, sleepless nights were more than a nuisance.

The president was in a bind. Berlin put to the test his ability to stall, dissemble, and bluff his way out of a crisis that could lead to nuclear war. This was not about a few small islands off the coast of China and restraining Chiang Kai-shek or steering clear of a land war in far-off Asia. In Berlin, US and Soviet troops could very quickly face each other in a direct confrontation. In European capitals and in Washington, there had always been some question about whether the United States was willing, as the expression went, to "trade Boston for Bonn." Khrushchev's missile-wagging ultimatum threatened to make that hypothetical question real. Many years later, John Eisenhower recalled the surreal feeling of White House national security meetings, which he attended as Goodpaster's notetaker. At one session on contingency planning for Berlin, an official from the Treasury Department discussed measures to restore the dollar exchange rate after a "general war." The president cut him off. "We're not going to be worrying about the exchange rate," Ike said. "We're going to be grubbing for worms."[8] Eisenhower's mood ranged from tetchy to gloomily philosophical. His wartime comrade, nemesis, and rival, British field marshal Bernard Law Montgomery, had raised the president's hackles that autumn by publishing a memoir in which he claimed that he could have ended World War II in the fall of 1944 by driving straight to Berlin, if only Eisenhower had let him. Eisenhower was so incensed at this claim that, on New Year's Day 1959, he drafted a letter to his fellow American generals proposing that they take an entire week at Camp David to match memories and confer about how to rebut Monty. Ike calmed down a couple of days later and thought better of it.[9] But he was clearly on edge in the weeks after Khrushchev delivered his ultimatum.

In a diary entry after Thanksgiving weekend, Slats Slater remarked, with some ruefulness, on Ike's unrelenting quest for perfection on the links and at the bridge table. "It's unfortunate the bad shots annoy him so," wrote Slater.

> Most of us just slough it off, swear a little and recognize these poor shots are really part of our regular game. But in his case he has come to look for something close to perfection, and when it isn't there and he is involved, he blames himself.... There is something to this expectation of perfection. It applies equally as much as far as bridge is concerned. He will jump all over a partner for a bad play, or even for missing an easy trick—and not because the loss itself is important but because the player could have done better.[10]

John Eisenhower, a frequent partner at the bridge table during this period, felt his father's wrath one too many times. "Why did you do that?" Ike exploded after John misplayed his cards. "I don't know, I felt like it," John sullenly retorted—and never again played bridge as his father's partner. The only one willing to partner with the president at bridge, General Al Gruenther, Ike's successor as Supreme Allied Commander Europe and a tournament-quality player, put up with Eisenhower by sniping back, recalled John.

As he had before, Eisenhower used analogies between cards and larger strategic decisions. When he'd returned to the White House in early December, he'd told his advisers that it was necessary to make clear to the Soviets that Berlin was "no minor affair." He went on: "In order to avoid beginning with the white chips and working up to the blue we should place them on notice, that our whole stack is in play."[11] He meant that there would be no slow escalation through conventional to nuclear forces (white chips to blue), a reiteration of his bet on massive retaliation: no "limited wars," no "flexible response," but rather the threat of going all the way, right away. The Americans would "hit the Russians as hard as we could." The Russians "will have started the war, we will finish it. That is all the policy the

President said he had," recorded the official notetaker at the January 22 National Security Council meeting.[12]

The analogy to putting "our whole stack in play" was to poker, the game Ike had been forced to give up after he had pocketed the savings of too many of his army buddies. In the Berlin crisis, he also drew on skills derived from the more cerebral and complex game of bridge. At bridge, as in politics and war, Eisenhower was extremely patient, and he liked to win big, even running up the score. John Eisenhower noted that at the bridge table, George Allen, Ike's favorite betting foe, was a "born gambler" who relied on luck. Ike, on the other hand, counted cards and used his sharp memory and careful calculation of the odds to try to control the game.[13]

He could not do it alone. Bridge is a team game played by two sets of partners. The partners, sitting directly across the table from each other, are not allowed to speak directly; rather, they communicate through a kind of cryptic shorthand known as bidding. The bidding gives them a rough understanding of what cards they hold and where their opponents are strong. Success depends on the partners correctly anticipating each other's next move, working together through standard conventions and practiced intuition to outmaneuver and finesse the opposition. A foolish or unthinking move by one partner can undo a carefully conceived strategy; unequal affiliation can cause palpable tension at the table.

In his greater endeavors, Eisenhower was long accustomed to difficult partnerships. He had worked hand in hand with some of the biggest military egos of the twentieth century—MacArthur, Patton, and Montgomery, each almost hopelessly grandiose and unreasonable in his own way. In each case, Ike had to be the patient one, smiling genially, seemingly accommodating, but in fact tough-minded and determined to get his own way. Eisenhower operated as a peer to the towering statesmen of the century—Roosevelt, Churchill, and Stalin. It is hard to imagine anyone who better understood, intellectually and viscerally, the requirements of successful collaboration than Dwight Eisenhower.

Eisenhower had a number of potential partners as he maneuvered through the Berlin crisis. None of them was wholly reliable; several were dangerously hard to control. As was his wont, Eisenhower only obliquely revealed his true intentions and sometimes intentionally gave off confusing signals. His range of possible partners included the Joint Chiefs of Staff, who seemed to itch for a fight; his secretary of state, who wanted to posture and not compromise; and the prime minister of Great Britain, who desperately wanted to negotiate a peacekeeping deal.*

Yet Eisenhower's ultimate partner, he knew, had to be his nominal enemy, Nikita Khrushchev. The Kremlin chief was not really Eisenhower's foe in this final contest, though he certainly sounded and acted like one. Eisenhower's critical insight was that nuclear warfare had made war itself the enemy. As he had written in April 1956, one month after declaring his intention to seek a second term: *The problem is not man against man, or nation against nation. It is man against war.* Eisenhower needed to make Khrushchev his partner in the great cause of man against war. One can imagine what he thought, reading Ambassador Thompson's cable describing Khrushchev's histrionics with Hubert Humphrey. He

---

*By treaty, America's partners were the Western European countries of NATO. Eisenhower, and especially his secretary of state Dulles, spent countless hours tending to the Western Alliance. Eisenhower ultimately wanted Europe to have the capacity for self-defense; he was even willing to equip his old foes the West Germans with nuclear weapons. But in the short term, he feared a NATO troop buildup would only serve to signal to the Russians that the West was preparing to fight a conventional, not a nuclear, war, which Eisenhower feared would tempt the Kremlin to unleash its vastly larger Red Army. Rather than serve as an "umbrella," as Ike put it, a large NATO force would be a "lightning rod."[14]

could hardly have found a more difficult or vexing challenge.

At a January 29 National Security Council meeting, John Foster Dulles framed the showdown as a test of America's "moral courage." Bluffing and stalling, he was certain, would not work. Khrushchev's six-month ultimatum—to expel the West from Berlin—would expire on May 27, 1959 (known as "K Day" at the State Department). That was the day Khrushchev had vowed he would turn over control of the borders to the East Germans, ending the West's access to Berlin. The United States should not meekly withdraw from Berlin, Dulles emphasized. It should force the issue by provoking a conflict with the East Germans.[15]

That was fine with the Joint Chiefs. They were planning for a full-scale nuclear war on May 27, if it came to that. The Supreme Allied Commander Europe, General Lauris Norstad, wanted to send a "probe," an armored column, down the autobahn. Back in the early days of the crisis, on December 11, air force general Nathan Twining, chairman of the Joint Chiefs, had told his NATO counterparts: "We must ignore the fear of general war. It is coming anyway. Therefore we should force the issue on a point we think is right and stand on it. Khrushchev is trying to scare people. If he succeeds, we are through."[16]

Eisenhower did not mind having Dulles and the Joint Chiefs strain at the leash when it suited his purposes, but he pulled back at a National Security Council meeting on March 5. It was important "not to get hysterical," he said.[17] He ridiculed the army's plan to use force to keep the autobahn open. "A little pontifically," observed his son, who was taking notes at the meeting, the former five-star general pointed out that "holding an open access route involves more than just occupying the road from shoulder to shoulder." The army would have to essentially conquer East Germany, an operation that would require three or four army corps. The entire US ground forces in Europe consisted of two corps ("and weak ones at that," noted John).

Eisenhower had made it clear that he was not going to fight a conventional war in Europe, or as he had sarcastically put it at an earlier NSC meeting, when he was feeling badgered by Dulles and others to abandon his all-or-nothing strategy, "a nice, sweet, World War II type of war."[18] To emphasize the point, he told Congress in March that he wanted to draw down US forces in Europe — about 250,000 troops — by 55,000 men. "What would these 55,000 men do if we had them?" he asked Republican leaders.[19] He wanted to send a clear signal to the Soviets that the United States was not planning to fight with tanks, troops, and artillery. If fighting broke out, the only option was nuclear. But to many congressmen and some of his own advisers, Ike looked as if he was shying from a confrontation.

Inevitably, and in this case immediately, Ike's position, laid out at a secret White House meeting for top congressional leaders, leaked. Within hours, Capitol Hill lawmakers were muttering conspiratorially; in hallways, cloakrooms, and hearing chambers, the president—shades of Sputnik!—was accused of fatal irresolution. At a March 6 meeting with congressional leaders intended to patch things up, one senator asked if the president planned to resign. No, Eisenhower patiently explained, he would carry on as long as he felt up to the job. Lyndon Johnson, always alert to political opportunity, saw the chance to play the hawk: Why wasn't the United States sending more forces to Germany? (Senator Richard Russell wryly asked, "Can our Germans lick their Germans?") In response, Ike dusted off his poker analogy. "When we reach the acute crisis period, it will be necessary to engage in our rights...the question is whether we have the nerve to push our chips in the pot."[20]

The backlash was not restricted to the Capitol. Eisenhower's Democratic critics accused him of sleepwalking through the crisis. Dean Acheson, Harry Truman's secretary of state, had become the hawks' chief polemicist, and wrote a scathing story for the

Saturday Evening Post titled "Wishing Won't Hold Berlin." Counting on nuclear threats was "fatally unwise," wrote Acheson. The United States, he argued, needed to muster a large conventional army to be ready to fight a conventional war in Europe. On March 11, Army Chief of Staff Maxwell Taylor, Ike's old nemesis in the flexible response versus massive retaliation debate, testified before Congress that the allies should "at once" test the Soviets with a military probe. In the words of historian Campbell Craig, Taylor's testimony "bordered on political insurrection."[21]

The press was also restless. At a news conference on that same day, reporters badgered Eisenhower, demanding to know why he had not done more to face down the Soviets on Berlin. Chalmers Roberts, the *Washington Post* reporter who had luridly publicized the Gaither Commission warnings, wanted to know if Eisenhower was "sufficiently aware of the possibility of war in this situation." Eisenhower responded that he wanted to calm down the nation, not frighten it. "What I decry is: let's not make everything such an hysterical sort of proposition that we go a little bit off half-cocked," he said. Cornered by reporters, he tried an old fallback: confusion. Asked if he was prepared to use nuclear weapons to free Berlin, he responded with gobbledegook: "I must say, to use that kind of nuclear war as a general thing looks to me a self-defeating thing for all of us....I don't know what it would do to the world and particularly the Northern Hemisphere; and I don't think anyone else does. But I know it would be quite serious. Therefore, we have got to stand right ready and say, 'We will do what is necessary to protect ourselves, but we are never going to back off on our rights and responsibilities.'"[22]

Privately, Eisenhower grumbled about munitions makers and "fat cats" trying to make money off the crisis. With congressional leaders, he querulously demanded how they had suddenly become such "military experts," and suggested they had "fallen victim" to the "salesmanship" of the arms industry. He was feeling increasingly isolated. He needed to find a partner.[23]

On March 19, Eisenhower greeted an old wartime friend, Harold Macmillan, who had worked with Ike as the British representative in North Africa in 1943 and was now prime minister of Britain. The sad-eyed Macmillan was in some ways a parody of an English clubman, punning in Latin and delighting in Trollope. In his diary the next night, Macmillan described his first evening at Camp David: "We had a film, called *The Great Country* or some such name. It was a 'Western.' It lasted three hours! It was inconceivably banal."*24

But Macmillan was fond of Ike, whom he described as "open hearted and generous."[25] Macmillan, who had gone from Oxford to the trenches in World War I, where his pelvis had been shattered by gunfire, recalled that the Great War had begun because leaders had failed to meet to resolve their differences. He pleaded with his ally to call for a summit meeting. Macmillan had just been to Moscow, where Khrushchev had blustered and threatened. ("I fucked [Macmillan] with a telephone pole," Khrushchev crudely boasted to his comrades.)[26] The British prime minister kept repeating to Eisenhower that eight nuclear bombs would spell the end of Britain, that he feared for the Anglo-Saxon race. If there was to be war, he wanted time to evacuate all the children from the British Isles, he said with tears in his eyes.[27]

Eisenhower was stern with Macmillan, pointing out that America stood to lose more of its citizens than Britain in an atomic war. But, though he did not come out and say it, he too wanted to meet Khrushchev at a summit. Arms control talks had

---

*The movie was William Wyler's *The Big Country,* starring Gregory Peck and Charlton Heston. Ike saw it "at least three times," according to Ann Whitman.

bogged down over the difficult issue of verifying underground nuclear tests. Eisenhower was searching for some kind of agreement on nuclear testing that would at least slow the arms race.[28]

John Foster Dulles, as usual, was skeptical. He had softened on arms control, coming around to favor a test-ban treaty, but he remained wary of face-to-face diplomacy between Eisenhower and Khrushchev. The secretary always saw summit meetings as at best unproductive and at worst appeasement. He knew that Khrushchev wanted a stage for his bluster; why, he asked, should we give him one? Dulles always insisted that no summit meeting could take place unless the foreign ministers met first and achieved some substantial progress that could be ratified by the heads of state at a more or less ceremonial occasion.

Dulles was very sick by now, dying of abdominal cancer at Walter Reed Hospital. Macmillan and Eisenhower went to see the secretary of state. Macmillan described the scene in his diary:

Foster Dulles was sitting up, in his dressing gown, and although very thin and even emaciated, talked with conviction and vigour. But it was even more of a monologue than ordinarily, and his views much more inflexible than they seemed at our last talk. It was a strange scene.... Foster ... discoursed on Communism, Germany, Berlin, etc. He was *against* everything. He was strongly against the idea of a *Summit;* he did not much like the Foreign Ministers' Meeting. He thought we could "stick it out" in Berlin, and that the Russians would not dare to interfere with us. There would be no war—unless the Russians challenged it. The President did not say anything. I said a few words, which I afterward regretted, because I felt I ought not to have argued at all with this dying man.[29]

Eisenhower was shaken by Dulles's decline. "The president was in a queer mood, seemed to want only to be left alone, said he was 'talked out,' that he wanted to 'mope' around alone," Ann Whitman recorded in her diary after one of Eisenhower's frequent visits to the hospital in Bethesda that winter.[30] Though Eisenhower "does not dwell on death," Whitman noted, he was "hard hit" by Dulles's terminal illness. She recorded the president's ruminations: "It seems so wrong some how that a man who has given of himself as Secretary Dulles did must die in such a painful fashion, held up every moment in the world's prying eyes. Somehow it makes you wonder if it is all worth it."[31]

As the Washington spring flourished and Berlin

simmered, Eisenhower continued to telephone and call on Dulles. They kept debating the best way to fight the Cold War, with Dulles doubting that an arms control settlement was possible, and Ike insisting that "in the long run there is nothing but war— if we give up all hope of a peaceful solution." At 7:18 p.m. on April 15, at an hour when Ike and Dulles might have been enjoying an evening chat, Dulles called the president to say, "I just wanted to hear your voice." In May, Winston Churchill came for a visit, and Ike took him up to see Dulles, who looked "just awful and so thin" to Ike. The eighty-four-year-old former prime minister was in poor shape, too—"feeble and has difficulty talking," recorded Ann Whitman. Ike took Sir Winston on a drive to enjoy the azaleas in bloom and out to Gettysburg to see his cows and the Civil War battlefield. "The President treated him like a son would treat an aging father and was just darling with him," noted Whitman, though Ike was a manic golf-cart driver and Churchill had to "hang on for dear life." As he was leaving Washington for New York, Churchill was gently prodded by his wartime friend Bernard Baruch to say something—anything—to the cameras. "Bow wow, bow wow, bow wow!" said the old bulldog.

As Dulles lay dying at Walter Reed, General George Marshall, just down the hall, was also in his final days. In her diary, Ann Whitman recorded what

Ike told her about this last gathering of eagles: "It was so sad and ironic that two of the men he considered 'great' and he does not use the term lightly, were both at Walter Reed, both hopelessly ill, both could not recognize him—it really is the saddest thing."[32]

With a touch of irony he rarely countenanced in life, Dulles was buried on "K Day," May 27.[33] The three-hour funeral was "unbearably hot, the traffic was hideous, there seemed to be confusion," Whitman wrote in her diary. The next day, after saying goodbye to visiting dignitaries, "as quickly as decent, the President left for Burning Tree with George Allen, where he had a wonderful score, I am told," she recorded.*[34]

Though Khrushchev did not formally lift his ulti-

---

*Though Ike seemed to bounce back after Dulles's funeral, he later felt pangs of guilt that he had not tried harder to treat Dulles as a true friend as well as an adviser, recalled John Eisenhower. Ike wished he had offered Dulles a drink of whiskey at their frequent meetings at the end of the day. A shy man, Dulles may have felt slighted. In the winter of 1958, when Ike was staying at the Georgia hunting plantation of his pal and former treasury secretary George Humphrey, Dulles arrived to see the president on an urgent matter. The secretary of state conferred with the president from his official limousine; Dulles did not want to come inside, where he might intrude on the president's socializing with his hunting buddies.[35]

Eisenhower, Churchill, and Dulles (Dwight D. Eisenhower Presidential Library, Abilene, Kansas)

matum, the deadline passed without action or comment by the Kremlin. Khrushchev continued to blow hard to Western visitors. On June 23, Averell Harriman, the wealthy Wall Streeter and former governor of New York, went to Khrushchev's dacha outside Moscow for an all-day-into-the-night marathon harangue. Khrushchev played his usual ghoulish game. One bomb would be "sufficient" for Bonn, three to five would take care of France, Britain, Spain, and Italy. "If you start a war, we may die but the rockets will fly automatically." He insisted, "We are determined to liquidate your rights in Western Berlin. What good does it do you to have eleven thousand troops in Berlin? If it came to war, we would swallow them in one gulp.... Your generals talk of tanks and guns defending your Berlin position. They would burn."[36]

Winston Churchill, in his grand way, liked to paraphrase Samuel Johnson's aphorism that courage is the greatest virtue, because without it man can have no other. Eisenhower was not given to such philosophical pronouncements, but it's clear that he valued patience above all else. At the beginning of his presidency, he had invoked "honesty of purpose, calmness, and inexhaustible patience" as "the principles by which I try to live" in a letter to a friend who was fretting about Senator Joe McCarthy capturing the headlines. Tempered by delayed gratification—denied combat in World War I, held back in Washington by General Marshall at the outset of World War II—Eisenhower was long practiced in swallowing his ambition and disguising his guile. His patience, in public at least, was very nearly "inexhaustible."[37]

But time was running out on Eisenhower's presidency. He needed to start taking some positive steps toward defusing the tensions of the Cold War and slowing the arms race that seemed to be heading for some terrible last spasm. At an off-the-record dinner with *New York Times* columnist Arthur Krock in

July, he spoke of reducing the "plateau of tension" with the Soviet Union by getting some kind of arms agreement. It was "the one thing that he wanted to accomplish most of all," according to Krock's notes. The veteran newsman, who, along with a few other influential columnists, was occasionally invited for a private chat with the president, quoted Ike's opinion of Khrushchev: "shrewd, but not wise." Eisenhower passed on an erroneous estimate, presumably from the CIA, that the Kremlin leader suffered from diabetes "because his actions were like those of a patient not adjusted to his insulin intake." (The president, wrote Krock, "with some evident pleasure, pronounces his name 'Crook-chef.'")[38]

The more he pondered his Soviet adversary, the more Eisenhower wanted to meet face-to-face with him. He wanted to see if, by spending time with Khrushchev, he could somehow steer the Kremlin demagogue to a less confrontational course. Ike had known that he could outwait Joe McCarthy, that eventually the senator from Wisconsin would self-immolate. But waiting for Khrushchev to go down in flames risked seeing the whole world burn with him. He needed to spend time with him, to take his measure, to hear him out, to communicate in all the small personal, intangible ways that transcended the diplomacy of cables and demarches. "One of the things he always talked about was getting into the other man's head," recalled General Goodpaster. "That was an expression he tended to use, and it was a real process with him. He did try to get inside the heads of other people."[39] Ike wanted a summit meeting. But he did not want to be seen as going "hat in hand," as a supplicant. He was in an awkward position. He and, especially, John Foster Dulles had repeatedly declared there could be no summit meeting without tangible progress made beforehand at a foreign ministers' meeting.

The foreign ministers conferring in Geneva had made little headway. Ike wanted to end-run the slow-moving diplomatic machinery. But he had to be crafty about it, lest it seemed, as Dulles's successor, Christian Herter, sternly put it, that he was "kowtowing" to Khrushchev, who was ever eager to use a summit as a platform for his boasts and threats.[40] Still, there seemed to be an opportunity: Khrushchev had it let it be known that he was eager to visit America. Ike arranged to have Robert Murphy, a diplomat who had performed tricky clandestine missions for him in World War II, quietly approach the Soviets with the suggestion that Khrushchev would be welcome to visit America and spend some time with Eisenhower, not at a formal summit, but in a more relaxed, casual atmosphere. A meeting at Camp David, perhaps, and if the premier wished, a tour of some American "points of interest." Perhaps realizing that his late secretary of state would be rolling over in his grave at such a show of unstatesmanlike expedience, Eisenhower staged a face-saving charade. At a meeting with Under Secretary of State Douglas Dillon late that July, Ike feigned anger at Murphy for somehow failing to tell the Soviets that they must fulfill a precondition — progress at the foreign ministers' meeting — before their heads of state could meet. It was too late now; Murphy had extended the invitation to Khrushchev, and it had been accepted. Ike pretended to be "disturbed," mostly for the sake of his visitor from the State Department and for the historical record. (In his memoirs he perpetuated the fiction, treating the whole episode as a miscommunication.) In the movie version, Eisenhower might have seemed shocked that there was gambling in a casino; as Campbell Craig wrote, "he was complaining, Claude Raines like," about a situation he had largely contrived. Back in 1953, when Ike wrote about his "honesty of purpose," he had been perfectly sincere, but honesty of purpose did not always require honesty of means.[41]

22
Sweet Words

KHRUSHCHEV WAS SURPRISED and overjoyed to be invited to America by Eisenhower. Here was concrete evidence of the respect he craved. He was a little suspicious about Camp David. "*Kemp David?*" he asked. "What sort of camp is that?" He wondered if it was like Prinkipo Island in the Black Sea. In 1919, a Soviet delegation had been asked to meet with Western representatives on the bleak island, where, as he put it, "stray dogs were sent to die." The Kremlin leader was reassured that Camp David was Eisenhower's vacation dacha.

Khrushchev traveled to Washington nonstop on his giant new plane, a Tupolev Tu-114, despite warnings that the flight was risky: microscopic cracks had been found in the engines. Khrushchev insisted on the big plane, and the KGB demanded that Soviet warships line the route, just in case. (Khrushchev said that fishing boats and freighters would do.) The

Tupolev was fifty feet high — so tall, the excessively proud Khrushchev was pleased to hear, that the Americans did not have a ramp high enough to access it. He was not told that the reason for this design was that the engines had been elevated in order to avoid ingesting the stones, dirt, and debris that littered the typical Russian runway.[1]

The Tupolev was an hour late arriving at Andrews Air Force Base, outside Washington. Eisenhower and the welcoming delegation stood sweltering on a still, hot, mid-September midday. The president wore a gray suit and a Stetson; Khrushchev wore a black suit with military decorations. The Soviet leader wondered why Eisenhower was not wearing full military regalia for such an important occasion. On the motorcade into Washington, the crowds along the roads were large but subdued. Khrushchev suspected they had been ordered to remain silent. In late afternoon, Ike invited Khrushchev to take a helicopter ride over Washington at rush hour. He wanted the Soviet Socialist leader to see Americans in their cars on the way to their single-family homes. Khrushchev professed to be unimpressed, though he did ask to buy three helicopters. At the state dinner, the president wore white tie and the First Lady dressed in a long gown; Khrushchev wore a plain suit and his wife, Nina, wore a simple dress. Ike's favorite band, Fred Waring and the Pennsylvanians, struck up "Zip-a-Dee-Doo-Dah," and Khrushchev offered his toast: "It is true that you are richer than we are at present. But tomorrow we will be rich as you are. The next day? Even richer! But is there anything wrong with this?"[2]

In other words, it all went fairly well, or at least predictably, at first. In New York, Khrushchev met with capitalists and shadow-boxed with Governor Nelson Rockefeller. In Los Angeles, he met Marilyn Monroe, who had been instructed by her studio to wear her tightest dress. (He was, however, denied a trip to Disneyland, for security reasons.) The motorcade proceeded to Twentieth Century-Fox Sound Stage 8, where Khrushchev gawped at Shirley MacLaine dancing in *Can-Can*. Then it was on to San Francisco, where Khrushchev traded insults with labor bosses, and to a farm in the Midwest, where his host farmer threw corncobs at intrusive cameramen.[3]

Khrushchev's American minder on his tour was Henry Cabot Lodge, Jr., the tall, thin, Brahmin ambassador to the United Nations, who made an odd companion for the short, round Communist leader. They were accompanied by the Soviet ambassador, Mikhail Menshikov, known as "Smiling Mike" because he never smiled. (Eisenhower called Menshikov "evil and stupid.") Khrushchev appreciated his conveyances. In addition to the helicopters, he asked if he could buy three Boeing 707s and praised America's smooth highways, which, he said, were easier on his kidneys (he had stones) than Russia's bumpy roads.[4] But the conversation was often strained. Khrushchev spoke so often of nuclear war that the Russian translator began using a little mushroom cloud as a shorthand symbol in his notebook.[5]

In Washington, Eisenhower waited for Khrushchev to end his eventful ten-day coast-to-coast tour. Ike was feeling "lousy," as he so often did before momentous events, suffering from one of his frequent colds (the year before, he had been diagnosed with chronic bronchitis). At Camp David on the night of September 25, Eisenhower showed Khrushchev a film of the North Pole, taken by the nuclear power submarine *Nautilus,* and the movie *Shane.* As writer Peter Carlson has noted, there was an obvious subtext to the *Nautilus* home movies—our submarines can go anywhere! In *Shane,* a strong and silent hero stood up to the rustlers. Eisenhower wanted Khrushchev to know he would do the same in Berlin.[6]

The next day, Eisenhower and Khrushchev breakfasted together. Wagging his index finger, Khrushchev went on about how he had opposed Stalin in World War II, trying to stop the dictator from squandering hundreds of thousands of troops in futile frontal assaults against Hitler. Eisenhower was not quite sure what Khrushchev was getting at: that he and Eisenhower were fellow old soldiers standing up to reckless politicians? Or that Khrushchev had defied Stalin, so he could surely defy Eisenhower? In the morning, the two leaders went for a long walk in the woods, accompanied only by a translator. The conversation did not go well. At lunch, both men were grim. There had been no movement on Berlin; Khrushchev, Eisenhower whispered in Andy Good-paster's ear, had refused to lift his demand that the West get out. The president's staff secretary took out a piece of paper and scribbled "Impasse."

Eisenhower was steady and unemotional through-out the talks, and even Khrushchev controlled him-self. "The conversations were carried out in a generally dispassionate, objective, and calm tone," began a White House memo on Camp David. "There were no harangues or outbursts on the part of Chairman Khrushchev."[7] As ever, Eisenhower discreetly reserved his anger for safe targets. One was newspaperman Joe Alsop, who wrote a column comparing the pres-ident to Neville Chamberlain returning from Munich with his umbrella. Ike got on the phone to Secretary of State Christian Herter, who had made the mis-take of speaking to the despised Alsop. Ann Whit-man took notes: "The President in no uncertain terms said that [Herter] should never talk to that 'bastard' and he should keep him out of the State Department and warn everyone not to talk to him at cocktail parties. The President was unusually angry."[8]

Ike took a nap and had an idea. Maybe Khrushchev would like to visit Gettysburg, only a half hour away. The Kremlin leader agreed. Ike's intended destination was not the battlefield, but something more domestic: Ike's son lived with his wife, Barbara, and their four small children (David, eleven; Barbara Anne, ten; Susan, eight; and Mary Jean, three) in an old schoolhouse near Ike's farm. The president called Barbara and ordered her to scrub the children and present them on the president's glassed-in porch in a half hour or so.

Ike delighted in his grandchildren. They were nice American kids, unusually well behaved and accustomed to being trotted out by their proud but stern grandfather, who sometimes lectured young David on "deportment."* (Susan recalled Ike reaching out, with his huge hands, to straighten her shoulders.) Meeting the son of the American leader and his sweet

---

*The Eisenhower grandchildren were aware that they were props on a grand stage. As Khrushchev left, he handed each child a small plastic red star as a memento. When the Kremlin leader had gone, their mother collected the stars and threw them away before the kids could show them off at school. Khrushchev also handed out some Christmas ornaments, including one of a Soviet missile striking the moon, which the family kept.

family in the president's modest home seems to have touched something in Khrushchev, as Eisenhower must have guessed it would. The Kremlin boss gave each child his or her Russian name, except for Susan (apparently Khrushchev could not come up with a Russian translation for a name that, John noted, means "serenity" in the West). On the way back to Camp David, the Soviet leader seemed to soften. By the next day, he had ended his intransigence and agreed to abandon the ultimatum on Berlin. He invited Eisenhower to Russia. The way, it seemed, had been cleared for a summit meeting and perhaps an easing of the impasse on disarmament.[9]

Eisenhower had his breakthrough, or so it seemed. But at lunch that day Khrushchev was testy, fencing with Vice President Nixon. Two months before, in July, Nixon and Khrushchev had hotly debated each other at an exhibition of American consumer products in Moscow. The so-called Kitchen Debate had been, at times, less than lofty. Khrushchev had denounced a congressional resolution calling on the Soviet Union to free its "captive nations": the resolution "stinks like fresh horseshit and nothing smells worse than that!" Nixon had clumsily responded, "I'm afraid the chairman is mistaken. There is something that smells worse than horseshit—and that is pigshit!"[10] Now, over lunch in the Aspen Lodge at Camp David, Eisenhower found himself comically drawn into refereeing whose remarks were the most insulting and provocative, Nixon's or Khrushchev's. An expert in displaced anger, Ike saw that Khrushchev was venting his irritation on his own aides, who were displeased with their boss's concession on Berlin.

After lunch, Khrushchev flip-flopped again. He balked at issuing a communiqué declaring an end to the Berlin ultimatum. Now it was Eisenhower's turn to draw the line. "This ends the whole affair," he said, "and I will go neither to a summit, nor to Russia." Khrushchev was brought up short. He quickly offered that he needed time to explain his decision to the Politburo. Could President Eisenhower wait forty-eight hours? He could. The deal done, the motorcades of the superpower leaders raced back to Washington at eighty miles an hour so Khrushchev could address the American people on television. ("Goot bye! Goot luck!") Back in Moscow, Khrushchev exulted in what the press was calling "the Spirit of Camp David." He put away his rockets for the time being and played the role of peacemaker in a long speech to the Supreme Soviet that was interrupted fifty times by "stormy applause," as *Pravda* described it. He invited Eisenhower to Russia and suggested he bring his family, including his grandchildren. Russia had no golf courses, so Khrushchev ordered that one be built for Eisenhower.[11]

The American president was more cautious. He did not embrace the "Spirit of Camp David" slogan. He knew it wouldn't last; Khrushchev was too mercurial for that. "Those are sweet words, but he won't change his mind about anything," Ike had told Ann Whitman on the first day, when Khrushchev arrived in Washington brimming with conciliation and bonhomie. She nonetheless noted that after Khrushchev's visit the president was "relaxed and in the best mood for days."[12] Ike had gotten a good close-in fix on the Kremlin boss. Khrushchev was, he told Andy Goodpaster, "very powerful, determined, vital, rather crude, quite shrewd, quick as a flash, a man who obviously had the strength to battle his way to the top and stay there despite the danger he was in from Stalin." At the same time, Eisenhower noted Khrushchev's "defensiveness, sense of inferiority, and belligerence."[13] No doubt the Soviet leader would continue to be a difficult partner, but he was, of necessity, the only partner who really mattered in the dangerous game of the Cold War. In the spring, the superpower leaders would meet at a formal summit in Paris. It would be Ike's last chance to achieve détente, a word he had begun to use privately, although not publicly (hard-liners on the right might object; Ike had inflamed leading conservatives from William F. Buckley to Cardinal Spellman just by inviting the godless Kremlin boss to tour America).[14]

*　　*　　*

After Khrushchev had gone home, Eisenhower wrote
a grateful letter to Henry Cabot Lodge, praising the
Brahmin diplomat's "easy and friendly manner,"
"patience and self-control," around the stormy Kremlin leader throughout the ten-day trip. Ike's letter to
Lodge began: "It is always difficult for any male of
the Anglo-Saxon strain to pay a direct tribute or
compliment to another of the same sex and the same
blood."[15] As always, Ike prized restraint, even as he
apologized for it. Eisenhower's rage toward columnist Joe Alsop was always kept private, no matter its
ferocity. In that case and others, Ike's volatility—his
outbursts of temper, biting putdowns, and bouts of
moodiness—was well concealed from the public.
The newspaper correspondents who covered Eisenhower day to day marveled at the president's self-
control. Merriman Smith, the senior White House
wire service reporter, recalled how Ike kept his cool
at the 1952 Republican convention. A very conservative delegation from the Midwest confronted Ike,
who was still new to the rough-and-tumble of elected
politics, with the rumors that Mamie had a drinking
problem. "We hear she's a drunk," said one delegate.
Ike "just leaned back and said, 'Well, I know that
story has gone around, but the truth of the matter is
that I don't think Mamie's had a drink for something like 18 months.'" The general was "very bland.

Never ruffled him at all," Smith recalled; he was "amazed" that Eisenhower didn't even get "sore."[16]

Yet, as Ike's intimates well knew by 1959, there was nothing natural or easy about Ike's self-enforced calm. Ever since he had beaten his hands bloody on a tree as a thwarted schoolboy— prompting his beloved mother to quote from scripture about the virtues of self-discipline—Ike had made a moral contest of mastering his emotions. Asked how he quit smoking cold turkey in 1949, he liked to say, "I gave myself an order," but the truth was more complicated and revealing. At first he had tried by removing temptation by ridding his office of all cigarettes, matches, and ashtrays. When that failed, he tried the opposite approach. He recalled to a friend:

> I decided to make a game of the whole business and try to achieve a feeling of some superiority when I saw others smoking while I no longer did. So I stuffed cigarettes in every pocket, put them around my office on the desk and in other accessible areas and had cigarette lighters instantly available. I made it a practice to offer a cigarette to anyone who came in and I lighted each while mentally reminding myself as I sat down, "I don't have to do what that poor fellow is doing."[17]

Ike's staff was not fooled by his willed serenity. "He was a man of a lot of native animal energy," recalled Dillon Anderson, his national security assistant (1955–56), who briefed him every morning at nine. Television viewers saw a genial grandfather; his aides sat at the foot of Vesuvius. Ike needed to be constantly moving as he thought and spoke. The president would jump up to make a point. Out of respect, Anderson would stand up, too. "God damn it, sit down," Eisenhower would bark. Anderson never felt comfortable as the president nervously paced the office.[18]

Some White House reporters, kept at a distance, began to realize that Ike's cool manner was to some extent a facade, albeit a very impressive one. On his travels with the president, United Press's Merriman Smith talked on occasion to Ike's golf partners, particularly the pros at various clubs. One pro, Don January, swore to Smith that he would never set foot on a golf course with Eisenhower again because the president took outrageous "gimmes," improved the lie of his ball when he felt like it, and took liberties when he added his score. "Here was old Mr. Courtly Manners and good sportsmanship—he was about the lousiest sport who ever lived, in golf. Incredible!" Smith exclaimed in a 1968 oral history.[19]

The truth, of course, was that Eisenhower's house had many rooms, and that while he tried to keep his impetuous rage locked away in the attic, inevitably it burst forth in tantrums and other child-ish displays. Eisenhower could not afford to show his temper or his enormous ambition and ego in public—that was for weaker, lesser men like Khrushchev and Monty. He had to be the one to keep an even strain while others blustered and threatened. Ike's image of calm assurance was his political capital, at home and abroad. He may have felt, without much exaggeration or self-glorification, that world peace depended on it. After his heart attack in 1955, his ileitis episode in 1956, and his stroke in 1957, he had another incentive to stay calm: bottled-up anger could kill him. The catch, as he protested to his doctors more than once, was that his job, by its very nature, imposed a daily menu of vexation and stress.

So Eisenhower took out his frustrations and fears on the golf course and at the bridge table, or aimed his vitriol and impatience at the two people he could afford to abuse because they loved and cared for him unconditionally: his wife and his doctor.

Howard Snyder and Ike were doctor and patient, friends and rivals, sometimes all at once. Snyder was proud, even vain, and one can sense an undercurrent of resentment and jealousy toward the president in his otherwise straightforward medical diary. Dependent on Snyder, Ike was not above passive-aggressive baiting of his doctor punctuated by outbursts of anger. The tensions showed on the golf course. In September 1958, when Snyder tried to compliment Ike's golf game as the two men played for some low-stakes wager, Ike suspected his doctor was trying to jinx him. "My God, two pars and a birdie on the first three holes!" Snyder exclaimed as they played the Newport Country Club course. "The President retorted, 'Keep your God damn mouth shut, Howard,'" Snyder later wrote. He described the president seething on the next hole: "bad drive, double bogie—spoke to his caddie in a voice I could hear, 'Too God damn bad you have people around who shoot off their mouths.'"[20]

On April 11, 1959, when Ike was trying to escape the Berlin Crisis by golfing at Augusta, his inner tensions burst forth in spectacular fashion. Recalled Snyder:

The President's golf was reasonably good on the first nine, but the worst I have ever seen on the second nine. The President was so mad that on the 17th green when he made a bad explosion shot out of the trap and I yelled "Fine shot!", he got so mad he yelled, "Fine shot, hell, you son of a bitch," and threw his wedge at me. The staff of the club wrapped itself

Dr. Snyder (Dwight D. Eisenhower Presidential Library, Abilene, Kansas)

around my shins and the heavy wedge missed me; otherwise, I would have had a fractured leg. He apologized perfunctorily and said, "Oh, pardon me."[21]

As this scene suggests, Eisenhower's relationship with his physician was intimate but fraught. Snyder, who turned seventy-nine in 1959, was a military doctor, a former general surgeon who was so elderly that his hands shook when he gave his patient a shot. ("It hurt," Ike told son John.)[22] In the early hours of September 24, 1955, Snyder had almost certainly misdiagnosed Ike's heart attack as indigestion. But he knew and understood his patient's complicated psyche, and he was devoted, rarely far from his side night or day. In 1955, after the heart attack, Snyder began keeping a daily record of the president's health, medications, and mood. The diary tells a sometimes startling story within a story—how Snyder and Mamie kept the president physically and emotionally well enough to shoulder the immense burdens of his office. As the pressure grew on Ike to leave a legacy of peace for his successor and his country, the president was locked in a triangle of love, anger, and dependency with his wife and doctor.

As many people do, especially if they have suffered serious illnesses, Eisenhower worried about whether his minor ailments presaged much greater ones. A nosebleed made the president wonder: Would the brain lesion from his slight stroke ever be resolved? He was getting up at night to urinate ("pump ship," as Snyder sometimes wrote in his log). Did that suggest kidney illness? Why was he still "flubbing" words? Did that signal an incipient stroke? Snyder continually reassured his patient, but sometimes Eisenhower refused to be soothed. Fussing at the heart specialists who always projected clinical confidence, Ike never got over the suspicion that he alone grasped his own mortality.[23]

Eisenhower became obsessed about his blood pressure, which ran particularly high when tensions mounted. His pulse continued to skip, causing more alarm. He tried to make light of this. "Mamie was present when I took the President's blood pressure," Snyder wrote on October 16, 1958. "I told him 138/80, and she made a wry face. The president remarked, 'If it were any lower than that, I would forget my swear words,' and then he laughed." But at other times, he felt a sense of dread. As the Berlin crisis mounted in December 1958, so did Ike's blood pressure, to an unsettling 144/90. "He cursed the doctors who had encouraged him to accept a second term," wrote Snyder. To ease the president's mind, the doctor began slightly fudging with his patient, subtracting ten points or so from the results when reporting them to Ike.[24]

Eisenhower, too, wished to be less than fully forthcoming when informing the public about his health. He needed an operation on his enlarged prostate. Could he do it secretly, he asked, perhaps aboard a navy cruiser while he was on vacation? "Needless to say, the President is hypersensitive regarding any comment with reference to this part of the male anatomy," Snyder recorded.*[25]

Unremarkably, Eisenhower liked to be looked after by female caregivers, especially attractive ones. He maintained an affectionate correspondence with one of the army nurses, Lieutenant Lorraine Knox, who had stayed by his bedside at Fitzsimons hospital after his heart attack. Snyder shrewdly chose as his assistant a pretty army captain named Olive Marsh. Eisenhower teased her in a manner typical of male bosses of his era. Snyder recorded one exchange: "The President stopped in the office and asked Capt. Marsh where she got all the pretty clothes she wears, then said, 'Who is keeping you?' She laughed and replied, 'That's a hard question to answer, Mr. President.' He laughed and said, 'I guess so.'"[26]

Such laughter had its limits. Eisenhower expected his subordinates to be ready at all times. Stopping by Snyder's White House office to see Marsh on

---

*Eisenhower was mostly a good sport about publicly divulging intimate medical details, though he wondered if it was necessary to report on his bowel movements. Ike had a rueful sense of humor about the sorry state of his gut. "The only thing about which he complains now," wrote Snyder near the end of Ike's term, "is that when he sits for any length of time in his office or playing bridge, he has to get up occasionally and go out and turn loose the exceeding amount of flatus that develops in these periods, and he says you can hear him all the way to the Washington Monument."

March 25, 1959 (on a day when Mamie was telling Snyder that "the President was quite concerned about his health"), Eisenhower was informed that the captain "was gone." Ike blew up: "When I come in to see my girls, I want them to be here," he told Snyder.[27] It was the same for all members of his medical entourage.

One woman who was almost always there was Ike's secretary, Ann Whitman. Whitman, whose marriage collapsed during her time in the White House, was willing to make small and large sacrifices. In a later oral history, she would describe her boss as a "chauvinist" who was heedless of her need for a personal life, but she deeply admired his honesty and felt she could argue with the president about anything, from civil rights (she wanted the president to do more) to those squirrels wrecking his putting green (she wanted to save them).[28] On March 22, three days before Eisenhower's outburst to Snyder about the missing Captain Marsh, Whitman dutifully went to Camp David, where the president had gone for the weekend. Eisenhower never called on Whitman; she spent the weekend sitting in her cabin. "I don't know why I'm here, except that the President I think—and I do not think I'm being vain—just likes to have me around whether or not I ever see him," she wrote in her diary.[29]

Whitman's diary is a barometer of Eisenhower's

moods. As he paced about the Oval Office dictating letters, Ike occasionally revealed more than he wished to, at least to outsiders. On the day after Sputnik was launched, he began a letter to Time-Life publisher Henry Luce, whom the president regarded as a semi-friend and certainly an important figure to cultivate. Dictating to Whitman, the president spoke of "a grave mistake in my calculation as to what a second term would mean to me in the way of a continuous toll upon my strength, patience, and sense of humor. I had expected that because of the [post-FDR] constitutional amendment limiting a President's tenure to two terms, I could rather definitely in a second term be free of many of the preoccupations that were so time-consuming and wearing in the first term. The opposite is the case. The demands that I 'do something' seem to grow."

Eisenhower told Whitman to delete that part of the letter.[30] She knew he was reluctant to make a record of his restiveness, though he felt free to vent to her. The president "complains he never has time for himself," she had written in May.[31] Whitman, along with Snyder and the president's inner circle, increasingly tried to protect "the Boss" from political and other distractions, so he could have more time to think and to relax. They tried as hard as they could not to do anything that could trigger an eruption that might stress his heart and circulatory system. Yet Whitman was smart and sensitive enough to realize that there was a danger of overprotecting the president. In early January 1959 she noted how happy he seemed on returning from a reunion with his West Point classmates. She sagely observed in her diary: "I continue to think that the isolation that is necessary simply because he is President, plus the isolation that is inflicted upon him by watchfulness over his health, is psychologically very bad. He is in the best possible physical condition, and yet all of us tend to forget that and because we value him above all things, tend to treat him sort of in cotton wool fashion."[32]

Whitman knew to take his moods in stride. In early February 1959, when he was feeling weighed down by a bad cold and Berlin, she wrote: "More serious talk of possible war. The President at one point said, 'You might just as well go out and shoot everyone you see and then shoot yourself' —which indicates a remarkably depressed view for him to take. But this mood does not last, and routine matters go pretty much as usual."[33]

The First Lady had a harder time detaching her mood from the president's. She was constantly alert to her husband's maladies and naturally exaggerated them. As the Berlin crisis was erupting in March, Mamie told the gang that she was hoping Ike could truly relax in Augusta because his blood pressure was high. Slats Slater wrote in his diary: "Later Howard Snyder said the latest physical had showed the President in good condition and that Mamie was overly apprehensive. Mamie also said that she kept watching the President during the night, he seemed to be breathing heavily on his left side. There can be no question, Mamie is constantly worried over every little condition of the President—things that would be only vaguely alarming to the average wife."[34]

Mamie, of course, was not an average wife, just as Ike was not an average husband. With her mate gone for years at a time in the service and often preoccupied when at home, she had endured much. Though she had been thoroughly spoiled by her father as a girl, as the wife of a rising and ambitious military officer, "she had to get in line with everyone else," as her granddaughter and biographer, Susan Eisenhower, put it. As a matter of self-declared principle, she was the submissive wife ("He made his own decisions and I followed. I can't emphasize that enough," she recalled in a 1972 oral history).[35] But she was hardly meek. She was an "army wife," observed Susan. "She understood parallel command structures. The West Wing was Ike's; the mansion was hers. It was her command post." On his first visit, Field Marshal Montgomery looked around the first floor of the White House and declared, "Well,

Mamie and son John (Library of Congress, Washington, DC)

it isn't Buckingham Palace." Mamie instantly responded, "Well, thank goodness for that."[36]

Mamie pushed back if Ike bullied her. When, during a bridge game, he barked at her, "Why did you play that hand?" she shot back, "Because I felt like it." (The two rarely played bridge together after that.)[37] Often anxious, she was afflicted by asthma attacks, her chronic inner ear condition, frequent colds, fatigue, and stomach woes (often stress induced). Yet patient continued to act as doctor, no matter her condition. Snyder put up with Mamie's penchant for diagnosing her husband—he called her "Dr. Mamie. "

Snyder also witnessed or refereed a good number of their marital spats. As Ike was itching to get off to Thomasville, Georgia, in February 1958, Mamie urged him to wait a day or two, until the snowy weather and his lingering cold improved. The president "flew off in a rage and went to his dressing room where he remained all afternoon. He would have no part of Mamie. She was quite alarmed for fear his anger would induce a recurrence of cerebral trouble, but there was nothing she could do to correct the initial reaction."[38] A month later, Snyder recorded that the president was mad at the First Lady for "dictating." In June, he wrote that Ike "batted off Mamie's head in the lower hall. Went upstairs and blew off at me, and was in a frightful humor. Said he didn't have a minute to do anything. Jumped into bed with a scowl."[39] Eisenhower groused and grumbled at her and from time to time blew up.

And yet he needed his wife and counted on her. That October, during a dustup, Snyder wrote that the president "immediately bristled and accused her of nagging him so continuously he was a bit tired of it." The next day, the doctor recorded "another wrangle" on a trip to Denver, but then wrote, "Mamie snuggled up to the President in his single bed."[40] In January, with the Berlin crisis brewing, Snyder wrote,

"Mamie called me shortly after dinner last night and wanted to know what was the matter with the President. She said he was absolutely flattened and looked like a dark cloud. I assume this was simply because he was not particularly communicative when she addressed him." But in the same diary entry, Snyder noted that at 4 a.m., the president had awakened and noticed that Mamie was not by his side. She had gone to her dressing room to sleep in a different bed. He found her and crawled in beside her.[41]

23

A Regular Pixie

WHEN IT CAME to imbibing, recalled his son John, Eisenhower had a rule: no more than five ounces of Scotch a day. "He would have a couple of two-ounce drinks, then Moaney would bring him a short one just before dinner," recalled John.[1] But toward the end of his presidency, Eisenhower relaxed his regimen a bit. Howard Snyder kept records — alcohol drove up Eisenhower's blood pressure — and "several Scotches" became an increasingly familiar notation. "He had at least 7 ounces of Scotch and was feeling no pain," Snyder wrote in July 1958, a few days after the invasion of Lebanon. A month later, on a summer Saturday night at Gettysburg, Snyder memorably captured his patient's vexation when his newfangled outdoor electronic oven failed. "To hell with these gadgets, Howard. I think I'll get drunk," Ike said as he climbed the porch steps. "The President had loaded in three good

Scotches between 1815 and 2000 hours...," Snyder noted.[2]

On New Year's Eve 1958, "the President had 3 Scotches, sherry, Red and White wines, and a glass of champagne at midnight," Snyder recorded. More troubling, if understandable, was the president's growing dependence on sleeping pills. The president "not infrequently resorts to ¾ grain [one pill] of Seconal," Snyder wrote on March 19, 1958.[3] Ike was suspicious of his medications, which included blood thinners to guard against stroke, vitamins, and various digestive remedies. "I don't see why you keep experimenting on me and give me medicine all the time," Ike muttered in November 1958, as the Berlin standoff was starting up. He blew up at Snyder for substituting vegetable salt for his regular salt, and Mamie feared her husband would have another stroke. Yet even as he pushed his caretakers away, Eisenhower pulled them back. He increasingly fretted about his health, demanding chest X-rays when some pinkness appeared in his sputum and worrying that he was unable to empty his bladder at night. Snyder tried to calm his patient with good reports, although when speaking to the president he began to fudge the numbers on Ike's cholesterol count as well as his blood pressure. Ike fussed at his doctor for not doing more to relieve his pains. He "would not admit that the aspirin had relieved his headache, although I knew it had," Snyder wrote on August 18, 1958. "He was not in too pleasant a humor with me."[4]

The grousing and bickering, the extra cocktail and even the regular sleeping pill, were natural, not unusual for the time, and not necessarily harmful, particularly under the circumstances. But in late 1958 and the winter and spring of 1959, as the Berlin crisis deepened and John Foster Dulles grew mortally ill, Eisenhower's mood and health had declined. His relations with both Mamie and Snyder were often scratchy and strained.

Reexamining the events of Eisenhower's late presidency through the prism of Snyder's diary raises more questions than can be answered. For instance, most medical experts now believe that the barbiturates in Seconal may impair memory and judgment.[5] What was the effect of one or two Seconals, ingested after 2:00 a.m., on Ike's mental capacities? There is no way to know for sure, and it's perhaps too easy to jump to conclusions. Nonetheless, Snyder's record of Ike's health during that period bears reexamination.

In March 1959, as pressure grew to confront the Russians, Ike experienced chest pains and took a nitroglycerine pill, "which worried Mamie," Snyder recalled. It was a false alarm. "Mamie calls—very concerned about President's health," Snyder wrote a week later. "She thought the President was quite concerned about his health; that he said he had been telling me for weeks that he was not feeling as well as he should." A week after that, Ike vomited and took an enema, fearful that his ileitis had returned. Snyder reassured him, while noting a concern that Eisenhower was overdoing the Seconal.[6] It was only six days later that Eisenhower hurled his golf club at Snyder, almost breaking his leg.

On May 19, 1959, Snyder wrote, "The President said each morning he seems driven to such an extent that he is absolutely pooped by the time he gets home at noon. This is a comment repeated many times of late." Less than a week later John Foster Dulles was dead. The next day, Eisenhower seemed to sink into deep despondency. "Mamie said this morning that the President seemed quite depressed last evening; he has lost his optimistic outlook." Snyder continued: "The President spent 15 minutes in his dressing room looking at old golf balls collected by Moaney, some bearing the imprint, 'Get well Ike,' which were sent to him immediately after his heart attack in September, 1955. The President pawed them like a miser counting his gold."[7]

Such moments were sad if not pathetic, and worrisome to Snyder and Mamie both. But Eisenhower was an extraordinarily resilient man, and his good cheer always returned. On January 23, 1959, only two nights after Mamie told Snyder the president was "absolutely flattened and looked like a dark cloud," Snyder wrote that Ike "had a very convivial and enjoyable time at the Argentine embassy last night for dinner. Mamie said he was a regular pixie and stole the show."[8] For all her hovering and drama, Mamie knew how to cheer up Ike. The one-time party girl who had turned drab barracks quarters into "Club Eisenhower" to entertain friends still knew how to party. In the evening she would sometimes gather friends around the piano and lead sing-alongs. Ike joined right in, rumbling, a bit off-key, the old favorites.[9]

Toward the end of his presidency, Eisenhower increasingly used foreign travel to revive his spirits and show the flag. In late August 1959, before the Khrushchev minisummit, Eisenhower had flown to Europe aboard his own new plane, a Boeing 707, which delighted him with its speed and ease of travel. He was thrilled and "astonished" by huge crowds in Bonn, Paris, and London.[10] At Balmoral Castle, the royal estate in Scotland, Eisenhower seems to have enjoyed the plentiful libations ("two Scotches before lunch, sherry, white wine, champagne and port with lunch, at least two Scotches at tea, a few drinks and several wines and brandy at dinner"). As always, he was charmed by Queen Elizabeth. "During the evening, the President had sat between the Queen and the Queen Mother, and he really had the time of his life. He talked his head off," wrote Snyder. The only ill effect he reported was "dizziness"— quite probably the product of the alcohol flowing through his veins. Indeed, at Chequers, the official country house of Prime Minister Macmillan, Eisenhower imbibed at a Churchillian rate: "He drank several gin and tonics, one or two gin on the rocks... three or four wines at dinner," recorded Snyder.[11]

Meeting with Khrushchev at Camp David a month later, Eisenhower was under the weather again, complaining of a cold and telling the Russian foreign minister, Andrei Gromyko, about his heart condition. The superpower leaders seemed to have taken some comfort from sharing their infirmities. Khrushchev, reported by the CIA to have fainted at a reception in East Berlin in March, talked about his kidney stones.[12]

By December of 1959, both Mamie and Snyder were beginning to worry about the president's dependence on sleeping pills. On December 28, the First Lady told Snyder that Ike "has been taking two Seconal every night for a considerable period of time." Snyder wondered whether the pills were starting to interfere with his performance. Taking one and a half grains of Seconal—double the amount he'd been using previously—after 2:00 a.m. "has some effect on his temperamental reactions to the duties of his office," Snyder wrote on January 6, 1960.[13]

That winter of 1960, his usual bronchitis set in. By March, Eisenhower was fulminating, "By God, Howard, if you don't get rid of this cough for me, I'm going to get another doctor." Snyder wrote that the president was "as sore as a bear with an asshole full of bees." Snyder fretted that the hangover from the Seconal and skipping a decent breakfast were making Ike irritable — "but he won't change," Snyder wrote. Relations between doctor and patient grew increasingly difficult. Ike had complained to Snyder that his dressing room was drafty; Snyder said it was not. One noontime, Snyder found Ike in his dressing room with his naval aide, Captain Pete Aurand, who routinely walked the president back from his office to the Mansion for his prelunch nap. The two men were experimenting with smoke from Aurand's cigarette to show that the room was drafty, that Snyder was wrong. That night a peevish Snyder wrote in his log, "It is just another indication of the President's joy if he can ever find me in the wrong." In mid-March, Snyder wrote in his diary that he would cease meeting with Ike at noon as long as Aurand (an Ike favorite) was around. Snyder wanted a more "professional" relationship with his patient, and thereafter his diary entries became more reserved and impersonal.[14]

*   *   *

In 1959, millions of moviegoers were enthralled and terrified by *On the Beach,* the film version of Neville Shute's best-selling novel, a chilling account of global doom from post–World War III nuclear fallout. The same year, a former newspaperman named Pat Frank published a novel entitled *Alas, Babylon* that depicted the United States under a massive nuclear attack from the Soviet Union. In the novel (later made into a TV drama) the Soviets lob thermonuclear bombs from "hundreds" of submarines and "hundreds of intercontinental missiles." In the *New York Times,* reviewer Orville Prescott found *Alas, Babylon* less exciting than Shute's novel, but the reviewer did not question the premise, which he called "unfortunately not unimaginable."[15]

In fact, in 1959 the Soviets had no missiles capable of reaching the United States. The Soviets did have some long-range bombers, but vastly fewer than the Americans.* True, even one thermonuclear bomb contained more explosive power than all the bombs dropped in World War II (including the two atomic bombs), and a single Soviet bomber over an Ameri-

---

*By 1960, the United States had a dozen ICBMs and about 1,500 long-range bombers. The Soviet Union had two ICBMs and about 120 long-range bombers. The Soviets also had a small number of nuclear-tipped cruise missiles on submarines.[16]

can city threatened unthinkable harm. But during Dwight Eisenhower's term of office, the chances of the Soviet Union even trying to launch a nuclear attack on the United States were remote.

It is puzzling that Eisenhower did not do more to reassure his frightened countrymen. The public was routinely reminded of the grim consequences of nuclear war. One Sunday night on the *Ed Sullivan Show,* the highly popular TV variety program, viewers watched an animated film of an H-bomb attack that depicted melting flesh and eyeballs, accompanied by eerie music. When the film was over, Sullivan just nodded knowingly to the stunned studio audience.[17] Americans never heard from their president that the Soviets were highly unlikely to make such an attack, that the Kremlin utterly lacked the means to knock out America before US forces could devastate the Soviet Union with a far greater onslaught.

Some Cold War scholars have suggested that through most of the 1950s, the Eisenhower administration (and not just some Senate hawks) cynically hyped the danger. Eisenhower, the theory goes, was trapped by his own apocalyptic vision of perpetual struggle with global Communism. America needed to remain in a state of constant alert, if not anxiety, to shoulder the burden of what a later president called "the long twilight struggle."[18] Indeed, Cold Warriors had at times alarmed the public in order to generate support for administration policies. The Truman administration had exaggerated the threat of a Soviet invasion of Europe in 1948 to pressure Congress to appropriate money for the Marshall Plan to rebuild Europe.[19] A believer in the power of psychological warfare, Eisenhower was not above playing some scary notes of his own when he wanted to alert the public (before World War II, some of his fellow army officers referred to him as "Alarmist Ike"). The president spoke darkly of an indefinite "age of peril" in which the nation stood exposed to "the threat of destruction."[20] Over time, reinforced by bureaucratic logic and imperatives, hype can become a mind-set. But Eisenhower was more likely to steer away from the opportunity to play on the public's fear, most notably after Sputnik.

Shortly after Sputnik was launched in the fall of 1957, Vice President Richard Nixon met with Eisenhower to urge the president to use the public's anxiety over Sputnik to generate support for more defense spending. Nixon's relationship with Eisenhower had remained neither warm nor close, but Nixon reliably did Ike's bidding. A dutiful VP, Nixon was generally willing to assume whatever role Ike asked of him. He was ready to receive instructions to play Cassandra, but at this meeting Eisenhower appeared, in his way, cheerfully obtuse. Eisenhower agreed with Nixon that Sputnik had changed the public's mood, though not the military situation, which remained strongly in America's favor.

Nixon pressed: "My point was that we should use this change in public mind to advantage and get the maximum mileage out of it in additional support for his programs," the vice president recorded in a memo-to-file. Eisenhower did not appear to get Nixon's point, or want to. The two men continued to talk around the subject, with Eisenhower obliquely making references to "guns" versus "butter." Nixon wrote, in apparent frustration, "I did not gather too clearly what he had in his mind."[21]

Nixon's notes hardly portray a president who wanted to manipulate public fear; indeed, behind the scenes, Ike spent much of his time trying to hold down defense spending. Nixon had long experience with stirring up fear of the Red Menace. Yet in his speeches in the late 1950s, the vice president was careful to stress that America's forces were sufficient, though he added that the nation must always stay vigilant. Nixon outlined his own speeches, and his drafts show considerable crossing-out and rewriting as he struggled to get the right tone, neither too complacent nor too alarmist—Ike's tone, not his own.

That balance was crucial. Eisenhower could get riled if he was accused of intentionally *understating* the Soviet nuclear threat. "Has the administration misled the American people in any way?" he was asked at a press conference in February 1960. Was the administration covering up evidence of Soviet superiority? Ike knew from the U-2 overflights that the Soviets were actually weaker than was generally assumed. But he would not say so, because he could not reveal the existence of the U-2. Instead, he flared: "If anybody—anybody—believes I have deliberately misled the American people, I'd like to tell him to his face what I think of him. This is a charge that I think is despicable.... I don't believe we should pay one cent more for defense than we have to. But I do say this: our defense is not only strong, it's awesome, and is respected elsewhere."[22]

Years later, Ike's son tried to sort through why his father did not try harder to ease the sense of dread that so oppressed Americans in the late 1950s. "We never discussed it," recalled the younger Eisenhower, who said that he also did not talk to his own children about the fear of nuclear war. (His daughter Susan recalled only that her mother told her she could no longer make syrup-and-snow cones—the snow might contain radioactivity from nuclear testing. John and his wife, Barbara, briefly contemplated building a fallout shelter, but abandoned the idea.)[23] Working at the White House as General Goodpaster's deputy, John Eisenhower said that he himself was afraid of a nuclear war during the Berlin crisis.

He did not expect a Soviet surprise attack, but he thought the Soviets might try to grab Berlin by force, and that the Americans might use nuclear weapons to stop them, thus setting off World War III. "I never knew whether Dad would have used nuclear weapons," said John. "He would never say."

Eisenhower did not use his avuncular manner to calm the fears of the American people. Perhaps he believed that for the American nuclear threat to be credible to the watching Russians, the Americans, too, had to believe that nuclear war was a real (if remote) possibility. In any case, he made no real effort to tell his citizens that they should fear not, or at least not so much. He said very little to allay the anxiety generated in schoolchildren by all those frightening duck-and-cover drills. Eisenhower himself rejected the idea of building a fallout shelter at his farm in Gettysburg. Reluctant to embark on an all-out shelter-building program by the federal government, he grudgingly supported limited funding for civil defense.[24] The president expected the American people—and his own son—to trust him. By and large they did, but they were still afraid.

For all his common touch, Eisenhower had long lived in a world apart from his countrymen, and as his presidency drew to an end, the gap widened. On a summer's night in 1959, Ann Whitman made a telling notation in her diary after the president had driven back from playing golf on a busy commercial thoroughfare rather than by his usual route through upscale residential neighborhoods: "Last night the President was disturbed because so many of the people he saw on the street were dressed badly and didn't have shoulders back—he had come down Connecticut Avenue, something he never does, at the height of the rush hour."[25]

Weary commuters did not meet the president's parade-ground standards. Men were shedding hats and neckties; a few women were even wearing pants.* In *The New Yorker* magazine, James Thurber, who at sixty-six was two years younger than Ike, wrote that America had become a "jumpy" nation, "afflicted with night terrors," living on the edge of nuclear war. Herman Kahn, the rotund RAND theorist, had been traveling the lecture circuit, drawing large and morbidly curious crowds with five-hour speeches

---

*That same month, Mrs. Whitman wrote that the Postmaster General, Arthur Summerfield, had tried to stop the publication of *Lady Chatterley's Lover.* "He has convinced the President that it is a 'filthy' book," wrote Whitman. The book rose to number two on the *New York Times* best-seller list. By April of 1960, Ike was fuming at the New York State Court of Appeals for blocking the post office's censorship of the book.[26]

on living with the bomb, with catchy titles like "Will the Survivors Envy the Dead?" No wonder people were turning away from the humor of Thurber's (and Ike's) era and laughing darkly along with the new "sick comics," or "sickniks," like Lenny Bruce, Tom Lehrer, and Mort Sahl.[27]

The Democrats, meanwhile, were rediscovering poverty. A contender for the Democratic nomination, Senator John F. Kennedy, gave a speech in April declaring that seventeen million Americans went to bed hungry every night. Told about the speech at a meeting of Republican leaders, Ike remarked a bit callously, "They must all be dieting."[28] Ike was hardly a heartless man, and he had protected the welfare state from the Old Guard Republicans, who had been eager to dismantle the New Deal. But he was far removed from the liberal consciousness-raising that would dominate the decade to come.

In the Senate, another Democratic presidential contender, Lyndon Johnson, hammered away at Eisenhower for lacking vigor and verve. More eyes were on JFK. He was, Norman Mailer wrote, the man to fulfill the nation's deep romantic need for a "hero central to his time."[29] The 1960s had begun; Ike remained in an earlier era. He had little time to ponder the new age. He was still fighting rearguard struggles against the "missile gap" and trying to tame the Pentagon, which wanted to build more missiles and bombers to make the rubble bounce. At the annual white-tie Gridiron Dinner in March, Ike's old nemesis Stuart Symington spoke on the need for newer and better weapons. The president followed at the lectern. He described how, in 1953, the Joint Chiefs of Staff had been in his office asking for more funding before he had even hung up his pictures. Ike told the audience that he had paced the bare floors, looked out the window, and asked, "My God, how did I get into this?" He went on to give a speech about the heavy burdens of office that was uplifting and heartwarming, even to the cynical newspapermen who had come for the annual night of spoofing and song.[30]

In private, Eisenhower was beginning to contemplate his legacy. He was wary of the word "great." In June of 1959, when the Senate passed a resolution declaring that General George C. Marshall was the "greatest living man in the world," Ike "took exception," wrote Snyder. Even Christ, said Ike, was not recognized for centuries. On a slow evening in early January ("Let's get drunk," the president told his doctor, "there's nothing else to do"), the talk turned to past great presidents. "The President was electric with his answers—read all the bios," wrote Snyder. Ike rattled off "Washington, Jefferson, Madison, Monroe, Lincoln…Adamses, J. and JQA."[31] Eisenhower knew that if he was to have any hope of joining that list, he needed to do something definitive to reduce the threat of Armageddon. The first step remained at least a partial ban on testing. The endless arms control talks were again stuck: the Russians remained wary of inspections, which might reveal their true weakness. But Khrushchev was beginning to speak more openly about the need for disarmament, if only, the CIA suspected, to keep China from getting the bomb. Since his Camp David visit, Khrushchev had blustered less and spoken, genuinely it seemed, about the need to avert war. Eisenhower's advisers began talking, albeit with a note of skepticism, about "the Great Thaw." The President was serious. "We must get an agreement.…We cannot continue to refuse to go a part of the way.…It is in our vital interest to get an agreement," he told his advisers. Otherwise, there was "no hope for disarmament."

The place to break through would be at the next summit. After Eisenhower and Khrushchev had agreed at Camp David to call for a formal meeting among the great powers (the United States, the USSR, Britain, and France), months of negotiation and dickering had passed until all four agreed to convene in Paris in May 1960. "All the omens are good," Harold Macmillan wrote in his diary on

March 28 after meeting with Ike at Camp David. "He is *really* keen on this." To Charles de Gaulle, his other summit partner, Ike said — one great man to another — "What a splendid exit it would be for me to end up...with an agreement between East and West."[32] First, he wanted more intelligence about Soviet missiles.

24

"The Pilot's Alive"

THE CIA'S RICHARD BISSELL knew well the routine required to send a U-2 on a mission. Bissell would gather up his briefers with their charts and maps and, accompanied by a general or two and sometimes Allen Dulles, appear at the Oval Office for an audience with the president. Eisenhower would bend down over the maps, scrunching up his suit. His rubbery face alive and curious, he would frown and nod and deliver surprisingly precise instructions. ("I want you to leave out that leg and go straight *that* way. I want you to go from B to D, because it looks to me like you might be getting a little exposed over here...") Bissell wasn't always sure how Eisenhower was making his judgments; he seemed to be intuitive, guessing that danger might lie one way but not another.[1]

Overall, Eisenhower's gut told him to be very careful about sending spy planes over Soviet Russia. At an intelligence briefing in February 1960, he remarked, according to Goodpaster, that if a U-2 were lost while the United States was engaged in negotiations, "it could be put on display in Moscow and ruin the President's effectiveness." His remark would prove eerily prescient.[2] John Eisenhower later recalled that his father put great faith in his own hunches and regretted it when he listened instead to contradictory counsel from his advisers.[3] In the realm of Soviet strength, Ike was usually shrewder than the generals, who tended to overestimate Soviet armaments, sometimes for parochial reasons (to justify more resources) and sometimes out of genuine concern for national security.

Ike was under tremendous pressure to gather more intelligence, particularly about Soviet ICBMs. The director of Central Intelligence, Allen Dulles, was caught between military analysts, who were quick to credit Khrushchev's claim that Soviet factories would soon be stamping out missiles "like sausages," and more cautious analysts who saw no evidence that the Soviets had deployed even one missile. Dulles had inflamed matters by becoming confused about his estimates for congressional leaders.[4] Ike was eager to send the missile gap the way of the bomber gap and save the vast expenditures involved in catching up to chimeras. Only the U-2 could provide hard proof.

Nevertheless, he scoffed at air force generals who wanted to photograph more bridges and rail depots; Eisenhower believed the Strategic Air Command already had enough targets to destroy the Soviet Union. And he was extremely anxious about provoking a violent Soviet reaction, especially as the Berlin crisis deepened in the winter and spring of 1959. Eisenhower was always sensitive to the shoe on the other foot: he reminded his aides that "nothing would make me request authority to declare war more quickly than violation of our air space by Soviet air craft."[5]

The U-2 gave Ike fits. After sleeping (or not sleeping) on a decision to fly the U-2 over Russia in April 1959, he had twice reversed himself the next day and denied permission. Bissell's staffers, reflecting their boss, grew impatient; they began sardonically referring to the president as "Speedy Gonzales," after the cartoon character.[6] (It may or may not be a coincidence that the day of his second about-face — Saturday, April 11 — was when he threw his golf club at Howard Snyder, who earlier that week had spoken to the president about taking fewer Seconal sleeping pills.)[7]

Ever the technologist, Ike was waiting, with hard-won patience, for the next generation of spy-in-the-sky. The Corona project would launch satellites capable of photographing Soviet missiles on their launchpads right down to the rivets. But while the U-2 development had been fast and relatively simple under Bissell's skillful leadership, the Corona had turned out to be frustratingly snakebitten. A dozen times Corona flopped—its boosters or satellites spinning out of control, exploding, burning up in the atmosphere, vanishing without a trace into the ocean. According to the National Reconnaissance Office's secret history of the project, Eisenhower "personally upbraided" Bissell after the first failure, but he then characteristically showed patient faith in an undertaking that others might have shut down in exasperation. Goodpaster, who had the lugubrious role of reporting one Corona failure after another to the president, reminded himself that Ike had endured worse frustrations in World War II.[8] Bissell had a hard time being so stoical. The continued fizzles of the spy satellite, the CIA man later recalled, were "increasingly heartbreaking and frustrating."[9]

Bissell had too much to do in the spring of 1960. In addition to running the U-2 and Corona projects, he was the CIA's chief of covert operations, an enormously powerful post. Years later, after the scandals and disappointments, old spies would look back on a golden age of spying at the Agency. At the time,

Bissell (© Acme-Bettmann/Corbis)

the CIA was running operations against Communism all over the world. A new front had just opened in Cuba, where Fidel Castro had emerged as Moscow's man in the Western Hemisphere. On March 18, Bissell laid out to President Eisenhower and his advisers an elaborate, ambitious plan to raise a secret army of Cuban exiles to overthrow the Castro regime.[10] Success, Bissell knew, would guarantee him the job he aspired to as Allen Dulles's successor as director of Central Intelligence.

Bissell was supremely confident, bold to the point

of brashness, unafraid of risk. Just as he liked to sail in the foggy, rocky waters off Maine without any electronic instruments for navigation or depth finding, he was willing to take chances with the U-2. He had inordinate faith that he could calculate the odds and beat them.

Soviet air defenses were improving by 1960. On March 14, as Bissell was preparing to brief Eisenhower on Cuba, he was warned by the air force of a "high probability of a successful intercept" of the U-2 at its normal flying altitude of 70,000 feet.[11] As author Philip Taubman has observed, "These bell-ringing findings should have ended the overflights on the spot."[12] But Bissell brushed off the warning as bureaucratic timidity. To Arthur Lundahl, his chief photo interpreter, he described the air force heads-up as the best "hands on your ass memo" he had ever received.[13] He did not inform the White House of the warning. Instead he pressed for more U-2 flights.

Eisenhower had been "agonizing," as he put it, over authorizing spy flights over the Soviet Union. In February, urged by his advisory board on foreign intelligence to permit more U-2 flights, he had worried about a shoot-down on the eve of the Paris summit. Ike's greatest asset, he told the board, was his "reputation for honesty." He feared squandering it just before the most important meeting of his presidency.[14]

But he agreed to a flight in early April. The intelligence community believed that the Russians were about to go operational with their first ICBM sites, and Bissell and others argued that it was necessary to find them before they could be camouflaged. Eisenhower allowed himself to be swayed, suppressing his second thoughts, according to his son John. The president's son likened Ike's premonitions to those of a World War II bomber pilot stroking a rabbit foot and knowing that one day soon his luck would run out. Against this hunch were arrayed the technical and policy judgments of Bissell, Dulles, Goodpaster, JCS chairman General Nathan Twining, and the president's foreign intelligence consultants, men like General Jimmy Doolittle, who were much admired by Ike.[15] "He gave way, is what he did," recalled John, who was in the U-2 meetings as Goodpaster's deputy. "He had such an array—a unanimous array—of people he trusted, that he just gave in."[16]

Soviet MiG fighters armed with heat-seeking missiles rose to challenge the U-2 flight on April 9, but they were too late and flew too low. Soviet radar had picked up the U-2 almost the minute it crossed the border from Turkey. Bissell did not detail this close call to the White House. He subsequently reasoned that the threat to the U-2 did not appear grave: the MiGs could not fly high enough, and the guidance system on the Soviet surface-to-air missiles was poor above 60,000 feet.[17]

Although his CIA aides joked about the Richard Bissell Air Force (and even gave him an RBAF mug emblazoned "Our Leader"), Bissell, for security reasons, kept his distance from the pilots, who knew him only as "Mr. B."[18] With his fondness for calculating odds, Bissell told President Eisenhower that the chance of a U-2 pilot surviving a shoot-down was "one in a million." Inside a fake silver dollar given each U-2 pilot was a stickpin dipped in poison; the pilots could instantly take their lives with a prick of the skin. The pilots were not ordered to use the lethal pins, but it was hoped they would anyway; there was little chance of keeping secrets under KGB interrogation. In any case, Bissell explained to Eisenhower, the fragile plane breaking up would probably kill a U-2 pilot before he could parachute.[19] The pilots were not told they were expected to die. They were instructed to toggle a switch that would blow up the plane (or at least destroy its sensitive cameras) after a several-second interval and to then hit the eject button. They would, it was explained, have time to get clear of the plane before the destruct mechanism went off.

Bissell had no reason to believe the pilots would commit suicide. Still, he pressed Eisenhower for "just one more" flight before the Four Powers Paris Summit in May. The CIA wanted to get good photos of a suspected ICBM launch site at Plesetsk, in northern Russia. The angle of sunlight in the northern latitudes would be right only through July, and Bissell figured Eisenhower would shut down the U-2 after the summit for most of the summer.

As with earlier U-2 flights, the Russians said nothing publicly about the April 9 mission across their border. In his diary, Ike's science adviser George Kistiakowsky noted that the Soviets made no public protest, "thereby virtually inviting us to repeat the sortie." Khrushchev, it was assumed, had his own reasons for keeping the intrusion a secret—because acknowledging the failure to shoot down the U-2 would be an embarrassing admission of weakness, and the Kremlin did not want to raise a ruckus before the summit.[20] It was the Soviet leader's version of Tell No One.

Eisenhower deliberated for a few days, but on April 25 he granted Bissell's request for one last flight, with the proviso that the window would close on May 1.[21] Bissell code-named the flight Operation Grand Slam. It would proceed over the ballistic missile launchpads at Tyuratam and head north over Plesetsk before landing in Bodo, Norway, a journey of some 3,788 miles. Operation Grand Slam would be the twenty-fourth and boldest U-2 flight over the Soviet Union. Weather caused delays, but on the morning of May 1, 1961 — May Day in Communist Russia — Francis Gary Powers, the CIA's veteran U-2 pilot, said to be a cool hand, took off from Peshawar, Pakistan. The delicate craft climbed to over 70,000 feet, where the blue sky begins to turn space black.

The Soviets were waiting for him. Near Sverdlovsk, in the Ural Mountains, a surface-to-air missile blasted off. Powers felt a dull thud and saw a bright flash. His plane began shaking uncontrollably. As the U-2 spun and tumbled earthward, the pilot removed his cockpit hatch and was half sucked out of the airplane. He would later testify that he was unable to reach the destruct switch.[22]

The downing of the U-2 was "stupendous" news, Khrushchev exulted, but his enthusiasm was forced. The Kremlin leader was faced with a dilemma. He had spent the past six months extolling the promise of détente, as well as specifically praising the American president as a man of peace. The temptation was to say nothing at all and let the Paris summit go ahead. But given the chance to score propaganda points, Kremlin hard-liners were unlikely to let go so easily. Khrushchev was on the spot; his position was hardly so secure that he could ignore such a blatant provocation from the West. In an oral history years later, Charles Bohlen, the expert Kremlin watcher, exactly described Khrushchev's bind: the Soviet leader regarded the resumptions of the U-2 flights in the spring of 1960 as "almost a personal insult. More than that, I think it made him out a fool. He'd been telling obviously all the other leaders that Eisenhower was a good, solid guy and you could trust him, and then—*whambo*—this plane comes over, and this shook a lot of Khrushchev's authority in the Soviet Union."[23]

Ever the showman, Khrushchev decided to put on a spectacle. With great fanfare he would extol the shoot-down of the U-2 but not reveal that the Soviets had captured the pilot alive. The Soviets would sit back and wait for the American response—no doubt a passel of lies. Then Khrushchev would spring the trap and produce the pilot. The Kremlin boss wanted to humiliate the West and extract an apology from Eisenhower, but he did not want to torpedo the summit. He had staked his political future on détente.

Indeed, Khrushchev wanted to give Eisenhower an out, a chance to pin the blame on "militarists" in his own government. On May 2, as the commissars and apparatchiks of the Supreme Soviet shouted, "Shame! Shame!" he heaped scorn on the U-2 flight. "What *was* this? A *May Day* greeting?" he demanded with an exaggerated sneer. But he went on: "The question then arises: who *sent* this aircraft across the Soviet frontier? Was it the American Commander-in-Chief who, as everyone knows, is the President? Or was this aggressive act performed by Pentagon militarists without the President's knowledge?...Even now," said Khrushchev, "I profoundly believe that the American people—except for certain imperialist and monopo-

Khrushchev and U-2 wreckage (© Corbis)

listic circles—want peace and friendship with the Soviet Union....I do not doubt President Eisenhower's sincere desire for peace."[24]

In his role as deputy staff secretary at the White House, John Eisenhower was often given the task of delivering bad news, on the mistaken assumption that Ike would take it better from his own son, or perhaps just because other staffers did not want to get yelled at. The younger Eisenhower was in Denver visiting his ailing grandmother when he heard about Khrushchev's speech. He called the White House and got his mother. He asked how his father liked the news. Mamie relayed his question to the president and reported the peevish answer: "He said, 'Do you think I *ought* to like it?' "[25]

Ike was in a foul temper. He had spent the morning suffering through the annual Operation Alert, the exercise of transporting all the top administration officials to the giant bomb shelter in High Point, North Carolina. The practice drill had been a dark comedy of errors. CIA director Dulles's car broke down; Defense Secretary Tom Gates forgot his ID and was barred at the gate by a marine; General Twining, chairman of the Joint Chiefs, did not show up at all.[26] On Sunday, when the CIA received the coded report that the U-2 had failed to complete its mission ("Billy Bailey didn't come home"), the government had put out a prearranged press release that a weather plane had crashed in Turkey.[27] Now the story was amended—the weather plane had strayed off course into the Soviet Union.

The story would have to be changed again.

On Saturday, May 7, Khrushchev once more summoned the Supreme Soviet to the Great Hall of the Kremlin. "Comrades, I must let you in on a secret. When I made my report two days ago, I deliberately refrained from mentioning that we have the remnants of the plane—*and we also have the pilot, who is quite alive and kicking!*"

Gleefully, to repeated roars and cries of disbelief, Khrushchev detailed the contents of the pockets of the captured spy. "He was to jab himself with this poison pin, which would have killed him instantly. *What barbarism!*" Khrushchev held up a picture of the pin. "Here it is! The latest achievement of American technology for killing their own people!" ("Shame! Shame!") Then there were two gold watches and seven gold ladies' rings (for local bribes, should the pilot survive). "Perhaps he was supposed to have flown still higher, to Mars, and seduced Martian ladies!" More laughter followed. He went on ridiculing the weather-plane cover story and asking how the Americans might have felt if a Russian plane had flown two thousand kilometers into American territory. "Perhaps these outraged people would rather seek the answer from Allen Dulles.... The whole world knows Allen Dulles is a great weatherman!"[28]

Allen Dulles had already heard the doleful news. On the night of Thursday, May 5, the CIA director had been at a black-tie stag dinner at the Alibi Club, a favorite haunt of the Washington elite not far from the White House. He was called to the phone. When he returned he was shaken and ashen faced. He turned to the CIA aide sitting beside him and muttered, "The pilot's alive."[29] A Soviet diplomat had been overheard suggesting that the spy plane pilot had been captured. The Agency had not been sure the report was true, but Khrushchev's confirming speech two days later instantly spawned mocking headlines all over the world.

Eisenhower was standing on the glassed-in porch of his farm at Gettysburg, staring out toward the battlefield where, not quite a century before, Pickett's Charge had failed, when John arrived with the further bad tidings from Moscow. "Unbelievable," said the president.[30] In the Great Game of spying, nations do not admit to espionage on other nations. It is understood that nations *do* spy on each other, but to acknowledge the fact invites diplomatic flaps and, in extreme cases of violated sovereignty, war. But after Khrushchev played show-and-tell with the downed U-2 and its pilot before the Supreme Soviet, the United States could no longer preserve the code of silence it had followed since 1776. At Allen Dulles's office and later at the State Department on Saturday, May 7, officials hotly debated what to say. With Eisenhower's lukewarm approval ("Worth a try"), a State Department spokesman trotted out a tortured half lie. Yes, a spy plane had "probably" flown over the Soviet Union, but "there was no authorization for any such flight." The government was still practicing what intelligence officials called "plausible deniability"—allowing the president to "plausibly deny" any knowledge of CIA activities.

The denial was not, however, very plausible, and newspapers all over the world scoffed or professed moral outrage. In Ike's favorite newspaper, the *New York Herald Tribune,* columnist Walter Lippmann reasonably asked, if a spy plane could fly over the Soviet Union without authority, what was to stop someone flying there with a hydrogen bomb? Lippmann's fellow high priest of establishment journalism, James Reston of the *New York Times,* zeroed in on Eisenhower's detached presidency (it did not help that Ike had been golfing in Gettysburg on Saturday while his aides huddled in Washington). "In denying that it authorized the flight, the Administration has entered a plea of incompetence," wrote

Reston. "It seems as if the country has been humiliated by absentmindedness in the highest quarters of the government."

Sunday, May 8, was Mother's Day, and Ike wore a carnation to church and smiled for the reporters. He was miserable. "Mamie and Ike sat around in the West Hall and got into some conversation about which Ike blew up in anger," Howard Snyder wrote in his medical diary that night. Ike had complained of "bowel trouble" to Mamie, who blamed his Metrecal diet (the president was trying to lose weight).[31] But Ike's stomach was roiled by more profound concerns. From his West Point days on, he had been taught that commanders take responsibility. As Supreme Allied Commander, he had steeled himself to take the blame if D-day failed. On Saturday, when Allen Dulles had offered to fall on his sword and resign, Andy Goodpaster had instantly responded, "That's the last thing the president would want. The president isn't in the business of using scapegoats." General Goodpaster, a fellow West Pointer, hadn't needed to check with Eisenhower; he understood his boss and their mutual code of honor.

On the other hand, Ike knew that if he announced personal responsibility for authorizing the U-2 flight, the Paris summit was probably doomed. So the president told his advisers to put out yet another amended statement—the fourth one in five days—this time stating that the U-2 had been flown under a broad presidential authority to gather information on the Soviet Union. The statement, still not the whole truth, avoided directly tying Ike to the flight that was shot down. Eisenhower wanted to preserve some shred of deniability for Khrushchev to grasp, to justify going ahead with the summit.[32]

By then it was almost too late. When Khrushchev read the Americans' latest statement, "he simply boiled over," recalled his son Sergei. "If they had set out to drive him out of his wits, they had achieved precisely that result." This was a "betrayal by General Eisenhower, a man who had referred to him as a friend, a man with whom he had only recently sat at the same table...a betrayal that struck him in his very heart. He would never forgive Eisenhower for the U-2." Yet despite his gamesmanship, his elaborate trick to trap the White House in a lie, Khrushchev did not really have a well-thought-out strategy. He was "simply enjoying the game," Sergei recalled, with "no definite plan" for how it would turn out. In truth, he was not having much fun. He knew he had as much to lose as Eisenhower if the summit collapsed and renewed Cold War wiped away détente. At a reception at the Czech embassy on Monday, May 9, Khrushchev continued, in his irrepressible and coarse way, to taunt the American president about the U-2: "It is impossible to admit it, but also impossible to deny it. It's like the famous story about the spinster who isn't a spinster—she has a baby." At the same time, he whispered to the American ambassador, Tommy Thompson, "I must talk to you. The U-2 thing has put me in a terrible spot. You have to get me off it."[33]

When the president arrived at the Oval Office on Monday morning, May 9, he said to Ann Whitman, "I would like to resign." Mrs. Whitman knew not to take him literally. She was accustomed to hearing Eisenhower's bleats, feigned and real. Still, this one was worrisome. "He seemed very depressed in the morning," she wrote in her diary. And yet, she went on, "by afternoon he had bounced back with his characteristic ability to accept the bad news, not dwell on it, and so go ahead."[34] Ike had gone to a long-scheduled lunch with West Point classmates, always a pick-me-up, and he felt more at ease now that he had taken at least general responsibility for the U-2 program. That afternoon he summoned the National Security Council and said, "Well, we're just going to have to take a beating on this—and I'm the one, rightly, who's going to have to take it." With more philosophical acceptance than he may have actually felt, he said that "one had to expect that the

Explaining the U-2 showdown; John (on couch) worries.
(Eisenhower National Historic Site, Gettysburg, Pennsyl-
vania)

thing would fail at one time or another.... We will now just have to endure the storm."[35]

Allen Dulles was sent to Capitol Hill to talk to Senate leaders, who were furious about having been kept in the dark about the U-2. He took along Arthur Lundahl and told him to give "the briefing of your life." With maps and giant blown-up images, Lundahl showed how the spy-in-the-sky had been tracking Soviet missile progress, or lack thereof, all along. The senators were impressed enough that they gave him a standing ovation. "Dulles was so surprised by the senators' reaction that his lighted pipe tumbled in his lap and set his tweed coat on fire," recalled Dino Brugioni, Lundahl's deputy. "Lundahl, equally surprised, did not know whether to stand there and accept the senators' acclaim or find a glass of water to throw on his flaming director."[36]

25

"I'm Just Fed Up!"

U NLESS ASKED, JOHN EISENHOWER generally did
not offer his father advice on affairs of state.
But as the presidential jet flew toward Paris on
the night of May 14, John summoned his gumption
and went to the presidential cabin, where Ike was
resting. The younger Eisenhower said something to
the effect that Allen Dulles had "screwed up worse
than ever." Assuring the president that the U-2 pilot
would not survive a shoot-down had been a "lie."
Dulles should be fired, said John. Eisenhower "blew
up," his son later recalled. "He was yelling at the top
of his voice for me to drop dead." Eisenhower's rea-
soning boiled down to "I'm the president and you're
not," John recalled, but he sensed that his father was
so mad because he regretted not having fired Dulles
long before. The son's guess was "not far from the
mark," wrote historian Michael Beschloss, who

interviewed all of Ike's top national security advisers for his 1986 book on the U-2 episode. According to Beschloss, the president told Goodpaster and Gordon Gray that he never wanted to see Dulles again.[1]

As Khrushchev flew to Paris, he, too, became agitated. "My anger was building up inside of me like an electric force which could be discharged in a great flash at any moment," Khrushchev remembered. Actually, as his biographer William Taubman noted, the die was cast back at Vnukovo-2 Airport before Khrushchev departed Moscow: the presidium of Kremlin leaders had decided that Khrushchev could meet with Eisenhower at the summit only if the American president made a public apology for the U-2.[2]

That was not going to happen. By the time Ike arrived in Paris, he had worked himself into a mental state somewhere between righteous indignation and grim resignation. In his memoirs, written five years later, Ike stiffly declared, "For me, attendance had become a duty. It might prove to be unpleasant, but I had no intention of evading it. Indeed, I welcomed the opportunity to uncover more Soviet hypocrisy."[3]

On the afternoon of May 15, Eisenhower met with his Western summit partners, Macmillan and de Gaulle, as well as West German chancellor

Konrad Adenauer, who had come for the expected bargaining over Germany. Ike was all defiance. "I hope that no one is under the illusion that I'm going to crawl on my knees to Khrushchev," said Ike. "No one is under that illusion," said de Gaulle, the most erect of leaders. De Gaulle had tried Ike's patience in World War II, but now he gave him heart. "With us it is easy," he said to the American president as the meeting broke up. "You and I are tied together by history."[4]

On Monday, May 16, President de Gaulle ushered Khrushchev and his delegation up the broad marble staircase of the Elysée Palace to a high-ceilinged room set with tables arranged in a square, overlooking the garden. Khrushchev shook hands with the British prime minister. But when Eisenhower entered the room, the American president and the Kremlin leader did not shake hands. The verbal jousting began right away. De Gaulle motioned for Eisenhower to speak, and Khrushchev immediately objected, saying he had been the first to request the floor. De Gaulle glanced over to Eisenhower, who looked displeased but nodded.

Khrushchev flew off in a rage, real or manufactured. For forty-five minutes, the Soviet leader ranted on about Eisenhower's alleged perfidy. "At one point he became so vehement that I could not help grinning," wrote Eisenhower. "He happened to notice this, and thereafter kept his eyes glued to the text of his speech."[5] Macmillan, too, groped for a sense of ironic detachment as he watched the Kremlin leader wreck the West's hopes of détente. The British prime minister saw Khrushchev, his eyebrow twitching and hand trembling, as a character out of Dickens, a "Mr. Micawber" who pulled a large wad of papers from his pocket and began "to pulverize Ike (as Micawber did Heep) with a mixture of abuse, vitriol and offensive, and legal argument."[6]

From the diplomats' seats along the wall, Chip Bohlen could see "the top of Eisenhower's head beginning to turn red, which was a sure sign that he was beginning to lose his temper. But he held it marvelously and didn't give tongue to it."[7] Khrushchev's voice grew louder, until de Gaulle admonished him: "The acoustics in the room are excellent. We can all hear the chairman. There is no need for him to raise his voice."

When it came time for the American president to speak, he was subdued and matter-of-fact about why his government needed to conduct espionage on the Soviet Union to guard against surprise attack. Eisenhower said the overflights had been suspended and would not be resumed. The meeting broke up shortly before 2 p.m.; the summit agenda—arms control—had barely been mentioned. As Eisenhower walked out of the meeting, General de Gaulle touched his elbow and said, "Whatever happens, *we are with you*."[8]

Back at the American embassy, John Eisenhower was waiting anxiously. "As the car pulled up to the drive, we all peered out the window. Andy Goodpaster was riding in the back seat with the Boss, and Andy's grim look told the story that things had not been a success. Dad appeared completely unperturbed."[9] But once inside, Eisenhower vented. Khrushchev, he declared, was a "son of a bitch." "I'm just fed up! I'm just fed up!" Eisenhower shouted.

Macmillan, calling on Eisenhower later that evening, recalled that the president seemed "very much shaken." (Certainly Macmillan was; it was "the most tragic day" of his life, he wrote in his diary.)[10] Jet-lagged, Eisenhower tossed and turned as he contemplated the demise of détente. The next day, Howard Snyder recounted in his diary: "Tough night. Slept til 0200, takes Seconal, lies awake til 4, sleeps til 9..." Sergeant Moaney had to awaken the president. Khrushchev didn't show at the next meeting, and the summit was over before it really began. Ike must have been deeply disappointed, and yet, as ever, he regrouped. "He seemed in excellent form. He was bubbling over," wrote Snyder that night.[11] Ike went sightseeing at Notre-Dame and Sainte-Chapelle the next day and cooked steaks in the embassy garden. John Eisenhower recalled: "The Old Man, a gourmet, loved to cook, and he went about this hobby with the same concentration he brought to bear on everything else. It had a therapeutic effect on him, and Mother has remarked that whenever something important occurred, Dad's inclination was to head for the kitchen."*

Mamie Eisenhower was waiting for her husband at Andrews Air Force Base when he returned from Europe on May 20. The newsmagazine reporters, standing close by, could see that she had tears in her eyes. Her husband caught her eye and looked away, blinking hard.[12]

Khrushchev railed all the way home. "The American president committed treachery. I repeat the word—treachery!" he cried in East Berlin. Ike's invitation to visit Russia was withdrawn. "A man doesn't go to dinner in a place he has fouled," said Khrushchev.[13] But while he was full of earthy scorn, he knew that his own standing had been shaken. From now on, he believed, he would have to show that he

---

*The younger Eisenhower recalled that in 1941, on hearing the news of Pearl Harbor, "Dad went straight to the kitchen and began making vegetable soup."

could not be lulled and taken in by Western leaders.* The Cold War was about to enter its bleakest and riskiest phase, and President Eisenhower would only be in office for nine more months to help contain it.

In his memoirs, Eisenhower played down the meaning of the collapse of the Paris summit. He came to believe, or convinced himself, that Khrushchev intentionally sabotaged the meeting because he was under pressure at home for showing weakness toward the West. The U-2, he rationalized, was just an excuse.[15] Many years later, John Eisenhower argued that the significance of the U-2 shoot-down and the aborted summit has been overplayed by historians. "Things between [the United States and Soviet Union] weren't that great before, and they weren't that bad after," he said.[16]

Maybe so. Perhaps the Cold War had to steer its dangerous course toward the Cuban Missile Crisis in October 1962; perhaps even without the U-2 cri-

---

*Khrushchev was later criticized by some Kremlin leaders for overreacting, for trying too hard to show his defiance by browbeating the American president. "That was no way to deal with Eisenhower," recalled deputy premier and Khrushchev's longtime Kremlin colleague Anastas Mikoyan. "Because our anti-aircraft missile finally accidentally shot down the U-2, Khrushchev engaged in inexcusable hysterics....He simply spat on everyone....He was guilty of delaying the onset of detente for fifteen years."[14]

sis, Eisenhower's skill at personal diplomacy could not have slowed the arms race. But after he returned from Paris in May 1960, Eisenhower felt a personal sense of defeat and at times despair over the lost opportunity. He bravely masked his discouragement, but his inner circle could not miss the symptoms. In late June, Ann Whitman wrote in her diary: "The President has spent two weekends at the farm, and one weekend at West Point. He has been, almost without exception, in a bad humor—with me, that is—but on the surface has managed to hold his temper and control his emotions far better than I ever thought he could."[17]

Ike let down his guard with George Kistiakowsky, his science adviser. Kistiakowsky was alone in the Oval Office with the president "some time after the Paris Summit," talking about another matter, when Eisenhower suddenly changed the subject to the U-2. Ike charged that "we scientists had failed him," Kistiakowsky wrote in his diary.

> I responded that the scientists had consistently warned about the U-2 eventually being shot down and that it was the management of the project that had failed. The President flared up, evidently thinking I accused him, and used some uncomplimentary language. I assured him that my reference was to the bureaucrats who ran

the show. Cooling off, the President began to talk with such feeling about how he had concentrated his efforts the last few years on ending the cold war, how he felt that he was making big progress, and how the stupid U-2 mess had ruined all his efforts. He ended very sadly that he saw nothing worthwhile left for him to do now until the end of his presidency.[18]

Even after Eisenhower forbade any more U-2 flights over Russia, Richard Bissell petitioned the White House to keep the program alive, in case the spy plane was needed in an emergency. The memo bore the notations "disowned by the Director" and "to be destroyed after reading." Aware of his own precarious position, Allen Dulles wanted nothing further to do with the U-2.[19]

Bissell's willfulness bordered on the manic. Fortunately, in August, the long-awaited Corona satellite succeeded after a dozen failed attempts. It finally proved what Eisenhower had long suspected: the only missile gap ran the other way. While the Americans were building ICBMs by the score by 1961, the Soviet Union had deployed a grand total of four SS-6 rockets, and they were already obsolete.[20]

In an interview after he retired, Eisenhower said the biggest regret of his presidency was "the lie we told about the U-2. I didn't realize how high a price we were going to pay for that lie."[21]

In his role as chief of all covert operations, Bissell was pressing on another front: the assassination of foreign leaders. In the summer of 1960, the CIA began plotting the death of Cuba's Fidel Castro and the Congo's Patrice Lumumba, both regarded as dangerous stooges of Moscow. Neither assassination happened. A myriad of plots against Castro, including hiring the Mafia to stage a "gangland-style" slaying, all failed. The CIA case officer ordered to kill Lumumba threw the poisons (which included spiked toothpaste) into the Congo River in disgust over what he regarded as a foolish mission.[22]

For years intelligence officials, politicians, and journalists have argued over the role of President Eisenhower in the assassination plots. There is no doubt that Eisenhower granted considerable license when it came to covert action. At the beginning of his presidency, in a letter to John Foster Dulles, he broadly defined psychological warfare as "anything from the singing of a beautiful hymn to the most extraordinary kind of physical sabotage."[23] Throughout his presidency, Ike remained influenced by his first "psy ops" coordinator, C. D. Jackson, who had spelled out these simple elements for success: "(a) money no object; (b) no holds barred; (c) no questions asked."[24]

Nonetheless, Goodpaster, Gray, and John Eisenhower all hotly denied that Ike ordered the assassinations, or that he was morally capable of such a thing.[25] Goodpaster recalled that when an aide jokingly referred to bumping off Lumumba, Ike reddened and sternly declared, "That is beyond the pale. We will not discuss such things. Once you start that kind of business, there is no telling where it will end."[26]

For his part, Bissell always insisted that he was operating at the direction of "higher authority," as the Agency described the president, but that the orders were conveyed "circumlocutiously," i.e., indirectly, in order to preserve plausible deniability.[27] It is true that Eisenhower could speak loosely, in a way that could be interpreted as condoning assassination. A Goodpaster memo from mid-May 1960 quotes Eisenhower disparaging both Castro and Dominican Republic strongman Rafael Trujillo and remarking that he "would like to see them both sawed off."[28] Ike may have actually said at a National Security Council meeting in August that he wanted to see Lumumba "eliminated," as one former official later alleged, but the suggestion was greeted with silence and the discussion moved on.[29]

Bissell did not need much encouragement. An

offhand comment from the president, relayed by Allen Dulles, would do. Chester Cooper, a senior CIA official, said that Bissell could see authorization in a double negative: "I think the fact that Eisenhower didn't say 'don't do it' was enough for Bissell." There is no doubt that Eisenhower failed to exercise sufficient control over the CIA. White House oversight—the so-called 5412 Committee, or Special Group—remained weak. Thomas Parrott, the CIA official assigned to record all approvals and authorizations given the CIA by the executive branch, recalled that "Bissell couldn't have cared less what the Special Group talked about. He was bored by it. I don't think he even read the minutes."[30]

It may seem strange that the president, so badly burned in the U-2 affair, was negligent about reining in the CIA official most directly responsible for that fiasco. But Eisenhower was, as he admitted to friends, running out of energy by the summer of 1960. He was playing golf almost daily, if he could, and grousing about his duties. Returning to the Residence after a National Security Council meeting at 12:55 p.m. on July 7, late for his noontime nap, he grumbled to Howard Snyder, "I wish someone would take me out and shoot me in the head so I wouldn't have to go through this stuff." Later that day, after dinner and a movie, Eisenhower stayed up until 11:45

"BS'ing with George Allen, whom he sees only about a thousand hours a month," wrote Snyder.[31]

A week later, Snyder observed:

I have noticed for several days, and particularly today, that the President has lost his sparkle. His facial expressions at most times seem grim and determined. This, I think, is because his "empire of glory" seems to be crumbling about his head, due to the press reaction to his management of the Cuba situation, the Russian RB-47 incident [the Soviets had shot down a low-flying American spy plane at least fifty miles off the Russian coast], the Congo situation, the slippage of the OAS [Organization of American States] program, etc....Many of the President's friends were criticizing him for his absence from Washington, and particularly the fact that [Press Secretary James] Hagerty announced on more than one occasion that he had delivered important international messages to the President on the golf course.[32]

A half century later, John Eisenhower was still wrestling with the question of whether his father was fully present and engaged in the last six months of his presidency. "I think the caretaker element comes in," he said. "He did not let down completely. But he did let down. He did not stack arms."[33] He always bounced back, or nearly. On July 17, Snyder wrote, "The President has lost that terrible grim look he has had for several days." But Eisenhower's inattention had costs, at home as well as abroad. Driving back to the capital one day from Camp David, the president was surprised to see the gash of highway construction on the outskirts of Washington. Eisenhower had intended the roads of his massive federal highway program to run between cities, not into them, where they destroyed neighborhoods. When Ike complained, he was told that the only way the program could win enough votes in Congress was by building highways that cut through inner cities. It was too late to stop.[34]

Eisenhower was keen to help Richard Nixon get elected president in November. In part, he viewed the election as a referendum on his own presidency. He had a low opinion of the Democratic nominee, John F. Kennedy, whom he regarded as the callow scion of a bootlegger's dynasty. Sitting around with his gang at Pete Jones's Newport estate in July, he disparaged patriarch Joe Kennedy. To his friend Ben Fairless of U.S. Steel, Ike said over the phone on August 19, "Motorcades kill me, but I'm going to do them to try to arouse enthusiasm. I'll do almost anything to avoid turning over my seat and the country to Kennedy."[35]

Eisenhower was grateful to Nixon for his loyal service and admired his canniness, but the two men were not naturally close, and even after years of working together their relationship was at best formal and correct. On August 30, after visiting Nixon in the hospital, where the vice president was recovering from an infected knee, Eisenhower remarked to Ann Whitman that "there was some lack of warmth" in Nixon's manner. Nixon has "very few friends," Ike noted. In her diary, Whitman added her own opinion that "the Vice President sometimes seems like a man who is acting like a nice man rather than being one."[36]

For all his protestations that he was not a politician like Nixon, Ike had shrewder political instincts about reaching voters. He advised Nixon not to debate Kennedy and thus give the upstart senator a stage, possibly because he correctly guessed how the candidates would match up on TV. But try as he would to do useful things for and say nice things about Nixon to reporters, Eisenhower had a way of undoing his assistance and praise by betraying his ambivalence. On one occasion in August, reporters were badgering Ike for some evidence of Nixon's role in shaping foreign policy. The questions seemed to imply that Eisenhower himself might not be the man in charge anymore, a sensitive point. Ike was happy to allow himself to be underestimated, but he did not want to appear irrelevant. When Eisenhower bridled at a reporter, Charles Mohr of *Time*, Mohr persisted, "We understand that the power of decision is entirely yours, Mr. President. I just wondered if you could give us an example of a major idea of his that you had adopted in that role, as the decider and final—" Eisenhower cut him off: "If you give me a week, I might think of one. I don't remember." With that, he signaled an end to the press conference.

Eisenhower knew that he had erred badly, and he called Nixon to apologize. As a form of conciliation, he leaned on his millionaire friends to financially support Nixon's candidacy and pledged to stump vigorously for the vice president in October.[37] But then health issues intervened. In Detroit on October 17, Eisenhower was receiving a key to the city and making some brief remarks to the Republican Women of Michigan when Snyder noticed, as he later recorded in his diary, that Ike's "lips were so tight he could hardly smile. He stumbled for words and did not express himself well." The doctor took his patient's pulse and blood pressure and decided, with some alarm, that the president was experiencing a "bizarre cardiac reaction....He was having

Nixon and Eisenhower in 1960. (Library of Congress, Washington, DC)

ventricular fibrillation, which is very dangerous." (The condition was probably in fact atrial fibrillation, which is less threatening.)[38]

Snyder thought that Ike may have been upset by reading an AFL-CIO leaflet that declared, "A vote for Kennedy is a vote for liberty; a vote for Nixon is a vote for bigotry." It is hard to imagine that a mere pamphlet could set him off, but Ike was in a fragile state. Mamie had been worried about the strain of campaigning all along. Back in July, just before Ike was to appear at the Republican Convention, he experienced a nightmare so extreme that he screamed and jumped up "almost out of bed," wrote Snyder. Mamie went to the president's doctor, who recorded: "She said I had to prevent his writing any more speeches because the tension that built up in him was so great, she feared for his health. She said the President had taken two red pills [Seconal] at about 0300 hours in the morning, which has become his regular habit. She criticized me for letting him have them, said they were habit forming. I told her they were the lesser of two evils."[39]

When Eisenhower scheduled a last bout of speech-making for Nixon in the final days of the campaign, the First Lady again appealed to Snyder. "Mamie was plugging at me to tell the President he had to quit speaking and working for Nixon—that he might pop a cork. I have been cautioning him in this regard during the past several weeks since he became involved in a direct effort to elect Nixon," Snyder wrote on October 28.[40]

According to Richard Nixon's memoirs, on October 30, eight days before the election, Mamie approached Pat Nixon, the vice president's wife, and told her that more campaigning might overstrain the president's heart.* She wanted Pat to go to the vice president, to find a way to relieve Eisenhower of his burden without tipping the First Lady's hand. Snyder was apparently in on the plot, because according to Nixon he weighed in to stop further campaigning by the president, saying, "either talk him out of it or just don't let him do it—for the sake his health."[42]

A sad misunderstanding followed. At an Oval Office meeting with Nixon on October 31, Eisenhower was "animated" about expanding his campaign appearances. Nobly, in Nixon's retelling, the vice president searched for arguments to keep the president on the sideline, without divulging the real reason. Nixon was awkward and uneasy; Ike was hurt, then angry. After Nixon had left, the president turned to Leonard Hall, the GOP chairman, and asked, "Why didn't Dick pay attention to what I was saying?" Hall, also surprised, stammered, "He was uptight, Mr. President." Eisenhower burst out, "Goddammit, he looks like a loser to me!"[43]

---

*Mamie's granddaughter Susan disputed this story, telling the author that before she died, Mamie denied having gone to Mrs. Nixon. It would be uncharacteristic for Mamie to interfere in her husband's affairs; on the other hand, she was aggressive when it came to protecting his health. On October 29, citing "Mamie's wrath," Ike wrote an adviser he was reluctant to make an extra appearance in New York. Yet he did wind up campaigning there.[41]

Eisenhower did not stay up to hear the election results. On the morning after, as Nixon conceded the close race, Mamie went to Snyder and said that Ike had told her "there was only one other occasion in his life when he felt that life wasn't worth living, and that was the occasion when it was determined that he could not play football anymore because of his injured knee."[44] John Eisenhower went to the Oval Office and sat with his father. "I rarely saw him so depressed," the younger Eisenhower later wrote. Ike said to his son, "All I've been trying to do for eight years has gone down the drain. I might just as well have been having fun." Eisenhower had to decide whether to stay in Washington and meet Nixon when he returned that evening from California or fly to Augusta right away to play golf. "Almost physically, I shoved Dad into his car and rode out with him to the airport. His conscience assuaged," John wrote, "Dad needed little urging."[45] On the plane, he told his pals that he had just suffered the greatest defeat of his life, then sat down to play bridge. In his memoirs, he wrote about the day, "To waste time mourning the loss of any contest is never profitable."[46]

26

The Underestimated Man

O N NOVEMBER 25, three weeks after the election, science adviser George Kistiakowsky briefed President Eisenhower on the Single Integrated Operational Plan (SIOP), the blandly bureaucratic name for the US scheme designed to destroy the Soviet Union, Red China, and the Soviet satellite states in a single cataclysmic blow if the United States were attacked. Under the SIOP, the United States would shoot the works, firing off its entire strategic arsenal of 3,500 weapons.* The plan was

---

*The Strategic Air Command's General LeMay argued that he needed thousands of bombers to get through the Soviet Union's air defenses (about 6,000 fighters and 1,000 surface-to-air missile sites). But by 1959, SAC had figured out how to evade Soviet radar by flying in low and popping up to drop their bombs.[1]

an exercise in "overkill," said Kistiakowsky. It would, the science adviser said, "kill four or five times over somebody who is already dead." Coming back from the briefing for his noon nap, Eisenhower told his naval aide, Captain Pete Aurand, that the SIOP "frightens the devil out of me."[2]

The SIOP had been Ike's idea, part of his all-or-nothing strategy. He did not want military commanders (or presidents) choosing from a menu of options under the illusion that they could fight a limited nuclear war. He wanted the choice to be clear: use the entire arsenal or not. Nonetheless, he had lost control over the size and variety of that arsenal, and it deeply bothered him.

For eight years, Eisenhower had watched with alarm as nuclear arsenals grew ever larger. When he arrived in office, the United States had about 1,000 atomic bombs. When he left, the number of nuclear weapons, counting tactical weapons (bombs, artillery and antiaircraft shells, undersea mines, and torpedoes), was closer to 20,000. At various times, Ike called the numbers "fantastic," "crazy," and "unconscionable."[3] Again and again, the record shows the president asking why the United States was engaged in "overkill," as nuclear planners began referring to arsenals that would, if triggered, make the rubble bounce. On April 1, 1960, Eisenhower listened as defense officials made the case for increasing from 150 to 400 the number of Minuteman missiles, the solid-fuel ICBMs that would replace the first-generation Atlas missiles. "Why don't we go completely crazy and plan for a force of 10,000?" asked the president with "obvious disgust," Kistiakowsky wrote in his diary that night.[4]

Was the president powerless to stop the madness? It's true that Eisenhower was reluctant to fire subordinates, even when they exceeded their authority, as his experience with the CIA makes regrettably clear. And his own staff was grumbling about his disengagement. In late July, Gordon Gray, Ike's special assistant for national security, complained to Kistiakowsky about their boss's absences. "He said he didn't mind the president playing golf and understood he needed it for his health," Kistiakowsky wrote in his diary, "but he found it unfortunate that the President never had enough time even when in the city to discuss matters thoroughly."[5]

Eisenhower felt a "definite sense of disappointment" with his failure to slow the arms race, as he put it in his Farewell Address on January 17, 1961. By the end, it seems, he was losing the will and energy to even try. But if Eisenhower was worn out from fighting with the bureaucracy, he can perhaps be forgiven. For eight years he had been struggling with the generals and admirals and their allies and minions on Capitol Hill, not to mention the defense industry and its legion of lobbyists, to hold back spending on wasteful or unnecessary weapons. This was, it bears emphasizing, a far more complicated task than just saying no. Eisenhower, the boyhood student of ancient militarists who followed the Roman aphorism *Si vis pacem, para bellum* ("If you want peace, prepare for war"), demanded a strong defense.[6] Needing to pick his weapons wisely, the president was torn by difficult choices and conflicting advice and information. More of the same was rarely the answer.

Ike regularly proclaimed the lesson he had learned from studying Clausewitz and commanding an army: that war is not static, but competitive and evolving, an endlessly mutating monster. Eisenhower often invoked Pearl Harbor, not just the literal surprise by the Japanese but their innovation of carrier-based airpower. He could have cited his own experiments after World War I as a young officer (along with his comrade George Patton) using the tank, the breakthrough weapon of the next war.

Ike wanted to develop a full range of armaments because, as he told the National Security Council in August 1960, "the one axiom that is trustworthy in time of war is that whatever comes and however it happens will be a surprise."[7] Still, as president, Ike was bothered by the proliferation of tactical nuclear weapons (at least fifteen different systems in three services) and the risk that an accidental firing of one would precipitate general war. Control of nuclear weapons was not a simple matter, despite Eisenhower's desire to reserve sole discretion to the president. By late 1959, Ike had formally "pre-delegated" authority to use the weapons if communications with Washington failed after a nuclear attack.[8]

Eisenhower seems to have believed he could control the use of nuclear weapons despite their proliferation and his "pre-delegation" of authority. He may have wanted America's enemies to be ever more fearful, in effect warning them that there are so many weapons, with such a range of lethality, in so many hands—don't even think about tempting their use! But it was a risky strategy and almost by definition only the sort of thing a leader with Ike's experience, stature, and confidence could try. It is perhaps no wonder that Ike's successors were inclined to move in a different direction, toward options that gave them more choices before going nuclear.

Eisenhower continued to be his own secretary of defense. He had to be, because all three of his secretaries (Charles Wilson, Neil McElroy, and, to a lesser degree, McElroy's successor, Wall Street banker Thomas Gates) were either shunned as outsiders or consumed by the Pentagon machine. In any case they had little to say about strategy.[9] Eisenhower's battles were lonely ones. In his first term, he had alienated many of his old army comrades. Army Chief of Staff Matthew Ridgway essentially accused Ike of ruining the profession of arms by adopting massive retaliation, which targeted civilians and relegated the army to the role of cleaning up after nuclear war.[10] Standing up to his own service, to his old comrades in arms, took remarkable gumption; it's safe to say that no other modern president would have been so boldly peremptory with an entire branch of the armed services. In his first term Ike had allies like Admiral Radford, the Joint Chiefs chairman and a tough bureaucratic infighter.[11] But in his second term Eisenhower did not get much help from the Joint Chiefs, who at times seemed joint in name only and failed to resolve interservice rivalries or to control freelancing generals.

Hardest to tame was the Strategic Air Command. General Curtis LeMay's SAC had one war plan, as a naval officer described it in 1954: to leave the Soviet Union "a smoking, radioactive ruin in two hours."[12] SAC was the sole instrument for destroying Russia until, at the end of the 1950s, the navy developed the Polaris submarine, capable of firing guided medium-range missiles off the enemy coast. Before long the two services were vying with each other, with overlapping targets and missions. Eisenhower ordered the Joint Chiefs to prepare one overall plan of attack, but the actual work fell to SAC, which had the computers and the targeting experience at its Omaha headquarters. The navy objected that it was being cut out, and Eisenhower was drawn into playing referee. General Thomas Power, LeMay's successor as SAC commander, was as hard-edged as the blustery "Iron Ass," but he was colder and, some thought, scarier.[13] Power shooed away any interference from the Joint Chiefs and did his best to ignore the navy. Admiral Arleigh Burke, the chief of naval operations, complained that air force leaders were "using exactly the same techniques as the Communists" to win power struggles in the Pentagon.[14] When Gordon Gray, "treading on eggs" as he put it, reported the friction to Ike in October, the president said that he was "not surprised." He held Power in low regard and could believe that he was behaving arrogantly. The president remarked, not for the first time, that the Joint Chiefs should step up and do their job. That job was not only to work together for the sake of the United States but to respect Eisenhower's authority.*[15]

The SIOP presented to Eisenhower on November 25 was almost entirely a SAC creation, with minimal navy input. The SAC targeters ignored or exceeded the instructions and limitations decreed by the Joint Chiefs. Eisenhower was appalled. "The sheer numbers of targets, the redundant targeting, and the enormous overkill surprised and horrified him," wrote nuclear historian David Rosenberg. Wasn't there a way to allow SAC "to have just one whack—not ten whacks" at each target? Ike wondered to Pete Aurand on the walk back to the Residence for his noontime rest. Snyder's diary quoted Eisenhower grousing to Aurand about General Power and suggests that Eisenhower was thinking about

---

*Eisenhower nearly despaired over the Joint Chiefs. On June 30, 1960, he had met with General William Westmoreland, former commander of the 101st Airborne (and later destined to be commander of US forces in Vietnam), who was on his way to take over as superintendent at West Point. Amid the war stories and pleas that "Westy" do something to improve the faltering army football team, Eisenhower complained about the fecklessness of the JCS. As Westmoreland later recalled the conversation, Ike remarked that the Joint Chiefs nowadays "tend to kowtow to the Congress and to make speeches inconsistent with the decisions of their superiors." Ike wanted the new military academy superintendent to tell the cadets "the old simple rule that after a decision is made, officers must be loyal to their commander."[16]

refusing to sign off on the SIOP. But it was too late to change the plan in any substantial way before the new administration took over. He had done what he could.[17]

On January, 19, Eisenhower greeted his successor, President-elect Kennedy, and told him about the man with the satchel—the naval officer carrying the briefcase, later known as the "football," that contained the communications equipment to reach SAC and the missile forces. The man with the satchel, Eisenhower explained, would shadow him for all of his days in office. Kennedy had been briefed on the SIOP in December.[18] Sometime later, after another SIOP run-through, the young president-elect would remark to his secretary of state, Dean Rusk, with a mixture of wonder and disgust, "And they call us human beings." But Kennedy and the presidents who followed him throughout the Cold War and beyond did not trim back the SIOP. It in fact grew more complex and fantastically apocalyptic.[19]

It's not clear who first coined the term "military-industrial complex," but Ike's aides were long accustomed to hearing him vent on the subject.[20] Staff Secretary Andy Goodpaster routinely recorded Ike's gripes about the coziness between defense contractors and congressmen. (Goodpaster later said that Eisenhower would have referred to the "military-industrial-congressional complex," but left out Congress "out of respect for the other branch of government.")[21] The president's aides were on the alert for proof of Cold War profiteering. Jim Killian, Ike's first science adviser, remembered Eisenhower "repeatedly" growing angry over "the excesses, both in text and advertising, of the aerospace-electronics press, which advocated ever bigger and better weapons to meet an ever bigger and better Soviet threat they had conjured up."

For at least two years, Eisenhower had contemplated following the example of his hero George Washington, who in 1797 had delivered a farewell address warning the nation against alliances abroad. The modern armsmakers' ads, and the presidential scorn for them, helped stir White House speechwriter Malcolm Moos to begin drafting an address about the dangerous alliance of the defense industry with the military, scientists, and policy makers. Around the first week of November, Moos showed the draft to Eisenhower, who said, "I think you've got something here." The speech went through twenty-nine drafts, heavily edited by Ike and his brother Milton, all built around the theme of the "military-industrial complex."[22]

In later years the speech would be regarded as a classic, a solemn warning from a soldier-prophet. At the time, it was respectfully received and then overlooked or ignored. A more powerful trope about Ike's legacy, far less flattering, had already entered the popular imagination. The jokes had been spreading for some time. In the mid-1950s, until Sherman Adams was disgraced over the Goldfine affair, wags declared that while it would be terrible if Eisenhower died and Nixon became president, it would be worse if Adams died and *Eisenhower* became president. "Eisenhower proved we didn't need a president," snickered the Democrats, while Georgetown wits described the Eisenhower administration as "the bland leading the bland."[23]

Granddad in a golf cart, the do-nothing, platitude-spouting, syntax-mangling, over-the-hill oldest man ever to occupy the White House—JFK's followers and admirers jeered and mocked, the better to accentuate the vigor and youthful eloquence of their champion. Reporters and pundits, particularly Joe Alsop, who was so close to Kennedy that the new president visited his house late on Inauguration Night, picked up the refrain. The hatchet job was one of the most lasting and effective in political history. A few observant journalists eventually saw through it. One of the most perceptive, Murray Kempton, wrote an article entitled "The Underestimation of Dwight D. Eisenhower" in *Esquire* in September 1967. Kempton saw that Ike had been far more in control than reporters realized; he was "the great tortoise upon whose back the world sat for eight years." The sophisticates in the press had failed to recognize "the cunning beneath the shell," wrote Kempton.[24] As presidential archives opened over time, scholars would discover Ike's hidden hand. Still, the misimpression of Ike as pleasantly ineffective has been remarkably enduring.

Eisenhower was mindful of the rap against him. He did not entirely dispute it. In August 1960, Henry Luce, the Time-Life publisher and Eisenhower's friend, wrote a *Life* editorial praising Ike as a unifier and "guardian of world peace." But, Luce acknowledged, there was some "substance to the charge that Ike had rather reigned than ruled. He has tended to assume, as you can in the Army but not in the White House, that an order once given is self-executing.... He has been an easy boss." Eisenhower sent Luce a thoughtful and revealing private response. "I plead guilty to the general charge that many people have felt I have been too easy a boss," he wrote. The president went on ("I do not mean to defend, merely to explain") to note that he was operating with a divided and complex government that required cooperation and compromise. He concluded, on a more personal note:

Of course I could have been more assertive in making and announcing decisions and initiating programs. I can only say that I adopted and used those methods and manners that seemed to me most effective. (I should add that one of my problems has been to control my temper—a temper that I have had to battle all my life!)

Finally, there is the matter of maintaining a respectable image of American life before the world! Among the qualities that the American government must exhibit is dignity. In turn the principal government spokesman must strive to display it. In war and in peace, I've no respect for the desk pounder, and have despised the loud and slick talker. If my own ideas and practices in this matter have sprung from weakness, I do not know. But they were and are deliberate or, rather, natural to me. They are not accidental.[25]

As Eisenhower was preparing to leave office, he noted the fawning press coverage of his glamorous successor and likened it to a "cult." But after meeting twice with Kennedy in December and January, he lowered his guard and softened his attitude toward his successor. He found Kennedy thoughtful and respectful, a good listener, though he later concluded that Kennedy had not paid enough attention to his warnings, and he never got over his feeling that Kennedy was "immature."[26]

On January 19, the day before his inauguration, Kennedy came to the White House to discuss the transfer of power with Eisenhower. High on the agenda was the small Southeast Asian country of Laos, which was collapsing in civil war and seemed headed toward a Communist takeover. Kennedy asked Eisenhower which option he preferred: armed intervention by the United States or settling for a coalition government that would include Communist representatives, possibly controlled by Beijing. Neither, responded Eisenhower. Armed intervention would cast the United States as colonialists, and a coalition government could lead to a Communist takeover that would spread throughout the region. Kennedy was confused. If intervention or a compromise was not the answer, then what was? Eisenhower said he doubted the Chinese wanted a major war. The record of the meeting does not show if Eisenhower smiled, or concealed a smile, but according to the notetaker, "The President further stated that it is like playing poker with tough stakes and there is no easy solution." In other words, if Ike were president, he'd take a hard line — and bluff. At least that's what Ike seemed to be signaling. But he was cryptic and opaque, and Kennedy's advisers, hearing what they wanted to hear, later claimed Ike had urged JFK to send in the troops.[27]

*　　*　　*

At noon the next day, Eisenhower, after a half century of public service, would become a private citizen. As he pondered giving up power to men he did not entirely trust, his battered body rebelled in familiar ways. When Ike presented General LeMay (now Air Force Vice Chief of Staff) and Convair (charter member of the military-industrial complex) an award on December 5 for development of the Atlas missile, his blood pressure "was out of whack," recorded Howard Snyder. After meeting President-elect Kennedy two days later, Ike experienced such a severe attack of intestinal gas on the golf course that he came back to the White House and gave himself an enema.[28]

For years, Eisenhower had talked about how much he longed to be free of the burdens of office, to have all the time he wanted to go fishing or just laze about. But as he sat in the Oval Office in the days before January 20, he grew morose listening to the bang and clatter of construction workers erecting temporary stands for the inaugural parade. To a visitor, he gloomily remarked, "it's like being in the death cell and watching them put up the scaffold." Eisenhower had been serving his country continuously since he had arrived as a plebe at West Point in 1911. His life had been devoted to duty. He didn't know what else to do.[29]

THE UNDERESTIMATED MAN

Ike puzzled President Kennedy by asking to revert to his five-star military rank, which among other things meant that he would be referred to as "General," not "Mr. President." No extra money or greater benefits were involved, though as a general he could keep Sergeant Moaney on as his valet.[30] But Ike saw himself more as a soldier than as a statesman. His legacy as president, he knew, would not be nearly so glorious or easily mythologized as his triumphs as Supreme Allied Commander, which had won him the presidency in 1952 virtually by acclamation. In 1946 he had written his clear, crisp memoirs of World War II in ten months. After leaving the White House, he struggled over his presidential memoirs for three years, and the two-volume product is turgid. He could write in an unemotional, straightforward way about waging war; the art of diplomacy and statecraft was harder to explain, especially when Ike remained wary of revealing his hidden hand. Ike was more comfortable as a soldier, yet his greatest victories were the wars he did not fight.

Epilogue
Peace

RICHARD BISSELL SEDUCED the Kennedys, for a time. JFK was introduced to Bissell in August 1960, at a dinner party given by their mutual friend Joe Alsop at his house in Georgetown. Over brandy and cigars, Alsop praised the CIA man for his brilliance and toughness. After the election, a member of Kennedy's transition team said to the president-elect, "There must be someone you really trust within the intelligence community. Who is that?" Kennedy answered, "Richard Bissell." In February, shortly after the inauguration, Allen Dulles put together a little dinner at the Alibi Club for the top men at the CIA and White House so they could get to know one another. Bissell was the star of the evening. "I'm your basic man-eating shark," said the CIA's chief of covert operations, with just the right mix of bravado and self-mockery to charm the New Frontiersmen.

JFK regarded national security meetings as a "waste of time," and his national security adviser, McGeorge Bundy, slashed away at Eisenhower's cumbersome (but thorough) planning process. The Kennedys would be vigorous and "forward leaning," in a phrase of the day, not poky and bureaucratic like the previous administration. With very little questioning or debate, Bissell was able to persuade Kennedy to sign off on a CIA-backed invasion of Cuba by an exile force in April.

The Bay of Pigs was a disaster, in many ways worse than the U-2 shoot-down of the previous spring. More than a thousand of the invaders were killed or captured. The American role, at first denied, was soon exposed. As the invasion failed, the president was seen wandering the South Grounds of the White House at 4:00 a.m., head lowered, hands thrust in his pockets. When he awoke in his bed at dawn, he was weeping.[1]

That morning, April 19, President Kennedy called Eisenhower in Gettysburg and asked to meet him at Camp David for a postmortem. Kennedy had never visited the presidential retreat, so, oddly, Eisenhower, the ex-president, acted as host, showing his successor around the simple cabins on the wooded Maryland mountainside. The young president was chastened. "Well, just somewhere along the line I blundered, and I don't know how badly," Kennedy told Eisenhower. "Everyone approved—the JCS, the CIA, my staff." Eisenhower started asking a series of pointed questions to learn precisely what the military had said about the CIA plan. Uncomfortably, Kennedy admitted that the Joint Chiefs of Staff had only offered "guarded approval."

Gingerly, Eisenhower pressed a little further. "Mr. President," he addressed Kennedy, "before you approved the plan did you have everyone in front of you debating the thing so you could get the pros and cons yourself and then make a decision, or did you see these people one at a time?" Kennedy smiled ruefully and admitted that he had not forced a full or formal airing of the invasion plan.

Eisenhower said nothing more, but he knew from long experience what had really happened: the Bay of Pigs was a CIA show; the military had signed off without *truly* approving because the Joint Chiefs knew that the CIA would take the blame if the operation failed. Kennedy, a junior officer in World War II, lacked Eisenhower's practiced judgment in these matters—Ike's ear for the inaudible dog whistle used by generals sidestepping responsibility. It had not helped Kennedy that the CIA's Bissell had suppressed skeptical views of some lower-level military officers. Trying to hide the American hand, Kennedy had at the last minute unwisely canceled US air cover for the invasion. Eisenhower had known about—indeed, encouraged—the CIA's plotting against the Castro regime, but he had made it clear that he would not agree to back a rebel force unless he was sure of success. Now he repeated to Kennedy his basic philosophy in military matters: all or nothing. Go in to win or don't go. "There is only one thing to do when you get into this kind of thing: make sure it succeeds," Ike admonished. "Anything like it in the future will succeed," replied the chastened Kennedy. "Well, I'm glad to hear that," said Ike.*[2]

During the presidential campaign, Kennedy had rejected Eisenhower's doctrine of massive retaliation in favor of "flexible response," the capacity to fight small wars. General Maxwell Taylor, who as Army Chief of Staff had unsuccessfully beseeched Ike to build up conventional forces, was now JFK's main

---

*Eisenhower tried to cover his own tracks on the Bay of Pigs, which were not insignificant. Ike believed there would be no trace of his involvement in the early planning because he had ordered that no records be kept, so he was taken aback when Gordon Gray, his special assistant for national security, informed him that he had kept notes. When the documents showed Eisenhower's involvement in plans for raising an exile force, Eisenhower asked that Gray rewrite his notes to omit the word "planning." "We did no military planning," Eisenhower insisted. On rare occasions, Eisenhower tinkered with correspondence he planned to reproduce in his memoirs. When his son caught him at it, Ike huffed, "What's the matter, I can't misquote myself?"[3]

military adviser.[4] The key to Ike's all-or-nothing doctrine was his personal credibility. He had been able to bluff because of who he was and what he had done—the man who had liberated Europe in World War II and repeatedly faced down Soviet and Red Chinese aggression in the Cold War. Former lieutenant Kennedy had no such bona fides. Khrushchev decided to test the young president right away. At an informal summit meeting in Geneva in June, the Kremlin leader renewed his ultimatum on Berlin.

Suddenly Kennedy was confronted with dangerous choices. Was he *really* willing to fight the Russians over Berlin? He could send tanks down the autobahn, as some of his advisers wanted to do, but how could he be sure the fighting would not quickly escalate, forcing the terrible decision to go nuclear? Kennedy soon discovered that he did not have any good options. The Joint Chiefs of Staff informed him that the Russians would crush NATO forces on the ground; after a four-month mobilization, the US Army might hold off the Red Army for five days, perhaps fifteen if the NATO allies helped out. Dean Acheson, summoned to the Oval Office to advise the new president, told JFK to think very carefully about when to resort to nuclear weapons, and then "tell no one at all what his conclusion was." For Kennedy it was a crash course in the burdens of his office, that loneliness of nuclear command.

The Berlin Wall, perversely, took Kennedy off the hook. In August, when the Soviets began throwing up concrete and barbed wire along the divide between the East and West sectors of the city, the wall stopped the steady stream of East Berliners fleeing to the West and defused the crisis. There were some tense confrontations between Soviet and American tanks in October, but the moment passed. Neither side wanted to push to the brink.[5]

In Southeast Asia, Kennedy managed to work a settlement with the Communists in Laos, but in South Vietnam, the North Vietnamese–backed Vietcong were making inroads against the US-backed regime of President Ngo Dinh Diem. In the fall of 1961, General Taylor advised President Kennedy to send 8,000 US combat troops to Vietnam. Kennedy was reluctant. "The troops will march in; the crowds will cheer; and in four days everyone will have forgotten. Then we will be told that we have to send in more troops. It is like taking a drink. The effect wears off, and you have to take another," he told Arthur Schlesinger.[6] But Kennedy could not resist the pressure from the Pentagon and his advisers, and before long the 800 military advisers who were serving in Vietnam during the Eisenhower administration became 15,000 combat troops (the number would ultimately exceed 500,000).

Eisenhower was briefed on the escalation by John

McCone, who had replaced Allen Dulles as CIA chief after the Bay of Pigs (Bissell was fired, too). Eisenhower was "very disturbed" by the troop increase, McCone later said in an oral history. The former president was "bitterly critical" of JFK and then Lyndon Johnson as America slowly fed troops into the widening war.[7] But he kept his criticisms quiet. He believed that ex-presidents should support the man in office.

To escape the raw Pennsylvania winters, Eisenhower began spending January to March in the California desert. Robert McCulloch, a Texas oilman, built a house for Ike and Mamie on the 11th fairway at the Eldorado Country Club, a luxuriant golf course at the foot of a craggy ridge officially dubbed "Mount Eisenhower." The nonstop games of golf and bridge distracted the former president, but at times he seemed to drift into some inner world of his past. Ike kept an office at the nearby ranch owned by Jackie Cochran, the woman who had helped persuade him to run for president in 1952. Cochran recalled finding Ike all alone in his office one Sunday, not reading, not working. "He came here year after year," she remembered, "and I frankly never understood him."[8]

By summer, Ike would be back on the farm in Gettysburg. The evening routine was always the same: dinner on TV trays served by Sergeant Moaney promptly at 7:30 p.m. Then began the ritual that Ike's treasured grandson, David, observed as a boy spending summers with his grandparents. Ike would start fiddling with his favorite new toy, the remote channel changer, impatiently switching channels every ninety seconds or so, and occasionally hitting the wrong button so the TV would cycle through all the channels. "Ike," Mamie would plead, "make up your mind." David later recalled, "I tried to be inscrutably enthusiastic about everything. Mamie would interrupt, and Granddad would resume punching the remote."[9]

The scene on the glassed-in porch was anything but relaxed. Ike would gnaw at his glasses, as he always did when Mamie kept him waiting or irked him in some way. But the two were inseparable, joined by affection and long years of shared sacrifice. The bond was obvious to Ike's female admirers. Clare Boothe Luce, wife of the Time-Life publisher and a beautiful and accomplished diplomat and playwright, liked to flirt with the president. (In 1953, Ike's appointments secretary, Tom Stephens, noted that Luce got more time with the president than other ambassadors; "golden curls have more leverage than striped pants," he observed.)[10] But Mrs. Luce recognized Ike's fierce attachment to his wife. "You can't talk to Ike, at least I can't talk to Ike, for more than three minutes before he says, 'Mamie and I.' You know he thinks in terms of himself and his wife. It's always 'Mamie and I,'" she later observed.[11]

Mamie understood her husband, loved him, put up with him, and didn't try very hard to change him or explain him. In 1962, Darryl Zanuck produced *The Longest Day,* his epic movie about the invasion of Normandy. Ike declined Zanuck's offer of a starring role playing himself, but he did consent to view a screening. A few minutes into the movie, Eisenhower turned to Mamie and said he was leaving. "Ike, you can't do that," his wife said. "The hell I can't," said Eisenhower, and walked out. David Eisenhower asked Mamie what had bothered his grandfather about the movie. "Oh, you know," she breezily responded. "Literary license."[12]

President Lyndon Johnson, in his oleaginous way, courted and flattered Eisenhower, sending him fawning notes and often seeking his advice. Eisenhower recoiled from LBJ's glad-handing. ("He's using me," Ike once grumbled to his aide Bryce Harlow as a limo transported him to the White House.) Yet once in the Oval Office, Ike was all smiles and geniality with the president. Johnson wanted Eisenhower's approval, and he got it from a variety of public statements by the former president. But privately, and tragically, the two men talked past each other on

LBJ and Eisenhower (Dwight D. Eisenhower Presidential Library, Abilene, Kansas)

the subject of Vietnam. Eisenhower's advice was always the same: if you fight, fight to win. But LBJ was a politician more accustomed to half measures and compromises, and he didn't really listen to what Ike was saying. In the fall of 1966, Secretary of Defense Robert McNamara and his deputy, Cyrus Vance, went to visit Ike at Walter Reed, where the ex-president was resting after his second heart attack. "Why don't you declare war?" demanded Eisenhower. "Take Hanoi," he urged. Johnson's men didn't know what to say. "Those two turned blue and got out of there," recalled John Eisenhower. Vietnam was precisely the sort of brushfire war Eisenhower had managed to dodge during his presidency. But once in, he believed, the United States had to go all the way.

Eisenhower was beginning to slow down. His heart was failing; from time to time he became depressed. He was appalled by draft-card burners and long-haired student protesters. In 1967, he roused himself to write an article for *Reader's Digest* called "We Should Be Ashamed," deploring the "growing disrespect for law and order."[13]

The heart attacks kept coming: four more by the winter of 1969, when he was seventy-nine. By then Ike had made his home in Ward Eight of Walter Reed, the VIP suite now decorated in Mamie's pinks and greens. He listened to "Climb Ev'ry Mountain," over and over, and flirted with the nurses. "Mamie monitored the nurses like a hawk," recalled grandson David. "Major Philips, a slim, pert redhead, was Granddad's favorite. She aroused a slight jealousy in Mamie. Years later, Mamie recalled, 'He was an old man, but after all he'd survived, you never know.'"

He would not give up. As his heart deteriorated, he lay under a machine he called "the Bulldozer," his head barely visible, wires and tubes snaking around him. He was in too much pain to say more than a few words. Finally he said to his son, "I've had enough, John. Tell them to let me go." To his wife he growled, "Now, Mamie, don't forget that I have always loved you."[14] On March 28, 1969, summoned by Ike, his son and grandson formed up to stand at rigid attention. Eisenhower looked at his son and said, "I want to go; God take me." He lapsed into unconsciousness. Three hours later, shortly after 12:30 p.m., he died. He was buried in an eighty-dollar soldier's coffin next to his first son, Icky, in a small chapel in Abilene. A decade later, Mamie joined them.[15]

As Eisenhower lay dying in 1969, he contemplated his memorial. "Just don't let them put me on a horse," he muttered.[16] Eisenhower may not have wanted to be placed on a pedestal, but he had fretted over his legacy. The peace and prosperity that marked his two terms in office "didn't just happen, by God," he complained more than once. But he had difficulty articulating just how they had happened. He never could admit that he had pulled off a giant bluff, that he had kept the peace by threatening all-out war. His all-or-nothing strategy worked brilliantly. The Russians did not look at Ike and see a humble farm boy from sleepy turn-of-the-century Abilene, Kansas, recalled John Eisenhower, but rather "Wild Bill Hickok," the gun-toting US marshal from the Abilene of the earlier Wild West.[17] It is likely that Eisenhower had no intention of ever using nuclear weapons, as his closest aide, Andy Goodpaster, believed. But the president never said as much to Goodpaster or anyone else. Years later, scholars would puzzle over Ike's real intentions. Robert Bowie, chief planner at the State Department, told Richard Immerman, a leading Cold War scholar and his coauthor of *Waging Peace,* one of the more insightful books on the Eisenhower era, that he was sure Ike would have been willing to use nuclear weapons in a crisis (say, if Red China moved on Taiwan). But Milton Eisenhower, the president's brother and a true White House insider like Goodpaster, told Immerman that Ike never would have used nuclear weapons. "Milton would just sort of smile," recalled Immerman.[18]

Through endless meetings on how to maintain credible deterrence, Ike resolutely kept his own counsel, understanding that the key was to "tell no one" whether he would be willing to use nuclear weapons. Eisenhower was equally adept at controlling his own military by simply denying it the means to fight small wars. But he did not advertise his strategy. Rather, he spoke in bromides about peace through strength.

Eisenhower's approach worked only for Eisenhower. Kennedy and Johnson could not have pulled it off even if they had wanted to. They lacked the credibility that was uniquely Eisenhower's; they had not liberated Europe or made enormous life-and-death decisions on the battlefield. Instead, believing that neither side would engage in nuclear war ("mutual assured destruction," or MAD, as it was articulated by JFK's defense secretary Robert McNamara), Kennedy and Johnson adopted a policy of "flexible response" that made possible the small wars Eisenhower did his best to avoid. The result was Vietnam.

During the course of his life, Eisenhower walked the battlefield at Gettysburg over and over again. As a West Point cadet in 1915, he came to the Pennsylvania farm town with his entire class to see where the Union had repulsed the Confederacy at Little Round Top on July 1, 1863, and to solemnly walk along the line where Pickett made his fatal charge on the third and decisive day. At the end of World War I, Ike was based in Gettysburg at Camp Colt, training men in maneuver warfare with a single tank and some trucks.

In 1950, Eisenhower had bought his farm not far from the battlefield where the Civil War turned, where the Union triumphed, and where Abraham Lincoln gave his most memorable address. Eisenhower seemed more preoccupied with the South's defeat than with the Union's great victory. His glassed-in porch looked out on the ridgeline where the Confederates retreated on the second and third days of the battle. The original farmhouse (largely rebuilt by Mamie) had been used as a Confederate aid station for the wounded. The ground where Ike practiced his putting had been wetted with Confederate blood.

To Eisenhower, as he took famous visitors on tours of the hallowed ground, Gettysburg was a lesson in how *not* to fight. Field Marshal Montgomery, taking the role of General Robert E. Lee, asked Ike, "What would you have done if I gave the order to Pickett to charge?" Eisenhower answered, "Fired you." Ike revered Lee but could not forgive the uncharacteristic passivity of the Confederate general's instruction to Pickett: "Do it if you can." In oral histories recorded by the US Park Service, which maintains the Eisenhower farm, Secret Service men recalled taking Eisenhower to the battlefield again and again.[19]

Despite his blunder, Lee remained a hero to Ike. But his greater hero was Abraham Lincoln, the "master of men" of Ike's favorite biography, by Alonzo Rothschild. In his first year in the White House, Eisenhower had reread the story of how the Civil War president, by guile and patience, by a subtle mix of moral, mental, and physical strength, had bent to his will some outsize figures. In the small office at the back of Ike's farmhouse in Gettysburg where he went to take secure telephone calls, there was but one picture, a portrait of Lincoln. In the glassed-in porch, on top of the TV set, sat a small bust of Lincoln. In retirement, as he punched impatiently at the remote control, Ike looked at Lincoln's bust for hours every night.

Like Lincoln, Eisenhower could be moody and temperamental. But also like Lincoln, he was supremely confident. His was not the confidence of the weak, the arrogance of the vain and needy. Rather, he had the kind of confidence that allowed him to be humble. He was willing to appear slower and sweeter than he really was in order to get other people to do his bidding. He knew the nation and the world needed a reassuring and calming figure as it entered the nuclear age. He did not have to be the smartest person in the room, to show off or assert his moral superiority. He listened to Frost: *The strong are saying nothing until they see.* Eisenhower knew he was strong, and that he could see around corners. He did not feel the need to constantly prove his strength. Eisenhower never compared himself to Lincoln; he was no Great Emancipator, and he did not pretend to be. But his challenge, as he understood it, was no less great. Lincoln went to war to save the Union. Eisenhower avoided war to save the world.

Eisenhower was a great peacekeeper in a dangerous era, when rival superpowers were developing ways of war that could end civilization itself. The United States was blessed to be led by a man who understood the nature of war better than anyone else, and who had the patience and wisdom, as well as the cunning and guile, to keep the peace. Ike was a deceptively simple man in his sayings and his tastes. Nothing, his faithful secretary Ann Whitman noted, pleased him more than having lunch and telling stories with his old West Point classmates. Maybe that is because Eisenhower understood, with profound insight, the moral ambiguities, the wrenching dilemmas, the dreary expediencies, and the quiet moral courage required of a life of duty, honor, country. Ike was humbled by a higher power, but he believed above all in himself. He should be remembered for that beaming smile, even if it was at times a mask. That he could be, as he made his lonely and sometimes inscrutable way, so resolutely cheerful, so determinedly optimistic, was a kind of miracle born of faith.

Acknowledgments

President Eisenhower's granddaughter Susan, who is an able historian, spoke to me many times about her grandparents, whom she knew well as a girl growing up in the 1950s and '60s. Warm, open, and candid, she has an unusual capacity to be objective about her family.

Perhaps her sense of perspective comes from her father, John Eisenhower, who observed his father at close range both professionally and personally. In long interviews at his home in Maryland and during several phone calls, Eisenhower gave me an invaluable feel for his father and for life inside his father's White House, where he served as deputy to the president's staff secretary, General Andrew Goodpaster. Thanks, too, to David Eisenhower, who, with his wife, Julie, wrote a wonderful memoir of life with his grandfather and shared his memories and observations with me.

Popular historians depend on the work of scholars. My understanding of President Eisenhower's nuclear policy was strongly influenced by the work of Campbell Craig, author of *Destroying the Village*. I spent valuable time talking to Fred Greenstein, the Princeton professor who first discovered that Ike was not the genial, syntactically challenged, grandfatherly president he sometimes appeared to be, but rather a sharp, tough-minded genius at "hidden-hand" governance. Equally helpful to me was Richard Immerman of Temple University, the academic scholar who, along with Greenstein, knows Ike best. Both Immerman and Greenstein read my manuscript and offered important corrections and critical comments. So, too, did my friend and colleague at Princeton Paul Miles, a historian both genial and shrewd.

I was very fortunate to have help from Daun van Ee, the former Library of Congress archivist and scholar who edited Eisenhower's presidential papers. Daun read my manuscript with a close and discerning eye, and provided some key documents. He is a generous and able man.

I was lucky to have Mike Hill, my friend and first-rate researcher with me as we traveled to the Eisenhower Presidential Library in Abilene, Kansas. Mike has been my right hand now through four books; there is no one more patient or more adept at digging up historical material. We are very grateful to all the staff at the Eisenhower Library, especially Valoise Armstrong, archivist; Chalsea Millner, archives technician; Catherine Cain, archives technician; Kathy Struss, audiovisual archivist; David Haight, retired archivist; and Karl Weissenbach, the library's director, and Tim Rives, his deputy. The Eisenhower Library is a well-run, welcoming, important institution (and the Eisenhower administration kept good records).

Incredibly, those records are still being declassified more than a half century later, long after the Cold War ended. In the search for new documents, I was greatly helped by William Burr, senior analyst at the National Security Archive at the George Washington University in Washington — a very valuable resource, as many researchers know. My efforts to understand the strange world of nuclear weaponry were greatly advanced by David Rosenberg, a brilliant student of nuclear overkill. Two more scholars — Conrad Crane and Andrew Erdmann — helped me sort out Eisenhower's mind-set on nuclear strategy and provided research leads or documents.

Mike and I want to thank Jeffrey Flannery, head of the Manuscript Reading Room at the Library of Congress, and Carol Hegeman, supervisory historian at Eisenhower National Historic Site in Gettysburg. Carol gave us the tour with Susan Eisenhower, and helped with photos and oral histories. At Princeton, I want to thank Dan Linke, who runs the invaluable Mudd Manuscript Library, home of the John Foster Dulles papers. At the Nixon Library at Yorba Linda, California, I had help from the former director, Tim Naftali, and archivist Meghan Lee; at the Central Intelligence Agency, I received useful guidance from historians David Robarge and Nicholas Dujmovic, who helpfully referred me to Chris Pocock, an independent historian of the U-2. For my own book on the early years of the CIA, I interviewed Richard Bissell at length, and I want to thank his assistants, Fran Pudlo and Jonathan Lewis, for aiding me in that effort. The chief historian at the National Security Agency, Michael Warner, was very helpful to me, just as he had been in his earlier incarnation as a historian at the CIA.

I enjoyed discussing Ike with my fellow Eisenhower authors Michael Korda and Jim Newton, and I'm especially grateful to David Nichols, who read and commented on parts of the manuscript. Irwin Gellman, who knows more about the documentary record of Richard Nixon than anyone, was helpful on numerous occasions. He very generously read my manuscript with a sharp eye.

Thanks, too, to Ted Barreaux, an old government hand who knows a great deal about intelligence and shared some intriguing tips; and to Elbridge Colby, a rising young star in the realm of national security who introduced me to an early master of game theory and nuclear war, Thomas Schelling. I first started this project after talking to John Newhouse, the former *New Yorker* writer and historian who gave me useful information from an old and trusted source, the late Andy Goodpaster. Thanks also go to Goodpaster's daughter, Susan Sullivan, and to her niece, Sarah Nesnow. At the Marshall Foundation, home to Goodpaster's papers, my thanks go to the head archivist, Paul Barron. I am grateful for the encouragement of Carl Redell, director of the Eisenhower Memorial, and for a sober-minded reading of the manuscript by Anna Nelson of American University, a scholar who knows much about the politics of the Eisenhower era.

I have been lucky to have great writers, editors, and historians as my friends. Jon Meacham, Walter Isaacson, and Michael Beschloss offered me their usual wise guidance, and Steve Smith applied his great editor's eye to a draft of the manuscript.

My editor at Little, Brown is truly gifted. Geoff Shandler must have spent weeks working on my manuscript. His deft touch is all over it. Thanks too for the support of the whole Little, Brown team: Michael Pietsch, the publisher; Liese Mayer, Geoff's assistant; Caroline O'Keefe, my able publicist; Peggy Freudenthal, the senior copyediting manager; Ben Allen, production editor; and my able copy editor, Chris Jerome.

ACKNOWLEDGMENTS

My agent, Amanda Urban, has been my friend and wise adviser for almost thirty years. My daughters, Mary and Louisa, and my wife, Oscie, are everything to me. Oscie is also one hell of a good editor. This book is for her.

Source Notes

Abbreviations

AWF	Ann Whitman File
CU	Columbia University
DDE	Dwight David Eisenhower
EL	Eisenhower Library
FRUS	*Foreign Relations of the United States*
LOC	Library of Congress
MF	Marshall Foundation
NA	National Archives
OH	Oral History
PDDE	Papers of Dwight David Eisenhower
PPP:E	Public Papers of Presidents: Eisenhower
PU	Princeton University

Introduction: Tell No One

1. PDDE, 15:780–1; Susan Eisenhower interview by author; 50th anniversary showing of DDE's farewell address, the Newseum, Washington DC, January 18, 2011.
2. David Bruce diary, January 12, 1955, David Bruce Papers, Virginia Historical Society.
3. Eisenhower, David, *Going Home to Glory*, 3.
4. Ambrose, *Eisenhower: The President*, 617.
5. Ambrose, *Eisenhower: Soldier and President*, 3.
6. Eisenhower, John, *Strictly Personal*, 3.

7. Ambrose, *Ike's Spies*, 7.

8. Ambrose, *Eisenhower: Soldier and President*, 96.

9. Eisenhower, John, *Strictly Personal*, 86.

10. Ambrose, *Eisenhower: Soldier and President*, 216.

11. Eisenhower, Dwight, *At Ease*, 292; Perry, *Partners in Command*, 409.

12. Olson, *Citizens of London*, 315.

13. Cutler, *No Time for Rest*, 261.

14. Eisenhower, David, *Going Home to Glory*, 18.

15. Ambrose, *Eisenhower: Soldier and President*, 246–7.

16. Kelly, *Tex McCrary*, 135.

17. Jackie Cochran OH, EL.

18. Griffith, *Ike's Letters to a Friend*, 99.

19. Alsop, *"I've Seen the Best of It,"* 338.

20. Ferrell, *The Eisenhower Diaries*, 218.

21. Stanley, *Paths to Peace*, 4.

22. Ferrell, *The Eisenhower Diaries*, 193.

23. Adams, Sherman, *Firsthand Report*, 44.

24. John Eisenhower interview by author; Eisenhower, John, *Strictly Personal*, 1.

25. Bundy, *Danger and Survival*, 375.

26. John Newhouse interview by author.

27. Craig, *Destroying the Village*, 60–1; Clausewitz, *On War*, 13–15.

28. PDDE, 17:2153.

PART ONE Duty: 1953–1956

Chapter 1: Confidence

1. Nixon, *RN*, 111.

2. Ambrose, *Eisenhower: The President*, 14.

3. Eisenhower, Dwight, *Mandate for Change*, 139–41; Greene, *Eisenhower*, 25; *Newsweek*, January 26, 1953; *New York Times*, January 21, 1953; *Washington Post*, January 21, 1953.

4. Rhodes, *Dark Sun*, 509; Kaplan, *Wizards of Armageddon*, 84.
5. Erdmann, "War No Longer Has Any Logic Whatever," 96.
6. Wittner, *Confronting the Bomb*, 75.
7. Cutler, *No Time for Rest*, 262; Greenstein, *The Hidden-Hand Presidency*, 40.
8. PDDE, 14:5.
9. Eisenhower, Milton, *The President Is Calling*, 340.
10. Eisenhower, Dwight, *Mandate for Change*, 151.
11. Nixon, *RN*, 92–110; Ambrose, *Nixon*, 278.
12. Nixon, *Six Crises*, 76, 160–3.
13. Eisenhower, John, *Strictly Personal*, 292.
14. Eisenhower, Dwight, *At Ease*, 51–2.
15. Ambrose, *Eisenhower: Soldier and President*, 65.
16. Bernard Shanley diary, preface, EL.
17. Thompson, *Portraits of American Presidents*, 148.
18. Lasby, *Eisenhower's Heart Attack*, 38.
19. Susan Eisenhower interview by author.
20. Eisenhower, David, *Going Home to Glory*, 29.
21. Ambrose, *Eisenhower: Soldier and President*, 121.
22. Thompson, *Portraits of American Presidents*, 102.
23. Olson, *Citizens of London*, 189, 198, 204.
24. Larson, *Eisenhower*, 37.
25. Olson, *Citizens of London*, 200.
26. Jordan, *Brothers, Rivals, Victors*, 160, 241, 270, 307, 529–42.
27. Ambrose, *Eisenhower: Soldier and President*, 73.
28. Eisenhower, Dwight, *At Ease*, 39–41, 185–7.
29. Ibid., 180–1.
30. Ambrose, *Eisenhower: Soldier and President*, 88.
31. Eisenhower, David, *Going Home to Glory*, 91.

Chapter 2: The Card Player

1. Donovan, *Confidential Secretary*, 43; PDDE, 14:31, 42.
2. John Eisenhower OH, CU.

3. Van Natta, *First Off the Tee*, 57–9, 75, 78.
4. Eisenhower, David, *Going Home to Glory*, 143.
5. Larson, *Eisenhower*, 166; Thompson, *Portraits of American Presidents*, 151.
6. Van Natta, *First Off the Tee*, 60.
7. Ibid.
8. Larson, *Eisenhower*, 165.
9. David Eisenhower OH, US Park Service.
10. West, *Upstairs at the White House*, 142.
11. Donovan, *Confidential Secretary*, 47, 58.
12. Adams, Sherman, *Firsthand Report*, 151.
13. Donovan, *Confidential Secretary*, 44–5.
14. Ibid., 2.
15. Ibid., 14.
16. Eisenhower, Susan, *Mrs. Ike*, 205–10.
17. Ferrell, *The Eisenhower Diaries*, 145.
18. Eisenhower, Susan, *Mrs. Ike*, 277.
19. John Eisenhower interview by author.
20. Mamie Eisenhower OH, EL.
21. West, *Upstairs at the White House*, 141; Ewald, *Eisenhower the President*, 182.
22. Lasby, *Eisenhower's Heart Attack*, 29.
23. Eisenhower, Susan, *Mrs. Ike*, 276.
24. West, *Upstairs at the White House*, 147, 142, 137, 153.
25. Eisenhower, Susan, *Mrs. Ike*, 235.
26. West, *Upstairs at the White House*, 129–32, 143; Cutler, *No Time for Rest*, 279.
27. Eisenhower, David, *Going Home to Glory*, 67.
28. Donovan, *Confidential Secretary*, 68–9; Manchester, *The Glory and the Dream*, 654; Adams, Sherman, *Firsthand Report*, 425.
29. PDDE, 14:430.
30. Eisenhower, David, *Going Home to Glory*, 38.

31. Ibid., 27.
32. Slater, *The Ike I Knew,* 34–7.
33. Eisenhower, Dwight, *At Ease,* 9, 21, 23, 26, 176; John Eisenhower interview by author; D'Este, *Eisenhower,* 25, 72–3, 96, 145, 149, 262.
34. John Eisenhower interview by author; *Time,* November 6, 1953.
35. Greenstein, *The Hidden-Hand Presidency,* 26; Andrew Goodpaster OH, EL; Susan Sullivan (Goodpaster's daughter) interview by author.
36. Adams, Sherman, *Firsthand Report,* 72.
37. Melanson and Mayers, eds., *Reevaluating Eisenhower,* 17; Thompson, *Portraits of American Presidents,* 76.
38. PDDE, 14:20.
39. Ewald, *Eisenhower the President,* 13; Hughes, *The Ordeal of Power,* 117.
40. Susan Eisenhower interview by author.
41. John Eisenhower interview by author; Eisenhower, Dwight, *At Ease,* 341.
42. Manchester, *The Glory and the Dream,* 653.
43. Greenstein, *The Hidden-Hand Presidency,* 5, 15.
44. Adams, Sherman, *Firsthand Report,* 4; Bowie and Immerman, *Waging Peace,* vii, 53.
45. Andrew Erdmann interview by author; Eisenhower, Milton, *The President Is Calling,* 309.
46. Bowie and Immerman, *Waging Peace,* 258.
47. Showalter, *Forging the Shield,* 3.
48. Eisenhower, David, *Going Home to Glory,* 190.
49. Manchester, *The Glory and the Dream,* 624.
50. Eisenhower, David, *Going Home to Glory,* 144.
51. Larson, *Eisenhower,* 11.
52. Grose, *Gentleman Spy,* 381.
53. Greenstein, *The Hidden-Hand Presidency,* 92.

54. Ibid., 57, 92.
55. Greenstein, *The Hidden-Hand Presidency,* 147; Hughes, *The Ordeal of Power,* 57; Larson, *Eisenhower,* 27; Manchester, *The Glory and the Dream,* 652.
56. Adams, Sherman, *Firsthand Report,* 27, 29.
57. Ewald, *Eisenhower the President,* 254.
58. Eisenhower, David, *Going Home to Glory,* 192; Susan Eisenhower interview by author; private memorandum, conversation with DDE, April 7, 1960, Arthur Krock Papers, PU.

Chapter 3: Positive Loyalty

1. Hughes, *The Ordeal of Power,* 47; Emmet Hughes OH, PU.
2. Hoopes, *The Devil and John Foster Dulles,* 13, 36.
3. Beschloss, *Mayday,* 96.
4. See Immerman, *John Foster Dulles,* and Pruessen, *John Foster Dulles,* passim.
5. Hughes, *The Ordeal of Power,* 62; Brands, *Cold Warriors,* 10; Halberstam, *The Fifties,* 391; Immerman, ed., *John Foster Dulles,* 47–8.
6. Hoopes, *The Devil and John Foster Dulles,* 17, 40.
7. Sherman Adams OH, PU.
8. Bowie and Immerman, *Waging Peace,* 5.
9. Beschloss, *Mayday,* 96.
10. Eisenhower, John, "The Presbyterian: John Foster Dulles"; John Eisenhower interview by author; Dwight Eisenhower OH, PU.
11. Lyon, *Eisenhower,* 419.
12. Hoopes, *The Devil and John Foster Dulles,* 156–7.
13. Hughes, 38.
14. Adams, Sherman, *Firsthand Report,* 31; Ewald, *Eisenhower the President,* 58, 63.
15. Isaacson and Thomas, *The Wise Men,* 568.
16. PPP:E, 1953, 62.

17. Hughes, *The Ordeal of Power,* 81; C. D. Jackson diary, December 12, 1953, EL.

18. Hughes, *The Ordeal of Power,* 83; Emmet Hughes diary, April 19, 1953, PU.

19. Eisenhower, Milton, *The President Is Calling,* 318.

20. PDDE, 14:136–8.

21. Isaacson and Thomas, *The Wise Men,* 564–70.

Chapter 4: Cross of Iron

1. Eisenhower, Dwight, *Mandate for Change,* 187.

2. Holloway, *Stalin and the Bomb,* 218.

3. Taubman, William, *Khrushchev,* 237.

4. Cutler, *No Time for Rest,* 321.

5. Hughes, *The Ordeal of Power,* 88; Emmet Hughes diary, March 6, 1953, PU. See Hugh Farley to Robert Cutler, "CIA Estimate of 'Probable Consequences of the Death of Stalin,'" April 10, 1953, AWF, EL ("predicts exactly the opposite of what has happened so far").

6. Emmet Hughes diary March 16, 1953, PU.

7. Ledbetter, *Unwarranted Influence,* 37–41.

8. Eisenhower, Dwight, *At Ease,* 55.

9. Hughes, *The Ordeal of Power,* 92; Emmet Hughes diary, March 16, 1953, PU.

10. Hughes, *The Ordeal of Power,* 27.

11. Lasby, *Eisenhower's Heart Attack,* 24, 25, 40, 52.

12. Emmet Hughes diary, April 16, 1953, PU.

13. Eisenhower, *Mandate for Change,* 192.

14. Cutler, *No Time for Rest,* 322.

15. Lasby, *Eisenhower's Heart Attack,* 64.

16. West, *Upstairs at the White House,* 157, 138.

17. Manchester, *The Glory and the Dream,* 661.

18. Hughes, *The Ordeal of Power,* 96.

19. Immerman, *John Foster Dulles,* 55.

20. Ambrose, *Eisenhower: The President*, 88–9; Arthur Minnich notes of legislative meetings, April 30 and May 12, 19, 1953, AWF, EL.
21. Adams, Sherman, *Firsthand Report*, 21.
22. PDDE, 14:196.

Chapter 5: Gentleman's Agreement

1. Manchester, *The Glory and the Dream*, 565, 567.
2. Cutler, *No Time for Rest*, 302–5; Dwight Eisenhower doodle file, EL.
3. Jordan, *Brothers, Rivals, Victors*, 129.
4. FRUS, 1952–4, 15:770.
5. Tannenwald, *The Nuclear Taboo*, 93–144.
6. FRUS, 1952–4, 15:770.
7. Ibid., 827.
8. Eisenhower, Dwight, *Crusade in Europe*, 442; Eisenhower, John, *Strictly Personal*, 97; Greene, *Eisenhower*, 10, 45.
9. Tannenwald, *The Nuclear Taboo*, 152.
10. Rose, *How Wars End*, 130–1, 139, 145–7.
11. Halberstam, *The Coldest Winter*, 628–9.
12. Rose, *How Wars End*, 136.
13. FRUS, 1952–4, 15:975–9.
14. Ibid., 1068.
15. Foot, "Nuclear Coercion and the Ending of the Korean Conflict," 98–9; Dingman, "Atomic Diplomacy During the Cold War," 87.
16. Foot, *Substitute for Victory*, 110.
17. Carl Spaatz diary, August 27, 1944; Eisenhower to Spaatz, August 24, 1944; Spaatz to Hap Arnold, August 27, 1944, Carl Spaatz Papers, National Archives, courtesy Conrad Crane and Daun van Ee. See Crane, *Bombs, Cities, and Civilians*.
18. Ambrose, *Eisenhower: Soldier and President*, 169, 183, 184.

19. Ferrell, *The Eisenhower Diaries*, 175–6.
20. Crane, "To Avert Impending Disaster," 73.
21. FRUS, 1952–4, 15:1059–68; Tannenwald, *The Nuclear Taboo*, 147; Foot, *Substitute for Victory*, 99; Eisenhower, Dwight, *Mandate for Change*, 229–30; Conrad Crane interview by author.
22. FRUS, 1952–4, 15:977; Tannenwald, *The Nuclear Taboo*, 146.
23. Erdmann, "War No Longer Has Any Logic Whatever," passim; Bundy, *Danger and Survival*, 243; Tannenwald, *The Nuclear Taboo*, 148.
24. Korda, *Ike*, 53.
25. Adams, Sherman, *Firsthand Report*, 102.
26. Eisenhower, Dwight, *Mandate for Change*, 230.
27. John Eisenhower interview by author.
28. Gaddis, *We Now Know*, 108.
29. Zhai, *The Dragon, the Lion, and the Eagle*, 132; Foot, *Substitute for Victory*, 105–6, 112.
30. Rose, *How Wars End*, 123–5.
31. Manchester, *The Glory and the Dream*, 663.
32. PDDE, 15:1825.
33. Van Natta, *First Off the Tee*, 69.
34. John Eisenhower interview by author.
35. Deane Beman interview by author (Beman, former commissioner of the PGA Tour, was in the foursome).
36. John Eisenhower interview by author.

Chapter 6: Deception

1. Bernard Shanley diary, 8, 10–13, 488, 549, 555–6, 575, 583, 614, 671, 1021, 1280, 1610, 1750, 1830, EL.
2. D'Este, *Eisenhower*, 24.
3. Howard Snyder diary, January 4, 1960, EL.
4. PDDE, 14:113, 15:726–7, 847.
5. Kornitzer, *The Story of the Five Eisenhower Brothers*, 45–6.

6. Eisenhower, Dwight, *At Ease,* 39.
7. Ambrose, *Ike's Spies,* 80–9, 98–100, 125–9.
8. Rothkopf, *Running the World,* 75.
9. Weiner, *Legacy of Ashes,* 45–66.
10. Bair, *Jung,* 73.
11. Fisher Howe interview by author.
12. Thomas, *The Very Best Men,* 73.
13. Ambrose, *Eisenhower: The President,* 21.
14. Crosswell, *Beetle,* 36.
15. Karl Harr OH, PU.
16. Thomas, *The Very Best Men,* 64.
17. Helgerson, *CIA Briefings of Presidential Candidates,* 25–38.
18. Rothkopf, *Running the World,* 73.
19. Mosley, *Dulles,* 294.
20. C. D. Jackson diary, June 2, 1954, EL.
21. Roosevelt, *Countercoup,* 115–16.
22. FRUS, 1952–4, 10:693; Kinzer, *All the Shah's Men,* 158.
23. FRUS, 1952–4, 10:748.
24. Roosevelt, *Countercoup,* 170.
25. Kinzer, *All the Shah's Men,* 163–81, 202; Roosevelt, *Countercoup,* 209.
26. President Eisenhower memo to file, October 8, 1953, AWF, EL.
27. Eisenhower, *Mandate for Change,* 211–12.

Chapter 7: Learning to Love the Bomb

1. Rhodes, *Dark Sun,* 524–5.
2. Gaddis, *We Now Know,* 237.
3. Schwartz, *Atomic Audit,* 151–4.
4. Eisenhower, Dwight, *Mandate for Change,* 145–6; Bowie and Immerman, *Waging Peace,* 224–5; Newhouse, *War and Peace in the Nuclear Age,* 92.
5. FRUS, 1952–4, 2(2):1056, 1066.

6. Oppenheimer, "Atomic Weapons and American Policy," 529.
7. FRUS, 1952–4, 2(1):397.
8. Bernard Shanley diary, July 9, 1953, EL.
9. Boyer, *By the Bomb's Early Light*, 67, 326.
10. Manchester, *The Glory and the Dream*, 575.
11. *Newsweek*, October 19, 1953.
12. C. D. Jackson diary, June 1, 1953, EL.
13. Eisenhower, Milton, *The President Is Calling*, 187; PDDE, 15:846.
14. FRUS, 1952–4, 2(1):457.
15. Emmet Hughes diary, September 15, 1953, PU.
16. PDDE, 14:505.
17. NSC meeting, September 24, 1953, EL.
18. NSC 5440/1, December 28, 1954, EL.
19. Rosenberg, "The Origins of Overkill," 32.
20. Taubman, William, *Khrushchev*, 332.
21. Ambrose, *Ike's Spies*, 160.
22. PDDE, 17:2153.
23. Bowie and Immerman, *Waging Peace*, 47, 64.
24. PDDE, 14:315.
25. Sherman Adams OH, EL.
26. Cutler, *No Time for Rest*, 273, 278; Ewald, *Eisenhower the President*, 2; Killian, *Sputniks, Scientists, and Eisenhower*, 50.
27. Cutler, *No Time for Rest*, 307–9; Bowie and Immerman, *Waging Peace*, 125.
28. Ann Whitman diary, July 16, 1953, AWF, EL.
29. Eisenhower, Dwight, *At Ease*, 31–2, 36; Branigar, "No Villains—No Heroes."
30. Bowie and Immerman, *Waging Peace*, 123–38; Bose, *Shaping and Signaling Presidential Policy*, 34–41.
31. Brands, *Cold Warriors*, 117–22.
32. Lear, "Ike and the Peaceful Atom," 87–94.
33. PDDE, 14:253.
34. Colville, *The Fringes of Power*, 654, 684.

35. C. D. Jackson diary, May 20, 1953, EL.
36. Colville, *The Fringes of Power*, 654, 683–8.
37. Lear, "Ike and the Peaceful Atom," 99.
38. Dwight Eisenhower diary, December 12, 1953, "Speech before the United Nations," AWF, EL; Melanson and Mayers, *Reevaluating Eisenhower*, 247; Susan Eisenhower interview by author.
39. Hoopes, *The Devil and John Foster Dulles*, 199–200.
40. Bowie and Immerman, *Waging Peace*, 199; PDDE, 15:805–6.
41. J. F. Dulles to Dwight Eisenhower, October 20, 1953, AWF, EL.
42. Hoopes, *The Devil and John Foster Dulles*, 194.
43. Bundy, *Danger and Survival*, 249, 254; FRUS, 1952–4, 2(1):447, 521, 533, 546.

Chapter 8: The Chamber Pot

1. Van Natta, *First Off the Tee*, 74–5.
2. Slater, *The Ike I Knew*, 57–8.
3. Arthur Minnich notes of legislative meeting, December 19, 1953, AWF, EL.
4. PDDE, 14:760, 788, 793.
5. Slater, *The Ike I Knew*, 57–8, 65.
6. *Newsweek*, January 18, 1954; public tour, Eisenhower Museum, Abilene, Kansas.
7. Larson, *Eisenhower*, 136, 154.
8. Parmet, *Eisenhower*, 262–3.
9. Morgan, *Valley of Death*, 158.
10. Ibid., 249.
11. Eisenhower, Dwight, *Mandate for Change*, 412.
12. FRUS, 1952–4, 8:949.
13. Morgan, *Valley of Death*, 309–10.
14. Arthur Radford OH, PU; Billings-Yun, *Decision Against War*, 20, 33, 35, 49.

15. Morgan, *Valley of Death*, 312; Billings-Yun, *Decision Against War*, 36.

16. NSC meetings, March 18, 25, and April 1, 1954, AWF, EL.

17. Ferrell, *The Eisenhower Diaries*, 190.

18. FRUS, 1952–4, 8:1163.

19. Ferrell, *The Diary of James C. Hagerty*, 35; Billings-Yun, *Decision Against War*, 60.

20. Billings-Yun, *Decision Against War*, 61–79.

21. Ibid., 80–81; FRUS, 1952–4, 8:1200–2.

22. Ferrell, *The Diary of James C. Hagerty*, 39.

23. Billings-Yun, *Decision Against War*, 84–6. But see Immerman, "Between the Unobtainable and the Unacceptable," 120–54.

24. Morgan, *Valley of Death*, 406–7.

25. Slater, *The Ike I Knew*, 58.

26. West, *Upstairs at the White House*, 155.

27. Billings-Yun, *Decision Against War*, 100.

28. Manchester, *The Glory and the Dream*, 686.

29. FRUS, 1952–4, 8:1250–65.

30. Billings-Yun, *Decision Against War*, 106–7; Manchester, *The Glory and the Dream*, 684.

31. "Ike doodles," Ann Whitman diary, April 6, 1954, AWF, EL.

32. FRUS, 1952–4, xiii, 1431–45.

33. Morgan, *Valley of Death*, 478–9. But see Immerman, "Between the Unacceptable and the Unobtainable," 140.

34. Donovan, *Confidential Secretary*, 47, 54.

35. FRUS, 1952–4, 8:1447; Bundy, *Danger and Survival*, 270; Betts, *Nuclear Blackmail and Nuclear Balance*, 51; Ambrose, *Eisenhower: The President*, 184.

36. Burke and Greenstein, *How Presidents Test Reality*, 111.

37. Truman and Acheson, *Affection and Trust*, 55.

38. Larson, *Eisenhower*, 12.

39. Billings-Yun, *Decision Against War*, 101. Billings-Yun may give Ike more credit for deviousness than he deserves. See also Immerman, "Between the Unacceptable and the

Unobtainable," 120–54; Anderson, "Dwight Eisenhower and Wholehearted Support of Ngo Dinh Diem"; Lawrence, "Explaining the Early Decisions"; Burke and Greenstein, *How Presidents Test Reality*, 1–115.

40. Herken, *Brotherhood of the Bomb*, 252–99; Bundy, *Danger and Survival*, 305.

41. Ferrell, *The Diary of James C. Hagerty*, 20.

42. Ann Whitman memo on DDE call to William Rogers, March 2, 1954, AWF, EL.

43. Ann Whitman diary, March 3, 1954, AWF, EL.

44. Ibid., April 1, 1954.

45. Greenstein, *The Hidden-Hand Presidency*, 155–227; Adams, *Firsthand Report*, 145–52.

46. DDE memo for record, February 10, 1954, AWF, EL.

47. FRUS, 1952–4, 15(2):1844–5.

48. Ferrell, *The Diary of James C. Hagerty*, 100.

49. Adams, Sherman, *Firsthand Report*, 128.

Chapter 9: Strange Genius

1. Eisenhower, Milton, *The President Is Calling*, 309; PDDE, 16:1879.

2. Immerman, *The CIA in Guatemala*, 133; Ambrose, *Eisenhower: The President*, 228, 192; Eisenhower, Dwight, *Mandate for Change*, 195, 504.

3. Grose, *Gentleman Spy*, 372.

4. E. S. Whitman, "Outline of Discussion Points at General Eisenhower's Luncheon," January 14, 1953, Edward Bernays Papers, Library of Congress.

5. PDDE, 15:889, 966.

6. Ambrose, *Eisenhower: The President*, 197.

7. Eisenhower, Dwight, *Mandate for Change*, 506.

8. Thomas, *The Very Best Men*, 119. See Cullather, *Secret History*, for the best account of the Guatemala operation.

9. Eisenhower, Dwight, *Mandate for Change,* 425.

10. Ibid.

11. Ibid., 509–10.

12. Weiner, *Legacy of Ashes,* 104. See FRUS, 1952–4, *Guatemala,* 417–26, 437–9.

13. Thomas, *The Very Best Men,* 128.

14. John Eisenhower interview by author.

15. Jim Kellis to DDE, May 14, 1954, AWF, EL; Weiner, *Legacy of Ashes,* 19.

16. Paul Carroll to Jim Kellis, June 3, 1954, AWF, EL.

17. Karalekas, *History of the Central Intelligence Agency,* 50–2; Ambrose, *Ike's Spies,* 187.

18. Ann Whitman memo, October 19, 1954, AWF, EL.

19. Osgood, *Total Cold War,* 6–7, 73–103.

20. Powers, *The Man Who Kept the Secrets,* 101; Thomas, *The Very Best Men,* 60–4, 134.

21. Taubman, Philip, *Secret Empire,* 89.

22. Ibid., 23.

23. Killian, *Sputnik, Scientists, and Eisenhower,* 68.

24. Taubman, Philip, *Secret Empire,* 12; Ambrose, *Ike's Spies,* 254.

25. Taubman, Philip, *Secret Empire,* 20–2.

26. Killian, *Sputnik, Scientists, and Eisenhower,* 69.

27. Taubman, Philip, *Secret Empire,* 28.

28. Hall, "Clandestine Victory: Eisenhower and Overhead Reconnaissance in the Cold War," 119–49.

29. Burrows, *Deep Black,* 68–70.

30. Brugioni, *Eyes in the Sky,* 97.

31. Thomas, *The Very Best Men,* 82–93, 165–71, 337.

32. Pedlow and Welzenbach, *The CIA and the U-2 Program,* 17–32.

33. Killian, *Sputnik, Scientists, and Eisenhower,* 82; Taubman, Philip, *Secret Empire,* 82–3, 90–102.

34. Taubman, Philip, *Secret Empire,* 107; Ann Whitman diary, November 22, 1954, AWF, EL.

35. Thomas, *The Very Best Men,* 166.
36. Bissell, *Reflections of a Cold Warrior,* 100.
37. Andrew Goodpaster memo of conversation, November 24, 1954, AWF, EL.
38. Allen Dulles OH, PU.

Chapter 10: "Don't Worry, I'll Confuse Them"

1. Slater, *The Ike I Knew,* 82.
2. PDDE, 15:1492.
3. Hughes, *The Ordeal of Power,* 95.
4. PDDE, 15:1158.
5. William Knowland conversation with DDE, Ann Whitman diary, November 23, 1955, AWF, EL.
6. FRUS, 1955–7, 2:279.
7. Pakula, *The Last Empress,* 593–4.
8. Adams, Sherman, *Firsthand Report,* 119.
9. FRUS, 1952–4, 14:598.
10. Beedle Smith–DDE telephone call, Ann Whitman diary, September 4, 1954, AWF, EL.
11. Ambrose, *Eisenhower: The President,* 231.
12. PPP:E, 1955, 57.
13. Ferrell, *The Diary of James C. Hagerty,* 196–7.
14. Newhouse, *War and Peace in the Nuclear Age,* 105.
15. Jones, *After Hiroshima,* 253.
16. Eisenhower, Dwight, *Mandate for Change,* 568.
17. FRUS, 1955–7, 2:347–9.
18. PPP:E, 1955, 332.
19. Tannenwald, *The Nuclear Taboo,* 170.
20. Eisenhower, Dwight, *Mandate for Change,* 570.
21. Bundy, *Danger and Survival,* 253.
22. Jones, *After Hiroshima,* 259–60.

23. Ambrose, *Eisenhower: The President*, 240.
24. PPP:E, 1955, 357–8.
25. Eisenhower, Dwight, *Mandate for Change*, 570.
26. Ambrose, *Eisenhower: The President*, 240, cites only "interview" as source.
27. Greenstein, *The Hidden-Hand Presidency*, 70.
28. Ferrell, *The Diary of James C. Hagerty*, 219.
29. Jones, *After Hiroshima*, 269.
30. Arthur Krock memo, May 15, 1955, Krock Papers, PU.
31. Bernard Shanley diary, 670–1, EL.
32. PDDE, 16:1636.
33. Brands, "Testing Massive Retaliation," 130.
34. Jones, *After Hiroshima*, 278–82.
35. Zhai, *The Dragon, the Lion, and the Eagle*, 175–7; see Chang, "To the Nuclear Brink," and Soman, " 'Who's Daddy' in the Taiwan Strait?"
36. Eisenhower, John, "The Presbyterian: John Foster Dulles."

Chapter 11: Meeting Mr. Khrushchev

1. Divine, *Blowing on the Wind*, 46.
2. Manchester, *The Glory and the Dream*, 725.
3. Ibid., 725, 759.
4. Ambrose, *Eisenhower: The President*, 250–1.
5. Lewis Strauss–DDE conversation, February 23, 1955, Ann Whitman diary, AWF, EL; Ferrell, *The Diary of James C. Hagerty*, 205–6.
6. Memorandum of discussion, National Security Council meeting, August 5, 1955, EL.
7. Ferrell, *The Diary of James C. Hagerty*, 187–8.
8. Herring, " 'A Good Stout Effort,' " 220.
9. Memo of conversation between J. F. Dulles and DDE, Ann Whitman diary, January 7, 1954, AWF, EL.

10. Robert Bowie OH, PU.
11. Divine, *Blowing on the Wind,* 60
12. Leonard Hall OH, PU.
13. Adams, Sherman, *Firsthand Report,* 177, 91.
14. Sherman Adams OH, PU.
15. Eisenhower, John, *Strictly Personal,* 178; John Eisenhower OH, CU.
16. Newhouse, *War and Peace in the Nuclear Age,* 115.
17. Sheehan, *A Fiery Peace in a Cold War,* 283.
18. Bernard Shanley diary, 1811, 2000–1, 2088, EL.
19. PDDE, 15:1193.
20. John Eisenhower interview by author.
21. Eisenhower, John, *Strictly Personal,* 175–6.
22. Stewart Alsop OH, PU.
23. Eisenhower, John, *Strictly Personal,* 178–9; Eisenhower, Dwight, *Mandate for Change,* 612, 620.
24. Ibid., 621.
25. Beschloss, *Mayday,* 104.
26. Ibid., 164–8.
27. Taubman, William, *Khrushchev,* 333, 336–7.
28. Bohlen, *Witness to History,* 369–70.
29. Taubman, William, *Khrushchev,* 332.
30. Khrushchev, Nikita Sergeevich, *Khrushchev Remembers,* 395; Khrushchev, Sergei, *Nikita Khrushchev and the Creation of a Superpower,* 83.
31. Taubman, William, *Khrushchev,* 350, 331.
32. Khrushchev, Nikita Sergeevich, *Khrushchev Remembers,* 397.
33. Charles Bohlen OH, CU.
34. Goodpaster, "Cold War Overflights: A View from the White House," 11.
35. Sheehan, *A Fiery Peace in a Cold War,* 282.
36. Bernard Shanley diary, 2003, EL.
37. Donovan, *Confidential Secretary,* 87.
38. Ibid., 88.

Chapter 12: The Devil's Grip

1. Burrows, *Deep Black*, 64; see also memorandum of discussion, National Security Council meeting, April 29, 1955, EL.
2. Brugioni, *Eyes in the Sky*, 87.
3. Taubman, William, *Khrushchev*, 243.
4. Sheehan, *A Fiery Peace in a Cold War*, 150–1.
5. Ibid., 218–9.
6. Kaplan, *Wizards of Armageddon*, 63–8, 108–10.
7. Sheehan, *A Fiery Peace in a Cold War*, 171, 216.
8. Rhodes, *Dark Sun*, 563.
9. Bacevich, *Washington Rules*, 43–55; Kaplan, *Wizards of Armageddon*, 43.
10. Eisenhower, David, *Going Home to Glory*, 146.
11. Memorandum of discussion, National Security Council meeting, August 4, 1955, EL.
12. Sheehan, *A Fiery Peace in a Cold War*, 288–99.
13. Ann Whitman diary, August 29, 1955, AWF, EL; Donovan, *Confidential Secretary*, 90.
14. Howard Snyder memo ("Draft of DDE's Heart Attack"), September 24, 1955; Snyder to Wilton Persons, September 29, 1955, Howard Snyder Papers, EL; Lasby, *Eisenhower's Heart Attack*, 70–110.
15. Donovan, *Confidential Secretary*, 91–3.
16. Eisenhower, *Mandate for Change*, 638.
17. Lasby, *Eisenhower's Heart Attack*, 71, 128–9; Ann Whitman diary, October 11, 25, 1955, AWF, EL.
18. Lasby, *Eisenhower's Heart Attack*, 21.
19. Cutler, *No Time for Rest*, 399.
20. Lasby, *Eisenhower's Heart Attack*, 50.
21. DDE to Paul Dudley White, DDE to Thomas Mattingly, November 17, 1955, AWF, EL.
22. Donovan, *Confidential Secretary*, 98.

23. Slater, *The Ike I Knew*, 110.
24. Lasby, *Eisenhower's Heart Attack*, 133.
25. DDE to Charles McAdam, November 28, 1955, AWF, EL; PDDE, 16:1908.
26. Bernard Shanley diary, 2012, EL.
27. Donovan, *Eisenhower: The Inside Story*, 397–8.
28. Nixon, *RN*, 168.
29. Slater, *The Ike I Knew*, 107; Eisenhower, John, *Strictly Personal*, 183–5.
30. Lasby, *Eisenhower's Heart Attack*, 125, 189.
31. Eisenhower, John, *Strictly Personal*, 183–4.
32. Ferrell, *The Diary of James C. Hagerty*, 242.
33. Griffith, *Ike's Letters to a Friend*, 153, 156–7.
34. Eisenhower, John, *Strictly Personal*, 184.
35. Nixon, *Six Crises*, 131–81; Nixon, *RN*, 164–6.
36. John Eisenhower interview by author; Ann Whitman diary, October 12, 1955, AWF, EL; Donovan, *Confidential Secretary*, 96.
37. Nixon, *RN*, 167–8.
38. Eisenhower, John, *Strictly Personal*, 184–5; Nichols, *Eisenhower 1956*, 90.
39. PDDE, 16:1850.
40. Lasby, *Eisenhower's Heart Attack*, 192, Nichols, *Eisenhower 1956*, 119.
41. Susan Eisenhower interview by author.
42. Bernard Shanley diary, 2171, EL.
43. Lasby, *Eisenhower's Heart Attack*, 155.
44. PDDE, 16:1949.
45. DDE diary, January 11, 1956, AWF, EL.

Chapter 13: Bows and Arrows

1. PDDE, 16:1949.
2. Craig, *Destroying the Village*, 56; FRUS, 1955–7, 19:188–91.

3. Eisenhower, David, *Going Home to Glory,* 173–4.

4. Shepley, "How Dulles Averted War."

5. Brands, *Cold Warriors,* 17.

6. Robert Donovan OH, PU.

7. Nichols, *Eisenhower 1956,* 95.

8. Craig, *Destroying the Village,* passim. See also Roman, *Eisenhower and the Missile Gap,* 63–111.

9. Preble, *John F. Kennedy and the Missile Gap,* 31–3.

10. Eisenhower's notes on John S. D. Eisenhower memo, undated, memo file of Andrew Goodpaster, 1957, Goodpaster Papers, MF.

11. Clausewitz, *On War,* xxvi–xxix, 3–31; Craig, *Destroying the Village,* 44; Trachtenberg, *History and Strategy,* 138; Gaddis, *Strategies of Containment,* 133; Dockrill, *Eisenhower's New-Look National Security Policy,* 4.

12. Craig, *Destroying the Village,* 58.

13. Ibid., 57; FRUS, 1955–7, 19:202–4.

14. Craig, *Destroying the Village,* 61.

15. FRUS, 1955–7, 19:302.

16. Ibid., 312.

17. Ibid., 313.

18. Craig, *Destroying the Village,* 59–70; see memorandum of discussion, National Security Council meeting, January 22, 1959, EL.

19. Gaddis, *We Now Know,* 234.

20. Lasby, *Eisenhower's Heart Attack,* 208–10.

21. Ibid., 185–7.

22. Ibid., 223–9.

23. Donovan, *Confidential Secretary,* 107.

24. Howard Snyder diary, July 19–20, 1956, EL.

25. PDDE, 17:2211–12.

26. Hughes, *The Ordeal of Power,* 154–5.

27. Lasby, *Eisenhower's Heart Attack,* 227.

28. Eisenhower, John, *Strictly Personal,* 189.

Chapter 14: Rising Storm

1. Manchester, *The Glory and the Dream*, 759, 773–4; Halberstam, *The Fifties*, 509, 573.
2. Andrew Goodpaster memorandum of conversation, February 18, 1960, AWF, EL.
3. Brugioni, *Eyes in the Sky*, 104–5, 163.
4. Thomas, *The Very Best Men*, 91–2, 189–90.
5. "Spy in the Sky," *American Experience*, PBS.
6. Beschloss, *Mayday*, 106–12.
7. Taubman, *Secret Empire*, 176–7.
8. Eisenhower, Dwight, *Waging Peace*, 545.
9. Pedlow and Welzenbach, *The CIA and the U-2 Program*, 100–12; Taubman, *Secret Empire*, 180–9; Bissell, *Reflections of a Cold Warrior*, 110–14; Andrew Goodpaster memorandum of conference with DDE, May 28, 1956; Goodpaster memoranda for record, July 3, 5, 6, 7, 11, 13, and October 3, 1956, AWF, EL.
10. Brugioni, *Eyes in the Sky*, 154–9.
11. FRUS, 1955–7, 16:653–4.
12. Nichols, *Eisenhower 1956*, 244.
13. Weiner, *Legacy of Ashes*, 127.
14. Eisenhower, John, "The Presbyterian: John Foster Dulles."
15. Allen Dulles OH, PU.
16. Nichols, *Eisenhower 1956*, 248, 256, 222–3, 249.
17. Ibid., 321.
18. Howard Snyder diary, October 24–November 25, 1956, EL.
19. Eisenhower, Dwight, *Waging Peace*, 67; Grose, *Gentleman Spy*, 437; memorandum of discussion, National Security Council meeting, October 26, 1956, EL.
20. Nichols, *Eisenhower 1956*, 263–4; Howard Snyder diary, October 14–16, 1956, EL.
21. Emmet Hughes diary, October 28, 1956, PU; Hughes, *The Ordeal of Power*, 185–6.

22. Nichols, *Eisenhower 1956,* 271–5.
23. John Eisenhower interview by author.
24. Emmet Hughes diary, October 30, 1956, PU; Hughes, *The Ordeal of Power,* 187–9.
25. FRUS, 1955–7, 19:873–4; Arthur Flemming oral history, EL.
26. Nichols, *Eisenhower 1956,* 285.
27. Eisenhower, Dwight, *Waging Peace,* 78–9.
28. Weiner, *Legacy of Ashes,* 129.
29. Brugioni, *Eyes in the Sky,* 180–4.
30. Emmet Hughes diary, October 31, 1956, PU; Hughes, *The Ordeal of Power,* 192.
31. Nichols, *Eisenhower 1956,* 292; Ann Whitman diary, November 1, 1956, AWF, EL.
32. Nichols, *Eisenhower 1956,* 297, 301.
33. Howard Snyder diary, November 1, 1956, EL.
34. PDDE, 17:2353–9.

Chapter 15: Subtle and Brutal

1. Slater, *The Ike I Knew,* 141–3.
2. Thomas, *The Very Best Men,* 142.
3. Taubman, William, *Khrushchev,* 296.
4. Eisenhower, Dwight, *Waging Peace,* 82. Memorandum of discussion, National Security Council meeting, November 1, 1956, EL.
5. Weiner, *Legacy of Ashes,* 130. But see Johnson, *Radio Free Europe and Radio Liberty,* 91–112.
6. Eisenhower, Dwight, *Waging Peace,* 95.
7. Nichols, *Eisenhower 1956,* 329.
8. Donovan, *Confidential Secretary,* 109.
9. Emmet Hughes diary, November 5, 1956, PU; Hughes, *The Ordeal of Power,* 194.
10. FRUS, 1955–7, xix, 982–1002.

11. Lasby, *Eisenhower's Heart Attack*, 238; Howard Snyder diary, November 5–6, 1956, EL.

12. FRUS, 1955–7, 19:1014; Eisenhower, Dwight, *Waging Peace*, 91.

13. Andrew Goodpaster memorandum of conversation, November 6, 1956, EL.

14. FRUS, 1955–7, 19:1016–17.

15. Ann Whitman diary, November 6, 1956, AWF, EL.

16. FRUS, 1955–7, 19:1025–7.

17. Yergin, *The Prize*, 471.

18. FRUS, 1955–7, 16:1012–13; Macmillan, *Riding the Storm*, 164; Kunz, *Butter and Guns*, 84–93.

19. Daun Van Ee interviewed by author.

20. Gaddis, *The Cold War*, 66.

21. Hughes, *The Ordeal of Power*, 198–9.

22. FRUS, 1955–7, 19:1040–2.

23. Adams, Sherman, *Firsthand Report*, 257.

24. Grose, *Gentleman Spy*, 429–32.

25. Mosley, *Dulles*, 6.

26. Allen Dulles OH, PU.

27. Beschloss, *Mayday*, 129.

28. Srodes, *Allen Dulles*, 485–6.

29. Sherman Adams OH, EL.

30. Schlesinger, *Robert Kennedy and His Times*, 455–6. See report posted on CIA website at www.foia.cia.gov/helms/pdf/cov_ ops.pdf.

31. John Eisenhower interview by author.

32. Thomas, "Spymaster General."

33. Jablonsky, *War by Land, Sea, and Air*, 180.

34. Karalekas, *History of the Central Intelligence Agency*, 51.

35. Beschloss, *Mayday*, 131.

36. PDDE, 18:62–3.

PART TWO Honor: 1957–1961
Chapter 16: Dark Star

1. PDDE, 7:764–5.
2. Ambrose, *Eisenhower: Soldier and President,* 542.
3. Nichols, *A Matter of Justice,* 104.
4. David Nichols interviewed by author.
5. Howard Snyder diary, August 16, 1959, EL. ("He loved having the jokesters around and I guess their sense of humor.... They [Gosden and Allen] enjoyed slightly off-color humor I think, southern." David Eisenhower OH, US Park Service.)
6. Sig Larmon OH, CU.
7. Merriman Smith OH, CU.
8. Sig Larmon OH, CU.
9. Richard Immerman interviewed by author.
10. PDDE, 19:922.
11. PDDE, 16:1986.
12. Eisenhower, Dwight, *Mandate for Change,* 290–5; Eisenhower, David, *Going Home to Glory,* 105–6, citing an interview with Attorney General Brownell. The words are usually attributed to Justice Felix Frankfurter.
13. John Eisenhower interview by author.
14. PDDE, 17:2086, 2104, 2189–90.
15. Nichols, *A Matter of Justice,* 142–68; Caro, *The Years of Lyndon Johnson: Master of the Senate,* 918–19.
16. Ewald, *Eisenhower the President,* 242.
17. Nichols, *A Matter of Justice,* 169–213; PDDE, 18:578.
18. PDDE, 18:551.
19. Rothkopf, *Running the World,* 73.
20. Dickson, *Sputnik,* 22; Howard Snyder diary, October 5–6, 1957.
21. Brzezinski, *Red Moon Rising,* 21.
22. Taubman, William, *Khrushchev,* 380–3.

23. Hall, "The Truth About Overflights," 36–8.
24. Taubman, William, *Khrushchev*, 360–7.
25. Brzezinski, *Red Moon Rising*, 96–7.
26. Ibid., 26, 39–44, 111.
27. Taubman, Philip, *Secret Empire*, 210–11; Brzezinski, *Red Moon Rising*, 129.
28. Brzezinski, *Red Moon Rising*, 128–9, 146–7, 159.
29. Ibid., 171–3; Manchester, *The Glory and the Dream*, 788–90.
30. Adams, Sherman, *Firsthand Report*, 415.
31. Andrew Goodpaster memorandum of conversation, October 16, 1957, AWF, EL.
32. Taubman, Philip, *Secret Empire*, 217; FRUS, 1955–7, xix, 598–600, xi, 755.
33. PPP:E, 1957, 719–30.
34. Brzezinski, *Red Moon Rising*, 182.
35. Killian, *Sputnik, Scientists, and Eisenhower*, 8.
36. Brzezinski, *Red Moon Rising*, 176.
37. *Time,* October 21, 1957.
38. Brzezinski, *Red Moon Rising*, 204.
39. Divine, *The Sputnik Challenge*, 43–4.
40. Brzezinski, *Red Moon Rising*, 216.
41. Divine, *Blowing on the Wind*, 16.
42. Manchester, *The Glory and the Dream*, 789.
43. Dickson, *Sputnik*, 234.
44. *Burt the Turtle* civil defense film, Eisenhower Museum, Abilene, Kansas.
45. Memorandum of discussion, National Security Council meeting, April 28, 1960, EL.
46. Killian, *Sputnik, Scientists, and Eisenhower*, 10.
47. Ewald, *Eisenhower the President*, 287.
48. FRUS, 1955–7, 19:608.
49. PPP:E, 1957, 789–99.
50. Eisenhower, Dwight, *Waging Peace*, 225–6.
51. PDDE, 18:576–8.

Chapter 17: The Great Equation

1. Howard Snyder diary, December 31, 1958, EL.
2. Ibid., November 19, 1957, EL.
3. Ann Whitman diary, November 24, 1954, EL.
4. Howard Snyder diary, November 19, 1957, EL.
5. Ibid., November 25, 1957, EL; Donovan, *Confidential Secretary*, 118.
6. Adams, Sherman, *Firsthand Report*, 196–7; Eisenhower, John, *Strictly Personal*, 195–7; Howard Snyder diary, November 25, 1957, EL; Eisenhower, Dwight, *Waging Peace*, 227–9.
7. West, *Upstairs at the White House*, 182.
8. Eisenhower, John, *Strictly Personal*, 197.
9. Lasby, *Eisenhower's Heart Attack*, 242–5.
10. Ann Whitman diary, November 22, December 3, 1957, AWF, EL.
11. PDDE, 19:734.
12. Howard Snyder diary, November 30–December 3, 1957, EL.
13. Brzezinski, *Red Moon Rising*, 90–2, 235; Halberstam, *The Fifties*, 607–12.
14. Taubman, Philip, *Secret Empire*, 207.
15. Divine, *The Sputnik Challenge*, 71; Taubman, Philip, *Secret Empire*, 35.
16. Manchester, *The Glory and the Dream*, 813.
17. Howard Snyder diary, December 7, 1957, EL.
18. Thompson, Nicholas, *The Hawk and the Dove*, 165.
19. Memorandum of discussion, National Security Council meeting, April 8, 1955, EL.
20. Schwartz, *Atomic Audit*, 314.
21. Carlson, *K Blows Top*, 52.
22. Showalter, *Forging the Shield*, 23.
23. Memorandum of discussion, National Security Council meeting, August 18, 1956, EL.
24. Adams, Valerie, *Eisenhower's Fine Group of Fellows*, 198.

25. Ibid., 2.
26. Abella, *Soldiers of Reason*, 84.
27. Adams, Valerie, *Eisenhower's Fine Group of Fellows*, 171.
28. Ibid., 174, 92.
29. Ibid., 23, 90; Kaplan, *Wizards of Armageddon*, 222–3.
30. Rosenberg, "The Origins of Overkill"; Abella, *Soldiers of Reason*, 86, 91–2.
31. Abella, *Soldiers of Reason*, 93–4.
32. Andrew Erdmann interview by author.
33. Andrew Goodpaster memorandum for record, November 7, 1957, EL; Kaplan, *Wizards of Armageddon*, 84–143.
34. Thompson, Nicholas, *The Hawk and the Dove*, 164.
35. Herken, *Counsels of War*, 114.
36. FRUS, 1955–7, 19:620–61.
37. Memorandum of conversation, November 4, 7, 9, 1957, Ann Whitman diary, AWF, EL; Abella, *Soldiers of Reason*, 112; Kaplan, *Wizards of Armageddon*, 150; Adams, Valerie, *Eisenhower's Fine Group of Fellows*, 180–1.
38. Thompson, Nicholas, *The Hawk and the Dove*, 165.
39. Herken, *Counsels of War*, 116.
40. Eisenhower, Dwight, *Waging Peace*, 221.
41. Thompson, Nicholas, *The Hawk and the Dove*, 166; Kaplan, *Wizards of Armageddon*, 153.
42. Brzezinski, *Red Moon Rising*, 222.
43. Caro, *The Years of Lyndon Johnson: Master of the Senate*, 1021.
44. Killian, *Sputnik, Scientists, and Eisenhower*, 9.
45. Divine, *The Sputnik Challenge*, 61–7.
46. Ibid., 78.
47. Caro, *The Years of Lyndon Johnson: Master of the Senate*, 1028.
48. Memorandum of conversation, Ann Whitman diary, November 6, 1957, AWF, EL.
49. Slater, *The Ike I Knew*, 151.

Chapter 18: The Strong Say Nothing

1. Divine, *The Sputnik Challenge,* 119.
2. Brzezinski, *Red Moon Rising,* 252.
3. Eisenhower, John, "The Presbyterian: John Foster Dulles."
4. Hughes, *The Ordeal of Power,* 215–6.
5. Ann Whitman diary, February 5 and March 1, 1958, AWF, EL.
6. Killian, *Sputnik, Scientists, and Eisenhower,* 234.
7. Ann Whitman diary, February 15–18, 1958, AWF, EL.
8. Slater, *The Ike I Knew,* 171.
9. Eisenhower, Dwight, *At Ease,* 168.
10. PDDE, 17:2255–6.
11. Memoranda of discussions, National Security Council meetings, December 6, 1957, and January 6, 22, 30, 1958, EL.
12. Andrew Goodpaster memorandum of conversation, January 31, 1958; Ann Whitman diary, January 31 and February 1, 1958, AWF, EL.
13. Arthur Minnich notes of legislative meetings, January 28 and February 3, 1958, AWF, EL.
14. Andrew Goodpaster memorandum of conversation, March 5, 1958, AWF, EL.
15. Arthur Minnich notes of legislative meeting, March 25, 1958, AWF, EL.
16. Adams, Valerie, *Eisenhower's Fine Group of Fellows,* 174, 186.
17. Cutler, *No Time for Rest,* 361–2.
18. Roman, *Eisenhower and the Missile Gap,* 125–7.
19. Ambrose, *Eisenhower: Soldier and President,* 453–4.
20. Caro, *The Years of Lyndon Johnson: Master of the Senate,* 1029.
21. PDDE, 16:2114.
22. Gaddis, *We Now Know,* 228–9.
23. Taubman, William, *Khrushchev,* 347.

24. Phone conversation between DDE and J. F. Dulles, April 16, 1958; between DDE and Thomas White, April 24, 1958, Ann Whitman diary, AWF, EL.

25. See Lucius Clay OH, CU.

26. Greene, *Eisenhower*, 50.

27. Ibid.

28. Donovan, *Confidential Secretary*, 50.

29. Ambrose, *Ike's Spies*, 91.

30. Greene, *Eisenhower*, 24, 46, 87.

31. FRUS, 1955–7, 20:538.

32. Ibid., 589, 616.

33. Bernard Shanley OH, PU.

34. Greene, *Eisenhower*, 110–17.

35. Divine, *Blowing on the Wind*, 113–57; Ledbetter, *Unwarranted Influence*, 74–86.

36. Arthur Minnich notes of cabinet meeting, June 3, 1957, AWF, EL; Greene, *Eisenhower*, 115.

37. Herken, *Counsels of War*, 118.

38. Greene, *Eisenhower*, 127–32.

39. J. F. Dulles memorandum to DDE, April 30, 1958, AWF, EL.

40. Marquis Childs OH, PU.

41. DDE diary, January 24, 1958, AWF, EL.

42. Marks, *Power and Peace*, 23–4; Richard Immerman interview by author. The most sympathetic biography is Pruessen, *John Foster Dulles*.

43. Eisenhower, John, "The Presbyterian: John Foster Dulles."

44. Slater, *The Ike I Knew*, 150.

45. Greene, *Eisenhower*, 163.

46. Ambrose, *Eisenhower: The President*, 18.

47. Ibid., 479–80.

48. David Rosenberg interview by author.

49. Ibid.

50. See Rosenberg, "The Origins of Overkill."

51. Andrew Goodpaster memoranda of record, March 13, 1956, and July 29, 1958, AWF, EL.

52. Ann Whitman diary, July 31, 1958; memorandum from DDE to Neil McElroy, July 31, 1958, AWF, EL.

Chapter 19: Guns of August

1. Slater, *The Ike I Knew*, 180.

2. Manchester, *The Glory and the Dream*, 834–43.

3. Donovan, *Confidential Secretary*, 126.

4. PDDE, 16:2125.

5. Ewald, *Eisenhower the President*, 260; Adams, Sherman, *Firsthand Report*, 447; Ann Whitman diary, July 15 and September 4, 17, 1958, AWF, EL.

6. Eisenhower, Dwight, *Waging Peace*, 311–17.

7. Ann Whitman diary, July 12, 1958, AWF, EL.

8. Thompson, ed., *Portraits of American Presidents*, 48.

9. Cutler, *No Time for Rest*, 363; Eisenhower, Dwight, *Waging Peace*, 270.

10. Slater, *The Ike I Knew*, 178; Donovan, *Confidential Secretary*, 122.

11. Melanson and Mayers, *Reevaluating Eisenhower*, 192–216; Immerman, *John Foster Dulles*, 169.

12. Zhai, *The Dragon, the Lion, and the Eagle*, 180.

13. Taubman, William, *Khrushchev*, 341.

14. Zhai, *The Dragon, the Lion, and the Eagle*, 181.

15. Eisenhower, Dwight, *Waging Peace*, 293.

16. Memorandum of conversation between DDE and J. F. Dulles, September 5, 1958; Ann Whitman diary, AWF, EL; Craig, 78–87.

17. Zhai, *The Dragon, the Lion, and the Eagle*, 188.

18. Eisenhower, Dwight, *Waging Peace*, 304.

19. Zhai, *The Dragon, the Lion, and the Eagle*, 207; Taubman, William, *Khrushchev*, 393.

20. Manchester, *The Glory and the Dream*, 820–1.
21. Thompson, *Portraits of American Presidents*, 104.
22. Weiner, *Legacy and Ashes*, 144.
23. Memorandum of deliberations, National Security Council meeting, April 24, 1958, EL; Weiner, *Legacy of Ashes*, 144–52; Thomas, *The Very Best Men*, 157–9.
24. Weiner, *Legacy of Ashes*, 139.
25. Ambrose, *Ike's Spies*, 256–7.
26. Brugioni, *Eyes in the Sky*, 152.
27. Grose, *Gentleman Spy*, 463.
28. Ibid., 451.
29. Karalekas, *History of the Central Intelligence Agency*, 62; memorandum to Robert Cutler from Bureau of Budget, date obscured (probably December 1958), AWF, EL.
30. John Eisenhower interview by author.
31. Thomas, *The Very Best Men*, 162–5; Grose, *Gentleman Spy*, 464.
32. Andrew Goodpaster memoranda of conversations, February 7, August 8, November 5, 1958, AWF, EL; Taubman, Philip, *Secret Empire*, 238, 267.
33. Ann Whitman diary, March 17, 1958, AWF, EL.
34. See Baker Report, July 25, 1958, "Scientific Judgments on Foreign Communications Intelligence," EL (heavily redacted).
35. Gordon Gray memorandum of conversation, August 16, 1958, AWF, EL.
36. Briefing notes on President's Board of Consultants on Foreign Intelligence, October 30, 1958; Gordon Gray memorandum of conversation, November 3, 1958, AWF, EL; Gordon Gray memorandum of conversation, October 17, 1958, AWF, EL.

Chapter 20: Missile Gap

1. Burrows, *Deep Black*, 92; Divine, *The Sputnik Challenge*, 177.
2. Divine, *The Sputnik Challenge*, 178; Beschloss, *Mayday*, 5.

3. Merry, *Taking on the World,* 363.

4. Thompson, *Portraits of American Presidents,* 103.

5. Cutler, *No Time for Rest,* 317–19; Joseph Alsop OH, CU.

6. Arthur Minnich notes of legislative meeting, August 12, 1958, AWF, EL.

7. Divine, *The Sputnik Challenge,* 179; Kaplan, *Wizards of Armageddon,* 163.

8. Garthoff, *A Journey Through the Cold War,* 46–7; Kaplan, *Wizards of Armageddon,* 162–3; Roman, *Eisenhower and the Missile Gap,* 36; Divine, *The Sputnik Challenge,* 172–9; Burrows, *Deep Black,* 94.

9. DDE memorandum of record, August 25, 1958, AWF, EL.

10. Roman, *Eisenhower and the Missile Gap,* 37, 218; Bundy, *Danger and Survival,* 337; Goodpaster memorandum of conversation, August 30, 1958, AWF, EL.

11. Brugioni, *Eyes in the Sky,* 183.

12. Memorandum of discussion, National Security Council meeting, December 6, 1958, EL.

13. Thompson, *Portraits of American Presidents,* 19.

14. Beschloss, *Mayday,* 153; Halberstam, *The Fifties,* 706.

15. Pedlow and Welzenbach, *The CIA and the U-2 Program,* 131–44; Andrew Goodpaster memorandum of conversation, September 9, 1958, AWF, EL.

16. Divine, *The Sputnik Challenge,* 175; Beschloss, *Mayday,* 160; see Garthoff, "Estimating Soviet Military Intentions and Capabilities," 135–85.

17. Brugioni, *Eyes in the Sky,* 271.

18. Thomas, *The Very Best Men,* 168–9; DDE to Anthony Eden, May 17, 1956, AWF, EL; Pocock, *The U-2 Spyplane,* 125.

19. C. D. Jackson to Walter Guzzardi, May 9, 1955, C. D. Jackson Papers, EL.

20. Merry, *Taking on the World,* 243.

21. Thomas, *The Very Best Men,* 105.

Chapter 21: Looking for a Partner

1. Taubman, William, *Khrushchev,* 360.
2. Burr, "Avoiding the Slippery Slope."
3. Taubman, William, *Khrushchev,* 407; FRUS, 1958–60, 8:148–52.
4. Beschloss, *Mayday,* 172.
5. FRUS, 1958–60, 8:46; Craig, *Destroying the Village,* 91.
6. John Eisenhower interview by author; Eisenhower, John, *Strictly Personal,* 211–13.
7. DDE phone conversation with J. F. Dulles, November 27, 1958; Ann Whitman diary, AWF, EL.
8. John Eisenhower interview by author; see memorandum of discussions, National Security Council meeting, January 22, 1959, EL.
9. PDDE, 19:1271–6; Ann Whitman diary, November 21, 23, 1958, AWF, EL.
10. Slater, *The Ike I Knew,* 184.
11. FRUS, 1958–60, 8:172–7.
12. FRUS, 1958–60, 8:174, 178.
13. Eisenhower, John, *Strictly Personal,* 211; Steve Hoglund (bridge expert who reviewed Eisenhower's hands) interview by author.
14. Trachtenberg, "A 'Wasting Asset.'"
15. Burr, "Avoiding the Slippery Slope," viii, 301–2.
16. Craig, *Destroying the Village,* 93.
17. FRUS, 1958–60, 8:424.
18. Memorandum of discussion, National Security Council meeting, May 1, 1958, EL.
19. Eisenhower, John, *Strictly Personal,* 222–6; memoranda of discussions, National Security Council meetings, March 5 and April 23, 1959, EL; Arthur Minnich notes on legislative meetings, March 5 and April 23, 1959, AWF, EL.
20. Craig, *Destroying the Village,* 97; FRUS, 1958–60, 8:428–37.
21. Craig, *Destroying the Village,* 98; FRUS, 1958–60, 8:450.

22. Craig, *Destroying the Village*, 99.
23. Arthur Minnich notes of legislative meetings, March 10 and June 2, 1959, AWF, EL.
24. Macmillan, *Riding the Storm*, 645; Ann Whitman diary, March 22, 1958, AWF, EL.
25. Beschloss, *Mayday*, 174.
26. Taubman, William, *Khrushchev*, 412.
27. Eisenhower, Dwight, *Waging Peace*, 354; Macmillan, *Riding the Storm*, 645; FRUS, 1958–60, 8:520–1.
28. Ambrose, *Eisenhower: The President*, 522–3; Craig, *Destroying the Village*, 101.
29. Macmillan, *Riding the Storm*, 644.
30. Ann Whitman diary, February 14, 20, 1959, AWF, EL.
31. Donovan, *Confidential Secretary*, 134.
32. DDE–J. F. Dulles phone conversation, April 7, 15, 1959, AWF, EL; Ann Whitman diary, May 4, 5, 18, 19, 1959, AWF, EL.
33. Craig, *Destroying the Village*, 102.
34. Ann Whitman diary, May 27, 28, 29, 1959, AWF, EL.
35. John Eisenhower interview by author; Richard Immerman interview by author.
36. Taubman, William, *Khrushchev*, 414.
37. PDDE, 14:275.
38. Memorandum of conversation with DDE, July 27, 1959, Arthur Krock Papers, PU.
39. Andrew Goodpaster OH, EL.
40. FRUS, 1958–60, 8:971–7.
41. Craig, *Destroying the Village*, 105; Eisenhower, Dwight, *Waging Peace*, 399–408.

Chapter 22: Sweet Words

1. Taubman, William, *Khrushchev*, 421–4.
2. Eisenhower, Dwight, *Waging Peace*, 440; Carlson, *K Blows Top*, 70–5, 81–5.

3. Carlson, *K Blows Top,* 141, 151, 159, 161, 186, 215; Ann Whitman diary, September 21, 1959, AWF, EL; memorandum of conversation, N. Khrushchev and H. C. Lodge, September 29, 1959, AWF, EL.

4. Memorandum of conversation, N. Khrushchev and H. C. Lodge, September 19, 1959, AWF, EL.

5. Carlson, *K Blows Top,* 106.

6. Ibid., 229.

7. Memorandum of conversation between DDE and N. Khrushchev at Camp David, undated (September 1959), AWF, EL.

8. Memorandum of phone conversation between DDE and Christian Herter, Ann Whitman diary, September 30, 1959, AWF, EL.

9. Eisenhower, Dwight, *Waging Peace,* 442–7; Eisenhower, John, *Strictly Personal,* 260–3; Carlson, *K Blows Top,* 236–41; Kistiakowsky, *A Scientist at the White House,* 89–94; Susan Eisenhower OH, US Park Service; Barbara Eisenhower-Foltz OH, EL.

10. Carlson, *K Blows Top,* 9.

11. Ibid., 243, 248–9.

12. Ann Whitman diary, September 16, 28, 1959, AWF, EL.

13. Andrew Goodpaster OH, EL.

14. Beschloss, *Mayday,* 6, 425.

15. PDDE, 20:1683.

16. Merriman Smith OH, CU.

17. DDE to J. Campbell Palmer, June 30, 1964, post-presidential file, EL.

18. Dillon Anderson OH, CU.

19. Merriman Smith OH, CU.

20. Howard Snyder diary, August 18 and September 1, 1958, EL.

21. Ibid., April 11, 1959.

22. John Eisenhower interview by author.

23. Lasby, *Eisenhower's Heart Attack,* 281; Howard Snyder diary, January 13, 1958, and August 2, 23, November 31, 1958, EL.

24. Ibid., October 16 and December 3, 1958.

25. Ibid., February 19, 1958, March 4, 1959, and December 29, 1960.

26. Ibid., August 5, 1958.

27. Ibid., March 25, 1959.

28. Ann Whitman OH, EL.

29. Ann Whitman diary, March 22, 1959, AWF, EL.

30. Ibid., October 8, 1957.

31. Ibid., May 23, 1957.

32. Ibid., January 12, 1959.

33. Ibid., February 5, 1959.

34. Slater, *The Ike I Knew,* 186.

35. Mamie Eisenhower OH, EL.

36. Ibid.

37. Susan Eisenhower interview by author.

38. Howard Snyder diary, February 11, 1958, EL.

39. Ibid., June 24, 1958.

40. Ibid., October 18, 1959.

41. Ibid., January 22, 1959.

Chapter 23: A Regular Pixie

1. John Eisenhower interview by author.

2. Howard Snyder diary, June 20 and July 26, 1958, EL.

3. Ibid., December 31, 1957, and March 19, 1958.

4. Ibid., February 8 and April 1, 1958; Lasby, *Eisenhower's Heart Attack,* 259–60.

5. See trialx.com/treatment/barbiturates-seconal-and-luminal -indications-side-effects-dosage-interactions-information/.

6. Howard Snyder diary, March 17, 25, 31, and April 1, 5, 1959, EL.

7. Ibid., May 19, 27, 1959.

8. Ibid., January 22, 23, 1959.

9. Barbara Eisenhower-Foltz OH, EL.

10. Ambrose, *Eisenhower: The President*, 537–40.

11. Howard Snyder diary, August 28, 30, 1959, EL.

12. Synopsis of intelligence material reported to the president, April 17, 1959, AWF, EL.

13. Howard Snyder diary, December 28, 1958, and January 6, 1960, EL.

14. Ibid., March 15, 1960, and August 30, 1959.

15. "Books of the Times," *New York Times*, March 20, 1959.

16. Podvig, *Russian Strategic Nuclear Forces*, 1–5, 122, 138–9.

17. www.thedailyzombies.com/2011/07/short-vision-animated -nuclear.html.

18. Chernus, *Apocalypse Management*, 102–3.

19. Isaacson and Thomas, *The Wise Men*, 439–42.

20. Chernus, *Apocalypse Management*, 9, 102–3.

21. Richard Nixon memorandum to file, December 3, 1957, Nixon Library.

22. PPP:E, 1960–1, 198.

23. John Eisenhower, Susan Eisenhower, interviews by author.

24. Susan Eisenhower interview by author; Eisenhower, Dwight, *Waging Peace*, 223.

25. Ann Whitman diary, July 8, 1959, AWF, EL.

26. Ibid., July 23, 1959; Howard Snyder diary, April 1, 1960, EL.

27. Kaplan, *1959*, 54–5, 62–3.

28. Arthur Minnich notes of legislative meeting, April 26, 1960, AWF, EL.

29. Kaplan, *1959*, 14, 238.

30. Ambrose, *Eisenhower: The President*, 562.

31. Howard Snyder diary, June 6, 1959, and January 4, 1960, EL.

32. Beschloss, *Mayday*, 218, 232, 7; memorandum of discussion, National Security Council meeting, February 18, 1960, EL.

Chapter 24: "The Pilot's Alive"

1. Bissell, *Reflections of a Cold Warrior*, 114–15; Beschloss, *Mayday*, 6, 140; Richard Bissell OH, CU.
2. Watson, *History of the Office of the Secretary of Defense*, 719.
3. John Eisenhower interview by author.
4. Roman, *Eisenhower and the Missile Gap*, 139.
5. Andrew Goodpaster memorandum of conversation, February 12, 1959, AWF, EL.
6. Pocock, *The U-2 Spyplane*, 150.
7. Andrew Goodpaster memorandum of conversation, April 7, 11, 1959, AWF, EL.
8. Taubman, Philip, *Secret Empire*, 271, 290.
9. Bissell, *Reflections of a Cold Warrior*, 137.
10. A Program of Covert Action Against the Castro Regime, March 16, 1960; Andrew Goodpaster memorandum of conversation, March 18, 1960, AWF, EL.
11. Pedlow and Welzenbach, *The CIA and the U-2 Program*, 168; Richard Bissell OH, EL.
12. Taubman, Philip, *Secret Empire*, 290.
13. Brugioni, *Eyes in the Sky*, 316.
14. Andrew Goodpaster memorandum of conversation, February 8, 1960, AWF, EL.
15. Brugioni, *Eyes in the Sky*, 343.
16. John Eisenhower interview by author.
17. Pedlow, *The CIA and the U-2 Program*, 170; Bissell, *Reflections of a Cold Warrior*, 123; Taubman, Philip, *Secret Empire*, 299; Richard Bissell OH, EL.
18. Beschloss, *Mayday*, 17, 147.
19. Bissell, *Reflections of a Cold Warrior*, 129; John Eisenhower interview by author.
20. Kistiakowsky, *A Scientist at the White House*, 328.
21. Andrew Goodpaster memorandum of conversation, April 25, 1960, AWF, EL.

22. Pedlow and Welzenbach, *The CIA and the U-2 Program*, 174–7; Taubman, Philip, *Secret Empire*, 306–7.
23. Charles Bohlen OH, CU.
24. Beschloss, *Mayday*, 44.
25. Eisenhower, John, *Strictly Personal*, 270.
26. Memorandum of discussion, National Security Council meeting, May 5, 1960, EL.
27. Thomas, *The Very Best Men*, 218; Andrew Goodpaster memorandum of conversation, May 2, 1960, AWF, EL.
28. Beschloss, *Mayday*, 59–60.
29. Grose, *Gentleman Spy*, 484.
30. John Eisenhower interview by author.
31. Howard Snyder diary, May 8, 1960, EL.
32. Beschloss, *Mayday*, 243–53.
33. Taubman, William, *Khrushchev*, 455, 458.
34. Ann Whitman diary, May 9, 1960, AWF, EL.
35. Eisenhower, John, *Strictly Personal*, 271; Kistiakowsky, *A Scientist at the White House*, 321; Eisenhower, Dwight, *Waging Peace*, 551.
36. Brugioni, *Eyes in the Sky*, 350–1.

Chapter 25: "I'm Just Fed Up!"

1. John Eisenhower interview by author; Beschloss, *Mayday*, 271.
2. Taubman, William, *Khrushchev*, 460.
3. Eisenhower, Dwight, *Waging Peace*, 552.
4. Beschloss, *Mayday*, 278.
5. Eisenhower, Dwight, *Waging Peace*, 555.
6. Taubman, William, *Khrushchev*, 462.
7. Charles Bohlen OH, CU.
8. Eisenhower, Dwight, *Waging Peace*, 555–6.
9. Eisenhower, John, *Strictly Personal*, 274.
10. Taubman, William, *Khrushchev*, 464.

SOURCE NOTES

11. Howard Snyder diary, May 16, 17, 1960, EL.
12. Eisenhower, John, *Strictly Personal,* 278; Beschloss, *Mayday,* 304.
13. Taubman, William, *Khrushchev,* 467–9.
14. Ibid., 468.
15. Eisenhower, Dwight, *Waging Peace,* 558.
16. John Eisenhower interview by author.
17. Donovan, *Confidential Secretary,* 156.
18. Kistiakowsky, *A Scientist at the White House,* 375.
19. CIA memorandum, "Future of the Agency's U-2 Capability," July 7, 1960, EL.
20. Brugioni, *Eyes in the Sky,* 356, 378.
21. Weiner, *Legacy of Ashes,* 160.
22. "Memories of a CIA Officer," *New York Times,* February 24, 2008.
23. PDDE, 14:600.
24. PDDE, 13:1148–9.
25. Ewald, *Eisenhower the President,* 271–80.
26. Ambrose, *Ike's Spies,* 295.
27. Richard Bissell interview by author.
28. Andrew Goodpaster memorandum of conversation, May 16, 1960, AWF, EL.
29. "Did Ike Authorize a Murder?," *Washington Post,* August 8, 2000.
30. Thomas, *The Very Best Men,* 231.
31. Howard Snyder diary, July 7, 1960, EL.
32. Ibid., July 16, 1960.
33. John Eisenhower interview by author.
34. Ambrose, *Eisenhower: The President,* 548; DDE memorandum for record; Ann Whitman diary, April 8, 1960, AWF, EL.
35. Slater, *The Ike I Knew,* 229; Ann Whitman diary, August 19, 1960, AWF, EL.
36. Ibid., August 30, 1960.

37. Ambrose, *Eisenhower: The President*, 599–601.
38. Howard Snyder diary, October 17, 1960, EL; Lasby, *Eisenhower's Heart Attack*, 286.
39. Howard Snyder diary, July 26, 1960, EL.
40. Ibid., October 28, 1960.
41. Susan Eisenhower interview by author; PDDE, 21: 2143–4.
42. Lasby, *Eisenhower's Heart Attack*, 284–5.
43. Ewald, *Eisenhower the President*, 312.
44. Howard Snyder diary, November 12, 1960, EL.
45. Eisenhower, John, *Strictly Personal*, 285.
46. Eisenhower, Dwight, *Waging Peace*, 602.

Chapter 26: The Underestimated Man

1. Keeney, *Fifteen Minutes*, 3, 221.
2. Rosenberg, "The Origins of Overkill."
3. Ambrose, *Eisenhower: Soldier and President*, 517; Roman, *Eisenhower and the Missile Gap*, 125–7; Watson, *History of the Office of the Secretary of Defense*, 448–57, 475–7, 481.
4. Kistiakowksy, *A Scientist at the White House*, 293.
5. Ibid., 374.
6. Jablonsky, *War by Land, Sea, and Air*, 142.
7. Gordon Gray, memorandum of conversation, August 25, 1960, AWF, EL.
8. Bundy, *Danger and Survival*, 323; Watson, *History of the Office of the Secretary of Defense*, 450–1; www.gwu.edu/~nsarchiv/news/19980319.htm.
9. Kinnard, *The Secretary of Defense*, 44–71; Watson, *History of the Office of the Secretary of Defense*, 8.
10. A. J. Bacevich, "The Paradox of Professionalism," 303–4.
11. John Eisenhower OH, EL.

12. Rosenberg, "A Smoking, Radiating Ruin," 11.

13. Rhodes, *Dark Sun,* 571.

14. Burr, ed., "The Creation of SIOP-62," 14.

15. Gordon Gray, memorandum of conversation, October 7, 1960, AWF, EL; memorandum of discussion, National Security Council meeting, October 6, 1960, EL; Howard Snyder diary, November 25, 1960, EL.

16. Ambrose, *Eisenhower: The President,* 592.

17. Watson, *History of the Office of the Secretary of Defense,* 490–4; Roman, *Eisenhower and the Missile Gap,* 100–3; Schwartz, *Atomic Audit,* 201; Howard Snyder diary, November 25, 1960, EL.

18. Eisenhower, Dwight, *Waging Peace,* 617; memorandum of discussion, National Security Council meeting, December 8, 1960, EL.

19. Thomas, Evan, and John Barry, "The Doomsday Dilemma."

20. Ann Whitman OH, EL.

21. Andrew Goodpaster, memorandum of conversation, February 13, 1959, AWF, EL; Andrew Goodpaster OH, EL; Roman, *Eisenhower and the Missile Gap,* 131.

22. Ledbetter, *Unwarranted Influence,* 95, 96, 109, 111, 116; Malcolm Moos OH, EL; "Farewell Address" drafts, January 6–16, 1961, AWF, EL; Newton, "Ike's Speech."

23. Greenstein, *The Presidential Difference,* 45, 57.

24. Kempton, "The Underestimation of Dwight D. Eisenhower."

25. PDDE, 21:2043–4.

26. John Eisenhower interview by author.

27. Greenstein and Immerman,"What Did Eisenhower Tell Kennedy about Indochina?"; Wilton Persons memorandum of conversation, January 19, 1961, EL.

28. Howard Snyder diary, December 7, 1960, EL.

29. Lyon, *Eisenhower,* 825.

30. Eisenhower, David, *Going Home to Glory,* 15.

Epilogue: Peace

1. Thomas, *The Very Best Men*, 237–63.
2. Eisenhower, David, *Going Home to Glory*, 32–3; Thomas, *The Very Best Men*, 250.
3. Rasenberger, *The Brilliant Disaster*, 109; Ambrose, *Eisenhower: The President*, 640; Gordon Gray OH, EL; Eisenhower, David, *Going Home to Glory*, 120.
4. Jones, *After Hiroshima*, 391.
5. Craig, *Destroying the Village*, 122–51.
6. Schlesinger, *Robert F. Kennedy and His Times*, 705.
7. John McCone OH, EL.
8. Ewald, *Eisenhower the President*, 318.
9. Eisenhower, David, *Going Home to Glory*, 139.
10. C. D. Jackson diary, December 31, 1953, EL.
11. Clare Boothe Luce OH, CU.
12. Eisenhower, David, *Going Home to Glory*, 78.
13. John Eisenhower interview by author; Eisenhower, David, *Going Home to Glory*, 168, 170, 199–200, 205, 210.
14. Ibid., 251–75.
15. Eisenhower, John, *Strictly Personal*, 336–7.
16. Susan Eisenhower interview by author. "I really don't want a memorial. But if they do anything, I *hope* they don't make a statue of me," Eisenhower told Mamie's secretary, Ethel Wetzel. Ethel Wetzel OH, US Park Service.
17. John Eisenhower OH, EL.
18. Richard Immerman interview by author. See also Jackson, "Beyond Brinksmanship"
19. Tour of Gettysburg by author; Ethel Wetzel OH, US Park Service.

Bibliography

Manuscript Collections

Dwight D. Eisenhower Presidential Library, Abilene, Kansas

Papers of George Allen

Papers of Richard M. Bissell, Jr.

Papers of Herbert Brownell

Eleanor Lansing Dulles Papers

John Foster Dulles Papers

Dwight Eisenhower Papers as President: Diary Series, including national security briefings and memoranda of Andrew Goodpaster and John Eisenhower

Gordon Gray Papers

James Hagerty Diary and Papers

Bryce Harlow Papers

C. D. Jackson Papers

John McCone Papers

Arthur Minnich Papers

Malcom Moos Papers

Lauris Norstad Papers

Bernard Shanley Diary and Papers

Walter Bedell Smith Papers

Dr. Howard McCrum Snyder Papers

Ann Whitman Diary Series—Dwight Eisenhower Papers as President

BIBLIOGRAPHY

George C. Marshall Foundation, Lexington, Virginia

Andrew Goodpaster Papers

Princeton University, Special Collections

John Foster Dulles Papers
Emmet Hughes Diary and Papers
Arthur Krock Papers

Virginia Historical Society, Richmond, Virginia

David Bruce Diary and Papers

Oral Histories

Eisenhower Presidential Library, Abilene, Kansas

George Allen
Herbert Brownell
Jackie Cochran
Dwight Eisenhower
John Eisenhower
Mamie Eisenhower
Barbara Eisenhower-Foltz
Arthur Flemming
Andrew Goodpaster
John McCone

Columbia University Oral History Project

Dillon Anderson
Charles Bohlen
Lucius Clay
John Eisenhower
Sig Larmon
Clare Boothe Luce
Merriman Smith

BIBLIOGRAPHY

Princeton University

Sherman Adams
Stewart Alsop
Robert Bowie
Marquis Childs
Robert Donovan
Allen Dulles
Dwight Eisenhower
Leonard Hall
Karl Harr
Emmet Hughes
Arthur Radford

Dwight Eisenhower National Historic Site, Gettysburg, Pennsylvania

David Eisenhower
Susan Eisenhower

Books and Articles

Abella, Alex. *Soldiers of Reason: The Rand Corporation and the Rise of the American Empire.* Orlando, FL: Harcourt, 2007.

Adams, Sherman. *Firsthand Report: The Story of the Eisenhower Administration.* New York: Harper, 1961.

Adams, Valerie. *Eisenhower's Fine Group of Fellows: Crafting a National Security to Uphold the Great Equation.* Lanham, MD: Lexington Books, 2006.

Allen, George E. *Presidents Who Have Known Me.* New York: Simon and Schuster, 1960.

Alsop, Joseph. *"I've Seen the Best of It."* Edinburg, VA: Axios Press, 2009.

Ambrose, Stephen E. *Ike's Spies: Eisenhower and the Espionage Establishment.* Jackson: University of Mississippi Press, 1999.

BIBLIOGRAPHY

———. *Eisenhower: The President*. New York: Simon and Schuster, 1984.

———. *Eisenhower: Soldier and President*. New York: Simon and Schuster, 1991.

———. *Nixon*, vol. 1, *The Education of a Politician*. New York: Simon and Schuster, 1987.

Anderson, David L. "Dwight Eisenhower and Wholehearted Support of Ngo Dinh Diem." In David L. Anderson, ed., *Shadow on the White House: Presidents and the Vietnam War, 1945–1975*. Lawrence: University of Kansas Press, 1993.

Bacevich, Andrew. *Washington Rules: America's Path to Permanent War*. New York: Metropolitan Books, 2010.

———. "The Paradox of Professionalism: Eisenhower, Ridgway, and the Challenge to Civilian Control, 1953–1955." *The Journal of Military History*, April 1977.

Bair, Deirdre. *Jung: A Biography*. Boston: Little, Brown, 2003.

Beinart, Peter. *The Icarus Syndrome*. New York: HarperCollins, 2010.

Beschloss, Michael R. *Mayday: Eisenhower, Khrushchev, and the U-2 Affair*. New York: Harper and Row, 1988.

Betts, Richard K., and Bruce K. MacLaury. *Nuclear Blackmail and Nuclear Balance*. Washington, DC: Brookings Institution Press, 1987.

Billings-Yun, Melanie. *Decision Against War*. New York: Columbia University Press, 1988.

Bissell, Richard, Jr. *Reflections of a Cold Warrior: From Yalta to the Bay of Pigs*. New Haven: Yale University Press, 1996.

Bohlen, Charles. *Witness to History, 1929–1969*. New York: W. W. Norton, 1973.

Bose, Meena. *Shaping and Signaling Presidential Policy: The National Security Decision Making of Eisenhower and Kennedy*. College Station: Texas A&M Press, 1998.

Bowie, Robert R., and Richard H. Immerman. *Waging Peace: How Eisenhower Shaped an Enduring Cold War Strategy*. New York: Oxford University Press, 2000.

BIBLIOGRAPHY

Boyer, Paul, S. *By the Bomb's Early Light: American Thought and Culture at the Dawn of the Atomic Age.* Chapel Hill: University of North Carolina Press, 1994.

Brands, H. W. *Cold Warriors: Eisenhower's Generation and the Making of American Foreign Policy.* New York: Columbia University Press, 1998.

————. "Testing Massive Retaliation: Credibility and Crisis Management in the Taiwan Strait," *International Security* 12, no. 4 (Spring 1988).

Branigar, Thomas. "No Villains—No Heroes." *Kansas History* 170 (Autumn 1990).

Brendon, Piers. *Ike: His Life and Times.* New York: HarperCollins, 1986.

Brugioni, Dino A. *Eyes in the Sky: Eisenhower, the CIA, and Cold War Aerial Espionage.* Annapolis, MD: Naval Institute Press, 2010.

Brzezinski, Matthew. *Red Moon Rising: Sputnik and the Hidden Rivalries That Ignited the Space Age.* New York: Times Books, 2007.

Bundy, McGeorge. *Danger and Survival.* New York: Vintage, 1990.

Burke, John P., and Fred Greenstein. *How Presidents Test Reality: Decisions on Vietnam 1954–1956.* New York: Russell Sage Foundation, 1991.

Burr, William. "Avoiding the Slippery Slope: The Eisenhower Administration and the Berlin Crisis, November 1958–January 1959." *Diplomatic History* 19, no. 2 (April 1994).

————, ed. "The Creation of SIOP-62." National Security Archive, Washington, DC: The George Washington University, 2004.

Burrows, William E. *Deep Black: Space Espionage and National Security.* New York: Berkley Books, 1988.

Byrne, Malcolm, and Mark J. Gasiorowski. *Mohammad Mosaddeq and the 1953 Coup in Iran.* Syracuse, NY: Syracuse University Press, 2004.

BIBLIOGRAPHY

Carlson, Peter. *K Blows Top: A Cold War Comic Interlude Starring Nikita Khrushchev, America's Most Unlikely Tourist*. Washington, DC: PublicAffairs, 2009.

Caro, Robert. *The Years of Lyndon Johnson: Master of the Senate*. New York: Vintage, 2003.

Chang, Gordon H. *Friends and Enemies: The United States, China, and the Soviet Union, 1948–1972*. Palo Alto, CA: Stanford University Press, 1990.

———. "To the Nuclear Brink: Eisenhower, Dulles and the Quemoy-Matsu Crisis." *International Security* 12, no. 4 (Spring 1988).

Chernus, Ira. *Apocalypse Management: Eisenhower and the Discourse of National Security*. Palo Alto, CA: Stanford University Press, 2008.

Childs, Marquis. *The Ragged Edge: The Diary of a Crisis*. Garden City, NY: Doubleday, 1956.

Clausewitz, Carl von. *On War*. Oxford, UK: Oxford University Press, 2008.

Cohen, William A. *Heroic Leadership: Leading With Integrity and Honor*. San Francisco: Jossey-Bass, 2010.

Colville, John. *The Fringes of Power: 10 Downing Street Diaries, 1939–1955*. London, UK: Hodder & Stoughton Ltd., 1989.

Craig, Campbell. *Destroying the Village: Eisenhower and Thermonuclear War*. New York: Columbia University Press, 1998.

Crane, Conrad C. *Bombs, Cities, and Civilians: American Airpower Strategy in World War II*. Lawrence: University of Kansas Press, 1993.

———. "To Avert Impending Disaster: American Military Plans to Use Atomic Weapons During the Korean War." *Journal of Strategic Studies* 23, no. 2 (June 2000).

Crosswell, D. K. R. *Beetle: The Life of General Walter Bedell Smith*. Lexington: University of Kentucky Press, 2010.

Cullather, Nicholas. *Secret History: The CIA's Classified Account of Its Operation in Guatemala, 1952–1954*. Palo Alto, CA: Stanford University Press, 2006.

Cutler, Robert. *No Time for Rest*. Boston: Little, Brown, 1966.

D'Este, Carlos. *Eisenhower: A Soldier's Life*. New York: Holt, 2003.

Dickson, Paul. *Sputnik: The Shock of the Century*. New York: Walker & Company, 2011.

Dingman, Roger. "Atomic Diplomacy During the Cold War." *International Security* 13, no. 3 (Winter 1988).

Divine, Robert A. *Blowing on the Wind: The Nuclear Test Ban Debate, 1954–1960*. New York: Oxford University Press, 1978.

———. *The Sputnik Challenge*. New York: Oxford University Press, 1993.

Dockrill, Saki. *Eisenhower's New-Look National Security Policy, 1953–61*. Hampshire, UK: Palgave Macmillan, 1996.

Donovan. Robert J. *Confidential Secretary*. New York: Dutton, 1988.

———. *Eisenhower: The Inside Story*. New York: Harper Brothers, 1957.

Dyer, Gwynne. *War: The Lethal Custom*. New York: Carroll and Graf, 2004.

Eisenhower, David. *Eisenhower: At War, 1943–1945*. New York: Vintage Books, 1987.

———. *Going Home to Glory: A Memoir of Life with Dwight D. Eisenhower, 1961–1969*. New York: Simon and Schuster, 2010.

Eisenhower, Dwight D. *At Ease: Stories I Tell to Friends*. Garden City, NY: Doubleday, 1967.

———. *Crusade in Europe*. Garden City, New York: Doubleday, 1948.

———. *Mandate for Change, 1953–1956*. Garden City, NY: Doubleday, 1963.

———. *Papers of Dwight David Eisenhower: The Presidency.* Vols. XIV-XXI, Louis Galambos and Daun van Ee, eds. Baltimore, MD: Johns Hopkins University Press, 1996–2001.

———. *Waging Peace, 1956–1961: The White House Years.* Garden City, NY: Doubleday, 1965.

Eisenhower, John, *Strictly Personal.* Garden City, NY: Doubleday, 1974.

———. "The Presbyterian: John Foster Dulles." Unpublished essay provided to the author.

Eisenhower, Milton. *The President Is Calling.* Garden City, NY: Doubleday, 1974.

Eisenhower, Susan. *Mrs. Ike: Memories and Reflections on the Life and Times of Mamie Eisenhower.* New York: Farrar, Straus, Giroux, 1996.

Erdmann, Andrew P. N. "War No Longer Has Any Logic Whatever." In John Lewis Gaddis, Philip H. Gordon, Ernest May, and Jonathan Rosenberg, eds., *Cold War Statesmen Confront the Bomb: Nuclear Diplomacy Since 1945.* Oxford, UK: Oxford University Press, 1999.

Ewald, William Bragg, Jr. *Eisenhower the President: Crucial Days, 1951–1960.* Englewood Cliffs, NJ: Prentice-Hall, 1981.

Felzenberg, Alvin Stephen. *The Leaders We Deserved (and a Few We Didn't).* New York: Basic Books, 2008.

Ferrell, Robert H. *The Diary of James C. Hagerty: Eisenhower in Mid-Course, 1954–1955.* Bloomington: Indiana University Press, 1983.

———. *The Eisenhower Diaries.* New York: W. W. Norton, 1981.

Foot, Rosemary. *Substitute for Victory: The Politics of Peacemaking at the Korean Armistice Talks.* Ithaca, NY: Cornell University Press, 1990.

———. *The Wrong War: American Policy and the Dimensions of the Korean Conflict, 1950–1953.* Ithaca, NY: Cornell University Press, 1985.

BIBLIOGRAPHY

———. "Nuclear Coercion and the Ending of the Korean Conflict." *International Security* 13, no. 3 (Winter 1988).

Foreign Relations of the United States, 1952–1954. Vol. 3, *Eastern Europe, Soviet Union and Eastern Mediterranean.* Washington, DC: Government Printing Office, 1988.

———. *Guatemala.* Washington, DC: Government Printing Office, 2003.

———. *1952–1954.* Vol. 2. *National Security Affairs.* Washington, DC: Government Printing Office, 1984.

———. *1952–1954.* Vol. 5, *Western European Security.* Washington, DC: Government Printing Office, 1983.

———. *1952–1954.* Vol. 15. *Korea.* Washington, DC: Government Printing Office, 1984.

Gaddis, John Lewis. *The Cold War: A New History.* New York: Penguin, 2006.

———. *Strategies of Containment: A Critical Appraisal of American National Security Policy During the Cold War.* New York: Oxford University Press, 2005.

———. *We Now Know: Rethinking Cold War History.* New York: Oxford University Press, 1998.

Garthoff, Raymond L. *A Journey Through the Cold War: A Memoir of Containment and Coexistence.* Washington, DC: Brookings Institution Press, 2001.

———. "Estimating Soviet Military Intentions and Capabilities," in Gerald K. Haines and Robert E. Leggett, eds., *Watching the Bear: Essays on CIA's Analysis of the Soviet Union.* Washington, DC: Central Intelligence Agency, 2004.

Goldworthy, Adrian. *Caesar: Life of a Colossus.* New Haven, CT: Yale University Press, 2006.

Goodpaster, Andrew. "Cold War Overflights: A View from the White House," in R. Cargill Hall and Clayton D. Laurie, eds. *Early Cold War Overflights, 1950–1956: Symposium Proceedings.* Washington, DC: Office of the Historian, National Reconnaissance Office, 2003.

Gordin, Michael D. *Red Cloud at Dawn: Truman, Stalin, and the End of the Nuclear Monopoly.* New York: Farrar, Straus and Giroux, 2009.

Greene, Benjamin P. *Eisenhower, Science Advice, and the Nuclear Test-Ban Debate, 1945–1963.* Palo Alto, CA: Stanford University Press, 2006.

Greenstein, Fred I. *The Hidden-Hand Presidency: Eisenhower as Leader.* New York: Basic Books, 1982.

———. *The Presidential Difference: Leadership Style from FDR to George W. Bush.* Princeton, NJ: Princeton University Press, 2004.

Greenstein, Fred I., and Richard H. Immerman. "What Did Eisenhower Tell Kennedy about Indochina? The Politics of Misperception." *Journal of American History*, September 1992.

Griffith, Robert W. *Ike's Letters to a Friend, 1941–1958.* Lawrence: University of Kansas Press, 1984.

Grose, Peter. *Gentleman Spy.* Amherst: University of Massachusetts Press, 1996.

Haines, Gerald K., and Robert E. Leggett, eds. *Watching the Bear: Essays on CIA's Analysis of the Soviet Union.* Washington, DC: Central Intelligence Agency, 2004.

Halberstam, David. *The Coldest Winter: America and the Korean War.* New York: Hyperion, 2007.

———. *The Fifties.* New York: Villard Books, 1993.

Hall, R. Cargill. "Clandestine Victory: Eisenhower and Overhead Reconnaissance in the Cold War." In Dennis E. Showalter, *Forging the Shield: Eisenhower and National Security for the 21st Century.* Chicago: Imprint, 2005.

Hall, R. Cargill, and Clayton D. Laurie, eds. *Early Cold War Overflights, 1950–1956: Symposium Proceedings.* Washington, DC: Office of the Historian, National Reconnaissance Office, 2003.

———. "The Truth About Overflights." *Quarterly Journal of Military History* 9, no. 3 (1997).

BIBLIOGRAPHY

Helgerson, John L. *CIA Briefings of Presidential Candidates.* Washington, DC: Center for the Study of Intelligence, 1996.

Herken, Gregg. *Brotherhood of the Bomb*: *The Tangled Lives and Loyalties of Robert Oppenheimer, Ernest Lawrence, and Edward Teller.* New York: Holt, 2003.

———. *Counsels of War.* New York: Oxford University Press, 1987.

Herring, George. "'A Good Stout Effort': John Foster Dulles and the Indochina Crisis, 1954–1955." In Richard H. Immerman, ed., *John Foster Dulles and the Diplomacy of the Cold War.* Princeton, NJ: Princeton University Press, 1992.

Holloway, David. *Stalin and the Bomb: The Soviet Union and Atomic Energy, 1939–1956.* New Haven, CT: Yale University Press, 1996.

Hoopes, Townsend. *The Devil and John Foster Dulles.* Boston: Little, Brown, 1973.

Hughes, Emmet John. *The Ordeal of Power: A Political Memoir of the Eisenhower Years.* New York: Atheneum, 1963.

Huntington, Samuel P. *American Politics: The Promise of Disharmony.* Cambridge, MA: Harvard University Press, 1981.

Immerman, Richard H. *The CIA in Guatemala: The Foreign Policy of Intervention.* Austin: University of Texas Press, 1983.

———. "Between the Unacceptable and the Unobtainable." In Richard Melanson and David Mayers, eds., *Reevaluating Eisenhower: American Foreign Policy in the Fifties.* Urbana: University of Illinois Press, 1989.

———, ed. *John Foster Dulles and the Diplomacy of the Cold War.* Princeton, NJ: Princeton University Press, 1992.

Isaacson, Walter, and Evan Thomas. *The Wise Men: Six Friends and the World They Made.* New York: Simon and Schuster, 1997.

Jablonsky, David. *War by Land, Sea, and Air: Dwight Eisenhower and the Concept of Unified Command.* New Haven, CT: Yale University Press, 2010.

Jackson, Michael Gordon. "Beyond Brinksmanship: Eisenhower, Nuclear War Fighting, and Korea, 1953–1968." *Presidential Studies Quarterly* 35, 1 (March 2005).

Johnson, A. Ross. *Radio Free Europe and Radio Liberty: The CIA Years and Beyond.* Palo Alto, CA: Stanford University Press, 2010.

Johnson, Paul. *Heroes: From Alexander the Great and Julius Caesar to Churchill and De Gaulle.* New York: Harper Perennial, 2008.

Jones, Matthew. *After Hiroshima: The United States, Race and Nuclear Weapons in Asia, 1945–1965.* Cambridge: Cambridge University Press, 2010.

Jordan, Jonathan W. *Brothers, Rivals, Victors: Eisenhower, Patton, Bradley, and the Partnership That Drove the Allied Conquest in Europe.* New York: NAL, 2011.

Kaplan, Fred. *1959: The Year Everything Changed.* Hoboken, NJ: Wiley, 2009.

Kaplan, Fred, and Martin J. Sherwin. *Wizards of Armageddon.* Palo Alto, CA: Stanford University Press, 1991.

Karalekas, Anne. *History of the Central Intelligence Agency.* Laguna Hills, CA: Aegean Park Press, 1977.

Keegan, John. *The Mask of Command.* New York: Viking, 1987.

Keeney, L. Douglas. *15 Minutes: General Curtis LeMay and the Countdown to Nuclear Annihilation.* New York: St. Martin's Griffin, 2012.

Kelly, Charles J. *Tex McCrary: Wars, Women, Politics: An Adventurous Life Across the American Century.* Lanham, MD: Hamilton Books, 2009.

Kempton, Murray. "The Underestimation of Dwight D. Eisenhower." *Esquire,* September 1967.

Khrushchev, Nikita Sergeevich. *Khrushchev Remembers.* Boston: Little, Brown, 1971.

Khrushchev, Sergei. *Nikita Khrushchev and the Creation of a Superpower.* State College: Pennsylvania State University Press, 2001.

Killian, James R. *Sputnik, Scientists, and Eisenhower: A Memoir of the First Special Assistant to the President for Science and Technology.* Cambridge, MA: MIT Press, 1982.

Kinnard, Douglas. *The Secretary of Defense.* Lexington: University of Kentucky Press, 1981.

Kinzer, Stephen. *All the Shah's Men: An American Coup and the Roots of Middle East Terror.* Hoboken, NJ: Wiley, 2008.

Kirsch, Beth. *War and Peace in the Nuclear Age.* New York: Knopf, 1989.

Kissinger, Henry. *Crisis: The Anatomy of Two Major Foreign Policy Crises.* New York: Simon and Schuster, 2003.

———. *Diplomacy.* New York: Simon and Schuster, 1994.

Kistiakowsky, George B. *A Scientist at the White House: The Private Diary of President Eisenhower's Special Assistant for Science and Technology.* Cambridge, MA: Harvard University Press, 1976.

Korda, Michael. *Ike: An American Hero.* New York: Harper Perennial, 2008.

Kornitzer, Bela. *The Story of the Five Eisenhower Brothers.* New York: Farrar, Straus & Cudahy, 1955.

Kunz, Diane B. *Butter and Guns: America's Cold War Economic Diplomacy.* New York: Free Press, 1997.

Larson, Arthur. *Eisenhower: The President Nobody Knew.* New York: Charles Scribner's Sons, 1968.

Lasby, Clarence G. *Eisenhower's Heart Attack: How Ike Beat Heart Disease and Held on to the Presidency.* Lawrence: University Press of Kansas, 1997.

Lawrence, Mark Atwood, "Explaining the Early Decisions: The United States and the French War, 1945–1954." In Mark Bradley and Marilyn Young Blatt, *Making Sense of the Vietnam Wars.* New York: Oxford University Press, 2008.

Lear, John. "Ike and the Peaceful Atom." *Reporter,* January 12, 1956.

Ledbetter, James. *Unwarranted Influence: Dwight D. Eisenhower and the Military-Industrial Complex.* New Haven, CT: Yale University Press, 2011.

BIBLIOGRAPHY

Lee, R. Alton. *Dwight D. Eisenhower: Bibliography of His Times and Presidency.* Ann Arbor, MI: Scholarly Resources, 1991.

Lyon, Peter. *Eisenhower: Portrait of a Hero.* Boston: Little, Brown, 1974.

Macmillan, Harold. *Riding the Storm.* London, UK: Macmillan, 1971.

Manchester, William. *The Glory and the Dream.* New York: Bantam, 1974.

Marks, Frederick W. *Power and Peace: The Diplomacy of John Foster Dulles.* Westport, CT: Praeger, 1995.

Melanson, Richard A., and David Mayers, eds. *Reevaluating Eisenhower: American Foreign Policy in the Fifties.* Champaign: University of Illinois Press, 1989.

Merry, Robert W. *Taking on the World: Joseph and Stewart Alsop and the American Century.* New York: Penguin, 1997.

Morgan, Ted. *Valley of Death: The Tragedy at Dien Bien Phu That Led America into the Vietnam War.* New York: Random House, 2010.

Mosley, Leonard. *Dulles: A Biography of Eleanor, Allen, and John Foster Dulles and Their Family Network.* New York: Dell, 1979.

Newhouse, John. *War and Peace in the Nuclear Age.* New York: Vintage, 1990.

Newton, Jim. *Eisenhower: The White House Years.* New York: Doubleday, 2011.

————. "Ike's Speech." *The New Yorker,* December 20, 2010.

Nichols, David A. *Eisenhower 1956: The President's Year of Crisis— Suez and the Brink of War.* New York: Simon and Schuster, 2011.

————. *A Matter of Justice: Eisenhower and the Beginning of the Civil Rights Revolution.* New York: Simon and Schuster, 2008.

Nixon, Richard. *RN: The Memoirs of Richard Nixon.* New York: Simon and Schuster, 1990.

————. *Six Crises*. Garden City, NY: Doubleday, 1962.

Olson, Lynne. *Citizens of London: The Americans Who Stood with Britain in its Darkest, Finest Hour*. New York: Random House, 2011.

Oppenheimer, Robert. "Atomic Weapons and American Policy." *Foreign Affairs* 31, no. 4 (July 1953).

Osgood, Kenneth. *Total Cold War: Eisenhower's Secret Propaganda Battle at Home and Abroad*. Lawrence: University of Kansas Press, 2008.

Pach, Chester J., and Elmo Richardson. *Presidency of Eisenhower*. Lawrence: University of Kansas Press, 1991.

Pakula, Hannah. *The Last Empress: Madame Chiang Kai-shek and the Birth of Modern China*. New York: Simon and Schuster, 2010.

Parmet, Herbert S. *Eisenhower and the American Crusades*. New York: Macmillan, 1972.

Paul, T. V., Patrick M. Morgan, and James J. Wirtz. *Complex Deterrence: Strategy in the Global Age*. Chicago: University of Chicago Press, 2009.

Pedlow, Gregory W. and Donald E. Welzenbach. *The CIA and the U-2 Program*. Washington, DC: Center for the Study of Intelligence, 1998.

Perret, Geoffrey. *Eisenhower*. New York: Random House, 1999.

Perry, Mark. *Partners in Command: George Marshall and Dwight Eisenhower in War and Peace*. New York: Penguin, 2008.

Pocock, Chris. *The U-2 Spyplane: Toward the Unknown: A New History of the Early Years*. Atglen, PA: Schiffer, 2000.

Podvig, Pavel, and Frank von Hippel. *Russian Strategic Nuclear Forces*. Cambridge, MA: MIT Press, 2004.

Powers, Thomas. *The Man Who Kept the Secrets: Richard Helms and the CIA*. New York: Alfred A. Knopf, 1979.

Prados, John. *Keepers of the Keys: A History of the National Security Council from Truman to Bush*. New York: William Morrow, 1991.

BIBLIOGRAPHY

Preble, Christopher. *John F. Kennedy and the Missile Gap.* DeKalb: Northern Illinois University Press, 2004.

Pruessen, Ronald W. *John Foster Dulles: The Road to Power.* New York: Free Press, 1982.

Rabe, Stephen. "Eisenhower Revisionism: A Decade of Scholarship." *Diplomatic History* 17, 1 (Winter 1993).

Radford, Arthur William. *From Pearl Harbor to Vietnam: The Memoirs of Admiral Arthur W. Radford.* Palo Alto, CA: Hoover Institution Press, 1980.

Rasenberger, Jim. *The Brilliant Disaster: JFK, Castro, and America's Doomed Invasion of Cuba's Bay of Pigs.* New York: Scribner, 2011.

Reeves, Thomas C. *The Life and Times of Joe McCarthy: A Biography.* New York: Stein and Day, 1982.

Rhodes, Richard. *Dark Sun: The Making of the Hydrogen Bomb.* New York: Simon and Schuster, 1996.

Rigden, John S. *Rabi: Scientist and Citizen.* New York: Basic Books, 1987.

Roman, Peter J. *Eisenhower and the Missile Gap.* Ithaca, NY: Cornell University Press, 1996.

Roosevelt, Kermit. *Countercoup: The Struggle for Control of Iran.* New York: McGraw-Hill, 1979.

Rose, Gideon. *How Wars End: Why We Always Fight the Last Battle.* New York: Simon and Schuster, 2010.

Rosenberg, David Alan. "The Origins of Overkill: Nuclear Weapons and American Strategy, 1946–1960." *International Security* 7, no. 4 (Spring 1983).

Rosenberg, David Alan, and W. B. Moore. "'Smoking Radiating Ruin at the End of Two Hours': Documents on American Plans for Nuclear War with the Soviet Union, 1954–55." *International Security* 6, no. 3 (Winter 1981).

Rothkopf, David J. *Running the World: The Inside Story of the National Security Council and the Architects of America's Power.* New York: PublicAffairs, 2006.

BIBLIOGRAPHY

Rothschild, Alonzo. *Lincoln: Master of Men: A Study in Character.* Boston: Houghton Mifflin, 1966.

Schlesinger, Arthur. *Robert Kennedy and His Times.* Boston: Houghton Mifflin, 1978.

Schwartz, Stephen I. *Atomic Audit: The Costs and Consequences of U.S. Nuclear Weapons Since 1940.* Washington, DC: Brookings Institution Press, 1998.

Sheehan, Neil. *A Fiery Peace in a Cold War: Bernard Schriever and the Ultimate Weapon.* New York: Vintage, 2010.

Shepley, "How Dulles Averted War." *Life,* January 16, 1956.

Showalter, Dennis E. *Forging the Shield: Eisenhower and National Security for the 21st Century.* Chicago: Imprint, 2005.

Slater, Ellis D. *The Ike I Knew.* Baltimore, MD: Ellis D. Slater Trust, 1980.

Smith, Jean Edward. *Eisenhower in War and Peace.* New York: Random House, 2012.

Soman, Appu K. " 'Who's Daddy' in the Taiwan Strait? The Offshore Island Crisis of 1958." *Journal of American-Asian Relations* 3, no. 4 (Winter 1994).

Srodes, James. *Allen Dulles: Master of Spies.* Washington, DC: Regnery, 2000.

Stanley, Elizabeth. *Paths to Peace: Domestic Coalition Shifts, War Termination, and the Korean War.* Palo Alto, CA: Stanford University Press, 2009.

Stassen, Harold, and Marshall Houts. *Eisenhower: Turning the World Toward Peace.* St. Paul, MN: Merrill/Magnus, 1990.

Tannenwald, Nina. *The Nuclear Taboo: The United States and the Non-Use of Nuclear Weapons Since 1945.* Cambridge: Cambridge University Press, 2008.

Taubman, Philip. *Secret Empire: Eisenhower, the CIA, and the Hidden Story of America's Space Espionage.* New York: Simon and Schuster, 2004.

Taubman, William. *Khrushchev: The Man and His Era.* New York: W. W. Norton, 2004.

BIBLIOGRAPHY

Thomas, Evan. *The Very Best Men: The Daring Early Years of the CIA.* New York: Simon and Schuster, 2006.

———. "Spymaster General." VanityFair.com, March 31, 2011.

Thomas, Evan, and John Barry. "The Doomsday Dilemma." *Newsweek,* April 10, 2010.

Thompson, Kenneth W. *Portraits of American Presidents: The Eisenhower Presidency.* Lanham, MD: University Press of America, 1984.

Thompson, Nicholas. *The Hawk and the Dove: Paul Nitze, George Kennan, and the History of the Cold War.* New York: Henry Holt, 2009.

Trachtenberg, Marc. *History and Strategy.* Princeton, NJ: Princeton University Press, 1991.

———. "A 'Wasting Asset': American Strategy and the Shifting Nuclear Balance, 1949–1954." *International Security* 13, 3 (Winter 1988–89).

Truman, Harry S., and Dean Acheson. *Affection and Trust: The Personal Correspondence of Harry S. Truman and Dean Acheson, 1953–1971.* New York: Alfred A. Knopf, 2010.

Van Natta, Don, Jr. *First Off the Tee.* New York: PublicAffairs, 2004.

Watson, Robert J. *History of the Office of the Secretary of Defense: Into the Missile Age, 1956–1960.* Washington, DC: Historical Office, Office of the Secretary of Defense, 1997.

Weiner, Tim. *Legacy of Ashes: The History of the CIA.* New York: Doubleday, 2007.

West, J. B. *Upstairs at the White House.* New York: Warner Books, 1973.

Wills, Garry. *Bomb Power: The Modern Presidency and the National Security State.* New York: Penguin, 2010.

Wittner, Lawrence. *Confronting the Bomb: A Short History of the World Nuclear Disarmament Movement.* Palo Alto, CA: Stanford University Press, 2009.

BIBLIOGRAPHY

Yergin, Daniel. *The Prize: The Epic Quest for Oil, Money, and Power.* New York: Free Press, 2008.

Zelizer, Julian E. *Arsenal of Democracy: The Politics of Security from World War II to the War on Terrorism.* New York: Basic Books, 2008.

Zhai, Qiang. *The Dragon, the Lion, and the Eagle: Chinese, British, American Relations, 1949–1958.* Kent, OH: Kent State University Press, 1994.

About the Author

Evan Thomas is the author of several best-selling works of history. He has frequently appeared as a commentator on television and radio, and he teaches writing at Princeton. He lives in Washington, DC.